'*The Consciousness Network* is an illuminating journey into the depths of our internal universe, unraveling the mysteries of the human mind with clarity and depth. Prepare to be captivated by Pennartz' brilliant exploration of the brain's intricate workings and their profound implications for our understanding of our subjective reality.'

Steven Laureys, MD, *neurologist, author and past president of the Association for the Scientific Study of Consciousness, Belgium*

'If you want a comprehensive update on the relation between brain functions and consciousness, read this book. Written by an expert neuroscientist it provides deep insights into the functional organisation of the human brain, critically reviews philosophical positions on the mind-matter problem and illustrates the multiple facets of consciousness with fascinating clinical examples on altered states of consciousness.'

Wolf Singer, *Max Planck Institute for Brain Research, Frankfurt, Germany*

'This highly engaging and thought-provoking book stands out in its accessibility and broad approach drawing on multiple sources of knowledge, and its original view on consciousness endorsing a modern scientific version of Spinoza's monism.'

Kathinka Evers, *Professor of Philosophy, Uppsala University, Sweden and Honorary Professor at the Universidad Central de Chile, Chile*

The Consciousness Network

What is the relationship between consciousness and our brain? Are they one and the same? Who are we really? *The Consciousness Network* presents a novel account of one of the greatest scientific challenges of the twenty-first century: understanding the connection between brain and mind.

The book explores remarkable cases of patients who demonstrate how our impression of reality is created by the brain. Age-old questions about dreams, colour perception, phantom sensations and hallucinations are illuminated by surprising discoveries from the latest brain research. How does consciousness differ from memory, emotions and behaviour? How did it develop during the evolution of life on earth, and does it serve a purpose? Does the brain leave room for free will? In this unique blend of philosophy, history, psychology and neuroscience, Cyriel Pennartz breaks new ground by presenting an original theory of brain and mind, substantiated by brain research in patients and healthy people. This theory, inspired by the seventeenth-century philosopher Spinoza, goes significantly deeper than current thinking based on computer models or artificial intelligence.

The Consciousness Network is essential reading for students working at the interface of neuroscience, cognitive psychology, philosophy of mind and cognitive science, as well as anyone interested in consciousness and the brain.

Cyriel Pennartz is Professor in Cognitive and Systems Neuroscience at the University of Amsterdam, The Netherlands. His research integrates neuroscience, theories and computer models of perception, memory and consciousness, psychology and philosophy.

The Consciousness Network

How the Brain Creates Our Reality

Cyriel Pennartz

Routledge
Taylor & Francis Group

LONDON AND NEW YORK

Designed cover image: Cortical Twilight © Greg Dunn Design

First published in English 2024
by Routledge
4 Park Square, Milton Park, Abingdon, Oxon OX14 4RN

and by Routledge
605 Third Avenue, New York, NY 10158

Routledge is an imprint of the Taylor & Francis Group, an informa business

© 2024 Cyriel Pennartz

Published in Dutch as *De Code van het Bewustzijn* by Prometheus 2021

British Library Cataloguing-in-Publication Data
A catalogue record for this book is available from the British Library

Library of Congress Cataloging-in-Publication Data
Names: Pennartz, Cyriel M. A., 1963- author.
Title: The consciousness network: how the brain creates our reality / Cyriel Pennartz.
Description: Abingdon, Oxon; New York, NY: Routledge, 2024. | Includes bibliographical references and index.
Identifiers: LCCN 2023055554 (print) | LCCN 2023055555 (ebook) | ISBN 9781032552149 (hardback) | ISBN 9781032552125 (paperback) | ISBN 9781003429555 (ebook)
Subjects: LCSH: Mind and body. | Mind and reality. | Consciousness. | Brain.
Classification: LCC BF161 .P46 2024 (print) | LCC BF161 (ebook) | DDC 128/.2--dc23/eng/20240229
LC record available at https://lccn.loc.gov/2023055554
LC ebook record available at https://lccn.loc.gov/2023055555

ISBN: 978-1-032-55214-9 (hbk)
ISBN: 978-1-032-55212-5 (pbk)
ISBN: 978-1-003-42955-5 (ebk)

DOI: 10.4324/9781003429555

Typeset in Galliard
by Deanta Global Publishing Services, Chennai, India

For Hanneke

To Ansje

In memoriam Paul

Contents

1 A dark dungeon for our brains

What is consciousness? On the curious connection between brain, mind and electricity

You lie in a dark, closed-off cavity and feel shocks running through you. You have no idea how you got into this situation or what will happen to you next. You have almost no room to move. But even if you did, you can't: you are completely paralyzed. After the first wave of panic, you can concentrate better: the shocks feel like electric currents of differing intensities. Isolated, occasional shocks alternate with clusters of pulses that rapidly dissipate. Because of the total darkness, you cannot see anything, but you also realize that you cannot even see that darkness. You see no darkness and no light: you see nothing at all. Your hearing is missing and you feel no sensation in your body. No pressure on your skin, no touch, but no pain either. You can't smell anything, and your mouth is free of all taste. In fact, you don't know if you have a mouth at all because you can't feel anything where a mouth should be. It is neither hot nor cold. There is no sense of heaviness; you have no idea whether you are lying flat on the ground, standing upright or hanging upside down. You might as well be floating, weightless, in an orbit around the earth. There are only these electrifying pulses, sometimes only a few, sometimes dozens per second. Where do they come from, what do they mean? You have no idea.

This nightmare evokes images from the horror story *The Pit and the Pendulum* by Edgar Allan Poe, in which a man is sentenced by the Spanish Inquisition to solitary confinement in a dark dungeon. He is exposed to a pendulum with a razor-sharp blade that moves ever closer over his body. What is depicted here also closely resembles the situation in which our brains constantly find themselves[1] – but without being terrified. Neuroscience has shown that electrical activity lies at the basis of how the brain works, while paradoxically, it is also the organ through which we see, feel, smell, move our bodies, have fun and experience grief.

It is a dry, anatomical fact that our brains are situated in the closed, dark cavity of our skull. Only when a neurosurgeon drills an opening in the cranium does light fall on this pinkish, blubbery and veined mass. The only way the brain can communicate quickly with the world outside of the skull is via a dozen cranial nerves and the spinal cord (Figure 1.1).[2] Like thin, white strands, our two optic nerves drill their way through the skull to merge into the bottom of the brain. The same is true for all the nerves and pathways that run down and up our spine:

DOI: 10.4324/9781003429555-1

Figure 1.1 Anatomy of the human nervous system. The figure shows how cranial nerves branch out in the body. Via these nerves, information from the senses is transported to the brain, and conversely, the brain sends commands for muscle movements and control of other processes to the body via the nerves. The spinal cord (not shown here) is involved in both forms of communication as well.

Source: *De Humani Corporis Fabrica, Libri Septem,* Vesalius, 1543 (woodcut). US National Library of Medicine.

they feed the brain with sensory information, or transfer information from the brain to our muscles or other bodily organs. Almost all this information is sent in the form of millions to billions of electrical pulses that flash across nerve fibres – the ultra-thin wires that make up nerves – every second. The brain receives these pulses directly as signals and it uses them to send messages. The macabre image of us being buried alive in our skulls, only to be subjected to power surges, therefore seems nothing short of logical. The paradox of the brain, however, is that we do not feel this electricity itself: in reality, we do in fact experience smells, colours, tastes, music, pain or pleasure. All those electrical pulses look similar, but they give rise to radically different experiences. Apparently, the brain is mysteriously able to make sense of all the electrical signals and ensure that we have experiences that could hardly be more different from electric shocks.

Despite this uncomfortable anatomical truth, how is it that we are aware of a vibrant and colourful world, in which we move with ease, with a body we can see and feel? Why, for example, does the transmission of electrical pulses by cells in our nasal cavity end up signalling the smell of coffee to us? Evidently, we are not that bothered by our brain's lonely, dark confinement to its cranial pan. How come we feel anything at all? When we contemplate how the grey matter is bombarded by millions of current pulses coming up from the spinal cord and the nerves, nothing seems to ensure we feel anything at all. The grey matter consists of some 150 billion cells (neurons), and we understand fairly well how these neurons work. At first glance, these cells appear to form a gigantic electrical circuit, much like a complex telephone switchboard, where incoming signals are relayed to stations that send commands to control our bodies. You might think: there is no need for any feeling or colour in all of this.

The discrepancy between the hard 'neuro'-reality of our brain and our personal experience of sensory information is referred to in consciousness research as the 'Hard Problem'.[3] Philosophers also refer to this problem as the *Explanatory Gap* – the abyss that looms before us as we attempt to bridge the world of conscious experience[4] and the world of nerve impulses, brain cells and physical manifestations of light and sound energy outside ourselves. In unravelling brain-mind relationships, philosopher David Chalmers distinguishes the Hard Problem from other issues that are easier to tackle. Among these 'Easy Problems' are, for example, brain mechanisms of memory, attention and decision making. Memory, too, is a colossal issue in itself, concerning thousands of researchers around the world. But this problem can at least be approached and tackled with the methods and computer models that we now have. The research field has been demarcated and we know what to look for. We have outlined important brain structures and we know quite a bit about the underlying biochemical and electrical processes. This is more difficult when it comes to consciousness. There are various theoretical schools of thought that approach the problem in fundamentally different ways, and it is not clear beforehand which experiments or models will provide the definitive verdict on one theory or another. In this book, however, I shall make the case that results from neuroscientific research do show us the way through this delta of rivers and marshes. It turns out to be possible to set up a framework that is consistent with both neuroscience and psychology.

To be honest, many of my colleagues in neuroscience are not very keen on the issue of consciousness. They consider it an unsolvable problem because the content of our consciousness is subjective and therefore cannot be described objectively. It would not produce results that other researchers could replicate. One can only say something meaningful about the consciousness of other people or animals by looking at their observable behaviour, they argue, and apart from this behaviour there is nothing to explain or investigate. When it comes to consciousness, the brain is a 'black box' that must remain closed. One of my colleagues recently sighed that the body-mind problem has been a headache for so many centuries that it will probably never be solved. Indeed, René Descartes, around 1641 – when his *Meditationes* were published in Amsterdam – was already battling with the issue, while long before him entire schools of thought such as those of Plato and Aristotle had emerged and gone out of fashion.

A standard argument against any kind of consciousness study is that all our experiences are subjective or private and therefore nothing can be said about them. If students let this objection slip to me after a lecture, I ask them whether they recognize – each individual for themselves – the experience that smelling is something completely different from seeing or hearing. A number of them stare at me with a slightly pitying or vacant expression on their face, and a few good-willed ones say: "Well, that's completely obvious. A truism." Some wonder whether they are in the right hall, and whether there isn't a confused man standing in front of the blackboard. For me, this is a positive sign to continue. The difference between seeing and smelling is so clear to everyone that most people don't feel the need to respond. Seeing, smelling and hearing are immediately recognizable as different experiences. The nice thing about this trivial observation is that it is a '*within-subject comparison*'.[5] In this case, it is not a problem that your experiences are private – only known to yourself – because you are comparing them within your own world of experience. Each person can express that their experiences can be radically different from each other. This experience of difference is confirmed between people: it is a repeatable, reproducible finding. I have never come across anyone in a healthy state of mind who found that smelling, seeing and hearing 'feel' the same.

Ultimately, the argument that we should see consciousness purely as an expression of behaviour makes no sense. If a person's behavioural utterances (including language) are always enough to indicate their state of mind, this means that nothing can be said about a person without perceptible utterances. Such a person might as well have no consciousness. This is contradicted by phenomena in patients with massive brain damage, which I will discuss in more detail later.

Let me give another example that shows why behaviour does not always reveal what a person experiences. In 1998, Charles Heywood, Alan Cowey and colleagues of the universities of Durham and Oxford described a 49-year-old patient with the initials M. S., who suffered from achromatopsia (total colour blindness) as a result of meningitis.[6] At the age of 21 he had contracted an infection with herpes simplex, and this virus had a devastating effect on parts of his cerebral cortex. The virus left him without colour vision, as he explained himself, and he was blind to part of his field of vision. Even with total colour blindness, a patient often retains normal perception of movement, shape, texture, faces, depth and other features of things we see. Brain scans in M. S. showed that a relatively large area in the upper parts of his visual cortex was damaged (these parts are not the primary stations for processing information from our eyes, but engage in more advanced processing). The damage was more extensive than the loss of a smaller area of the cortex that is considered a major brain station for seeing colours (area V4).[7] His visual world was contained in shades of grey and thus became much duller, but within the intact part of his visual field he could still clearly see shape, movement and light reflections on objects.

Then Heywood discovered something remarkable. He had M. S. sit down in front of a screen and showed him four discs in red, green or grey shades, all with the same brightness. Three discs were the same colour and one was deviant. As expected, the patient stated that he could not see any differences between the discs. Even when he was forced to tell which of the four discs had a different colour, his score was no better than might be expected from chance. But when M. S. was asked to make eye movements towards the outlier among the discs, he performed better than you would expect based on chance. This suggests that M. S.'s brain had a surreptitious shortcut for passing colour information to the brain areas that control the eyes, outside the brain's system for conscious colour experience. When M. S. was asked to pick out a deviant colour from a series of separate colour fields of equal brightness, or to name colours, he proved completely unable to do so. But if the colour areas were presented as a continuous whole, he could in fact pick out the deviant colour, and could even indicate the boundary between two different colours. He got this done, as he said, by tracing the edge between two surfaces that in his own perception nevertheless looked identical.

This remarkable result illustrates that observing one's behaviour – pointing out the boundaries between coloured areas – does not necessarily correspond to how one consciously experiences these areas. Fortunately, this patient was able to talk about his lack of colour experience – but had he not been able to speak, this deficiency might never have been noticed.

'Experience' and 'consciousness' are thus not superfluous concepts, and studying them is not an impassable path. Indeed, over the past 30 years, studies of patients, computer simulations and the electrical behaviour of brain cells have paved the way for in-depth research into the brain's mechanisms of consciousness. Of course, research on consciousness depends on the reliability of what people or animals reveal through their words or in their behaviour, but this dependence also applies to all kinds of other research in medicine and biology. When I began my degree in biology in 1982 in the eastern Dutch city of Nijmegen, it was not done to get mixed up with consciousness. Such vagueness belonged in philosophy, and perhaps, turning a blind eye, in psychology. Later, in Amsterdam, I decided to combine neurobiology with all subsidiary subjects in philosophy that contained even a wisp of mind-brain material. A delightful tandem, I thought, but not a direction in which you could continue your studies. You had to choose. I chose a research position in brain research and, with some regret and a heavy heart, turned my back on philosophy. But the problem continued to gnaw and ferment. I continued to read literature, keep notes and search for ways to reunite brain and mind. It was not until years later, when I was a postdoctoral fellow at the California Institute of Technology in Pasadena, that I attended an inspiring lecture by

Francis Crick, the scientist who, together with James Watson, discovered the structure of DNA.[8] Once he had grown grey hairs, Crick decided that the time was ripe for what he saw as the most perplexing, puzzling problem in biology. Arriving at his last slide, frowning his imposing white eyebrows, he displayed his final chord. On the slide were the two words '*Consciousness Now!*' – in a perspective that cast an ominous shadow towards the audience. The cause started rolling again and excited a growing number of neuroscientists. Crick teamed up with Christof Koch, who wrote a seminal and empirically minded book on consciousness.[9] Today, students can choose all kinds of directions in the Brain and Cognitive Sciences, with a customizable dose of consciousness.

Properties of conscious experience

When I ask people around me about it, they are usually very good at telling me when they were and when they were not in a conscious state during the past 24 hours. When we wake up in the morning, our brains leave their sleeping state and we become conscious. When asked, people are perfectly capable of naming and describing the things they are consciously aware of. It requires more brain-racking to describe what consciousness itself is, for ourselves or for others. When you are conscious, you are in a state of having experiences – memorable moments of taste, smell, music, warmth, pain, touch and compositions of colours, shapes and movement that fill up your visual field. But what is an experience? Attempts to define experience lead us back to consciousness itself, or related concepts such as 'realising', 'feeling' or 'noticing'. Is 'knowing' perhaps a good alternative? We can stare at a wall full of graffiti and see it consciously, without knowing or realising what it says.

Can consciousness or awareness[10] be captured by seeing it as a state of thoughtful action? "I was well aware of the quality and price of those shoes when I bought them", says a girl to her mother on suspicion of an impulse buy. But here she mainly means that she thought her decision through – not that she became sensorily aware of the smell or colour of the shoes, or how they fitted her feet. Consciousness is like a little ferret that, with its smooth fur, wriggles out of your hands every time you think you have caught it. This book is mainly about sensory consciousness – and how the extraordinary tissue of the brain, crackling with electrical activity, is able to make us experience the world with its wealth of qualities as a matter of course. Later, I will deal with other, more highly developed forms of consciousness such as self-consciousness, while consciously dealing with the big questions of life (climate awareness, etc.) will remain outside the scope of this book. 'Awareness' and 'consciousness' will be regarded as the same phenomenon here.

Apart from waking up, there is at least one other daily event that makes us collectively realize that we have a consciousness: we lose it when we fall asleep. When your eyes become heavy, you feel yourself slowly slipping away. But you miss the moment when you really fall asleep – because that is when you lose consciousness. You can't catch the tipping point: you could only catch it if your consciousness was still there. Consciousness is delimited by the realization that we lose it for a large part of the night. It is that grip on reality – on the situation you are in – that defines consciousness. Sleep takes us from a superficial stage to deeper waters, free of perception. Later in the night, the brain manages to work its way up from its state of deep sleep to a slumber or dream. A dream is something that we experience and, with a bit of luck, can remember when we wake up. Dreams, therefore, belong to the realm of consciousness, although they represent a peculiar condition that is different from fantasizing or daydreaming in a waking state. And the funny thing is: our body is largely paralyzed during dreaming: here, too, consciousness occurs essentially without behaviour![11] When we finally wake up in the morning, everyday life intrudes again – either suddenly, or through a slow awareness of where or who you are.

But through all this sleeping, dreaming and waking, the brain remained one and the same. It was constantly active, even in the deepest sleep. When an awake person is exposed to electrical stimulation of a nerve running from the hand to the brain, a response can be measured in the cerebral cortex: a series of waves of electrical activity. If the same person is put under anaesthesia, one might expect this reaction to cease due to the suppressive effect of the chemical inducing loss of consciousness, but here too the nerve continues to conduct tactile stimuli and the cerebral cortex continues to respond with electrical waves. Overall, the reaction remains more or less the same during loss of consciousness and in the awake state.[12] And yet, the test subject does not react to the stimulus and, upon awakening, is unable to report that she experienced anything. Most likely the test subject did not feel anything, but yet her cortex was active. What causes this difference?

Apart from the sleep-wake cycle, human consciousness manifests itself strongly in the moment, the split second in which you did or did not notice a red traffic light. Here too, a confusion of concepts lurks in the background. Take a motion detector in the garden that switches on a bright lamp when a burglar or cat passes by. Does the motion detector 'see' anything? Vision normally involves forming an image of the surroundings, complete with garden terrace, deck chairs, bushes and trees – and perhaps the cat. That is not the case here. 'Detection' in this context refers to all kinds of cases where living beings, devices or other objects react to a stimulus in their environment in a way that is perceptible to others. Detection is thus a much broader concept than consciousness: an animal or device does not have to be aware of something to be able to detect it.

Therefore, I shall save 'perception' for conscious processing of sensory stimuli. A smoke detector does not perceive smoke, it merely detects it. Via electronic circuits, the binding of molecules to a smoke sensor activates a pungent alarm. Does this mean the device is devoid of all forms of consciousness? The 'behaviour' of the thing – setting off a shrill sound – is so simple that there is no decent reason to assume consciousness. The internal circuitry is simple and does not suggest it could produce anything as complex as a percept. But

we will have to do some exploring to determine when living or artificial creatures *can* sustain perception, regardless of its simplicity. For now, nothing
seems to stop you from slapping the smoke detector when you get fed up with
that annoying alarm. We can safely assume the detector is not in pain. This
demarcation of concepts may seem like splitting hairs, but proves indispensable in the debate about which kinds of beings – animals, embryos, robots,
computers – have consciousness and which do not.

Smoke detectors and other down-to-earth sensors force us to confront that
conscious experience is always *about* something: an experience is not about
the electronic signal itself, or the vibration in the speaker that generates the
alarm sound, but about the scent of smoke that you smell. If we put ourselves
in the shoes of a dog who raises his wet nose to sniff the air, we can easily
imagine that this creature will experience something, in much the same way
as we ourselves experience something in a similar situation.[13] It must feel like
something to be that dog, but this 'feeling that the other is feeling something'
is missing in the case of the smoke detector. Olfactory cells in our nasal cavity
transmit electrical signals to an elaborate olfactory network in our brain, and
these brain cells generate a complex pattern of electrical activity, which apparently encodes an experience of something other than itself. Something that
moreover takes place outside the brain: we locate the smell of smoke in the
outside world. This key property of conscious experience is denoted as '*aboutness*' (or *intentionality*).[14]

Not only is perception part of our conscious life; imagination also contributes to it. Imagination is one of the most powerful, yet least understood,
phenomena produced by our brain. Without external stimuli and with our
eyes closed, we can conjure up a vivid image, a melody, a spoken sentence or
a complex social situation. Dreams, too, occur spontaneously, without external stimuli, and share with imagination the property of being generated from
within the brain. But while we ourselves can somewhat control what we imagine, dreams take their own course. With their often bizarre progressions and
emotional charges, in which elements present themselves through loose and
wild associations, dreams distinguish themselves from processes of the imagination, which are more easily regulated. Dreams withdraw from the logic of
our predictable everyday life.

Perception, imagination or dream: every experience revolves around
something, whether that something is real or not. These manifestations of
consciousness have something else in common: all three are a matter of interpretation. On 26 February 2015, the blue-or-white dress went viral on the
internet (Figure 1.2). Among the millions of tweets, Taylor Swift and Justin
Bieber stated that the dress was blue and black, while Katy Perry, Julianne
Moore and US Senator Chris Murphy insisted it was white and gold. Kim
Kardashian declared her solidarity with the white-and-gold camp and got into
an argument with her husband Kanye West, belonging to the blue-and-black
experiencers. A few chosen ones were able to switch their perception between
the two colour combinations. Entire families were split by frantic debate, as

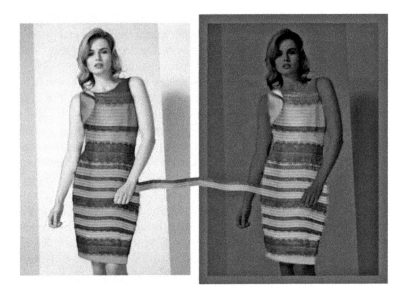

Figure 1.2 (Left) The blue-or-white dress designed by the British company Roman Originals. (Right) Same as on the left, but now all of the picture is darkened, except for the dress itself, which now 'lights up'. The ribbon connecting the two dresses illustrates that the same colour composition is maintained from left to right. People who see the left version in blue and black tend to have more of a white/gold impression when looking at the right.

Source: Justin Broackes, The Brains Blog, 23 March 2015, https://philosophyofbrains.com/2015/03/23/how-does-a-black-and-blue-dress-sometimes-appear-white-and-gold.aspx. Reproduced with permission from Justin Broackes and Hilary Brown, and Roman (Ian Johnson, www.roman.co.uk).

if it were about the election of Donald Trump or Hillary Clinton that was upcoming at the same time.

How does this striking difference in perception relate to that other, chilly image of the brain sitting underneath the skull cap, fed with millions of electrical impulses? In the case of the dress, the difference in colour perception is not subtle, like in a discussion with your neighbour who judges a shade of turquoise to be 'green' and you judge it to be 'blue'. From the eyes, with their retinas studded with protein molecules that capture light, electrical impulses are transmitted to the brain. These impulses are also called action potentials or *spikes* because of their sharp peaks that become visible if you plot electrical voltage against time. The strange thing about the blue-or-white dress is that it is one and the same sensory stimulus that evokes very different experiences, sometimes in the same person. The influx of spikes into the brain, distributed over some 1.5 million optical nerve fibres per eye, is relatively constant. But what our brain or mind makes of this is not the tsunami of spikes coming at it, but a colour. Apparently, the brain is able to interpret the stream of pulses as a colour. This is not an 'interpretation' as when we explain the plot of a novel in words, but a 'translation' of light-evoked pulse patterns into perception. This is already miraculous in itself, but the blue-or-white dress cranks it up a notch: with the same stimulus, two interpretations are evoked.

Thus, the squabbling over a dress underlines that consciousness is a very special state of our brain. Let us pause here and look back at the essential characteristics of consciousness that have come to pass so far. First and foremost, our consciousness displays an extraordinary wealth of sensory qualities. We are not only aware of what we see and hear, but we also have the sense of smell and taste, a sense of balance and all kinds of physical sensations from our skin, muscles and internal organs. The pain of a pinprick feels fundamentally different from a light caress. This richness is a fundamental characteristic of conscious experience. Colour sensation is radically different from the feeling of a brushstroke on your hand or the smell of an autumn forest. Physics teaches us to link colour to the wavelength of light falling into the eye, which allows us to express colour in a number – a quantification of colour. But this does not explain why we experience colour as a quality that is so obviously different from, for example, pitch, texture or movement. Like light, we can capture pitch in a number – the number of vibrations with which a sound wave travels through the air per second – but these numbers themselves do not reveal how differently we experience colour and sound, and why they are two different sensory qualities.

A second characteristic of consciousness: what we experience in terms of richness is open to interpretation. This interpretation is about something (*aboutness*): not about which neurons are active in our brain, but about what happens before our eyes and what other sensations we have beyond that. The blue-or-white dress illustrates this characteristic to the core. Besides richness and interpretation, at least three other characteristics can be distinguished that are applicable to conscious experiences of healthy people. If one loses consciousness, the processing of sensory stimuli continues to some degree, but it is no longer experienced. You feel nothing, and apart from your own body, which remains visible to others, you are absent – you are temporarily 'gone'. When you come back from 'being away', you realize your conscious state is characterized by the fact that you are always somewhere, that is, in a situation that takes place in space and time. When you wake up, you are not looking at your world from a distance – as if you were playing a third-person video game – but are in the middle of it. Inevitably and immediately you are 'immersed' in a situation.[15] I will refer to this third characteristic as 'situatedness' and 'immersion'.

You experience the situation you are in as an integrated unit. By this fourth characteristic – integration or unity – I mean that at each moment of our waking existence we experience only one situation or scene at a time. This seems trivial, but because we have, for example, two eyes that each provide a separate image of the environment, it is remarkable that our brain is able to merge the information from two separate retinas into one image. We see only one world.

When we scan our surroundings with our eyes – a series of movements that we are normally not aware of – we do not see a series of separate images that jump from one to another. Eye movements cause a different part of the visual field to be projected onto the retina each time (Figure 1.3). This would result in a chaotic series of ever staggering images each time – something that could easily make us dizzy and nauseous. But we see one stable image of the outside world. Apparently, there is something going on in the brain that corrects for these chaotic eye movements.

The integrative capacity of the brain applies to all senses that contribute to an experience, such as when we understand the words of an interlocutor from a combination of visual lip movements and sounds. What we hear is determined not only by sound waves reaching our ear, but also by what we see. The brain can easily be fooled. If we watch a ventriloquist with a puppet on his lap moving its lips, we experience the illusion that the spoken words come from the puppet's mouth. Our brains are forging two separate inputs – the sounds and visual lip movements – into a single experience, not an interpretation consisting of two separate experiences.

Finally, we perceive situations from a personal perspective. This fifth characteristic is experienced first and foremost as a visual perspective: the fact that we perceive the world based on the orientation of our eyes and head in relation to the outside world. You do not see the world from above, as if

Figure 1.3 Eye movements enable us to direct our gaze subsequently to different points in our field of view. When a test subject looks at the painting (left), our eyes move quickly from one part of the picture to another (right; white lines and dots). Notice how often the human gaze lingers on interesting parts such as faces and hands.

Adapted from: Yarbus (1967). Yarbus' original material has been adapted into the version shown here, by M. Neault "Tracking the gaze" (Art 21 magazine, 7 Jan. 2013; http://magazine.art21.org/2013/01/07/tracking-the-gaze/#.YBpWMi2ZM0o), as cited in: Alvare and Gordon (2015). The painting ('Unexpected Visitors') was made by Ilya Repin around 1884-1888.

you were looking down on yourself like a Pac-Man navigating a map. This perception from one's own perspective also applies to other senses, although this is often not immediately obvious. I do not smell a rose near my left big toe, but I experience its odour as being near my nose. I effortlessly locate a wasp sting on the back of my left thigh, even though I cannot directly see the spot where this occurs. We also experience our body as a spatial object, and our 'eyes' for this object are the sensors in our skin, muscles and internal organs.

These characteristics of consciousness (qualitative richness, interpretation and aboutness, situatedness and immersion, unity and perspective; Table 1.1) will be popping up again hereafter. They are closely interrelated. One of the key questions is how exactly these characteristics are connected and whether they can be captured in one overarching theory. They can be found in the various forms by which consciousness manifests itself: perception, imagination and dreaming. Perception is dependent on an external stimulus in a context that is consciously experienced. For imagination, we do not need an external stimulus: we close our eyes and can direct what we experience visually or hear as a *monologue intérieur*. This internal 'talking to yourself' also counts as imagination, even though we do not envision an 'image', and it is mainly our auditory system that is active here.

Table 1.1 Essential characteristics of consciousness

Essential features of consciousness	Description
1. Qualitative wealth	Consciousness is characterized by a wealth of diverse experiences in different kinds of senses (modalities): seeing, hearing, smelling, taste, touch, sense of balance and other sensations from the body. We do not experience sensory signals as one homogeneous mush of information.
2. Interpretation	The blue-or-white dress illustrates how a single sensory stimulus can lead to a big difference in perception. Brain activity linked to consciousness is about something – not about itself, but about something outside the brain.
3. Situatedness	What we consciously experience takes place somewhere – we are immersed in a situation set in space and time.
4. Unity	We can only have one conscious experience at a time: visually, for example, we do not experience two or more images or scenes simultaneously. Similarly, the various sensory modalities do not produce many experiences in parallel, but only one integral experience.
5. Perspective	We experience visual sensations from a personal point of view that depends on the orientation of our eyes and head in relation to the outside world. Also in other modalities, sensations depend on the positioning of sense organs in relation to our body and the outside world.

Consciousness: why now?

Bickering about a blue or white dress is amusing, but is that the only reason to talk about consciousness? If everything in our behaviour is regulated by brain cells and electrical activity anyway, if everything is ultimately just a dance of molecules and currents, why should we even bother with something as intangible as our mental life – our 'psyche'? There is more to this than that consciousness cannot be easily dismissed as a non-problem or elusive phenomenon. There is more to consciousness than meets the eye in a person's external behaviour. When people fall into a coma or vegetative state after an accident or a medical problem, their ability to express themselves is absent or extremely limited. A famous and tragic example is the fate of Terri Schiavo, who was 26 years old when she suffered a heart attack on 25 February 1990. Resuscitation could not prevent her brain from being exposed to prolonged oxygen deprivation. After two and a half months she was diagnosed as 'persistent vegetative': her body showed a sleep-wake rhythm and she could occasionally open her eyes, but her brain was irreparably damaged. At the request of doctors, she was unable to make voluntary movements such as lifting her arm, was unable to communicate through words or gestures and did not respond clearly or reliably to her mother's presence. The damage to her cerebral cortex was massive and it was highly doubtful whether she still had any consciousness – an inner perception of herself and the world around her. After 15 years of being fed artificially, her husband and parents feuded over whether she should be kept alive or not, culminating in a protracted legal battle from local Florida courts to the Supreme Court and back. President George W. Bush and his brother Jeb pushed for new legislation to stretch the lives of these patients, but in the end, the Federal Supreme Court allowed the feeding tube to be removed. Terri Schiavo died on 31 March 2005. Crucial to the court's decision to allow her life to end was not only whether Terri would have had the desire to die in her current situation, but also whether she would ever regain a functioning consciousness. Her case is one of many on a gradual scale ranging from brain death to a situation of complete lock-in. In locked-in syndrome, a person is fully conscious, but is unable to express her thoughts or feelings at all due to a nearly complete body paralysis. Usually, vertical eye movements are still possible. Across the full width of this scale, in addition to clinical tests, brain measurements are required to determine the extent to which a person is still conscious. For this group of people, the issue of consciousness has been ignored for too long.

Yet, the importance of consciousness is underlined just as much by the emotional life of healthy people as in extreme cases of deep brain damage. An example is a transgender person who has the body of a girl but who internally feels himself to be a boy inside. This conscious feeling does not correspond to physical appearance. An expert who has no interest in the phenomenon of consciousness and only looks at external physical characteristics, would conclude that this person is 100 per cent female. Fortunately, this external assessment is no longer the only thing that counts: gender identity is about a person's fundamental feeling of being male or female (or non-binary). The conscious feeling counts heavily, and rightly so.

Even if you are not transgender, it is interesting to know what goes on in the consciousness of yourself and of other people. When you take one of your nephews to the zoo and he begs for an ice cream, do you grant him one? And after much whining, do you give him an ice cream to jack up the glucose level in his blood or is it about giving him a pleasurable experience? Don't all the things that really matter to our lives – the things that bring us sorrow, pain, pleasure, love or joy – pass through our consciousness sooner or later? When I get on my bicycle, I am not interested in the pedal movements of my feet, but I am consciously concerned with my destination or what might happen there. I do not need to be aware of eye movements – but I do need to be aware of what my eyes are focusing on. Thus, our consciousness appears to be inextricably linked to everything that matters in our lives and that makes them worthwhile. Around the year 57, the apostle Paul wrote in his first letter to the Corinthians: "If I were to speak with the tongues of men and of angels, but had not love, I would be a sounding brass or a tinkling cymbal."[16] Or a smoke detector, to keep up with the times. There is an endless chain of examples illustrating that consciousness cannot be ignored. In the case of someone who considers euthanasia, a doctor does not assess whether her body is too sick or too old, but whether there is unbearable and hopeless suffering – again, a question of consciousness.

All in all, there is little reason to be downhearted about our brains as prisoners in their dark encasement, tortured with electric pulses. Apparently, our brain has figured out something miraculous: perception or interpretation of sensory information delivered by way of electrical spikes – but a perception of something other than the spikes themselves. We are not forced to feel buried alive. That's nice, but how do perception and interpretation actually *work*? Who or what in the brain is responsible for this? The more we deal with brain damage or disease, the more we realize what a fantastic, beautiful phenomenon consciousness really is. It seems like magic that the brain, with its rather uniform cells and electrical pulses, can produce such hugely different experiences. The smell of a cowpat is not comparable to listening to a song by The Beatles. Without wishing to resort to the supernatural, it seems that an illusionist is at work. And in a way, that is what we will ask ourselves: is the brain itself an illusionist?

This book is a travel guide for an adventurous journey through the deep valleys of the unconscious to the peaks of our most intense experiences – a journey that seeks to discover what consciousness is in essence, what it has to do with brain processes that regulate memory, emotion, motor movement or sensory sensitivity, and how it relates to the minuscule patterns of activity that take place in the mushy swamps of our brain cells. Like a medieval traveller plotting his path on ancient maps with dragons and sea monsters, we will be confronted with bizarre life forms that raise the question of how consciousness arose during the evolution of life on earth. The journey will take us past treacherous hallucinations, delusions and other misfits of consciousness, and will make us doubt fundamental certainties we think we have, such as the existence of ourselves and a reality outside ourselves. The quest will take us past the ravine of the Hard Problem, through the Woods of Expectation, and make us question whether it ultimately leads to the Holy Grail of the conscious computer, or whether this is just grandiloquence and hubris. This book is not a dry list of all the questions or possibilities that arise in exploring consciousness and the brain. It does not take a neutral stance but rather points out which paths are impassable and which lead to fertile grounds for further investigation. This is, in short, a guide to a journey that, while it can be undertaken from the comfort of an armchair, requires efforts of imagination and logical thought. This is not a book for the faint-hearted – it has been written for doubters, tinkerers, ponderers, trackers and others who are simply curious about what goes on in the top bunk of our body.

2 A phantom on the operating table

Descartes' quest in Amsterdam: the dissection of the body and the indivisibility of consciousness

The year 1641 is an exciting one for the Low Countries. The Seven Provinces are winning ground in the war against Spain. Governor and army commander Frederik Hendrik conquers cities in the province of Limburg, the city of Malacca capitulates to the Dutch expansionism in South-East Asia, the Dutch gain a foothold in Japan with their settlement of Deshima and at the peace of The Hague an alliance is forged with Portugal against Spain. Amsterdam is a bustling refuge for Protestants from Antwerp, Jews from the Iberian Peninsula and other dissenters who want to escape from living under the oppressive Catholic Spanish yoke. Amsterdam's pivotal position in trade makes merchants rich, and this attracts people who want to get a piece of the pie. Among them is Rembrandt van Rijn, who is busy painting *The Night Watch*. That year, his wife Saskia gives him a son, Titus.

At that moment, René Descartes has been living in the Low Countries for 13 years and publishes his *Meditationes*.[1] In it he expounds his body-mind philosophy and posits his immortal trinity of words: *Cogito ergo sum* ("I think therefore I am"). Why was this statement so shocking and revolutionary? When we are awake and healthy, it is quite normal to think. The fact that we are there – that we exist – is not surprising either. So what is the big deal?

In 1618 Descartes had already volunteered as a 21-year-old to join the Dutch army led by Maurice, Prince of Orange. The brand-new prince acted as a magnet for Descartes because of his successes in the nation's struggle for independence and his interest in mathematics, politics and engineering. René did not feel a need to fight very hard or to lead the way into battle. He wanted to gain experience, become a man of the world and was curious about the applications of mathematics in waterworks and fortifications. Irreverent gossip may have had it that Descartes was not a trigger-happy soldier, aversive to real combat. On the other hand, he was not afraid to share his insights on everything that interested him with all and sundry. As an intellectual glutton, he immersed himself in the mathematics of conic sections, the movement of celestial bodies, the free fall of stones in a vacuum or the idea that all art is intended to awaken emotions in us. Above all, Descartes wanted to go his own way and develop his thinking in freedom. As he left the Netherlands in 1619 to travel on through Europe, he wrote that he wanted to roam the world in

DOI: 10.4324/9781003429555-2

an attempt to be more of an observer than an actor in all the comedies that are performed there.[2]

Somewhere in the years before 1641, Descartes visits a hospital in Leiden. It is a dirty place; the staff members do not wash their hands in preparing for surgery and many of the sick are treated with a venesection. But it is here that Descartes discovers something essential about the relationship between body and mind. He meets a young girl who has had one arm amputated. In an attempt not to let this trauma hit her too hard, the staff does not tell the girl what has happened to her arm, and the wound is concealed from her view with a large bandage. Without knowing about the amputation, she tells them that she has pain, not in her arm stump but in her hand – sometimes in one finger and sometimes in another.[3] We now know this type of sensation as phantom pain. In the seventeenth century, this was a relatively unknown phenomenon, although surgeons in the bloodstained field hospitals of the European armies will have known it here and there because of the numerous amputations of limbs.

Descartes observes the girl's gestures and utterances, and realizes how deceptive sensations can be. She feels pain in a part of her body that is no longer attached to it. "For what can be closer to me than pain?" Descartes wonders. "But I once heard, from those who had a leg or arm amputated, that they still seemed to feel pain in the part of their body that was missing."[4] So the reliability of the senses must be doubted, and it is primarily our intellect that can unravel with rigid, mathematical precision how body and mind interlock. Deception of the senses has long been a theme in Descartes' work. A straight cane that sticks halfway into transparent water and halfway out of it seems to make an acute bend exactly on the surface of the water. He argues that this is based on a physical law of refraction that we now know as Snell's law, but which could have been attributed to Descartes as well. The law makes me think back to some less exciting physics lessons at high school – a subject for a lazy summer afternoon in a class where everyone is longing for a swimming pool – until I return to the present and realize with some embarrassment how special it was in Descartes' time to approach physical phenomena with mathematical equations. In seventeenth-century France, Descartes had been taught at the Jesuit college La Flèche in the Loire Valley, where he enjoyed mathematics. But there he was also confronted with a dominant and outdated scholastic philosophy that was unable to apply mathematical tools in practice, and lumped all physical phenomena together, without delineating natural laws. A mathematical treatise on the deflection of light rays at the transition from air to water was utterly lacking. That seemingly snapped stick is not an illusion resulting from a peculiarity of our senses and brains, but the consequence of a physical principle that fitted exactly into Descartes' geometric way of reasoning. A triumph of reason.

Now, in Leiden, there is more to it. The girl has lost her arm 'purely physically' but in her mind, to speak in the framework of that time, there is the sensation of one intact body. Descartes concludes: the body is divisible, but the mind is indivisible. So these two things must be separate, although they are somehow connected. At first sight, this is not an unreasonable conclusion. But it is not an inference based on a hard, geometrical proof such as Pythagoras' Theorem, which can be proved mathematically. It is a conclusion that fits in with Descartes' time, in which more and more attention is paid to logical thinking and independent observation of phenomena in nature – but also a time that still relies heavily in all respects on the unshakeable, Christian belief in an independent soul that lives on after the death of the body. Descartes has to play a completely different game here than he did with the law of refraction, but he sticks to his iron-clad mathematical principles. He develops his famous dualistic thesis: body and mind are two separate, essentially different substances. The body as something that occupies physical space, a *res extensa*, and the mind as a thinking thing that does not occupy space, the *res cogitans*.

The big problem Descartes continues to face is how the two connect. To this day, this is still an issue that the few remaining dualists are grappling with. Light, pressure on the skin and the heat of a campfire are phenomena in the external, physical realm that prompt our 'mind' to feel and recognize them.[5] When we feel hungry, our mind wants our body to move around and find food. The body influences the mind and the mind influences the body – but how? Assiduously, Descartes searches for a solution to this riddle. For much of his time in the Low Countries, Descartes lives in Amsterdam's Kalverstraat, where he dissects animal carcasses from the slaughterhouse. Every now and then, he goes out into the street to find some distraction. There he is confronted time and again with the horrible stench: of horse manure, rotting fish and human faeces dumped in the canals; of the countless pig farms, tanners and soap makers in the city. He tries to repress his olfactory sensations by chewing on tobacco and clove, freshly brought from the East Indies. The sound of hammers on anvils gets on his nerves.

On to the Sint Antoniesbreestraat, past the luxurious house of the painter Rembrandt, where he finds some relief in the play of light from the sun and clouds on the water. The wealth of sensory titillations makes him dizzy. Then he heads to the moored island of Vlooijenburg and the Houtgracht, where he mingles with a crowd of people who are just pouring out of the Portuguese synagogue. As he passes, he bumps into a boy of about nine years old, dressed formally in a black suit, white shoes and wearing a striking white, broad-brimmed hat.[6] The boy babbles something in Portuguese and scampers out of the way. Cheeky little brat, Descartes must have thought, everyone here is busy with themselves and can do what they like. With a hint of loneliness, he notes: I could live here all my life without ever being noticed by anyone.[7]

Descartes eventually arrives at the idea that the nerves that crisscross our bodies form a system of channels or conduits upon which the mind, sitting in the brain, exerts pressure in order to push 'animal spirit' through the body and convert it into muscular movement. In his view, this 'animal spirit' is a mysterious substance created by heating blood in the heart – something like the material a flame is composed of – and transported from there to the brain.

Descartes is clearly struggling here with the lack of knowledge in his time; today we would immediately replace 'animal spirit' with 'nervous activity'. In the seventeenth century it was not yet known that the nervous system runs on electricity, and it was not until 1780 that Luigi Galvani discovered that muscle movements could be induced by electrically exciting a nerve.

Where in the brain could the mind be? Descartes reasoned: the mind is uniform and must therefore consist of one piece, whereas most parts of the brain are present in duplicate, both in the left and right hemisphere. This is how he arrives at the pineal gland.[8] Named after its pinecone-like shape, in humans this organ is hidden under the cerebral cortex, up against the thalamus (Figure 2.1) – just over the midline that separates the two halves. But even with his astute intellect, Descartes cannot compete against the shadows of the era he lives in. It is not only the lack of biological knowledge and empirical testing that trips him up. It is also the dominance of the church that leaves no space to doubt the dogma of the separation of body and soul. However powerful his method of mathematical reasoning may be, he gets stuck with his pineal-gland-with-channels theory. He cannot clarify how the mind is housed, or how it manages to propel the 'animal spirit' through specific tubes. His project runs aground in disintegrated cadavers. In Descartes' time, too, critics were diligently sawing the legs from under his theory. Not long after Descartes, the Dutch naturalist and animal researcher Jan Swammerdam (1637–1680) carried out experiments that denied that the mind could drive muscles by means of a hydraulic or pneumatic system of tubes.

Yet Descartes continues to intrigue. His restless search, his stubbornness and creativity remain particularly contagious – even if the latter sometimes comes across as a bit clumsy in the way he tries to capture the complexity of the mind in plain mechanics. Even though in his time Descartes was forced to seek compromises with the church – which considered the immortality of the soul to be a given – it remains miraculous how he pulled himself out of the swamp by his own mathematical hair and bootstrapped his scientific approach.

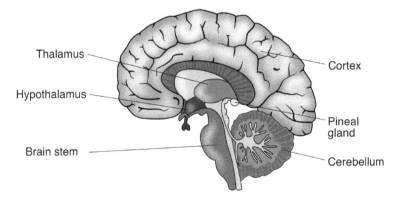

Figure 2.1 Location of the cortex, thalamus, pineal gland, hypothalamus, brainstem and cerebellum in the human brain.

In his book *Descartes' Error*, the Portuguese neurologist António Damásio criticizes the philosopher: with his emphasis on rational reasoning as the greatest good, Descartes would seriously neglect the role of emotions and moods in our mental lives. Descartes did indeed think that emotions such as love and sadness can disrupt the mind, but he recognized that emotions are part of the mind and did not see them as aberrations or disturbances.[9]

Descartes was no stranger to violent emotions. Not much is known about his private life, but we are fairly certain that around 1634 he had an extramarital affair for about a year with a maidservant, Helena Jans. Strangely enough, Descartes himself has documented when he fathered a daughter with her: on Sunday 7 September 1634, probably at the 'Westerkeerck Straet' in Amsterdam. The threesome stayed alternately in places like Deventer, Amersfoort, Santpoort and possibly Egmond. Although Descartes accepted the responsibility of his paternity and was present at Francine's baptism, the secret of his illegitimate parenthood had to be simultaneously concealed. What effect did this ongoing secrecy have on the couple? How did he feel about her? It is clear that the relationship came to an end, even though Descartes made efforts to arrange accommodation for mother and child. At the age of five, Francine was assigned a governess by her father who would take care of her education. Then the girl fell ill. Her body became covered in red-purple spots and she died of scarlet fever on 7 September 1640.[10] Descartes was inconsolable. Acknowledging his pain, he noted that he refused to believe that tears and sorrow belonged only to women. He was not the cold-hearted mechanic that some later made him out to be. After the death of his daughter, he would only have ten years to live himself. At the invitation of Queen Christina of Sweden, he left Egmond in 1649, but was caught in his new homeland by an exceptionally harsh winter. On 11 February 1650, after violent fever attacks and futile bloodletting, he gave up the ghost. In 1667 his body was taken to Paris, but Descartes' skull probably remained in Sweden until 1821.

For our understanding of the relationship between body and mind, his contribution remains above all: *Cogito ergo sum*. Even if you doubt all your senses and wonder what is real, at least one thing remains undisputed: doubt itself. I doubt and therefore I must exist. Bodily sensations and things in the outside world are uncertain, but our doubting mind is not. Descartes' genius lies in the twist by which he transforms his doubt into a positive observation – there must be something that does the doubting. That is Descartes' revolution: his big deal. But jumping ahead with the benefit of hindsight: to what extent is this something, the mind, really a unity? And what is the 'I' that has nestled itself almost unnoticed in this train of thought? Is having a mind, or consciousness, equal to having an indivisible 'I'?

At one side, Descartes' ideas hinge on modernity, with its advanced natural science, and at the other, on medieval philosophy, rooted in antiquity with Plato and Aristotle as its central figures. From the perspective of the twenty-first century, Descartes' preoccupation with the pineal gland and its hydraulic tube system may seem bizarre, but his orientation towards the brain was in any case heading in the right direction. In the fourth century BC, Aristotle and his contemporaries saw the brain as a ventilation device, intended to cool the blood with inhaled air. The soul had to reside in the heart, because that organ reacts palpably to stimuli that move us.

Beyond Descartes: the dissection of body and mind

So actually Descartes' quest was not so bad. How should philosophy and science proceed after his death? There was no systematic neurology that linked brain damage to loss of functions such as locomotion, sensation, vision or consciousness. Surgeons and medics had anecdotal evidence that roughly linked brain damage, often from a blow to the skull or a fired musket ball, to deterioration in the victim's mental functioning. But this inaccurate evidence got little further than the knowledge the ancient Egyptians already had, who left us papyrus scrolls from the seventeenth century BC in which they already described how an open wound in the skull could lead to abnormal eye movements or a shuffling gait. It was in this context of medical ignorance that the German doctor Franz Joseph Gall came up with a new approach at the end of the eighteenth century: cranioscopy or phrenology. Lacking knowledge about the structure and function of the brain, he turned to something he could measure well: the size and position of lumps on the skull of a test subject. He linked these nodules to special capacities of the same person and thus arrived at a map of the head on which functions such as caution and self-confidence were located.

In the twenty-first century, we feel somewhat smug when looking back on Franz Joseph Gall. With his phrenology, he made a valiant attempt to dissect the mind into separate functions and to link these to brain areas. If someone had a well-hung lump in the centre of the back of the head and was a good family man, it was concluded that the area of cerebral cortex under the lump had a strong predisposition towards love for offspring. Today's pitying look stems from the wild and erroneous conclusions Gall drew from his skull measurements. The assumption that skull thickening can be traced to detailed mental abilities tickles the funny bone of many contemporary neuroscientists. Yet today, with the blossoming of brain imaging techniques, there is something weird going on with phrenological thinking.

Suppose a test subject is placed into a magnetic resonance imaging (MRI) scanner and exposed to emotional images, such as pictures of bloody attacks and serious traffic accidents. In comparison, neutral images are offered, such as images of traffic intersections where nothing out of the ordinary happens. In response to the images, a hot spot is found in the amygdala,[11] meaning a place that at that moment shows increased metabolic activity. This activity is measured with a special variant of MRI that is sensitive to local oxygen consumption in brain areas, functional MRI (fMRI). The increased activity can be seen on an image of the brain as a 'hot' colour such as yellow or red. Eventually, a series of measurements on a group of test subjects will lead to a publication in which we will usually read that the amygdala is indeed the brain area where fear and dismay are located. But is this also what the brain scans show in this case? The amygdala is involved in many functions, including sexuality and pleasure. Moreover, fear is a complex phenomenon: it is an emotion that is not only constituted by a feeling, but is also accompanied by a propensity to action, with all sorts of physical reactions such as a quickened heartbeat and a lightning-fast analysis of the situation that arouses fear. This complex interplay requires activity in a network of at least a dozen other brain areas connected to the amygdala. It is therefore wrong to link 'fear and terror' to the amygdala on a one-to-one basis: seeing a bloody attack activates a whole network of areas that regulate many aspects of our emotional reactivity.

Every so often, newspapers report that the nucleus accumbens is a centre of delight, and dopamine is a substance giving pleasure. Are you shopping or sitting at the table with an exciting new date? All your pleasure is – wham! – explained by the release of a jolt of dopamine and the activation of your nucleus accumbens. It is hard to imagine a greater nonsense. A crucial mistake made here is that there would be a one-to-one link between a brain area or a chemical substance and an extremely complex and subjective thing like pleasure. Ironically, this popularizing way of doing science takes us back to Gall's very approach that was met with so much ridicule and mockery before. Even in the twenty-first century, there is a resurgence of phrenology – a 'neophrenology'. Scientists are still trying to attribute mental functions to one specific brain area – a land grab of the mind. For some functions, a direct link can be somewhat justified, but most mental capacities are too complex to be linked to one area.

If there is one mental function that is difficult to fathom, it is consciousness. If we want to connect this phenomenon to brain areas, where should we start? We can subject consciousness to the dissecting knife, but which cognitive functions count as essential, and which aspects are there for bacon and beans? In a broad sense, 'cognition' is different from consciousness. Traditionally, cognition is associated with our (conscious) thinking and the acquisition of knowledge, but in recent decades, the concept has fanned out to encompass all kinds of functions: perception, imagination, dreaming, working memory and long-term memory (including declarative and procedural memory), emotion, planning, decision-making, attention and language (Table 2.1). This list comprises essential cognitive functions but can be expanded at will. Some functions fall within the domain of consciousness, others can also take place unconsciously or are coupled to consciousness to a varying degree. Perception and imagination occur by definition consciously, but if I walk to the fridge and take out a cold beer, this series of planned actions may be largely unconscious if I am simultaneously talking on the phone. Small decisions, such as choices to turn left or right on a route through a city that you know all too well, do not stand out in your consciousness as long as you have your mind on anything else.

It is equally tempting to think of memory as being strongly linked with our consciousness. If you have an intense experience such as pain from a bee sting,

Table 2.1 Overview of cognitive abilities. Cognition is understood here in a broad sense and includes not only processes that have to do with 'knowing' or 'thinking', but also, for example, perception and emotion. The table is not exhaustive; only cognitive faculties that are explicitly discussed in this book are included. In the right-hand column, each function and its relation to consciousness are briefly explained.

Cognitive ability	Note
Perception	Sensory sensation that is by definition conscious and is triggered by a stimulus from outside the brain. Sensory information can also be detected unconsciously, but this process is not included in perception. 'Feeling' is included in the definition of perception and is usually based on stimuli from inside one's own body, but in colloquial language often refers to emotion.
Imagination	Ability to consciously and volitionally envision things or events in the absence of an external stimulus. This ability is not only expressed visually but also in other sensory modalities such as hearing and touch. Characteristically, we can control or direct what we imagine.
Dream	Spontaneous form of internally generated, conscious experience that usually occurs during REM sleep (a sleep phase in which rapid eye movement occurs). Unlike imagination, dream activity is much less under cognitive, volitional control.
Working memory	Short-term storage of information subserving the performance of a task or assignment. Information from the past is actively represented by the brain to help solve a problem or reach a decision. This type of memory is usually active on a time scale of seconds to minutes, depending on the task. Although working memory is used when we are in a conscious state, we are not necessarily aware of information in our working memory.
Long-term memory	Memory that is retained over the long term, usually on a timescale of hours to days and years. Unlike working memory, brain cells do not need to remain permanently active to contribute to long-term memory: storage is achieved through biochemical changes in cells and their connections. Two main forms of long-term memory are declarative and procedural memory.
Declarative memory	Narrative memory: memory for events that we have experienced ourselves, for facts and other matters of general significance. Episodic memory includes our own past experiences; semantic memory includes facts and matters of general significance. Recalling declarative memories occurs consciously by definition.
Procedural memory	Memory that enables us to convert sensory stimuli into associated physical movement (motor action). When a learned motor movement is performed very often, it becomes a habit. Usually a habit is executed automatically without being accompanied by consciousness.

(*Continued*)

Table 2.1 (Continued)

Cognitive ability	Note
Emotion	Reaction to a sensory stimulus (trigger) that is assessed as positive or negative. In addition to sensory sensation of the stimulus itself, cognitive appraisal of the stimulus and autonomous reactions in the body also play a role. Through sensory sensations, emotion can be linked to consciousness.
Planning	Ability to prepare one or more actions in sequence to achieve a goal in the context of expectations about events in the near future. Is related to consciousness, but not necessarily linked to it.
Decision-making	Selecting a particular action or strategy to solve a given problem or task. Selection usually occurs by considering a variety of information about the benefits and risks of different actions. Is related to consciousness, but not necessarily linked to it.
Attention	The ability to selectively focus on certain information while ignoring other matters. This ability is also known as 'concentration' or 'focus'. Attentional processes may occur unconsciously, but when perceiving or imagining, attention intensifies conscious experience.
Language	Communication system in which spoken or written words (or other symbols) are organized into a grammatical form to allow beings to exchange complex information with each other. Language often, but not necessarily, goes hand in hand with consciousness.

you will easily recall it the next day. But deep sleep, for example, is known to accommodate unconscious processes that help process and reinforce memories experienced during a previous waking period. Sometimes you find yourself pondering an issue just before you go to sleep, such as coming up with the best possible design for the flat you are going to move into. When you pick up the problem the next day, after a good night's sleep, you may solve it or approach it better than on the day before. This is not only because you are better rested, but also because unconscious processes have taken place during sleep that have increased your insight into finding a solution.[12] If I manage to do some mental arithmetic within a matter of seconds, I am mainly aware of the end result – the solution to the calculation that I say out loud or consciously imagine – while the intermediate steps in it remain hidden under the bonnet of my consciousness. This makes cognition a broader concept than consciousness.

So cognition is a collective term for all kinds of brain processes that enable people and animals to perceive, process and remember stimuli and to use them to solve problems and make decisions. This does not mean that cognition covers all forms of information processing. If a mosquito suddenly looms right before your eyes, sensors in the cornea send a signal to the brain that immediately causes the eyelid to close. This reflex is a matter of lightning-fast information processing and does not require any cognitive systems, let alone systems of consciousness.

Attempts to dissect the mind into cognitive functions, with their corresponding territories in the brain, inevitably represent a certain philosophy: the view that it is possible at all to subject the relationship between brain and mind to a dissection into smaller parts. In this case, the components are functional in nature and all fit under the wide umbrella of 'cognition'. This makes 'cognition' a handy connecting thread to string the more difficult concept of 'mind' on.[13] 'Mind' is thus understood as the total sum of cognitive capacities, whether or not consciously exercised. If one of these capacities is switched off, there are usually enough left to still be able to speak of mental activity ('mind'), even though the loss of capacity means cognitive decline. A person without emotions still has mental abilities but is indifferent and lacks the drive to react strongly and passionately to stimuli and events.

The very idea of a dissection of the mind into cognitive faculties goes against Descartes' indivisibility of the mind. Even though there is plenty of evidence today to analyze mental activity as a collection of sub-processes, one can still maintain that conscious experience comes in a single piece, a unity. From a wealth of sensory inputs the brain is able to construct an integrated unity: we perceive only one world at once, each from our own perspective. But as yet, this property of unity only applies to perception, and to its more introverted sisters, imagination and dreaming. This is not to say that other cognitive functions, such as memory or emotions, are also coming in one piece, or that all cognitive functions together would necessarily form a unity to which consciousness contributes. In the upcoming set of five chapters I will clarify how far we can get if we use the dissecting knife: what can we peel off from our mind – the totality of our cognitive functions – before we lose consciousness? We will not be able to examine all cognitive functions: the relationships between memory, emotions and consciousness are particularly interesting and instructive. And: to what extent is a non-cognitive process – physical body movement – essential for consciousness? During our diligent peeling work in Chapters 3 to 7, we will especially witness what consciousness is essentially *not* about; in the later chapters, we will discuss which brain processes consciousness *does* relate to. This order has not been chosen accidentally: to understand what consciousness is, and where it comes from, we first need to know what it is *not*.

Nearly always, our experiences take place in a situation. The framework of a situation consists of the space you find yourself in, such as the bedroom in which you wake up in the morning. This spatial framework is rather abstract and not directly observable, but you do see all kinds of objects that occupy a certain place in relation to yourself and each other. Therefore I find it more convenient to refer to conscious experiences as 'situational' and not to make a direct appeal to spatiality. But whoever yells 'space' must also call for 'time'. When you eat an apple, there is not just one instantaneous experience but a series of moments that unfolds from picking up the fruit, your first bite, the sweet and sour juice you taste and that drips down from your lips, to the bitter taste of the core. In 1899, the American psychologist William James characterized consciousness as "a stream, a succession of states, or waves, or fields [...] of knowledge, of feeling, of desire, of deliberation, etc., that constantly pass and repass, and that constitute our inner life".[14] Consciousness of the 'now' is embedded in a continuum of past and future. Embedding in the past is only possible if, through our memory, we have access to information about things from the past. And we can only anticipate the future if we combine information from the present with our past. The relationship between memory, time and the flow of consciousness calls for further unravelling.

Next we will let emotions and consciousness take their place on the operating table. There are strong arguments to say that we attach negative or positive value to our experiences and respond to them with joy, anger, fear, disgust or sadness. This list of basic emotions can easily be expanded to include other affective feelings such as desire, shame, pain and relief. If an American ex-president sends out an emotional tweet, it certainly indicates he is conscious. And we, readers of his tweets, are conscious too, as we experience the feelings and thoughts that the tweets produce within us. Pleasant and painful stimuli evoke emotions in us, and conversely, emotions give rise to sensations in our bodies – the feeling that your stomach turns at the sight of a horrible car accident. But are emotions always necessary for conscious experience to occur? If someone's emotions fade away or even disappear, does that mean that consciousness is also lost?

And what about motor skills? To what extent can we read consciousness from a person's behaviour – the body movements and facial expressions produced by a fellow human – as motor output from the brain? What proportion of our actions is carried out consciously, and which movements slip under the radar of consciousness? Stepping on the accelerator, blinking your eyes, breathing: you only notice the details when you pay attention. In spoken or written form, language can be considered an extension of body movement. Intuitively, there seems to be a connection between consciousness and thought, and thoughts unfold primarily in language. If you are aware of something, you can talk about it. And if you can talk about something, it means you are aware of it. Can we substantiate the intuition that language and consciousness are so intimately connected?

I wonder what René Descartes would have thought of all these developments in brain research. He would certainly have loved the flourishing of the neurosciences and cognitive sciences, but also artificial intelligence. He might have been disappointed to hear that the mind did not turn out to be as indivisible as he had thought, but as an empirically minded naturalist he would probably not have continued to believe in two strictly separate substances – body and mind. Miraculously, his thesis of the mind's indivisibility still holds true when we talk about conscious experience: no matter how diverse the sensory inputs our brain receives, we always concoct a single common experience from them, not a series of chunks of information that present themselves to us separately. In 2017, Philippe Charlier published an investigation into the shape and size of Descartes' brain, as deduced from his skull, which is kept in the *Muséum National d'Histoire Naturelle* in Paris.[15] He reconstructed a three-dimensional image of his brain on the basis of the imprint it had left on the inside of the skull. The erstwhile genius turned out to have a conspicuous bulge in his frontal lobe – the piece of cerebral cortex located just behind your forehead. This particular spot has been attributed a function in interpreting the meaning of words. Although this speculation is not out of keeping with the feel for language expressed in Descartes' writings, I suspect that, with today's knowledge, he would have turned in his grave because of this case of phrenology.

3 Memory absorbed

*How our awareness of the here and now can be
decoupled from the past and the future*

You wake up on a crisp spring morning. The curtains are flapping in the wind, spots of sunlight taking shape on the floor. You crawl out of bed and look for slippers and dressing gown. There is no one else in the house who would know where they are. You find them in the last room you visit. You go down the stairs to the living room, and in the kitchen you find a coffee machine. You look for the coffee can, look in the bread bin and make a sandwich with a cup of coffee. Then the doorbell rings. When you open the door, a young woman at the door says: "Hello, how are you?"

You don't know her by name, but she looks vaguely familiar. Although she might be up to something bad, you are not afraid and let her in. She is very polite and has brought cakes, says it is a 'special day' and makes you another cup of coffee. On the windowsill are a few framed photographs of young people who look familiar – who are they again? You talk to the lady about the weather and the trees full of buds, about to burst. She talks about your children and grandchildren. And whether you still remember who is coming to visit you later.

An hour later, the doorbell rings again. This time it is a friendly older woman who introduces herself as a doctor. After a third cup of coffee, you are presented with a stack of papers. She points to handwritten squiggles on a page and says: "Look, you have signed here." The scribble is your signature. Then words like 'living will' are used and you are asked if you still stand by it. You ask yourself: what exactly is this about? Is this about what I want now, or what I once wanted? Who do they mean when they speak to me? Where am I now, where am I going, what is the plan? You look at the cake and coffee on the table in front of you and say it's fine. You say, "This cake – that's what I want now."

Apart from the euthanasia issue at stake, this case[1] shows how Alzheimer's patients are still aware of their surroundings despite a severe loss of memory. The disease often manifests itself first in the brain areas that we associate with what we normally call our memory: areas such as the entorhinal cortex and hippocampus, located in the temporal lobe, tucked away deep beneath the tissue that rests against our skull (Figure 3.1). 'Memory' is a broad term that also includes the storage of information needed to perform automatic actions,

DOI: 10.4324/9781003429555-3

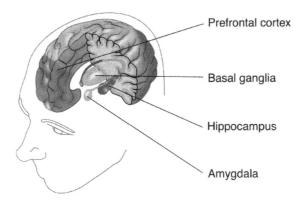

Figure 3.1 Location of the prefrontal cortex, basal ganglia, hippocampus and amygdala in the human brain. The prefrontal cortex is indicated in dark grey. The part of the cerebral cortex in which the hippocampus and amygdala are embedded is the temporal lobe. The nucleus accumbens is the part of the basal ganglia that faces the ventral or pharyngeal side and the eye sockets.

such as adjusting your posture when lifting something heavy. It also includes the information we have learned to carry out motor skills – a special category we call 'procedural memory'. In its early stages, Alzheimer's mainly affects the memory that is most precious to us – the memory of experiences we have consciously lived through and can talk about. Memories from our own lives, facts and figures gained through newspapers or smartphones. This is declarative memory, freely translated as narrative memory. It is the memory that allows us to tell stories about ourselves and the rest of the world. Declarative memory is a fantastic and stunning capacity. For example, it gives us the ability to think about our future, as we travel forward in time in our minds, and to explore our options when faced with difficult choices. This invention of evolution – from worm to human – is of staggering beauty and provides its owner with colossal advantages for survival in a complex world.

Alzheimer's is a cruel experiment that nature sometimes, if we are unlucky, imposes on us with advancing age – although it can also manifest itself at a younger age. After damaging the memory areas of the temporal lobe, it spreads to surrounding areas of the brain and wreaks even greater havoc there, progressively and exponentially. The formation of the characteristic plaques and tangles[2] can spread to the frontal lobe, parietal cortex and even occipital lobe (Figure 3.2), where vision is undermined. As Alzheimer's progresses, it becomes an increasingly non-specific disease, affecting a wide range of cognitive abilities, including perception, imagination and personality. To precisely determine the extent to which memory can be separated from consciousness, we need to look at patients with more specific brain damage.

Henry Molaison, also known as H. M., is perhaps the most studied patient in neuroscience. He suffered from epilepsy as a young man, and in 1953 he went to see neurosurgeon William Beecher Scoville in Hartford, Connecticut.

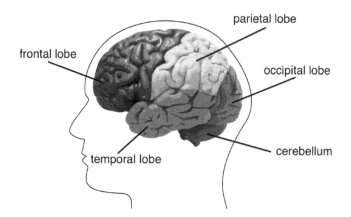

Figure 3.2 Division of the cerebral cortex into lobes.

His illness was attributed to a bicycle accident when he was nine years old and manifested itself in severe seizures, usually accompanied by loss of consciousness, incontinence, powerful spasms in his limbs and cramped jaws that could injure his tongue. After weighing Molaison's symptoms and limited treatment options, Scoville decides on a drastic and daring intervention. He concludes that the source of Molaison's disease is located in and around the hippocampus. He chooses to remove this seahorse-shaped structure from both the left and right hemispheres. Using a metal straw inserted at the eye socket, he sucks out brain tissue over a length of eight centimetres. The dissection is not entirely selective, as some hippocampal tissue remains and material from surrounding structures is removed en passant. This only becomes clearly visible during post-mortem examination, following Molaison's death in 2008.

After he is released from surgery and has recovered sufficiently, neuropsychologist Brenda Milner conducts a series of tests on him. She finds that most of Molaison's cognitive abilities, including speech and writing, are intact. His locomotor system is fine and he is able to master new motor skills. Milner asks him to look at his hand and a piece of paper through a mirror. On it is a pentagonal star with an inner and outer edge, and the task is to draw lines between these two edges with a pencil. Within a few practice sessions, spread over several days, he manages to do this. But even after he has completed this skill learning test for several days in a row, he cannot consciously put this back together in his mind. The learning effect is visible through his hand manoeuvring with the pencil, but he cannot recount his experience.

Molaison's memory of recent, consciously lived experiences is almost completely destroyed. After his surgery, Molaison is no longer able to store new, general facts or new events from his own life, or to recall them from his memory. He does not recognize the hospital staff and cannot find his way to the toilet, whereas before the operation this has not been a problem. Even two years after the procedure, Molaison hardly realizes that he has been operated on. He has also largely lost track of the events he had experienced in the last few years before surgery. He can, however, remember events from his childhood and teens, and recognizes his family members without any problem.[3]

After Molaison, other patients have been described with severe amnesia, usually caused by illness or accident. Many patients showed a similar pattern: inability to store and recall new, consciously lived experiences, but an intact memory for events in the distant past and an undamaged ability to learn new motor skills and habits. In terms of consciousness, these patients live on an 'island of the present': they cannot remember where they were a few minutes ago, how they got to where they are or what has happened in the world over the past few days. This group of patients does, however, have an intact short-term memory that allows them to remember experiences in a time span of seconds to minutes. Surprisingly, Molaison retained some spatial memory: for example, he could draw a map of the house he moved into in 1958 – five years after his operation. So he had not completely 'lost his way'.

A defective long-term memory makes it particularly difficult to build up expectations of what will happen later in the day: knowledge of the past is necessary to anticipate the future. As I write this, I am sitting in a hotel room in Stockholm full of stuff that reminds me of having to pack to catch my plane. The psychologist Endel Tulving has coined the term *'mental time travel'* for this. This is not a mysterious way of becoming a time traveller, but means that, with a healthy memory, you can imagine situations from your own past and future. What will it be like to go on holiday to Greece in a few months' time? You reminisce about long gone Mediterranean trips, beaches, sun, hot sand and hanging out in an easy chair. It is your memories that help you make a list of things to take along. Thus, declarative memory is an essential source for imagination, but also for planning.

Not all cases of amnesia resemble the severe form that Molaison revealed. In 1981, 30-year-old K. C. got on his motorbike to ride home from the factory where he worked. At an exit he skidded off the road. He was taken to hospital unconscious. An examination revealed extensive brain damage and, like Molaison, he was virtually unable to remember new information. Two years later, a student at the University of Toronto drew the attention of neuropsychologist Morris Moscovitch to the case; it would concern someone who was 'exactly like H. M.'. But closer examination revealed substantial differences with Henry Molaison. K. C. showed a particular loss of personal, autobiographical memories – the type of memory we call 'episodic' because it includes concrete episodes from our lives. This is an important part of declarative memory, with its more general scope. Declarative memory makes it possible to tell a story about our past, but this can either be a personal (episodic) story about what we ourselves have experienced in detail or a factual account that is independent of our own circumstances. We can dryly report what happened during the attacks on 11 September 2001, or we can remember in detail where we were ourselves when we heard the news, who was with us and what was going through our minds at the time. So, as a counterpart to episodic memory, our declarative memory contains another component that deals with 'impersonal' or 'objective' facts – semantic memory.[4]

K. C.'s semantic memory was reasonably intact, but his memory for personal events and circumstances was virtually destroyed. A few years before his accident, K. C.'s younger brother, from whom he had been inseparable, had died. This fact was still known to K. C. after his accident, but he did not remember anything about the circumstances under which he had received this tragic news – who told him, where he was or how he reacted. K. C. remembered events from the past, but they were stripped of the vivid, colourful details that made memories his own – that made them *his* memories. Characteristically, he could also hardly imagine the future – his capacity for 'mental time travel' was severely restricted. Although in K. C. it is not clear exactly which damaged brain structures are linked to his episodic memory loss, his case makes it clear that declarative memory consists of several elements, which can be affected separately.

But our key question about the relationship between memory and consciousness is: does consciousness continue to exist when memory fails? From all the tragic histories of patients such as Molaison, the answer is unequivocal: yes. There was no loss of consciousness in Molaison, K. C. and similar cases. Molaison was fully awake and aware of the people around him and of his surroundings, and he was able to talk about them or express himself through gestures and facial expressions. Nonetheless, we also witness how Molaison's consciously experienced world was impoverished because of the discontinuity with his past and future. In terms of temporal experience, his world of experience was less 'deep'. But despite this, his consciousness was not less present.

In advanced stages of Alzheimer's disease, there is erosion, and even disappearance of one's personality and identity. Was Henry Molaison subject to this? Who did he see when he looked in the mirror? Sue Corkin, who did a lot of research on him after Brenda Milner,[5] notes that the 'old' memories that he still possessed, still provided enough information to give substance to his 'self', his identity. He knew where he came from and who his parents were. Even after the operation, he continued to cherish his own beliefs and preferences. He was fond of crossword puzzles and believed that they enabled him to remember words better. He was genuinely happy that Scoville and his colleagues had learned about his own brain defects and could help other patients with the knowledge they had gained through him. When he looked in the mirror, he had got used to not seeing his younger self – the 'me' he had been in the years before the operation. He remarked dryly: "I am not a boy." That he was not surprised by the increased age of his face may have been due to regular re-encounters via the bathroom mirror. Moreover, the brain areas important for face recognition, and for the feeling that someone looks familiar, had probably remained intact after surgery.[6] Fortunately for Molaison, his sense of humour had also been preserved. When Corkin asked him during an interview, "What are you trying to remember?", he quipped: "I don't know, because what I was trying to remember I can't remember."

Over the years, I have heard and read a lot about Molaison, and repeatedly wondered: Why did he stay in such good spirits? Why wasn't he angry at Scoville and the entire neurosurgical community for the harm inflicted on him? He had lost a bloody part of his past – a part of his person and his life! And each time I have to remind myself that this 'suffering' was not present in him in the way a healthy person would experience it. You don't miss something if you don't have a memory of it.

Returning to the question of whether memory and consciousness are inextricably linked, it remains a predominant 'no'. Our declarative memory depends on a well-defined system: the hippocampus and adjacent areas in the temporal lobe, with some ramifications into other areas such as the frontal lobe. When damaged, this memory can vanish without losing consciousness. Memory and consciousness form a living apart together (LAT) relationship. Nonetheless, this relationship is quite intimate: without narrative memory, our consciousness becomes poorer, lacking temporal depth. Stripped of all memories, it lives on an island of the here and now, with no connection to our past and no expectations about the future. Without memory, consciousness becomes timeless; time exists only by virtue of memory. When we recollect traces from our memory, we become aware of them. This contrasts with our procedural memory, which allows us to automatically convert sensory input into motor output: we usually dig out this information before we realize it. The bow has already touched the violin strings before the music penetrates our mind.

4 Curses and deceit above the eye sockets

On emotions, consciousness and the tragic fate of their intimate relationship

Emotions and consciousness seem to be intimately connected. When we are angry or happy about something, or disgusted by an awful taste in our mouth, we are keenly aware of the sensory stimuli and the situation that evoke these emotions. Our conscious experience can be overwhelmed by intense feelings. Without consciousness, we feel nothing, and there is no emotion. Without consciousness, our face turns blank, devoid as it is of expressions, smiles or grimaces. When it comes to emotions, our face is the brain's signboard. Only in a conscious state does our face express fear, anger, joy, sadness, disgust, desire, pain, relief or shame. No matter what state of consciousness we are in – sharp perception, reverie or dream – we are always in some kind of mood or feel an emotional undertone – not always intense but often as an undercurrent of contentment or unease. For neurologist António Damásio, emotions, feelings and consciousness are irrevocably connected. He believes that emotions provide the raw material for feelings of which we become aware.[1] Consciousness would have evolved in evolution to give animals knowledge of what they are experiencing emotionally at any given moment, so that they can better adapt to their environment. But how hard is this link – is there no consciousness without emotion? What are emotions and feelings anyway?

In September 1995, Alan Davies and his wife Christine, from south Wales, were travelling in their car when Thomas Williams cut them off. There was a severe collision. Until that moment Alan and Christine had a warm relationship. Alan was a spontaneous, emotional man, who greeted his wife every morning with: "Good morning, I love you." When the accident happened, Christine cried out and was taken to hospital, where she was found to have suffered whiplash. Alan was in shock and thought his wife had been killed. He went home to recover, but when Christine rejoined him, he was still convinced that his wife was dead. Alan thought that the woman he was now dealing with was an impostor. He had flashbacks of how his wife had died, and he saw the person who now impersonated and dressed up like Christine as a strange person pretending to be his wife. He called her 'Christine Two'.[2] This became a painful situation also for Christine, who was in fact still his wife. She no longer felt any affection from her husband. He did not lay a finger on her and they no longer slept together. Alan's psychiatrist remarked that when the couple

DOI: 10.4324/9781003429555-4

visited him, he did not behave like he was sitting next to a human being of flesh and blood.

In the history of psychiatry, there have been very different views on this condition, first described in 1923 by Jean Marie Joseph Capgras and Jean Reboul-Lachaux, and known as Capgras syndrome. Freudian psychoanalysts have explained the phenomenon as the result of poor maternal bonding. This explanation has proven to be untenable, and it is more likely that the syndrome reflects a special form of disconnection between our brain systems for conscious perception and emotion. Patients with Capgras syndrome, like Alan Davies, can still see the alleged imposter, but no longer feel the affection, familiarity and warm feelings that seeing their loved one used to evoke.[3] Because the brain lacks signals associated with those feelings, it interprets the image of the person as a stranger. Capgras syndrome manifests itself especially when it comes to loved ones or family; patients do not lose all their feelings or emotions, and are still able to identify people they know, regardless of their emotional attachment to the patient.

How the connection between seeing and feeling is made in the brain is not precisely known, but research into Capgras syndrome is sufficiently advanced to suggest a plausible explanation. Neurons in the sensory areas of the cerebral cortex – the areas that process sensory information – send thin fibres (axons; Figure 4.1) to brain regions such as the amygdala, the prefrontal cortex and other members of the emotional network, such as the nucleus accumbens located in the basal ganglia (Figure 3.1). The same areas send information to memory areas in the temporal lobe. The case of Henry Molaison already showed that damage to the hippocampus in that lobe greatly affects our memory of consciously experienced events. With this memory, we can deduce a person's identity from their visual features and complex behaviour.

The same lobe houses even more areas, including the perirhinal cortex. This area is thought to help you remember if you are familiar with a person or thing. Riding your bicycle past a busy café terrace, you may realize in a flash that one person in the crowd looks familiar – without remembering all the details about that person, such as name, address or how you know her. The feeling of familiarity is usually hidden in the background of our consciousness, busy as we are deciding whether or not to wave at the person sitting over there. But the feeling is there. This feeling of *familiarity* is also known as the '*butcher on the bus*' phenomenon: you are on a bus and recognize the butcher among the passengers. But because you see the man outside his usual environment, you cannot remember what his shop looks like or what his name is. Memory areas such as the perirhinal cortex have strong connections with the amygdala and areas in the frontal lobe.

In Alan Davies' case, it is likely that the car accident caused damage to the connections between his sensory brain areas and his emotional centres. He still saw his wife as she physically was, but this visual experience no longer evoked a warm and loving feeling. Quite plausibly, the connections between the sensory brain areas and the memory system in the temporal lobe were damaged

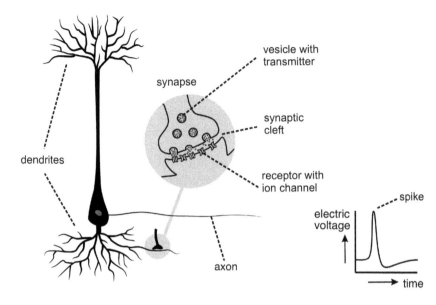

Figure 4.1 Structure of a neuron. Connected to the cell body (bottom left) are thick and thin branches (dendrites) on which the neuron receives electrical inputs from other cells. From the cell body originates an axon, a very thin fibre over which the output of the neuron is transmitted to other cells. This output consists of *spikes* or action potentials: very brief jumps in the electrical voltage across the cell membrane. The spikes are conducted to the axon ending, where a connection (synapse) is made with a receiving neuron. The neuron in this example receives a synapse on a dendrite on the lower left. If the synapse is magnified, it can be seen that in the axon ending (the presynaptic part of the synapse) there are vesicles containing a chemical messenger substance (transmitter). When a spike reaches this part, the transmitter is released into the tiny space between the axon ending and the membrane of the receiving neuron. This piece of membrane forms the postsynaptic part of the synapse and contains protein molecules (receptors) that bind the transmitter. As a result, an electrical reaction is triggered in the postsynaptic part: the receptors contain a channel through which charged particles (ions) start to flow. The electrical voltage change in the postsynaptic part propagates via the dendrites towards the cell body.

as well. Davies had the feeling he was dealing with a *stranger*. Seeing his wife no longer recalled a sense of familiarity. Whether this is due to the loss of connections to the perirhinal cortex, hippocampus or other temporal areas is difficult to say, but somewhere in this network the wiring or functioning of the neurons was probably impaired.

Apart from the problems that Capgras causes in love and family relationships, this syndrome brings us back to the question of how intimately consciousness and emotion are intertwined. We see a fracture, or at least a crack: the conscious percept remains, but the feelings of love, warmth and intimacy are gone. There is something to be said for an impoverishment of consciousness here too, although the element of love has given way to another sentiment: the delusion of deception.

There is no cure for Capgras syndrome. Mr Davies had to give up his teaching job and was prescribed medication – but continued to believe that his real wife had died. His psychiatrist concluded that his delusion would persist. As a cold comfort, a court case, three years after the accident, ruled that the reckless Thomas Williams had to pay the couple £130,000. He admitted guilt in the collision but denied having anything to do with Alan's psychological problems. The couple left the court walking a few steps away from each other. A divorce was being considered. It is sobering to note that the fascination entailed by neurological case studies has little to offer the patients themselves.

The disconnection between emotion and perception that is revealed by Capgras does not mean that consciousness would remain unaffected if emotions disappeared completely. What disappears is a specific emotionality experienced with a loved one or family member; the translation of a sensory input into an affective feeling is lost. Does damage to brain areas involved in evoking or regulating emotions perhaps lead to a weakened or diminished consciousness? Behavioural changes in people with permanent damage to their frontal cortex speak volumes. In the history of neurology, we come across the famous case of the American Phineas Gage, a foreman who, in 1848, when building a railway through the rocky forest landscape around Cavendish, Vermont, was given the job of blowing up rocks in order to pave the way for laying the tracks.[4] First, a hole had to be drilled in a rocky outcrop that was blocking the rails to be laid. Dynamite was pushed into this hole, and it had to be covered with sand, which was tamped with a long metal rod, about three centimetres in diameter.

On a crisp September day in the mid-nineteenth century, Gage probably forgot to apply the sand. The dynamite exploded too soon. The bar was launched, shot straight through Gage's left cheek, came out at the top of Gage's skull and landed about 25 metres away. Despite the enormous head wound, Gage presumably remained conscious. For a moment his body shook, but within a few minutes he could sit up straight. He began to talk again. The first doctor to see him was Edward Williams, who described the top of Gage's head as an inverted funnel. At first he could not believe that a rod had flown through Gage's head. Gage stood up and vomited. The pressure of his muscular contractions forced a brain mass the size of half a teaspoon through the skull opening, falling on the floor.[5]

John Harlow, the doctor who examined Gage shortly afterwards, confirmed that his patient was in good spirits and could talk 'rationally'. He could move his limbs, had no major problems with perception or language, could think and showed no dramatic decline in intelligence. He recognized his mother and uncle. During the first ten days after the accident, Gage seemed to recover and thought he could return to work soon. Harlow was more pessimistic given the colossal skull fracture Gage had suffered. A coffin was ordered just in case. But then Gage's skull wound and an abscess in his forehead began to heal. Gage picked himself up. His miraculous recovery made Gage a celebrity, but also gave rise to the myth that he had only minor problems. In other words, even if you suffer serious brain damage, you will not need to suffer from it in the long run.

As time went by, it became apparent that Gage's behaviour and personality did in fact get dented. Whereas before the accident he had been an exemplary, hard-working American, he was now impatient and impulsive. He regularly cursed and threw temper tantrums. If he had been rude or discourteous, he showed no signs of shame. He could no longer plan his work in a coherent way. '*He was no longer Gage.*' Strikingly, despite his intact narrative memory, he could no longer correctly assess the value of objects and money. When asked if he wanted $1,000 in exchange for a few stones he had found in an old riverbed, he refused.

Phineas Gage was fired by his railway company. The rest of his life is a sad story, stretching from performances at P. T. Barnum's freak show in New York to work as a coachman in Valparaíso, Chile, and as a farmhand in the fields of California. At Barnum he had a hard time competing with Josephine Clofullia, the bearded lady from Switzerland, or with Saunders Nellis, the Armless Wonder who could play the accordion and cello with his toes. Gage's health deteriorated, he could no longer find his footing and continued to suffer from his short fuse. Eventually he faced epileptic seizures and died in 1860, at the age of 38. Five years after his death, Dr Harlow dug up his skull, which, together with the fatal rod, was deposited in the museum of Harvard Medical School. In 1994, Hanna Damásio and her colleagues reconstructed the trail of destruction left by the rod: the orbitofrontal and medial prefrontal cortices were likely badly hit (Figure 3.1 and 4.2; the prefrontal cortex is the most frontal part of the lobe). The orbitofrontal cortex is part of the prefrontal cortex and is named after its position just above the eye sockets (Latin: *orbitae*). The medial prefrontal cortex is closely connected to the orbitofrontal part and lies close to the midline that separates the brain hemispheres. Hanna Damásio's reconstruction has been widely criticized. Gage's skull and the original drawings clearly show that the bone tissue was blown away so powerfully that it remains uncertain exactly how the rod passed through Gage's head.

Since the time of Phineas Gage, more cases of similar, though often lesser, prefrontal damage have come to light. They confirm the view that at first glance, given the extent of the damage, there is relatively little wrong with these people. Their intelligence, memory and language abilities are usually normal. In 1952 the neurologist Richard Brickner of the Mount Sinai Hospital in New York described patient Joe A., who had died a few years before. Joe A. was a stockbroker at the New York Stock Exchange and in 1929 he suffered more and more from headaches. His family found him increasingly absent-minded, and his memory deteriorated. This had little to do with the stock market crash of that year. In 1930, at the age of 41, A. suddenly fell into a coma and required an acute operation. An enormous tumour was found in his frontal lobes. The tissue was soft and mushy and extended to both hemispheres.[6] Large parts of his frontal brain were amputated. Joe A. came out of his coma and recovered.

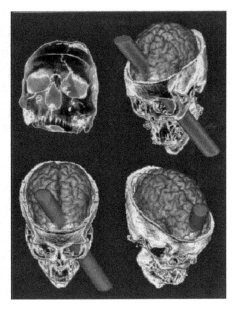

Figure 4.2 (Left) Portrait of Phineas Gage with the iron bar that shot through his skull. As a result of the accident, Gage was blind in his left eye. (Right) Reconstruction of the path that the iron rod took through Gage's brain. Entering through the bottom of the left eye socket, the rod smashed through the prefrontal cortex. According to this reconstruction, the orbitofrontal and medial prefrontal cortex were severely affected.
Source: (Left) Phyllis Gage Hartley. (Right) Adapted from Damásio et al. (1994).

Years later, he accompanied a couple of very experienced specialists on a tour of the hospital's neurological department. The tour lasted an hour, but they noticed nothing unusual about A., until someone explained his case. Under everyday circumstances, A. could behave quite normally. After his radical operation, his practitioners noticed that over a period of 14 years A. had developed a stronger tendency to take a bath and to brag about himself, but he also gradually suffered more from crying and tantrums. Like Gage, A. had difficulty controlling his emotional impulses. He was throwing around childish, negative comments and could not stop talking about his sexual adventures. He tended to touch women he found attractive and make obscene suggestions, but did not attempt to seduce them seriously. Apart from these periods of unrestraint, it was noticeable how little else he had changed, given the size of the brain mass that had been removed from him. His eyesight and hearing were also normal. However, his sense of smell had almost disappeared and he suffered from incontinence.

Patients with less obvious prefrontal damage often need in-depth, long-term testing to reveal defects in emotional and social functioning. When infants or toddlers suffer damage to their prefrontal cortex, they may lack moral awareness later in life and have difficulty abiding by social norms and rules. António and Hanna Damásio's group described a girl who was hit by a vehicle when she was 15 months old and who seemed to develop normally even after the accident. It was only after a few years that she was noticed to be insensitive to verbal spanking or other punishment. As a teenager she started to steal from family, from other children or from shops. She lied a lot, abused others and indulged in risky sexual behaviour, becoming pregnant at 18. She had very little to say about her plans for the future, and she jumped from one job to another. She hardly expressed empathy with the fate of others, including her own child. Other patients with early prefrontal damage show a similar pattern, accompanied by apathy, hanging in front of the TV all day and binge eating, with no awareness of the risks and long-term consequences.[7]

Superficially, this pattern looks a bit like the behaviour of some adolescents without prefrontal damage, but the lack of social awareness, remorse or shame nevertheless makes these patients afflicted in early childhood stand out as a special group. Empathy and the ability to adopt someone else's perspective are lacking, bordering on a psychopath's state of mind.[8] Phineas Gage's brain was damaged when it had already been fully developed, and despite his behavioural changes he knew the unwritten rules of social interaction; at least he could put these into words. But after early prefrontal damage, the child has great difficulty acquiring a moral database of facts and rules. When an underlying sense of empathy, plus a sense of what is or is not permissible, is lacking as early as the child's development, the foundation for learning to think socially and morally is shaky. The child is not ashamed if it does something morally wrong, and thus lacks an essential incentive to learn from its mistakes.

Joe A. showed that not all adults who suffer prefrontal damage undergo strong changes in personality. In a test lab, it is sometimes necessary to dig deep to find a defect. Patients with limited damage (lesions[9]) to the prefrontal cortex were placed in an experimental set-up where they had to learn to assess which of two decks of playing cards provided the highest probability of winning. The patient was given the opportunity to do this by taking a card from either deck and being told how much profit or loss he made per card. One card yielded a large profit (e.g. +$100), the next a low profit (+$10) or low loss (−$5), or in rare cases a large loss (−$100). What the patient was not told was that, on average, one deck eventually yielded a lower profit than another, although this was not immediately noticeable from the individual cards. The lower net profit came from the combination of a few cards that produced a substantial profit with relatively many cards that produced a mild loss. The other deck gave less spectacular, but more stable profits.

The game is similar to making a choice about an earnings model: would you rather try to earn your money by gambling in a casino or by filling shelves in a supermarket? However, there is an important difference with such a deliberately made choice. During the game, the test subject is aware of the cards he picks from the stacks and of the result his choices yield immediately, but the development of a preference for one of the two stacks is largely implicit and unconscious. Compared to healthy people, prefrontal patients preferred the stack with quick gains in the short term but low gains in the long term. The implicit aspect of this result lies in the fact that the patients (but also the control group of healthy subjects) could not clearly articulate the reason for their preference; it was more a matter of a gut feeling about what their favourite stack was.

The test offers a glimpse into a component of emotions that is usually lurking silently in the background in the face of intense stimuli that trigger an emotion. This component consists of autonomous, bodily responses to sensory stimuli, such as an increased perspiration at the sight of a random playing card. To measure the intensity of the sweat response, the skin's conductivity to electrical current was recorded in prefrontal patients and healthy subjects. In healthy people, perspiration increased when they saw a deck of cards that was covered but considered risky. The body signalled that some risky event was about to happen. With prefrontal lesions, this effect did not occur: the patient's body reacted as if nothing was at stake. An unconscious learning process – learning to assess the value of an object, in this case a deck of cards – was linked to an emotional response that is normally hidden from view – the secretion of sweat.

António Damásio regards this as an indication that autonomous bodily reactions – and the pattern of brain activity that triggers them – play a causal role in the unconscious assessments we make of people and things in everyday life. He calls the total pattern of this activity a 'somatic marker', a bodily signal that marks a situation or an object as safe or risky, or as good or bad. It is this feedback from the body to the brain that drives unconscious judgement. An argument against this idea is that value estimates and physical emotional reactions may just as well be controlled in parallel by the prefrontal cortex, without a causal link between them. Whether there is really a causal link between autonomous responses such as sweat secretion and unconscious judgement remains to be seen.

A number of characteristics of emotions have now come to pass, but what are emotions exactly? Emotions differ from moods such as melancholy or euphoria by their short-lived nature: in healthy people, an emotion often bubbles up suddenly and subsides again after some time. Suppose you come home from a presentation of your work to a group of people who are important for your future career. The panellists have questioned you critically and you are not sure what to make of their reactions. Stressed and sweating you come home. But then, after that big day, you see your loved one sitting at the table that is covered with cheeses, wine, salads and cold cuts. You plop down in your chair, tell your story and indulge in all the goodies. Everything tastes fabulous. You shed a tear and relax. A great feeling of relief, gratitude and love.

Where is the emotion in this story? Sometimes, our narrative on emotions focuses on one aspect, such as the feeling that accompanies the emotional event or the fact that we are ready to take action.[10] But an emotion exists above all as a totality of interlocking elements. First there is the sensory stimulus, such as the sight of your loved one and the table, which acts as a trigger to provoke a change in the state of our brain and body. Fear causes us to tense up, sweat and makes our heart beat faster. This points to a second element of emotions: the autonomous, involuntary reactions of our body, which help prepare us for what is about to happen. We notice these autonomous changes in our bodies through a third element: physical feelings. The sight of the lovingly laid table makes your body feel warm, languid and relaxed. The senses in and on your body signal to the brain how your body is doing, and the brain incorporates this information into your conscious experience, although you do not necessarily have to be strongly aware of it.

A sensory stimulus often evokes a fourth element: muscle tension and preparation for action. When experiencing fear or anger, you get ready to repel, fight or flee from the cause of the stimulus. While switching from stress to emotion and love, a big physical action is not always necessary, although a big hug would fit the story well.

The fifth and final component of emotions is cognitive appreciation. When you settle down in your chair and enjoy the moment, it is not just because of a piece of cheese on the table. You realize that your loved one has put effort into this; everything about the situation feels right and authentic. There is someone who understands your situation. Emotion is almost always accompanied by a stream of thoughts that value the sensory triggers. We value the impact of a sensory stimulus according to its context. A snake suddenly squirming into your field of view may seem very threatening at first, but if the animal turns out to be in a glass cage, it is not so bad. The cognitive aspect of emotional brain systems enables us to think about the meaning of a stimulus, to appreciate the overall situation and to dampen a primary fear response if necessary. In short, emotions are complex beasts with at least five legs (a sensory trigger, bodily reactions, the resulting feelings, preparation for action and cognitive appraisal).

To what extent is consciousness affected in patients with prefrontal damage? Damásio argues that emotions and consciousness are closely intertwined, and the role of the prefrontal cortex is to regulate that relationship through feedback from the body. But when it comes to sensory experiences – what the patients experience on a daily basis – they do not actually show a significant deterioration. They see, hear, taste, feel and talk normally, and their declarative memory, language capacities and motor skills are also intact (an exception to this is an impaired sense of smell, as occurred with Joe A.). Phineas Gage, too, did not suffer from a lack of emotional expression, but rather from overexpression and disinhibition: his lid on Pandora's emotional box rattled. Remarkably little goes awry with consciousness, unless we stretch this concept to include morality and social feeling.

Yet something has changed. Because prefrontal patients show fewer autonomous bodily responses, the sense organs in their bodies also transmit fewer signals to the brain. The function of that sensory feedback is to inform the brain about our internal physical state: is the body in a state of stress or relaxation? So something is missing from the palette of conscious experiences in prefrontal patients: not so much 'feeling' like the sensation of touch – the feeling that your skin is being touched or pressed by something – but rather the feelings from inside our bodies, such as tension or butterflies in your stomach, changes in heartbeat, and the sensations caused by sweating, coupled with cooling of your skin.

The loss of one kind of sensory experience does not mean a total loss of consciousness: a blind person is aware of his surroundings, although not through seeing them. But perhaps our view has been too narrow: have we focused too much on patients with relatively little prefrontal damage? Gage had suffered significant damage to several prefrontal areas, but is it possible that this was not yet large enough to establish a link between emotions and consciousness?

Twentieth-century psychiatry reveals a long-standing, though well-intentioned, aberration in which patients with depression, obsessive-compulsive disorder or schizophrenic delusions[11] were subjected to a procedure causing massive damage to the prefrontal cortex – the lobotomy. 'Lobotomy' literally means cutting away a lobe, but in the history of surgery it has become virtually synonymous with a deliberate surgical procedure that causes a large prefrontal lesion. The underlying idea was that the prefrontal cortex would be abnormally active and that its removal or disconnection would benefit the patient. This idea was fuelled by findings such as Joe A.'s, who was missing huge chunks of prefrontal cortex but seemed to be little affected. Couldn't the prefrontal cortex be something you could do without, like a bad toothache? Isn't it like an appendix: a useless part of your body but a source of painful inflammation?

Trials conducted in the 1920s had shown that chimpanzees kept in captivity for scientific study could, over time, develop aggressive and compulsive behaviour, and were reluctant to cooperate in tests. Housed in small cages, the monkeys became frustrated and reacted with compulsive behaviours such as stereotyped and repetitive biting, hitting, licking or head-banging against a wall. With the recent knowledge about frontal patients the researchers tried something new: in these chimpanzees most of their frontal lobes were removed.[12] The monkeys seemed to become more friendly and cooperative. The Portuguese neurologist António Egas Moniz took advantage of this fact to treat patients around 1935 with a 'leukotomy': the removal or severing of the white matter located at the front of the brain. Unlike grey matter, which consists of cell bodies and dendrites (Figure 4.1), white matter is composed of masses of axons – nerve fibres that transport electrical pulses from one brain region to another.

Following the monkey study, Moniz also claimed that his patients became calmer. A pioneer in psychosurgery, Moniz was awarded the Nobel Prize in Physiology or Medicine as early as 1949 – just 14 years after his first operation. At Georgetown University in Washington, DC, Walter Freeman was employed as a neurologist, and he simplified the technique into the now infamous frontal lobotomy. The procedure could be performed without a brain surgeon – on an outpatient basis – and took just over 15 minutes. Freeman briefly anaesthetized his patients, then hammered an ice pick into the top of the eye sockets and used it to pry up and down through the prefrontal tissue. The 'emotional' parts of this area in particular were irreversibly destroyed, both in terms of fibre tracts and cells from which the fibres originate. His patients, previously afflicted with emotional disorders and compulsive tendencies, seemed to be able to control themselves better now.

With his casket full of ice picks and hammers, Freeman travelled across North America performing thousands of operations, often several a day. Rumour had it that Freeman called his camper van the 'lobotomobile', but it is more likely that this nickname was coined after his death in 1972.[13] Thanks to the protests, books and films about the frontal lobotomy – such as Ken Kesey's *One Flew over the Cuckoo's Nest* – we now see all too clearly that patients did not become calm because of increased self-control, but because they lost essential capacities through the operation: spontaneity, emotionality and initiative in making decisions. Thousands of patients were more or less reduced to emotionless, docile zombies. With the wisdom of hindsight, it is easy to condemn Freeman for his overreaching, unbridled practice and lack of in-depth research into the long-term effects of his procedure. But he, Moniz and others began their work at a time when doctor's offices and hospitals were flooded with desperate patients and their families: no treatment was working.

Returning to the 1950s, there is every reason to remain critical of Walter Freeman and his practice. He found himself in an environment of colleagues and organizations all too sympathetic to virtually any treatment that had any effect on unruly patients. William Beecher Scoville, surgeon to 'memory patient' Henry Molaison, also tried to help psychotic patients. He did this by cutting away tissue in the temporal lobe in a manner similar to how he treated epilepsy, but this approach was not successful either and often resulted in dramatic memory deficits. Neither Scoville nor Freeman were required to conduct controlled clinical trials on limited groups of subjects. They were fulfilling an urgent, existing demand. When Freeman started, psychopharmaceuticals had yet to be developed and it would take until 1951 before the first effective drug against schizophrenia and psychosis became available: chlorpromazine. Not by chance, this event coincided with the rise of protests against lobotomy. The slogan became: "I'd rather have a bottle in front of me than a frontal lobotomy." Yet I keep asking myself: why did Walter Freeman not delve more deeply into his patients and the consequences of his interventions for their personal fate?

What conclusions can we draw if we combine these studies on the effects of massive prefrontal damage? The cognitive effects are very diverse and sometimes contradictory: in some cases (Phineas Gage, Joe A.) we observe emotional disinhibition or antisocial and impulsive behaviour, but in other cases dullness, lack of emotional expression and spontaneity (lobotomy). The overall lack of systematic changes can be explained by the fact that the damage was inflicted in an unfocused way: it was a matter of chance where exactly the cortex was damaged. In humans, the cortex is a few millimetres thick, and if all its windings (*gyri*) and grooves (*sulci*) were smoothed out as with an iron, it would look like a flattened layer cake with a diameter of 39 centimetres, one for each hemisphere. If you cut through this pancake and look at the inner structure from the bottom upwards, it turns out that most of the cortex is divided into six layers. Based on detailed differences in the presence and thickness of these layers, and in the density and type of brain cells in each layer, the prefrontal cortex is subdivided into at least 16 areas, distinguished on the basis of their anatomical architecture.[14]

Surveying the battlefield of prefrontal lesions, we should not be surprised that the undirected shooting of rods and ice picks through the tissue resulted in a mixture of emotional and cognitive defects. The net damage depends on the exact combination of areas and their wiring that was hit. Sometimes the white matter of the fibre tracts was destroyed, in other cases mainly the grey matter, but usually an undefined mixture of both. Through systematic and accurate studies in laboratory animals – which are still necessary because the precision required cannot be achieved by examining haphazard lesions in humans – it has become clear that the many territories of the prefrontal cortex perform different functions. These range from emotional regulation to object valuation, from control over urination and impulsive behaviour to focusing attention and making long-term plans. Doesn't that take us back to a naive form of phrenology? Well, to some extent it does – but not necessarily in a reprehensible or naive way. Now, it is no longer a question of linking something as complex as 'love' to a skull lump. Research shows that complex mental functions can be broken down into simpler sub-functions, and it is often feasible to associate these sub-functions with specific brain areas. An example of such an area is a part of the orbitofrontal cortex that researchers have been able to link to smell perception and that was probably damaged in Joe A.

Are brains and minds simply made up of more puzzle pieces than we thought? There is something to be said for this, but what makes the matter even more complicated is that even a sub-function depends on a network of areas. If we scrutinize the orbitofrontal region for olfactory perception, it is highly unlikely that this region on its own would be enough to 'produce' conscious smell. If a surgeon were to cut the area out of a patient and keep slices of the tissue alive in a culture dish outside the body – which is technically possible – the brain cells from the area can remain electrically active for hours or days. But is the production of electrical impulses by these cells – the 'firing' of spikes[15] – enough to produce a sense of smell? How would this blob of tissue know that its own activity is about odours, and not about something you taste or see? Why would it produce a conscious sensation of rose scent? The precise arguments for saying that it must be a network of areas that collectively produce a sensation of smell are put on hold for now, to emerge later again.

Apart from the awareness of sensations, there is a strong case to be made that a brain area can only perform its sub-function if other areas it connects to are intact. Returning to the five elements of emotions, it is the sensory triggers, autonomic reactions in the body, feelings, muscle contractions and cognitive appreciation together that give each element an emotional meaning. When I am confronted with a huge barking dog, my heart races, I break out in a sweat and my stomach is up in the back of my throat. My brain registers these changes and I become partially aware of them – a cramped, anxious feeling. I brace myself to ward off the beast. Until I realize I am dealing with the neighbour's dog – an animal that barks loudly but would not hurt a fly. For each part of this chain, several brain areas can be identified. If only our heartbeat is raised or lowered, this is already controlled by several areas. But that control only has any meaning for my anxiety if it is part of the whole emotional network of the brain – plus its offshoots that send information to the body or receive signals back from it.

Despite the diversity of effects, one more conclusion can be drawn: even after massive prefrontal damage, as deliberately inflicted by lobotomy, patients do retain consciousness. Even if a lobotomy makes a person meek, apathetic, lacking in initiative and emotion, his gestures, verbal utterances, posture, gaze and other reactions to sensory stimuli show that his consciousness has not disappeared. Therefore a flattened or eroded emotionality does not have to go hand in hand with a loss of consciousness. Capgras' syndrome already indicated that conscious sensation can be separated from emotion. At the same time, the findings suggest that the prefrontal cortex – regardless of its role in emotions and other processes – is not essential for consciousness. In this kaleidoscopic complex, there is no single area whose damage results in loss of consciousness (apart from olfaction). As we shall see, this contrasts sharply with the effects of damage in the posterior part of the cortex.

But when I talk to a colleague – such as Steven Laureys from the University of Liège – who treats patients straddling the borderline between coma and consciousness because of a head trauma or stroke, they often find that activity in the prefrontal cortex does seem to be important as an indication that the patient may regain consciousness. How is this possible? In these 'minimally conscious' patients, a neurologist must diligently look for any sign of consciousness, and this is done by asking the patient questions: Can you move a finger when you hear me? Can you say your name? Can you blink your eyes? These trials set the patient the task of responding in a voluntary, nonautomatic way to a command presented to him by the doctor. In this way, the doctor is testing something else besides the patient's consciousness: his ability to respond volitionally. And this exactly happens to be a cognitive ability that involves the prefrontal cortex, as lobotomy patients show. A commandresponse test alone is therefore insufficient to determine whether a brain structure is necessary for consciousness – although in clinical practice this test is indispensable for making a diagnosis.

Up to now, we have mainly looked at emotions and the brain through a 'prefrontal' lens. It would be an understatement to say that emotions have little to do with consciousness, as their interrelationship may only become clear if we look at other brain areas as well. The prefrontal cortex appears to be particularly important for our control over emotions and behaviour, but we have not yet got to the heart of the matter – the brain mechanisms for emotion itself. If there is one brain node that is important to explore further, it is the amygdala. Is this brain node key to the unravelling of consciousness?

5 Aurora and the almond

On psychic blindness and transactions on the emotional stock market

The following text accompanies the 'Master of Business Leadership's Executive Superpowers Program' by Phil Johnson.[1]

> Every time change moves us out of our comfort zone, we feel some type of discomfort. Usually this takes the form [of] increased fear or anxiety. We see the unfortunate results of these hijacks every day. The development of our emotional intelligence inhibits the effects of these amygdala driven hijacks and increases our ability to embrace rapid change and innovation. We are surrounded by numerous fear, safety and survival triggers that continually hijack our consciousness. The faster we learn to recognize these amygdala hijacks the easier it will be for us to minimize their damaging effects.

It is one of the many references to 'amygdala hijacks' that can be found on the internet when you search for terms like 'stress', 'management' and 'brain'. Within the world of courses and workshops on self-control, fear and tension in the workplace, the amygdala has acquired cult status. Perhaps this is because the use of anatomical concepts gives a scientific kick to the seemingly lawless chaos that seems to rule inside our heads, and jazzes the story up a bit. What's the truth behind it? Is the amygdala indeed a kind of 'gatekeeper' that shuts down our consciousness and lets our instincts take over? What exact research results are known about the amygdala, and how can we interpret them?

In the 1920s and 1930s, Heinrich Klüver and Paul Bucy at the University of Chicago investigated the function of the amygdala in rhesus monkeys. Klüver was born in Holstein, Germany, three years before the twentieth century began. At the age of 17, around the outbreak of the First World War, he enlisted in the German army. He disliked his job as an infantryman and was lucky to suffer only a minor injury during the war. Just when a massive Allied attack was imminent, he was transferred to a hospital. After the war he sought a safe haven by signing on with a cargo ship that took him, via the Panama Canal, to the United States. From the surviving documents I get the impression that Heinrich Klüver was a shy and withdrawn boy, much more interested

DOI: 10.4324/9781003429555-5

in his perception and 'inner world' than in a career that would enable him to leave an overwhelming mark on the outside world.

Klüver began his research in the hope of finding out how the psychedelic drug mescaline affects the brain. From Indian tribes in Mexico, this substance from the peyote cactus was known to induce hallucinations, and researchers in the Western world became curious about how its mind-blowing effects could be explained. Mescaline changes your thinking, your sense of time and your awareness of things around you. Users describe seeing striped patterns and multicoloured surfaces appear, while the sensory modalities (the types of senses we have, such as sight, hearing and touch) melt into one another. Heinrich Klüver also experimented with it, describing visual experiences of checkerboard-like patterns and other geometric structures, tunnels and spirals of repeating forms – while the boundaries between his 'I' and the outside world were blurring.

He found that a mescaline trip resembles the hallucinations of schizophrenic patients. Any clue to a brain mechanism of this disease could provide a breakthrough for treatment. When, around 1939, Klüver and his colleague, the American neurosurgeon Paul Bucy, set about cutting away the amygdala in both hemispheres of the monkey brain, they realized how crude and imprecise their approach was. The amygdala is tucked away deep in the temporal lobe (Figure 3.1) and it was virtually impossible to remove this nucleus without damaging the surrounding tissue. In practice, it turned out that adjacent parts of the temporal lobe were indeed affected. While Klüver hoped his experiments would shed light on the bizarre realm of mescaline trips and schizophrenic hallucinations, he found evidence of an entirely different phenomenon: 'psychic blindness'.

In the animal colony at the University of Chicago, there was a female rhesus monkey, named Aurora, who had started behaving aggressively in the run-up to the surgery. Other researchers considered her unruly and too risky to handle, but Klüver was known for his ability to deal with difficult animals. On the afternoon of 7 December 1936, Paul Bucy removed her left temporal lobe, incidentally with Klüver's knowledge. The next day Klüver inspected his monkey group and called Bucy excitedly: "What have you done to my monkey?" Bucy went to the lab and saw that Aurora had become tame.

The monkeys with temporal lobe lesions revealed a complex of behavioural changes. Objects that were new to them or would normally elicit a fear response were now approached without hesitation and elicited little or no emotional response. Normally, new objects elicit a 'neophobia' – a fear or reluctance to see and approach new objects. The monkeys operated on had a strong tendency to put objects in their mouths, as babies can do with rattles and other toys.[2] They also showed a marked increase in sexual behaviour, which was not specifically directed at a conspecific, but manifested itself in excessive masturbation. They started to eat more and became less choosy about the food they consumed. They reacted more impulsively to visual stimuli, with less distinction to the importance or meaning of the objects they were shown. This is what Klüver and Bucy meant by 'psychic blindness': in addition to the disinhibitions in food and sex, the animals were less able to judge the negative or positive value of objects. Their 'blindness' mainly concerned the emotional value of things such as objects and living creatures in their environment, while their eyesight and other senses were fine.

The work of Klüver and Bucy gave an enormous boost to research into psychosurgery before the Second World War. Towards the end of one of Klüver's lectures in the 1930s, Egas Moniz – the man who pioneered the lobotomy – stood up from the audience and asked him whether temporal lobe surgery could be a means of treating persistently aggressive individuals. Klüver was stunned. His lecture became an important impulse for Egas Moniz and others to vigorously extend their research on psychosurgery in patients.

Does 'mental blindness' also occur when the amygdala is damaged in humans? The answer depends on the size of the surrounding area that is excised. In many epilepsy patients, the part of the temporal lobe in which the amygdala is embedded is the source where seizures begin and spread to other brain structures. The abnormal brain tissue that is the source of epilepsy is unstable. Normally, the local network of neurons is in balance: cells stimulate each other to become electrically active (excitation) but also dampen each other's activity to about the same extent (inhibition). During an epileptic seizure, excitation takes over and waves of activity emerge from the epicentre, which propagate through other parts of the brain, somewhat like the vibrations of an earthquake, causing visible effects such as spasms and foaming at the mouth, often accompanied by loss of consciousness. When drugs for epilepsy do not work, neurosurgeons may decide to operate by cutting out the suspected source area. If this is in the temporal lobe, this often means the demise of the amygdala, but surrounding tissue is excised as well.

The patients with such severe damage show a very mixed picture that partly corresponds to the monkey studies. Many of them have difficulty reading negative emotions (fear, sadness) from faces and judging people as reliable or unreliable. Social contacts proceed less smoothly, which is understandable because many of our interactions are determined by underlying emotional ties such as friendship. There may be fear of meeting others, and often phobia and depression are lurking around the corner. As in Klüver and Bucy's monkeys, surgery in the temporal lobe can lead to hypersexual behaviour.

A research group in Istanbul described a teenage girl who suffered from epilepsy and began masturbating excessively in the schoolroom, the school bus and at family parties nine months after her operation.[3] She became so disinhibited that she rubbed her genitals against tables, rocks and other objects that lent themselves to it. Her family, from eastern Anatolia, was not particularly thrilled about this. They, but also the girl herself, were filled with intense shame and disgust. The child had crying fits but was also easily irritated and aggressive, withdrew from social life and suffered from depressive mood swings. It was not clear to the doctors whether these were a direct result of the operation or of all the stir among family and friends. Fortunately, the child responded well to the treatment she was prescribed, starting with an antide-pressant. The family was urged to deal with their daughter in a more positive way, to not put the blame on her and not constantly focus on her behaviour. After two months, things were already much better.

So far, there is little evidence that the amygdala acts as a gatekeeper that would deprive us of brain control or even consciousness. If this were the case, cutting out the amygdala would result in a diminished role of 'instinct' – a vague concept, but one that can be broadly equated with propensity for 'prim-itive behaviour' such as aggression and sexual impulses – and a strengthening of consciousness. Instead, we see more basic behaviour, such as eating and sexual activity – and an inability to judge whether objects and living creatures are risky or trustworthy. Perhaps the myth of the amygdala as the 'hijacker' of our brains and the driver of our instincts has something to do with the docile behaviour of the monkey Aurora after her operation. With the wisdom of hindsight, it is plausible that this was caused by the disappearance of fear and the ability to see other things as threatening.

In extreme cases, surgery in the temporal lobe can have legal consequences. Together with Oliver Sacks, who died in 2015, Julie and Orrin Devinsky, affiliated with New York University, described a 51-year-old man who had to undergo surgery for the second time because of persistent epilepsy.[4] When the man was still young, his disease presented in a mild form, as a series of 'déjà-vu-attacks'. A walk, a meal, a concert – it seemed as if he had experienced the moment before, when in fact he had not. Later, spontaneous musical hallu-cinations joined the orchestra of his inner world. In the absence of music in his environment, he heard songs so loud that it seemed as if they were being played in the room next door. This was not a normal musical imagination – 'internal humming' – but a powerful hallucination, a brain-created fake expe-rience that the man himself did not perceive as 'fake'. The attacks worsened, and he also began to smell 'pungent odours', have taste sensations and out-of-body experiences – as if he were stepping outside his body and looking at himself from a distance. Despite this, he still had a good social network during this period, and his wife considered him a good husband. They had a normal, healthy sexual relationship.

Around the age of 33, his condition worsened. He had his first temporal lobe surgery, but it did not help sufficiently, and six years later he had to undergo another operation. From that moment on, a Klüver-Bucy-like syn-drome began to manifest itself. He had a short fuse, began to eat excessively and became hypersexual, especially stimulated by poo.[5] His wife said that since then he always wanted to have sex with her, without foreplay, romance or warmth. A few seconds after his orgasm, he wanted it all over again. If she wasn't available or didn't want to, he would jerk off. It was as if the ther-mostat switch on his libido was broken. Sexually, he could only be 'hot' or 'cold', nothing in between. The cruise control was missing. He started watch-ing porn on the internet and became increasingly obsessed with child porn, which he downloaded. No one else knew about this, and he kept it a closely guarded secret. Eventually he was arrested by the federal police. During the court hearing, the prosecutor argued that the man's criminal behaviour was voluntary and deliberate. Therefore, there could be no question of a 'neurological cause'. His doctors argued that neurological disturbances, related to Klüver-Bucy syndrome, must have contributed well and truly. Was the man guilty of his criminal behaviour? Or was this actually the fault of the surgeons who – albeit with noble intentions – had damaged brain areas that normally tempered his sex drive? Or was this unfortunate turn of events nobody's fault – just a cruel twist of nature? The judge found the man guilty: 19 months in prison. The Klüver-Bucy argument weighed in only lightly, as a mitigating factor.

Beyond the actual issue of consciousness, there are a number of thorny issues in this case. One of the strangest aspects is that some guardians of our justice believe there can be no neurological (brain-localized) cause if behaviour is voluntary and conscious. But why should actions attributed to 'free will' have no cause or equivalent in the brain? This belief assumes a separation between brain and mind that has been problematic since the times of Descartes. Another, more ethical question is to what extent our knowledge of the causes of neurological and brain damage should contribute to the conviction and punishment of the accused. In this case of child pornography, there is a plausible link to the documented damage to the temporal lobe, also because the resemblance to the classical Klüver-Bucy syndrome is so strong. But what if someone downloads child pornography and there is no known brain abnormality? Paedophilia can also develop in people with a tumour in the prefrontal cortex, or in a special form of dementia where both the frontal and temporal lobes are affected (frontotemporal dementia). A paedophile can be behind bars before such a cause is known. If it is ever discovered at all. In other words, doesn't every sexual offence (or even every offence in general) have a cause somewhere in the brain – because it is the brain that controls almost every aspect of our lives? Does this fact make the delinquent less guilty? And, as the last of the legal bones of contention for the moment, should the question of guilt be leading in determining punishment – or are other factors, such as the protection of individuals in society, perhaps even more important?[6]

In addition to the two hypersexual patients reviewed here, there are other known cases of operations on the temporal lobe leading to changes in sexuality. As with the prefrontal cortex, the variety of effects is extremely wide, ranging from hyper- to hyposexuality (excess and lack of sexuality, respectively). What is striking about this type of surgery is that not only can the degree of sexuality change, but also someone's preference, or sexual orientation. After an intervention, a person's preference can shift from adults to children, but heterosexuality can also turn into homosexuality. The notion that sexual orientation is determined by processes in the hypothalamus (Figure 2.2) has been quite dominant in this research field.[7] The hypothalamus is a complex of 'lower' areas in the brain, located not far from the nasal cavity, which control all kinds of vital functions and basic behaviour such as our day-night rhythm, regulation of body temperature, secretion of hormones, but also sexual and aggressive behaviour. There is good evidence that the hypothalamus does indeed play a role in determining some male-female differences in sexual behaviour, but when it comes to sexual preference, recent studies indicate that mainly 'higher' areas are involved – that is, areas in the cerebral cortex, the amygdala and regions closely connected to it.[8] Just as the amygdala and the network in which it is embedded are important for assigning emotional value to sensory stimuli, this network also controls who we find sexually attractive.

Neurosurgeons do not necessarily aim to eliminate well-defined brain areas but try to remove the source of a brain disorder. Like the prefrontal cortex, the temporal lobe is a kaleidoscopic complex of anatomical puzzle pieces. Each piece appears to be made up of smaller, even more specialized parts, and you can zoom in further and further on each little part, right down to the microscopic level of the brain cell. In this respect, the brain resembles planet Earth, observed from a satellite. First the camera has the whole world in view, then it zooms in on a continent – a lobe of the brain. If you look at the Amazon in South America – comparable to a sub-area of the temporal lobe – you will see different regions of rainforest, each resulting in a river, or a cerebral blood vessel. Zooming in further, trees come into view, with branches that resemble the dendrites of neurons (Figure 4.1). The big difference is that trees do not enter into synaptic contacts with each other and do not form a rapidly communicating network. Neuroanatomists have shown that the amygdala alone consists of at least 13 subregions.[9] Diligent and systematic studies in animals have shown how these areas perform separate functions within the larger complex of the amygdala.

Joseph LeDoux and his colleagues from New York University implanted very fine electrodes in one of the areas within the amygdala of rats.[10] These electrodes can be used to detect the firing of electrical pulses by amygdala cells. The cells are located near the electrodes, which are somewhat similar to microphones that a researcher sinks into the sea to pick up sounds from fish or whales. Firing activity is monitored over the period of time during which a rat learns that a sound of one particular pitch is followed by a mild electric shock, administered via a grid floor – an unpleasant outcome that causes the animal to freeze in fear. When the rat hears the tone for the first few times, the electrical response of amygdala neurons to that tone is faint. As the rat learns that the tone has a constant, negative consequence, the response of the neurons becomes stronger (Figure 5.1). It is not that the cell as a whole changes and therefore fires more pulses. The key change is that the synapses – the contact points between brain cells – are strengthened.

The synapse can be likened to a very small hand clasped around the dendrite of a cell. When learning the link between the tone and frightening outcome, it begins to squeeze harder and harder (Figure 5.1B). This metaphor illustrates that synapses are plastic, or in other words changeable, and their reinforcement can be long-lasting. A reinforcement does not necessarily mean

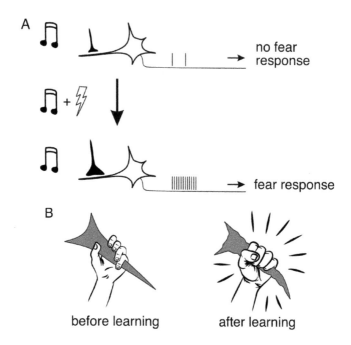

Figure 5.1 Brain mechanism for learning fear responses. (A, top) A neuron in the amygdala receives a weak synaptic input when the animal is offered a sound stimulus. In this initial situation, the tone has no consequences. The output of the neuron is correspondingly weak, shown as two spikes (vertical dashes) sent across the axon of the cell. (A, middle) The animal is repeatedly exposed to the tone accompanied by an electric shock. (A, bottom) Even without the electric shock, the animal starts to behave fearfully when hearing the tone. During this learning process, the synapse that transmits sound information is strengthened (symbolized by the larger synapse). The cell now fires more spikes in response to the sound signal. (B) The strengthening of a synapse is symbolized by a hand that, after learning, squeezes the dendrite more forcefully. In the brain, it is actually the strength of the electrical 'squeeze' by the synapse that is important, not a mechanical squeeze.

that the synapse also physically increases in size (as suggested in Figure 5.1A); this can also be achieved by a biochemical change in the synapse, resulting in a stronger electrical response. In this case, the cell-to-cell connections transmit the tone information to cells in the amygdala. Because the intensity of a cell's firing response is related to the negative consequences of the tone (and not to its pitch or other properties), we can conclude that the cells encode the (emotional) value of the sound stimulus. From the subregion that was recorded, electrical signals are sent to other structures in the amygdala, which determine how the animal reacts to the emotional stimulus in its behaviour and in its body's interior.

Despite the apparent fearlessness with which a Klüver-Bucy monkey faces the world, it is not the case that without the amygdala we would be totally free of anxiety or fearful behaviour. Basic, innate fear mechanisms are still present without a functioning amygdala – like shrinking back from a large object approaching you at breakneck speed, or ducking when a loud bang reaches your ear. It is especially the acquisition of the value of stimuli that depends on a healthy amygdala – and translating this value into a behavioural response appropriate to the situation. Moreover, dozens of publications on the amygdala show that it is not an anatomical complex that merely signals negative value. Spread across the nucleus are cells that become active when stimulated with a positive value, such as – in the case of monkeys – pieces of banana, grapes, pineapple, raisins and other sweet foods. The amygdala is there to learn associations of things with the sweet and the sour, grief and joy.

Do you remember when you, as a child, first became acquainted with banknotes? Growing up in the Netherlands, I still remember the somewhat grumpy Joost van den Vondel – a seventeenth-century poet and playwright – on the green five-guilder banknote, whereas kids in the United States or United Kingdom get acquainted with Andrew Jackson (on twenty-dollar bills) or King Charles III (on all pound sterling banknotes). Back then, a freshly printed banknote stood out because of its smooth and solid feel and crackling sound when folded – but initially not because of the economic value it represented. Once you learn that the banknote can be used to buy all sorts of delicious food and drink, and you eat all that with relish, the association that the banknote is *worth* something arises: it predicts all sorts of pleasant things you can do with money. If you then get another banknote right under your nose, it has become an attractive object – regardless of its visual and tactile features. The amygdala is important for this learned, emotional association. The example of banknotes can be extended to all sorts of objects in our environment that we learn to value: packaged food, cans of cola, cups of coffee, houseplants, cars, bicycles, Barbie dolls, trees, animals, computers, TV personalities, soccer balls and voices on the radio. The sight of an object is like a share on the stock market: it starts out as a piece of paper with a dry text with no intrinsic value, but it becomes a positive thing as soon as you start to believe that it stands for something valuable. Depending on our positive or negative experiences, the stock price rises or falls. The network in which the amygdala is embedded acts as a comprehensive valuation system on which – day in and day out – all important things are tirelessly weighed and appraised.

Here, too, the amygdala does not act alone. In estimating the attractiveness of objects, the amygdala works together with the orbitofrontal cortex, one of the areas affected in Phineas Gage and Joe A. While the amygdala mediates the basic learning process by which we make connections between neutral stimuli and – apart from its visual and tactile features – their unpleasant or pleasant consequences in the short term, the orbitofrontal cortex is more important for judging long-term value. It helps us to flexibly deal with things we encounter in a changeable environment, and to spontaneously change our strategy for coping with the outside world. When you go shopping somewhere in one of the Western countries of the European Union, you can blindly trust that a 50 euro note will be accepted as a currency, but in the interior of Sumatra, it will not get us very far. Instead of persisting with a strategy of using this note to pay for consumed food, we will have to look for a foreign exchange office first.

When the anatomical connections of the amygdala with brain structures other than the prefrontal cortex are mapped, it appears to be located in an extraordinarily central place: a spider in the web that also includes the more posterior areas of the cerebral cortex. From these areas in the back of our head, the amygdala receives sensory information and in turn sends back signals about the value of perceived objects. This feedback from the amygdala can be used to focus our attention on what is important to us. Thanks to its central position in the brain, the amygdala is not only able to influence behaviour such as trembling or sitting still, but also internal cognitive processes such as attention and memory.

What have we found out so far about the role of emotions in consciousness? Despite its suspected role in 'psychic blindness', the amygdala does not turn out to be the 'seat of the soul'. If it is wiped out, together with the surrounding tissue, all kinds of abnormalities come to the surface. But perception itself is still intact. Dream and imagination, as consciously experienced counterparts of our perception that are not dependent on external stimuli, keep on going as well. But the people (and monkeys) with Klüver-Bucy-like symptoms that passed by so far all had extensive damage to the temporal lobe, not just to the amygdala. Sporadically, patients with specific damage to the amygdala have been described. Do they provide a clearer picture of the functions of the amygdala than that described by Klüver and Bucy?

In 1998, Elizabeth Phelps, an expert on emotional memory, described a woman – patient S. P. – with amygdala lesions in both hemispheres. She also suffered from epilepsy and it was decided that the source, located in the temporal lobe of the right hemisphere, should be excised. Not only was the amygdala removed on that side, but also nearby memory structures such as the hippocampus. Brain scans also revealed previously incurred damage to the left amygdala. What was special about this patient was that her declarative memory was largely fine, probably because the memory structures in the left hemisphere were relatively intact and could compensate for the loss in the right hemisphere.

In a laboratory test situation, S. P. was exposed to two consecutive stimuli: an initially neutral, blue square on a screen, followed by an electric shock.[11] S. P. was allowed to set the intensity of the electric shock herself, which did not evoke a stabbing pain but rather aversion (essentially Phelps adopted the same classic experimental design that Ivan Pavlov used to condition his dogs in the late nineteenth century). As with the prefrontal patients we saw in Chapter 4, Phelps measured sweat secretion on the skin to see how strongly S. P.'s body responded to neutral or emotionally charged stimuli, which in this case were not pleasant but negative and somewhat frightening because each test resulted in an electric shock. Just like healthy test subjects, patient S. P. showed an increased sweat production when the electric shock was administered. This is logical, as the stimulus is unpleasant in any case.

But while a healthy person would also produce more sweat at the sight of the blue square – as a sign that she has learned the negative emotional meaning of this – S. P. did not show this learned reaction. Strikingly, she was fully aware of the situation: she was able to articulate very well how she anticipated the electric shock when the blue square appeared on the screen. "I knew it was going to happen. I expected that it was going to happen. So I learned from the very beginning that it was going to happen: blue and shock." What also stood out was that in her personal life S. P. was anything but emotionally deficient or suffering from 'psychic blindness'. Despite a history of severe epileptic seizures, she was a funny, sympathetic woman who enjoyed painting and writing poetry. She did not behave inappropriately and did not show extreme mood swings. Even fearful or panic-stricken voices were appropriately valued by her.

What do amygdala lesions tell us about emotions? Which of the five components – sensory trigger, bodily response, bodily feelings, preparation for action and cognitive appraisal – are affected when the amygdala fails? And what does this say about consciousness? S. P. lacked an autonomous bodily response to a stimulus with a learned negative value, and as a result her brain did not receive feedback from her body that would otherwise produce a sensation of cold sweat. But apart from this lack of subcutaneous appreciation, emotions were still very much present. Without an amygdala you do not become an emotional zombie. Patients still have consciously experienced feelings and can describe the emotional situation they are in without difficulty, also by virtue of their intact brain mechanisms for narrative memory. All in all, consciousness loses some shards and shells upon prefrontal or amygdala damage, but it continues to exist. This is also the case when the damage is so vast that emotionality is severely impaired or flattened, as in lobotomy patients. This adds to the mystery of where consciousness is seated in the brain (if anywhere at all) and leads us to explore other directions. In any case, a dysregulation of the amygdala – be it by lesion, epilepsy or overstimulation – can lead to behavioural changes, whether consciously noted or not, but does not wipe out or 'hijack' consciousness itself. But what happens to our consciousness when our behaviour, or the totality of our body movements, is itself at stake? Will the image of a rock-solid, untouchable consciousness then finally start to tip over?

Apart from his prison sentence, the case of the patient who indulged in child pornography had a relatively happy ending. The man did not cheerfully subscribe to a Master of Business Leadership centred on Amygdala Hijacks or Amygdala Healing Workshops. Instead, his psychiatrist prescribed psychopharmaceuticals that caused an unusually low libido. The man no longer had sex. He was no longer constantly harassing his wife, but he did develop a form of warm, intimate contact with her.

6   The genie out of the bottle

On what slipper animals, paralysis and dreams show us about the relationship between movement and consciousness

One of our heroes in the quest for consciousness is the sea squirt. This bagpipe-shaped creature can be found in almost all the world's oceans and seas. Adults attach themselves to rocks, sucking up seawater and filtering out plankton, and thus lead an unspectacular existence. Their body consists of little more than a mantle or hull, with an opening through which the water flows in or out, plus a kind of gill. There is no brain: their seated existence is so uncomplicated that a brain would be superfluous. But when these humble little creatures manage to reproduce, something sensational happens. From the fertilized egg a larva develops that looks a lot like a tadpole. This creature sets out into the seven seas and does in fact develop a nervous system – a thick nerve cluster connected to a primitive spinal cord. Unlike its parents, the youngster is confronted with rapidly changing sensory information – about temperature, sea currents, light, food, oxygen and the scent of possible predators – and must be able to react quickly by adjusting its behaviour. In this form, the animal does need a fast-switching centre – a kind of cockpit that quickly converts sensory information into physical movement. If, after all its wanderings, the larva manages to settle on a suitable rock, its nervous system degenerates. This unsightly creature holds up a mirror to us: doesn't the adult stage of the sea squirt suspiciously resemble the life of a bureaucrat, bound to a sedentary existence in office? Does not the promise and redemption of this creature lie in its procreation and the adventurous existence of its young?

Neurophysiologist Rodolfo Llinás of New York University[1] cites this ascidian to support one of his theses: consciousness and mind are inextricably linked to active movement. This is not unreasonable: when we decide to act – in any situation – this is generally accompanied by awareness of what we are experiencing and doing at that moment. We see, hear, feel the world around us, and know the position of our body in this world before we take action. But is the statement true – in its entirety or partially? How important is physical movement exactly for consciousness?

Here the sea squirt leaves the stage and our second hero appears: the slipper animal. This organism has an even simpler body structure than the previous one: it consists of only one cell. With a length of a quarter of a millimetre, it has, as its name suggests, the shape of the sole of a foot. If you put a drop

DOI: 10.4324/9781003429555-6

of ditch water under a microscope, there is a good chance you will see the creature manoeuvring through the water. That one cell is a marvel of multi-tasking. Through an oral groove in its body surface – a cell membrane that forms a 'skin' and is made up of fat-like molecules – it takes in food particles. Minuscule food pellets are digested in the cell's internal fluid, while in the meantime it moves on to new microscopic vistas. If this mini-animal bumps into a plant fibre, the cilia that cover its membrane change direction: it puts itself in reverse and starts moving in the opposite direction. If there is a spatial gradient of nutrients such as sugar in the ditch water – meaning that there is less sugar in one place than the other – sensors in the membrane effortlessly detect the difference and the system of cooperating cilia immediately adjusts itself to head in the direction of the highest sugar concentration. All this happens without a brain or even a nerve cell: there is only one cell and it takes care of everything (Figure 6.1).

The little slipper cell shows active behaviour and is able to initiate it. But is there any consciousness here – however slight? A collision with a straw fibre deflects the cilia, and sensors in the membrane transmit signals to other cilia, which then reverse their undulation. The entire behaviour of the animal can be explained by mechanical, chemical and electrical couplings that lead from a stimulus to a response: a system of automatic reactions, resulting in reflexes. In ourselves too, we recognize a reflex as a rigid, stereotyped form of behaviour that occurs quickly and independently of our stream of thoughts. The lower leg that shoots forward when the doctor taps the piece of tendon under your kneecap with a hammer. The hand that is already withdrawn from a gas flame before you even know it. Like no other behaviour, reflexes illustrate the existence of unconscious motor processes: they are an active form of movement that does not require consciousness. In the case of the gas flame, of course, we feel pain, but this sensation only arises clearly after we have already withdrawn our hand. Here, consciousness is playing catch-up. Why should we become aware of the stabbing pain at all? I will come back to this later, but for now, it seems very likely that the behaviour of the slipper animal is made up of reflexes without a need for consciousness.

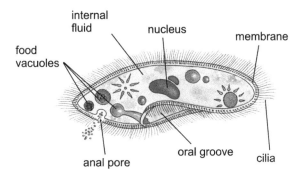

Figure 6.1 Construction of the slipper animal, a single-celled organism.

While Llinás proposed that even simple invertebrates have a seed of subjectivity – their own domain of experience, very primitive, but still – I think we should avoid vagueness and only speak of consciousness when there is a good reason to do so. An animal, or even an artificial make such as a computer, must provide at least one shred of evidence that it is capable of more than a reflex or other simple response to a sensory stimulus. First of all, this has to do with *Occam's Razor*, the 'razor' of the English Franciscan monk William of Ockham (c. 1287–1347). If there are competing ideas to explain a certain phenomenon, he reasoned, take the most 'efficient' or simplest explanation as a guide for further investigation, and cut away the rest as if they were superfluous beard hair. Your explanation should use as few assumptions or presuppositions as possible to explain the phenomenon you are interested in. If we apply Occam's razor to the slipper animal, is it necessary to assume that it is conscious? The interplay of sensors, electric currents, chemical reactions and cilia turns out to be sufficient to explain the animal's movement patterns.[2] What would you gain by dragging a complex phenomenon such as consciousness in by the hair? What could you explain more or better, on top of the mechanical and chemical processes that dictate the swaying movements of the cilia?

But couldn't this adorable single-cell organism have a bit of consciousness after all? This legitimate question raises the issue of whether consciousness is an all-or-nothing phenomenon, or whether it can manifest itself across a gradual scale, from little to much consciousness. How could this question be answered? Let us draw on consciousness here as a state in which we experience the world – and ourselves in it – as a wealth of sensory qualities, arranged in a spatial overview that we sense from our own perspective and in which we feel immersed. If we follow this description, might we not call the slipper animal a little conscious? Is this charming creature capable of interpreting the world around it in a totality of images, sounds and other impressions, woven together and ordered in space and time? In this particular organism, there is, all things considered, no reasonable ground to suspect a rich, complex world of experience behind the forest of whip hairs. There is, to quote philosopher Thomas Nagel, no reason to assume that being a slipper animal feels like anything.[3] If we were to cling to the idea that it is a bit conscious, what would this 'bit' explain about its behaviour that we did not already know? The creature has no eyes and will therefore not be able to form an image of its surroundings, as we have when our eyes open in the morning. When it comes to consciousness, the slipper animal fits better into the category of smoke detectors and other sensors in household appliances than among creatures to which we can ascribe an emotional life and a rich representation of the surrounding world. Do not let this be an insult to this living creature. Its behaviour, well adapted to its environment, makes it much more complex than a smoke detector, but in this case we are talking about consciousness. When it comes to living beings that actively move around, (conscious) experiences do not come for free. So no: although single-celled creatures deserve our deepest respect in many ways, there is no reason to attribute even a modicum of consciousness to them. Just as there is no reason to call the slipper animal, during sexual interactions with a fellow congener, a little bit in love.

And yet, especially among philosophers, there is much debate as to whether it is not arrogant and conservative to reserve consciousness for highly developed animals like ourselves. Is there a hard border between animals that can or cannot be conscious? Where should that boundary be drawn – with insects, reptiles, squids, birds or mammals such as cats and dogs? As any boundary seems arbitrary in advance, some say that everything in nature is conscious, from weak to strong or from little to much. This stance ('panpsychism'[4]) has a serious drawback: doesn't our practical experience show that consciousness is a state that we sometimes find in an animal or a human and sometimes not? We can be awake or deeply asleep – and only after a deep sleep do we notice that we have been 'away' for a while and conclude that we must have been asleep. After a blow to the head, a boxer may continue to fight or be knocked out. He loses consciousness, but only realizes this afterwards, when regaining it. In the hospital, a major operation is performed under general anaesthesia so that we do not have to consciously experience any painful cutting – and then we recover consciousness. It is in this contrast of conscious and unconscious states that the usefulness of the concept of consciousness comes into play. If everything in the universe is always conscious of everything, it is better to delete the word from your vocabulary. My conclusion on the panpsychism discussion is therefore sobering: attribute 'consciousness' only to a thing or a being that shows a manifest characteristic of it. This can be a certain behaviour, a particular type of brain activity or perhaps – also in the case of computers – a very complex concatenation of computations. The real discussion should be about which properties count as manifest or, in other words, provide a positive indication for consciousness.

The debate on the role of active movement and consciousness is not limited to sea squirts and slipper animals. In recent years, there has been a boom in ideas about consciousness that focus on interactions between humans or animals and their environment. We explore our environment by performing motor actions, such as eye and hand movements. Motor activity leads to changes in what we perceive. For instance, an eye movement brings an interesting object into view. By closing one of our hands, we feel the shape of the spoon lying in it. It is only by taking a deep breath that we notice a subtle sewer smell in the bathroom. If we turn a coin between our thumb and forefinger, it will alternately look elliptical or round. We gain new experiences by doing things, and the way we interact with the outside world determines how that outside world presents itself to us.

A central idea behind this school of thought is that our experiences are determined by a fixed, lawful link between movements and sensory changes induced by this motor activity. In the last decade, one of these theories – the motor-sensory theory of consciousness – has become somewhat of a hype.[5] When we perceive the colour green, it is not because our brain internally creates a picture (or other representation) of 'green', but because our eye movements cause a pattern of certain light particles[6] emitted from an object to impinge on our retina at that moment. It is not an 'internal picture' that determines what we are aware of, but the fixed relationship between movement and its effects on the information our senses process. In fact, there is no 'internal picture' at all, because when we open the brain and look inside, all we see are blood vessels, brain cells and a few other kinds of cells and tissue fluid. What we call 'consciousness' is nothing more or less than the cycle in which our body movements lead to changes in the signals we receive from the environment, which in turn result in a different processing of these signals by our sensory systems. These changes in sensory processing then give rise to new motor actions, and so on. Kevin O'Regan and Alva Noë, two authors favouring this motor-sensory theory, summarize their vision as: "Seeing is a way of acting. It is a particular way of exploring the environment." Motor activity and interaction with the environment as a basis for consciousness. Does this perhaps provide a foothold to fathom consciousness any better?

As with Descartes, neurological abnormalities provide a first benchmark to determine the validity of the theory. Radical adherents of the theory argue: we are already conscious of a thing the moment we perform a motor action that triggers a change in the processing of sensory information about that thing. This would mean that a slipper animal is indeed conscious when it bumps into a straw fibre and the sensors in its membrane transmit signals to the cilia that propel it forward. If you take this literally, this quickly gives rise to objections. People with paralysis would not be able to become aware of environmental stimuli because they cannot perform actions that would trigger the senses in their paralyzed body parts to signal changes. If damage to the nervous system leads to paralysis, there may indeed be sensory loss, but there does not have to be. The motor cortex is located in the part of the frontal lobe closest to the back of the head (Figures 3.2 and 12.1) and controls the skeletal muscles. If, as a result of a stroke, this part of the cerebral cortex is lost, the patient will retain his physical sensations, for example if someone touches the – now passive – body part with a finger. In the past, when trekking through the Amazon jungle, one risked being ambushed by an indigenous tribe who dipped the tips of blowguns in curare, a poison extracted from lianas. Curare can be so powerful that it completely paralyzes all body muscles, including those used for breathing. Thus, a heavy dose guarantees death by suffocation. But before that happens, the victim remains fully aware of his surroundings and his own paralyzed state. Again: consciousness without motricity.

The operating theatres of modern hospitals provide further evidence against a fixed one-to-one relationship between consciousness and physical activity. About one in every thousand patients who are subjected to general anaesthesia consciously undergoes the operation while their muscles are paralyzed.[7] The anaesthetic is apparently not working properly, but the staff in the operating theatre do not realize this because the patient's physical signals – such as heart rate and muscle weakness – match the image of a complete anaesthesia. This sounds like a nightmare, and that is how these patients experience it. After recovering from the operation, one of them tells how he heard a saw going back and forth as a surgeon opened his chest to remove a tumour near his heart. He tried to move and scream, but was unable to do so. During a heart operation, a female patient heard voices and experienced intense pain as she felt people were trying to tear her chest apart. Another woman who underwent a lung transplantation heard staff talking about the war in Afghanistan, and recalled that she disagreed with them but could neither move nor speak. A doctor listening to the story after treatment may think her patient was delirious and experienced a delusion about a surgical experience that was concocted from pure fantasies. But sometimes details emerge that match the events during the actual operation too well to be dismissed as a fabrication.

A stroke can cause such massive brain damage that almost the entire body is permanently paralyzed. Jean-Dominique Bauby was 43 years old and the editor-in-chief of *Elle* magazine in Paris when he was struck by this condition in 1995. After weeks in a coma, he woke up. He noticed that he could hardly move a thing in his body – only his head and eyes a little. His right eyelid had to be stitched shut, his left eyelid eventually became his strongest weapon. According to the motor-sensory theory, it is to be expected that his world of experience would shrink drastically in this locked-in situation. He may have been able to blink with that one eyelid, but his ability to gather diverse, rich sensory feedback from the environment with it was very limited. That feedback would have to come from the limited head and eye movements he could still make. When he opened his eye, he received light signals from the room he was lying in. When he closed his eye, it became dark. But did this dramatically reduce his consciousness? Shortly after the incident, it was impossible to determine.

Bauby gets help from a speech therapist with whom he learns to communicate using his one, active eyelid. They develop a system: the therapist reads the 26 letters of the alphabet in an order from frequently to rarely used letters, and Bauby blinks his eyelid at the letter he needs to form the word he wants. He manages to convert eyelid movements into letters, string them together into words, and thus compose an entire book. *Le Scaphandre et le Papillon* (The Diving Bell and the Butterfly) is his impressive sign to the outside world: even as a locked-in patient he has conscious experiences.[8] In 200,000 glances, he dictates his account of a rich inner world – a world of someone who is locked in a paralyzed body but still experiences all sorts of phenomena – sensations, memories and fantasies, accompanied by dismay, hope, despair, sadness and resignation. He realizes that he will be able to see his daughter Céleste and son Théophile, but can never hold them. Bauby died of pneumonia in 1997, shortly after the publication of his book. His tragic story not only expresses an enormous will to survive – the will to remain a complete human being despite a body that does not cooperate – but also shows that an almost total loss of motor function does not result in a gradual deterioration of consciousness in the long term.

Does the reverse also occur: motricity without consciousness? Particularly in children, epileptic seizures occur in the rather mild form of an *absence*, a mental absence which can be recognized in a patient by a vacuous, emotionless facial expression. The little patient glazes in the distance and does not react to signals from his surroundings, such as the calling of his name or a request to answer. As with a severe, prolonged attack in which the patient falls to the ground and jolts with his muscles – the type of attack that Henry Molaison was so often caught up in – an electrical tornado rages through the brain during an *absence*, only this phenomenon lasts, at most, tens of seconds. Some patients with absence epilepsy show automatisms: stereotyped and simple behaviours such as smacking their lips or fidgeting with clothes. Others show more complex behaviour: they take off their clothes and put them on again, catch a ball thrown to them, walk around as a sleepwalker would and follow moving objects with their eyes. But even during this more complex behaviour, they are unable to respond to a doctor's questions, read a text or make difficult decisions – and with their blank faces, they are still considered mostly 'unconscious' or 'absent' when observed in the clinic during a seizure.

Without wishing to detract from these patients, the image of 'zombies' – beings who behave normally but feel or experience nothing – comes to mind here. This image is fuelled by the absence of emotional expression. Recovering from an absence attack that was accompanied by a series of automatisms, the patient is surprised at the situation he has ended up in. He has no idea what has happened in the meantime, or how much time has passed. A memory defect caused by the epileptic seizure could play a role here: perhaps he has immediately forgotten what he experienced during the seizure. But this is contradicted by indications that at least some of the patients with automatisms were lacking consciousness. When memory tests are administered to patients to see what they have remembered of the things that were presented to them during their attack, some appear to be able to retrieve memories. This may seem contradictory, as narrative memory enables healthy people to remember things they have experienced consciously, but in this particular group of patients there is a disconnect: motor skills, no consciousness and still some memory.[9]

Thus, the evidence against an inseparable link between motor activity and consciousness is mounting. Our daily lives are characterized by an abundance of physical activity, but when we walk or cycle we are aware of things other than our habits and muscle contractions. Even when we sit still, our bodies remain active. We blink our eyelids but do not experience the darkness that, according to the motor-sensory theory, this should bring. In a perpetual cycle we breathe in and out, and the expansion of our chest certainly has an effect on the local sensory organs in the muscles and skin. Although these signals are passed on to the brain, they do not lead to a conscious experience (except perhaps during an exercise in mindfulness). Our heart beats and our intestines squeeze digested food forwards without our noticing – and why should we? With such a jumble of bodily signals, our conscious brain would be extremely busy. Conversely, we have daily experiences that do not involve physical inter-actions with our environment. We can comfortably lie cuddled up in bed day-dreaming and doing nothing else: our visual and auditory imagination lets us experience all sorts of things while our body remains still. Even when we fall asleep and really start dreaming, there is consciousness, roughly speaking, without body movement. Dreams often have a surrealistic nature and manifest themselves in a virtual reality created by our brain, but nonetheless they count as conscious experience.

When we go to sleep, our brain goes through several stages of activity that can be clearly distinguished by electrical signals on the scalp. These electroen-cephalographic (EEG) signals represent global variations in electrical voltage within the brain, and these fluctuations propagate ultrarapidly from the brain to electrodes applied to the scalp during an EEG measurement. When we are awake or slipping into a first, light sleep, the EEG shows irregular waves with little peaks and valleys. If we pass from superficial to deep sleep, slow electrical waves appear – a few of which fit within a second – and become increasingly stronger and more regular (Figure 6.2). When we awaken from deep sleep, this pattern loses its powerful waves, reminiscent of a sea that the wind is play-ing with, with small and ephemeral waves and an occasional foam head.

From deep sleep, the brain spontaneously ascends several times a night to dream sleep, which shows an electrical pattern very similar to the waking state. Often, but not always, our eyes flash up and down during dreams – a state of rapid eye movement (REM[10]). Dreams thus involve eye movements, but the rest of our body is paralyzed. In the brainstem (Figure 2.1) there is even a group of neurons that actively prevents us from living out our dreams in physical movement; apparently it is important that our body is paralyzed dur-ing the dream. The function of this dream paralysis probably lies in the risks that would be associated with the motor actions that you would undertake if your body did react to the content of your dream. A young deer that would physically express its reactions during dreaming could damage its limbs, and this motor activity could betray its hiding place in the bushes to a nearby wolf. In humans, the physical manifestation of an erotic dream can be problematic on a social or relational level. Dreams would make us wander around without actually seeing the obstacles in the outside world. The body paralysis contrasts with the experience that our body – virtually – can very much move actively within the dream. I sometimes dream of running, taking off and flying, wildly flapping my arms through the air. I am aware of moving limbs without them physically interacting with my surroundings.

Gradually, the picture is beginning to crystallize: consciousness and motor activity can in fact exist without each other. With its ingenious manoeuvres, the slipper animal makes it clear that we do not necessarily have to involve consciousness to explain behaviour. If we look higher up in evolution, then humans, in their daily grind but also in bizarre circumstances, show how phys-ical movement can be disconnected from consciousness. Paralysis, locked-in syndrome and staying awake under anaesthesia confront us with the continued

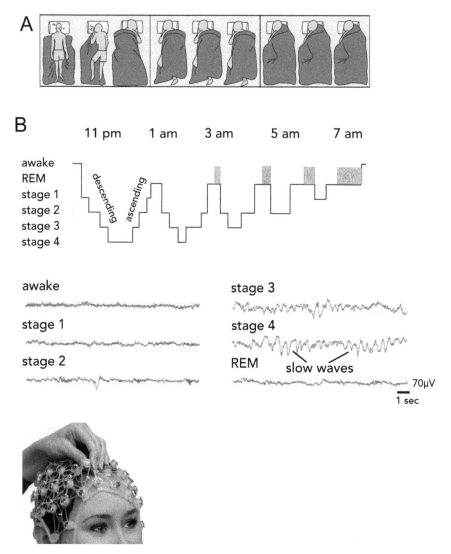

Figure 6.2 Brain signals during the sleep cycle. During the night, people go through a cycle that changes from the waking state to a state of light, superficial sleep (stage 1). This gradually deepens to stage 4 and then alternates with rapid eye movement (REM) sleep. Sleep stages 1 to 4 belong to non-REM sleep. The stepwise graph illustrates a typical time course from 23:00 in the evening to 7:00 in the morning. Shown below are electroencephalographic (EEG) signals derived from the scalp of a test subject. In the waking state, EEG signals do not show large waves in electrical activity, but this picture changes as sleep deepens to stage 4 where large, slow waves are expressed. A microvolt (μV) is a millionth of one volt.

Source: Adapted from Hobson (2005; A, top panel); Buzsaki (2006; B, other panels; EEG recordings in B are courtesy of A. A. Borbély.

existence of a consciously experienced reality in the absence of ostentation. In a healthy state, daily musings, nocturnal dreams and imagination bear the same witness. Conversely, all kinds of bodily movement take place without our awareness: our external behaviour is packed with unnoticed habits and reflexes, while also our internal organs continuously work to keep us alive, unobtrusively and without a cry for attention. And this adventurous sea squirt larva, doesn't it show that a good set of nerve cells is essential for an expeditious motor system? The larva may need a nervous system to translate sensory information into behaviour, but it does not lay claim to having conscious experiences. Thus, as we continue to peel away our brain functions and strip them of the shell of motor skills, consciousness seems only to become more enigmatic: where in the brain is it located, and how does it come about? If conscious experience is not acutely dependent on motor activity, is it after all an 'internal picture' or internal movie that is playing? Perhaps we are still looking at the problem too much through an old-fashioned lens. Shouldn't we be more generous in attributing consciousness to simpler forms of life than humans?

7 Feeling rich in what you do not have

How consciousness is related to corporeality, learning and language, but at the same time escapes these

Alongside the strong, radical motor-sensory theory of the previous chapter, a milder variant has been proposed that is no less interesting. According to this variant, conscious experience is not acutely dependent on an action performed at the particular moment we label 'now', but is related to motor-sensory processes we have undergone in the past. The emphasis shifts from our actions in the here and now to our personal past history. Suppose you are sitting on a café terrace in the light of a setting sun with a dish of coins in front of you. The radical motor-sentence theorist says: "If I move my head down while looking at the coins, this action results in intense flecks of light reflected from those coins into my eyes, and this interaction is what we call 'consciousness'." What is radical about this idea is that it actually places consciousness outside the brain (not accidentally is it called 'externalism'). The milder variant allows us to also experience situations without performing the corresponding movement at the very moment, using knowledge of past interactions with the environment: "With my eyes closed, I can imagine moving my head down and the light being reflected by the coins in my eyes." This mild, memory-dependent variant has the advantage of leaving room for our imagination as part of consciousness. Conscious experience does not necessarily require instantaneous physical actions that cause changes in sensory inputs to the brain. It is more about the knowledge that our brains accumulate throughout our lives about how bodily movements would change sensory inputs *if* performed. When we find ourselves in a certain situation, our perceptions are guided not only by our eye and head movements but also by the different scenarios or action options dug up from memory. There is a strong case to be made that our perception depends at least in part on how we move our body with its sensory organs.

What is also attractive about this milder variant is that it emphasizes the importance of brain development and learning processes for the formation of conscious experiences. By playing and doing, children learn how their perceptions are shaped and controlled by their own actions. A toddler who has discovered a tennis ball somewhere will repeatedly pick it up, bite it, throw it or drop it. She learns how the ball feels, how the visual shape of the ball changes when squeezed and how the elasticity of the ball ensures a funny bounce. Her brain learns to predict what she would experience *if* she squeezes it, even if she

DOI: 10.4324/9781003429555-7

doesn't physically do so. I still remember my own daughters tirelessly banging on the rattle in their playpen as babies, or how as toddlers they could spend hours trying to figure out how a candle fits in a candlestick. There is nothing wrong with calling this process 'playing'. But at the same time, it is a spontaneous, self-directed learning process, by which the child elicits feedback or information from the outside world through its own actions. It learns how the world works, and what the effect of its own actions is on things in that world. It construes a model of the world in which the material properties of candles and candlesticks are contained. But is this 'knowledge-by-action' variant more resistant to practical examples than the strong, acute variant of motor-sensory theory?

A. Z. has feelings that were not thought possible. She is a 44-year-old woman who was born without lower legs, feet, forearms and hands. In places where a normal body has arms and legs, she has cone-shaped stumps about 25 centimetres long. About a hundred and fifty years ago, she would have been an attraction in a travelling circus; now she is a student. As a child, A. Z. learned to pick up objects with her arm stumps, and with her stumps she learned to type. She writes with her mouth and eats using a fork attached to a ring around her right arm stump. To transport her body, she uses an electric wheelchair, which she also controls with her stump. Strangely enough, A. Z. regularly has feelings in body parts she has never possessed. She has no fingers, but it feels as if she does have them, and she can move her phantom fingers too. They do not feel like they are loose, like they are floating in the air, but are an integral part of her body. This has been the case for as long as she can remember. The sensations are nullified if an object or another person occupies the space where her virtual limbs are. Also when she looks at herself in a mirror, the phantom sensations are suppressed. If she palpates an object with her stump, she experiences her phantom fingers as stuck to her stump, not to the full phantom arm she is otherwise aware of. But if she then lets go of the object, her phantom fingers immediately switch back to the position at the very end of her virtual arm. Strikingly, the vividness and intensity of sensations in her phantom feet and legs are enhanced by stimulation of erogenous zones.

What does the case of A. Z., which is described by Peter Brugger at the University Hospital Zürich, Switzerland, and is an example of amelia (a congenital defect of missing one or more limbs), say about the relationship between consciousness and motor activity?[1] A. Z. is unable to move the limbs in which she experiences sensations, because they have never existed. Because she has never had the opportunity to actually move her limbs, her brain does not know the consequences of such movements for sensory experiences. But she does feel them. This seems to be in flagrant contradiction to the motor-sensory theory (both in its radical and milder variant). The girl with the amputated arm described by Descartes might have been able to experience phantom sensations because of her prior history of learning experiences from the time her arm was still attached to her body, but A. Z. never was able to build up such learning experiences. So where did A. Z.'s sensations come from?

Using a scanner, Brugger examines A. Z.'s brain, which turns out to be completely intact. For body sensations, areas around the central groove in the cerebral cortex are important (Figure 7.1). The area immediately to the occipital side of this groove (towards the back of the head), the primary somatosensory cortex, contains a map representing where sensory inputs from the body (soma) come in. Inputs from our legs, feet and genitals are mapped along the midline that separates the hemispheres, continuing through the trunk, head and hands to our face, tongue and digestive system. 'Primary' indicates that this area is the first cortical station where bodily information enters. From there, processed information is passed on to 'higher' areas such as the secondary somatosensory cortex. The map shows your face greatly enlarged, and our lips are even ridiculously magnified. When your lips touch something, cells in the corresponding lip area of your brain map become active. The larger the brain area for a body part is relative to the size of that part, the higher the sensitivity to stimuli, and the stronger your ability to distinguish stimuli in neighbouring places on your skin. It is as if the map presents you with a funhouse mirror: the brain knows exactly what is important to you!

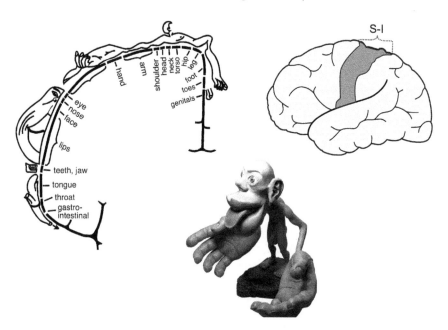

Figure 7.1 The cerebral cortex contains a map representing bodily sensations. On the right, the relevant area is shown in grey (S-I, the primary somatosensory cortex; the front of the brain is on the left side). On the left, the projections from body parts onto the cerebral cortex are mapped. Representations of feet, toes and genitalia lie along the midline that separates the two hemispheres. Below, a 'homunculus' with highly magnified body parts having a high density of tactile sensors (tongue, lips and hands).
Source: Left image adapted from Penfield & Rasmussen (1950).

The fact that in A. Z. the area of the cortex involved in physical sensations was intact indicates that her brain has a normal anatomical structure that provides a basis for her phantom sensations. The area could become active on its own, without external stimulation, and the activity of cells in that area could represent her sensations.[2] From birth, this area may have been able to develop autonomously, without sensory input from any limbs, to express a genetically programmed scheme of her body. In other words, this scheme would already be pre-programmed in our DNA. Brugger and his colleagues carried out additional tests to see if they could confirm the existence of an 'innate body map' in A. Z. They asked her, lying in the brain scanner, to move her phantom fingers at her own pace, rotating her virtual thumb to touch the tips of the other fingers on the same hand. As might be expected, areas in the motor cortex important for movement planning became active, but her (intact) somatosensory cortex remained relatively silent. At first glance this is surprising, because one would expect phantom sensations accompanying virtual movements to lead to activation of this area.

One of the higher cortical regions to which the somatosensory cortex sends its information is located in the parietal lobe. In contrast to the somatosensory cortex, that area was in fact active, in association with her self-directed but virtual finger movements. This suggests that it is not the primary somatosensory cortex that is directly related to conscious sensations, but the parietal cortex. The somatosensory cortex would, to put it bluntly, be merely a conduit or way station on the way to the higher regions that actually encode our experiences. If bodily information does not arrive at this intermediate station, as in A. Z., conscious sensation is still possible. The higher station can, with the help of information from other brain areas such as the motor cortex, in principle still produce the appropriate patterns of electrical activity. With this statement we make an important assumption: A. Z.'s brain itself produces patterns of activity that represent or encode her bodily sensations. Electrical activity in the cortex somehow corresponds to conscious experience. This is no small assumption, for it touches directly on the Hard Problem signalled by David Chalmers: the gap between our subjective, conscious experiences and the billions of electrical impulses that brain cells send to each other.

Amelia provides us with an intriguing insight into the origins of sensory experience: conscious sensations in body parts that were never there. It undermines the idea that conscious sensations are based on memories of motor and sensory activity produced by the brain and body in the past. Sometimes phantom sensations in people who have been missing limbs since birth have been put forward as evidence for a pre-programmed body map, but Brugger rightly expresses reservations about this. Apart from the hereditary factors that groom the cerebral cortex during embryonic development to form an active body map, external stimuli probably do play a role in eliciting phantom sensations. In A. Z.'s case, it is possible that observing other people with intact arm and leg movements, and talking about limbs, may have played a role. But anyhow: these stimuli do not fit the picture presented to us by the motor-sensory theory, even in its milder, memory-dependent variant. It assumes that feeling in your limbs coheres with the movements your own limbs make or have made, not with arm or leg movements of others.

The phenomenon of synaesthesia also provides ammunition against the harsh and mild variants of the motor-sensory theory. About 2 to 4 per cent of the population is familiar with the phenomenon whereby a stimulus in one sensory modality (e.g. a violin sound) evokes an experience in another modality (e.g. a colour). This 'jumping' between different types of sensory experience is also known to occur in non-synaesthetes, as is the case with an LSD trip, but a characteristic of synaesthesia is that the evoked experience is consistently linked to a specific stimulus that triggers the experience in the other modality. When the Hungarian composer and piano virtuoso Franz Liszt was court conductor in Weimar around 1842, he astonished his orchestra by exclaiming: "Please, gentlemen, a little more blue! This key demands it of you!" He could also demand a deep violet sound, or a little less pink. At first the members of the orchestra thought that Liszt was joking, but then they were getting that Liszt in fact saw these colours where they themselves only experienced sounds. In other synaesthetes it is not sounds that evoke colour experiences, but letters or numbers printed in black. Each symbol has a fixed colour. The physicist Richard Feynman experienced mathematical equations as a colourful whole in which the letter n was violet blue and the letter x dark brown.

Synaesthesia is not limited to the generation of colour experiences. For some people, a colour or a piece of music gives rise to a taste sensation; for one person, the word 'numbers' gives a chocolate taste, another will not utter it because it makes it taste awfully. Synaesthesia does not seem to have a distinct function or survival benefit. The phenomenon likely arises as a result of a special way the brain is wired during development,[3] through which signals from one sensory modality can influence information processing in another modality. However, when recognizing and remembering series of letters and numbers, such as Feynman's equations, it can be useful if symbols 'jump out' by their colour or taste.

But what does synaesthesia say about our key question: how do motor-sensory couplings in the present or past affect conscious perception? When a synaesthete scans a page of black letters with his eyes, moving his head and possibly other body parts, there is no reason why such movements should make the same 'T' look blue to one person and red to another – and black to a mere mortal. Yet it is a coloured T that is seen. There must be something special going on in the brain here to experience the seeing of a non-existent colour – something that does not come from our direct physical interactions with the environment. Nor can the phenomenon be explained by an association between body movements and colour or taste that we might once have learned.

There are more arguments against the various variants of the motor-sensory theory, but it is time to leave them for what they are. Undoubtedly, eye movements and other motor activities cause changes in sensory inputs, but this fact does not sufficiently explain why we become aware of these inputs. Even the mild variant, based on learning processes from our past, does not explain this. If my home is broken into, I try to imagine how the burglar got in and how he proceeded. All kinds of scenarios of possible actions and corresponding observations open up. I discover a broken window at the back door and imagine how he sneaked in and looked to the left, where a painting of a bunch of cows is hanging. But I can just as easily imagine that there is a painting of a gypsy girl with a big tear running down her red cheek. I can just as easily imagine something that I have never experienced, like a pink elephant on a monocycle – following in the footsteps of A. Z. who tangibly experiences things she never felt before. In short, the motor-sensory theory does not do justice to the enormous ingenuity and creativity of the brain, which takes us far beyond our actual interactions with our environment.

Consciousness, thinking and language

One of the charming but also complicated aspects of consciousness is that it is a rich and layered concept. The complication lies in the fact that different people can refer to different phenomena with it. Sometimes, during a conversation with someone, I find out only later that she means something different by 'consciousness' than the richly variegated sensory experience I have in mind. It turns out to mean, for example, 'thinking' or 'having control over your own behaviour'. Others mean 'self-consciousness', but this I see as a special, more highly developed form of consciousness that involves a distinction between an 'I' and the rest of the world, a form of reflection. Among neuroscientists, but also philosophers such as Ray Jackendoff,[4] the view of consciousness as a complex sensory experience is widely held, and it is this view that I will maintain here.

In philosophical debates, it is not unusual to link consciousness inseparably with thought and language. Peter Carruthers of the University of Maryland illustrated this with the example of following a well-known route in his car.[5] He drives along the route without accidents or fender bender, avoiding double-parked trucks and other obstacles, but in the meantime is thinking deeply about an article he is working on or fantasizing about his next summer holiday. He is not at all concerned with his immediate surroundings, absorbed as he is in his thoughts. In this situation, he reasons, he is mainly aware of his thoughts, not of the things he encounters along the way. He is constantly processing visual information about obstacles and bends in order to adjust his car, and although one may call this 'experience', it is not a conscious experience of those obstacles. In his view, an experience only becomes conscious when we have the conviction that the experience exists. The sensory data received by the brain are of a lower order and may admittedly give rise to a raw experience, but consciousness requires a higher-order realization that there is an experience we are undergoing. For Carruthers, this conviction is a form of thinking, and it is only through this linguistic activity that we become aware of an experience. A conscious mental state thus differs from an unconscious state in that it is available for reflection. Because we express our experience in language, as a conscious thought, it gives rise to other concoctions, such as: "that banana I am seeing is supposed to be yellow, but to me it actually looks green".

It is to Carruthers' credit that his story depicts how complicated patterns of behaviour allow us to move through the world without being strongly aware of it.[6] But do these automatically performed actions, which stimulate our senses but do not lead to awareness, mean that we necessarily have to be able to think about experiences in order to be aware of them? What is 'thinking' anyway? In the wake of many philosophers of language, Carruthers links thinking to language as an instrument used to express a conviction or belief – not only spoken language, but also language as a *monologue intérieure,* the 'talking within yourself'. Modes of thinking that are absent from this line of thought are visual imagination and other non-linguistic kinds of imagination, such as that of music. When asked to think of my paternal grandmother, I have no hesitation in imagining her – old but active, cooking currants to make jam. I think of her by evoking visual images, not with language. But visual imagination aside, how close is this relationship between language and consciousness?

Carruthers also applies his view to animals or, as he calls them, 'brutes': animals that do not have any form of conscious experience. Here the linguistic theory of consciousness turns out to have a nasty, chauvinistic streak. Because it is extremely unlikely that toads, mice, reptiles, fish or other 'lower' animals have language, Carruthers believes it is unreasonable to attribute consciousness to them. He finds it dubious that great apes could be conscious. An animal could only experience pain consciously if it can think or reflect on it. This has a dramatic consequence which he does not shy away from: we may, without moral objection, be indifferent to pain or distress in bio-industry, because it is unlikely that animals would experience it consciously.

It is precisely this example of pain that shows where the shoe pinches. Intense pain, as well as the experience of colours, tastes and smells, illustrates like nothing else what it is like to have a 'rough feeling' or 'rough sensation'. Pain can so completely dominate our consciousness that we cannot even get around to talk. You just want to scream out your pain, although this too is not necessary to experience it. Ludwig Wittgenstein wrote: "If I see someone who is writhing in pain with evident cause, I do not think: all the same, his feelings remain hidden from me."[7] This underlines that we can see in someone that he is in pain, even if he does not express it in words.

When pain is caused by an injury, blood appears. Do I not see that blood as intensely red until I have expressed a belief that the blood is red? Suppose the colour 'red' is usually available to the language system in our brain to express the belief that this blood is really red, but that this system is momentarily 'offline' and not working. Does the colour red then disappear from our experience of that bloody scene? The linguistic view of consciousness here ignores the raw, non-verbal quality of sensations. Colour sensations can hardly be captured in a language that should be understandable for people who do not know these raw sensations from their own experience – such as people who are totally colour-blind from birth.[8]

When the evolution of man is discussed, a bit of chauvinism pops up in the linguistic theory of consciousness as well. The theory reserves consciousness rather exclusively for modern humans, *homo sapiens*. It is estimated that language emerged in human evolution about 100,000 to 50,000 years ago.[9] On the time scale of evolution, which spans about 4 billion years since the emergence of first life, language appeared on the scene in the blink of an eye. What about the hominids before that time – were they not aware of anything at all? Or did their alarm calls and other primitive guttural sounds entitle them to a little consciousness? Did they behave as we expect of these primitive humans – hunting aurochs and other game, gathering berries, cooking food on a wood fire in a cave – without being aware of all this, like a bunch of zombies? It would be bizarre to assume that these hominids made a sudden leap when they began to have language at their disposal – as if the switch of consciousness had been turned acutely from 'off' to 'on'.

The great apes – and even the rhesus monkey Aurora – clearly have cognitive capacities and perceptions that closely resemble those of modern humans, including emotions, declarative memory, planning and deliberate behaviour, social interactions and empathy. That these mental properties belong to creatures that, because of the lack of language, would go through life totally automatically and unconsciously is not plausible. The anatomy and physiology of monkey brains is very similar to that of humans, for example in the changes brain signals undergo during the transition from waking to deep sleep, the dream state coupled to REM sleep or anaesthesia. It would be very strange to present the evolution of humans as marked by the rapid emergence of language as the 'big bang' of consciousness, and thus to dismiss apes and early humanoids as zombie-like creatures – wandering over the continents in eternal darkness. Or not even in darkness, for they had to be aware of this too in order to know about it. Moving on from human evolution to our development from embryo to adult, a similar argument bubbles up: language theory would dictate that babies and toddlers who have not yet mastered language go through life unconscious.

What is the fate of consciousness in people who lose their language ability? A friend once told me about his father, who suffered from global aphasia as a result of a severe stroke in his left hemisphere. Apart from some babbling, he could no longer utter words and sentences – a speech impediment of a motoric nature attributed to damage to Broca's area, which lies rather frontally in the cerebral cortex. Possibly the damage was so massive that also his system for hearing and understanding spoken language – Wernicke's area – was affected: when my friend talked to his father in short, simple sentences, he often frowned, as if he did not understand the message. It is clear that the language system consists of a larger network than just these two areas. Massive damage affects not only our understanding of language and our ability to speak, but also our linguistic thinking – talking to ourselves – because the difference between 'talking to yourself' and 'talking to others' lies primarily in the control of your vocal cords, throat and lips. In the case of my friend's father, the damage in the left hemisphere was accompanied by right-sided paralysis of his body, but apart from that he showed a normal body language. He sat up straight, had an alert look in his eyes, communicated through gestures and reacted normally to stimuli from his surroundings. His facial expressions showed emotions and moods, and in a speech test he made a visible effort to speak. Occasionally my friend discerned a reproachful expression on his face, as if to say: why did you let me live? As with other aphasic patients, the doctors and family had no doubt that the patient was conscious. Here too, the conclusion is clear: consciousness can exist without language.

During an absence seizure, epileptic patients perform automatic actions, most likely without being aware of them. In special cases, this involves language automatisms. During an attack, children may chat spontaneously – with a blank expression on their face, and afterwards without any memory of what they said. It is as if they are sleepwalking, but in spoken language. Surprisingly, epilepsy can also be accompanied by uttering words in a foreign language instead of the mother tongue. Three French men, with the source of epilepsy in their temporal lobe, spontaneously began to pronounce phrases in both English and French during an attack. One of them repeatedly said: "Mummy, I love you, because" and: "Je t'aime, maman." He pronounced his words in a flat and stereotypical way, without the emotional undertone you would expect from something so loving. After his seizures, he could no longer remember these expressions.[10]

All in all, these arguments are not good news for adherents of the language theory of consciousness: consciousness can exist without language, but language can also exist without consciousness. A faithful supporter might protest that there are perhaps other ways to put flesh on the bones of a conviction or belief about what one hears or sees, but that would profoundly change the nature of the theory. To keep it somewhat afloat, we would have to broaden the playing field to include non-linguistic forms of behaviour or cognition. Perhaps that is not such a bad idea.

Where are we now in dissecting mind and consciousness? The mind turns out to be 'peelable': cognitive capacities are not spread out over the whole brain, but are connected with anatomically distinct networks, delimited in territories. Cognition and anatomy do not interlock as envisaged by classical phrenology, with simple one-to-one relationships between a single brain structure and a highly specific capacity, such as parental love or fear. But we do see clearly how larger chunks of cognitive functions – such as narrative memory – can be linked to larger structures and networks of areas. In our search for consciousness, we have so far mainly seen which areas and networks are *not* directly involved. Memory, emotionality, motor skills and language can be lost or significantly altered, while consciousness remains essentially intact. This is not to say that these functions have nothing to do with consciousness. Even if there is no direct connection between overt behaviour and consciousness in general, it may still be the case that consciousness is related to a certain type of behaviour. The arguments against the motor-sensory theory may be strong – and convincing to my taste – but the question remains how the brain *does* get the job of conscious experience done.

This brings us to developments in artificial intelligence (AI) and robotics. The Boston Dynamics company came up with dog-like robots that can easily move through an office building and open doors to taste the freedom of the outside world.[11] Heralding a new era in AI, Yann LeCun, Yoshua Bengio and Geoffrey Hinton and their colleagues at the University of Toronto developed deep learning machines that learn to classify visual images into different categories of objects and scenes on their own, based on millions of sample images – more on this will follow later.[12] DeepMind, a Google subsidiary led by neuroscientist Demis Hassabis, built a computer algorithm, AlphaGo, that beat human world champion Lee Sedol 4-1 in the board game Go. Its successor, AlphaGo Zero, has since beaten the old programme 100-0.[13] Does an increase in intelligence – the ability to solve problems within a manageable time frame – go hand in hand with an increase in consciousness? Should we be worried about robots that are not only smart but can also experience pleasure, pain and desire for power? Inventor and future visionary Raymond Kurzweil estimated that AI will equal humans in intelligence around 2045, and he sees no reason why AI machines could not develop consciousness. From this supposed 'singularity' in human history, they will be able to improve themselves by designing even smarter robots, leaving humans bewildered and powerless.

Are there serious reasons to already restrain AI machines now, so they will not develop consciousness and take control of our lives? What the attempts to peel off the mind have made clear is that consciousness is something other than displaying 'interesting behaviour' or clever forms of cognition. News reports in the media frequently allege that the emergence of robot consciousness is only a matter of time. At some point, robots will show us that we will have no choice but to interpret their intelligent behaviour as a sign of consciousness. The general tone is: theorizing about consciousness is of little use – intelligent robots will show us through their behaviour along the way what artificial consciousness is. But the examples of decoupling consciousness from behaviour or movement are numerous.

I have saved a telling example of this until last. During a stroke, the primary visual cortex, located in the occipital lobe, is sometimes damaged. This area, also called V1,[14] is the first station in the cortex for processing information that enters the retina and reaches the cortex via an area in the thalamus (Figure 7.2). Once V1 has processed this information, it sends signals to many other areas in the cortex – especially to nearby areas in the back of the head that are also involved in vision. Total damage to V1 in both hemispheres leads to blindness: patients report that they can no longer see. This makes sense, since V1 is the station that supplies almost the entire cerebral cortex with visual information. But otherwise these people are still conscious: they smell, taste, feel, hear and have a sense of balance; only their visual sensations are lost.

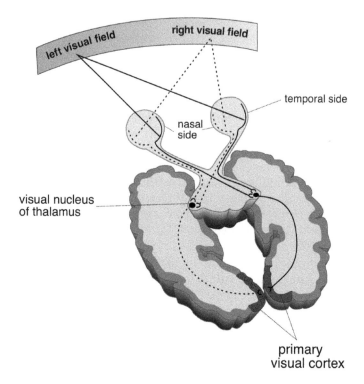

Figure 7.2 Pathways for processing visual information from the eyes to the cerebral cortex. Information from both eyes is sent to the primary visual cortex in both the left and right hemispheres. The optic nerves, which relay the outputs from both retinas to the visual nucleus of the thalamus, meet along the way and show a partial crossing from left to right. Light patterns from the left visual field are received by the nose side of your left eye and the outside of your right eye, that is the part closer to your right temporal bone. The inputs from the left part of your visual field (solid lines) lead to stimulation of your right hemisphere, while the opposite is true for the right part of your visual field (dotted lines).

Damage to V1 is often partial: patients say that they are blind to only part of their visual field, for example the right half of the normal visual field, or the lower left quadrant. When an object moves through this scotoma (the 'blind' part of the total visual field) and the patient is asked to guess which way the object is moving, her estimates turn out to be above chance level. This phenomenon is called "blindsight": you are blind but can still say something sensible about what is happening before your eyes. Somewhere in the brain are structures and pathways that can still process the visual stimulus and enable the patient to respond to it in a meaningful way. The visual information required for guessing is processed via a different route than that normally involved in conscious vision in healthy people, and via that hidden shortcut, manages to reach systems that control a specific motor behaviour (such as a speech response: "the movement goes to the left"). One would be tempted to think that a blindsighted patient might, after all, secretly need to see something of the stimulus in order to guess correctly. But these people are themselves utterly surprised when they are asked to take part in a test: "How can I look at something I haven't seen?"[15]

To find out how the brain mechanisms behind this remarkable phenomenon work, Petra Stoerig from Ludwig Maximilian University in Munich and Alan Cowey from Oxford University conducted a research project in which the primary visual cortex of monkeys was selectively damaged. In an initial behavioural test, they showed that, like people with V1 damage, they could detect visual stimuli within their blind field above chance level – something that can be deduced from their hand movements to the spot on a screen where the visual stimulus appeared. But in this experiment, the researchers cleverly built in an extra test that gave the monkeys a 'free choice' option to indicate whether they had seen a stimulus or not. If they did not offer a stimulus in the non-blind part of the visual field, the monkey would choose to touch a separate rectangle on the screen, indicating 'not seen'. If they then showed a stimulus within the blind area of the visual field, the monkey would again indicate 'not seen'. This test showed that these monkeys, just like people, are 'seeing blind'. They could guess quite decently what was going on in their blind field, but when given a free choice, they indicated they did not perceive the stimulus anyway. If we accept that monkeys do not have language, this result moreover provides some pretty strong evidence against the language theory of consciousness (and in favour of consciousness in animals).

Is consciousness always linked to 'interesting' behaviour? Stoerig and Cowey's experiment involves the detection and localization of visual stimuli, indicated by manual gestures, and even without consciousness this would pass as interesting behaviour in AI circles. But the argument becomes even more striking when blindsighted monkeys are released into a large enclosure where they can do as they please. Nicholas Humphrey of Cambridge University described monkey Helen, who went through life without a V1 but was nonetheless able to locate, grasp and distinguish visual objects in space. She was able to avoid obstacles – as long as they were not made of transparent Perspex.[16] With this behaviour, which requires light information, Helen leaves even the best robots today far behind, but without visual awareness. Later, Beatrice de Gelder of Tilburg University, the Netherlands, and her colleagues described a similar phenomenon in a man who had become blind as a result of two strokes that had destroyed his V1 areas in both hemispheres. Although in daily life he had learned to use a white cane to avoid obstacles in his path, he could also do without the cane or outside help in completing a trail full of boxes, chairs and other hurdles without collisions.[17] In doing so, he approached the navigation of today's best self-driving cars, but again without visual awareness. And do you remember M. S., the person who had become totally colour-blind due to a herpes infection? In his behaviour he could distinguish between coloured surfaces, but he experienced no difference in colour. It is becoming increasingly clear that people can exhibit all kinds of interesting and intelligent behaviour without being aware of the information required – and this need not be different for robots and self-driving cars. Intelligent behaviour is by no means proof of consciousness.

Interesting robot behaviour and impressive AI performances easily entice us to believe that the problem of consciousness is a non-problem, something that will disappear like snow in the sun as technology advances. The current generation of AI technologies is very good at harnessing the enormous processing power of supercomputers to solve expert tasks, but in approaching the problem of consciousness they have not even passed the outer shell of the problem. Take a self-driving car. An on-board computer is fed hourly with thousands of camera images, radar data, GPS coordinates and countless other sensors it uses to calculate how fast the car should take a turn, what kind of object is in front of the car and whether this is a reason to slam on the brakes. The device learns from the mistakes it makes. All incredibly clever, but does this mean that the on-board computer is aware of its surroundings? Perhaps not as aware as a human being, but still: a kind of 'automotive awareness'? Many people have a hunch that this would be too much honour for the on-board computer; not even the engineers of Uber or Google have claimed that their four-wheeled creatures are conscious of their experiences on the road. Or are we biased and just don't like the idea that machines can feel anything? There seems to be a strong case to say that our intuition is not deceiving us. But first, it is time to leave the loose, non-exclusive relationship between consciousness and outward behaviour and ask what consciousness is in fact really about.

8 Visual consciousness peeled off

Why one blindness is not the other, and what this tells us about brain hubs for visual perception

Just as Mr S. was recovering in a hospital room, he soon realized that something was wrong with his eyesight.[1] Not that he was blind, but he had great difficulty distinguishing shapes, such as the letters of the alphabet. A month earlier, in November 1966, the 25-year-old soldier had been found lying groggy on the floor of his bathroom. He was on leave and had taken a shower, unaware of a gas leak that had slowly dazed him with carbon monoxide. In hospital he regained consciousness, talked a little with his family, but sank into a coma the next day. For a few days he reacted only to pain stimuli, but this manifested itself only through abnormal bending or stretching of limbs, a symptom that indicates a failure of the cerebral cortex. This was followed by a phase of parkinsonian symptoms: his facial expression was straight and rigid and his hands were shaking. One month after the accident, S. reacted alertly to his surroundings and spoke again, but the doctor treating him thought he was blind. He was then transferred to the Veterans Hospital in Boston.

Two neurologists, Frank Benson and John Greenberg, decided to examine him systematically. In view of the observed blindness, they noticed that S. could manoeuvre his wheelchair remarkably well through the corridors of his ward. On a screen, they projected a variety of stimuli of different brightness, colour and size, and as long as these stimuli differed in one or more of these properties, he had no trouble telling them apart. But if the colour, brightness or size remained the same, he was unable to distinguish between two different shapes. He could not tell whether a bright blue circle was different from a bright blue square. Was it perhaps his cognitive ability to call things by their name that was impaired? Mr S. could pronounce words and sentences well and his memory and understanding of language were also fine. He was able to name colours, but he had problems with pictures of all kinds of objects, such as numbers and body parts. When he was asked to smell, hear or feel stimuli with his fingers, his ability to recognize and name things was confirmed to be intact. Effortlessly, a smell led him to the word 'rose', or feeling a round, squeezable object led him to 'ball'. When presented with a safety pin, he could tell from its colour and texture that it was something 'silvery' and 'shiny', but as for its shape he guessed it must be something like a watch or nail clipper (Figure 8.1). His physical motor skills and eye movements were fairly normal,

DOI: 10.4324/9781003429555-8

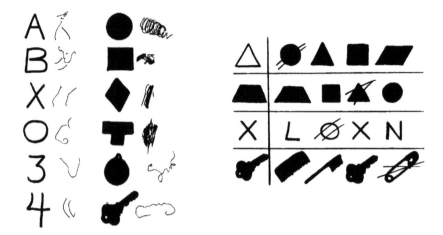

Figure 8.1 (Left) Result of a test in which patient S. was asked to draw letters, numbers and simple shapes. (Right) Test in which S. was asked to mark shapes that corresponded to the object shown to the left of the vertical line.
Source: Farah (2004). Reproduced with permission from the MIT Press.

but when confronted with a visual object, he did not fix his gaze on it; it wandered randomly over the object or its surroundings.

When the doctor and some relatives entered his room, he was unable to call people by their names – until they began to speak. When a photograph of family members was shown to him, even though he was thoroughly familiar with them, he was unable to say who was in it. When he looked at his own face in a mirror, he guessed that it was his doctor's. However, he did make clever use of visual details that could be uniquely linked to a person. If he saw a picture of a half-naked lady, he would scan the image carefully and conclude that it was probably a woman – based on the fact that there was no hair on her arms. He clung to the fleshy colour and smooth texture of her limbs. Shape recognition was completely absent: he could not indicate body parts and when asked to identify the woman's eyes, he pointed to her breasts.

They dug deeper to find out exactly what was wrong with Mr S.'s condition. Did his inability to identify shapes visually mean that he was no longer able to depict shapes himself, either by drawing them from memory or by copying them from pictures next to him? He was almost completely unable to recreate a simple, visible shape (Figure 8.1) and when asked to write down a letter or number, he did so very clumsily: he drew many letters backwards or mirrored them. Nevertheless, Benson and Greenberg found something hopeful in this test. When someone else drew a letter O or X slowly in front of Mr S.'s eyes, he had less trouble naming it. Also, when a complete letter was shown on a sheet of paper that was slowly moved back and forth in front of his eyes, his shape recognition improved. But as soon as the sheet of paper was again laid motionless before him, he had no idea what he was looking at.

Is there any way to help patients like Mr S. cope with their disability? Mr S.'s specific defect is called 'visual form agnosia' and falls into the larger family of agnosias. Where this designation is about 'visual form', it covers the scope well, but the label 'agnosia' is somewhat unfortunate here. From its Greek origin, agnosia stands for 'not-knowing' or 'ignorance', whereas it is not the understanding or naming of form that patients like Mr S. lack: they simply cannot see form. A name like 'form blindness' would fit Mr S. better. Prior to Benson and Greenberg, a neurophysiologist had already examined Mr S. once. "When I repeatedly drew a circular figure with a pencil", he wrote of a session with him, "he was apparently able to see the shape. There was one moment when his face lit up with pleasure and he declared that he saw the circle. After a few minutes, with the circle motionless before him, he was no longer able to name the object."

Mr S.'s brain was found to be so affected by carbon monoxide that all sorts of things were still working on his vision – seeing colour, brightness and texture, but also movement and shape-through-movement. Apparently, brain circuits for motion vision harbour a shortcut to smuggle in form information as well. This shortcut prompted Mr S. to adopt a strategy to make himself the agent in causing the object to move. When he was asked in yet another test to judge whether two lines on a flat surface were aligned in the same direction, the neurophysiologist saw how Mr S. scanned the lines by moving his head up and down. Asked to identify a complex figure, Mr S. repeatedly followed the outline of the object with his eyes, like a child who obsessively follows toy cars speeding down a race track. An intensive and slow way of working, but it did work for him.

The case of Mr S. is not an isolated one. When carbon monoxide poisoning does not cause death, the survivor may suffer from selective form blindness, while seeing colours and other visual properties such as movement remain intact. Shape-blind people show that they try to piece together the visual object information that they do still receive in order to guess its shape. They add up the information about colour, size, texture, gloss and other details, as it were, to infer the shape of the thing in front of their eyes. Brain scans in patients show scattered, diffuse damage in the occipital lobe and adjacent temporal lobe (Figure 3.2). Selective loss of shape vision appears bizarre to healthy people: when we look at the world around us, indoors or out, shapes always seem to be present. Without shapes, it seems that seeing cannot exist, but this is refuted by patients like Mr S. Perhaps we can intuit the condition better when we ourselves look at a picture that initially presents us with a jumble of spots – and when we make an effort to recognize the global shape in a figure (Figure 8.2).

Mr S. brings us to the second part of this book, where we will focus less on memory, emotion, motor skills and language and all the more on brain

Figure 8.2 (Left) If people are unfamiliar with this picture, they usually experience a black and white spot pattern, without recognizing a specific object. Later on, many experience a 'pop-out' of the Dalmatian. (Right) Brick wall from which some people spontaneously see a cigar pop out. Many people do not discern this shape by themselves, but once you have discovered the cigar it is almost impossible not to see it again (see https://slate.com/technology/2016/05/sometimes-a-cigar-isn-t-just-a-cigar.html).

processes that are essential for consciousness. It was not his whole consciousness that was permanently affected by carbon monoxide, but only one part of it – a shard of his total consciousness. The patient is unable to see still shapes, while consciousness for other visual features or attributes is unscathed. The patient has no problem with his hearing, smell, taste, touch, pain, internal bodily sensations or sense of balance. How to understand the case of Mr S., with his loss of form vision while preserving other sensory modalities and visual attributes? His condition becomes less bizarre if we scrutinize damage to lower and higher areas of the visual cortex.

This distinction between lower and higher regions of the visual cortex is preceded by a long history of neuroanatomy that began in the nineteenth century and – as cynical as it is – was given a huge boost by modern warfare early in the twentieth century. It is a cruel twist of fate that innovations in weaponry greatly contributed to our knowledge of the visual system. The bullets used in the Japanese-Russian War (1904–1905) and the First World War left a well-defined trail of destruction in the brain after piercing the skull. British army physicians such as Gordon Holmes and George Riddoch were confronted with the mental devastation that manifested itself on their operating tables and subsequently, during the rehabilitation programme, in the affected soldiers. When a soldier finally succumbed to his wounds, they still managed to rip some knowledge out of this pool of misery by reconstructing the bullet trail through his brain post mortem.

During a visit to the museum of the Royal College of Surgeons in Edinburgh, I became deeply impressed by a collection of pierced soldiers' brains, preserved in large glass cylinders. In these specimens, the trajectory of the bullets, from point of entry to exit, was clearly visible, outlined by a dark red rim of coagulated blood. I was reminded of John McCrae's famous poem, *In Flanders Fields*:

> We are the Dead. Short days ago
> We lived, felt dawn, saw sunset glow,
> Loved and were loved, and now we lie
> In Flanders Fields.

The poem is both moving and shocking: it takes on the perspective of the dead, coming back to live and speaking to the reader. It also clarifies what consciousness is, what it is to have experiences – feeling the morning twilight, seeing the glow of the sunset. It is as if we can sit fraternally between them and feel the warmth of the last rays of the sun on our faces. To be dead but still feel something. An impossibility that nevertheless appeals to us, perhaps because we long to have a soul that can survive the demise of the body.

During the wars of the early twentieth century, neurologists were mapping how a bullet passage through the primary visual cortex amounted to a loss of vision, either for the entire visual field or part of it. George Riddoch discovered patients who were allegedly blind in a limited part of their visual field, but who could still see movement in that part. Colours, shapes or visual details escaped them. They were thus aware of 'pure' movement, without seeing an object that moved.[2] Again, this is rubbing our intuition the wrong way, as we can hardly imagine seeing movement without seeing that *something* is moving. But this is what the patients told Riddoch. Later on in this book, we will again run up against the limitations of our imagination.

Riddoch's conclusions were confirmed in the 1970s and also led to the recognition of blindsight as a clinical phenomenon. The primary visual cortex receives its signals from the visual part of the thalamus, which is a large collection of nuclei that lies beneath the cortex. In turn, this visual thalamic nucleus receives its information from the retina. Also the retina, as a direct receiver of light signals, is in itself a processing station of staggering complexity – a kind of 'pre-brain' when it comes to visual inputs. The retina, the visual thalamus and the primary visual cortex are interconnected in such a way that information from both eyes is sent to both the left and right visual cortex (Figure 7.2). Along the way, a partial crossover takes place, so that inputs from the left part of your visual field lead to stimulation of your right hemisphere, while the reverse is true for the right visual field. For bullet damage to the left visual cortex, Riddoch observed failures in the right half of the visual field and vice versa for damage to the right visual cortex.

Your visual field is mapped within the visual cortex in great detail. The centre of your visual field – where you direct your gaze – is projected onto a greatly enlarged area at the very back of the primary visual cortex, while the peripheral edges of your visual field activate cells that lie further forward, that is towards your forehead, along a deep trench or fissure called the *calcarine sulcus.* Each spot on the retina has a corresponding place on the visual cortical map, all neatly organized in a topographic arrangement. As blindsight already revealed, damage to this area usually results in failure of all visual attributes that fall within the corresponding part of the visual field: not only information about shape but also colour, movement, texture and size of objects. Riddoch's discovery that only motion vision can be spared is an exception.

A roadmap of the visual system

Holmes' and Riddoch's neurological research was followed up with anatomical monk's work that involved injecting tracers into cortical areas such as V1: molecules that are absorbed in situ by brain cells and then transported via their axons (Figure 4.1) to areas where the signals from the same cells are received and processed. The presence of tracers in recipient areas is determined by sensitive chemical reactions to visualize the presence of these molecules. Conversely, anatomists investigated whether the recipient areas also send nerve fibres back to the original area, and how they provide inputs to various other areas further along the cortex. In this way it was discovered that areas of the cortex are not connected to each other randomly, but that there is a system within this interconnectivity. For example, V1 appeared to be a 'low' visual cortex area because of a specific pattern of back-and-forth projections relative to other visual areas in the cortex. Areas such as V2, V3, V4 and V5 (Figure 8.3; V5 is also referred to as 'MT', the Middle Temporal area) each have their own signature of projections to and from V1 and other areas, and were classified as 'higher' visual areas. It thus became clear that cortical areas are not all equally connected. Within the visual areas of the cortex, there is neither anarchy nor democracy nor equality. It began to dawn on us that the visual system of the cortex has a hierarchical order.

At the University of Texas in Houston and the California Institute of Technology in Pasadena, Dan Felleman and David Van Essen diligently built on this work with tracers. In 1991, they produced a 'road map' of the visual system of the cerebral cortex (Figure 8.4).[3] This map is reminiscent of an underground subway network of a metropolis, and indeed the little boxes are brain areas (stations) connected by black lines (bundles of axons). While the subway transports passengers from station A to station B, in our brain it is the *spikes* – the ultra-short electric pulses – that flash across the fibres at lightning speed. At the bottom of the network in Figure 8.4, axons spring from cells in V1, making contact with higher regions such as V4 and MT. From there, information is sent to even higher areas located in the temporal and parietal lobes.

When I present Felleman and Van Essen's famous scheme to students, it elicits mixed reactions: some students become intrigued, others fall asleep. Neuroanatomy is surrounded by a tinge of dullness and dustiness. But anatomical knowledge is absolutely fundamental to understanding the brain. If you lack this knowledge, you are like a stranger trying to navigate through an

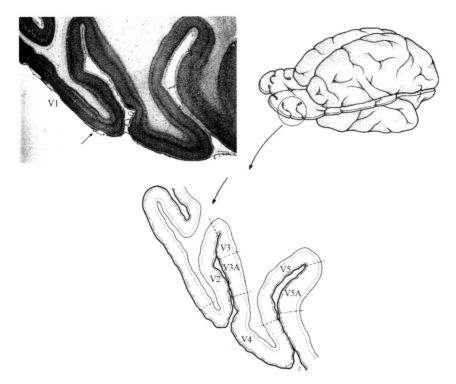

Figure 8.3 Horizontal section of the human cerebral cortex, particularly the occipital primary visual cortex (V1) and neighbouring areas such as V2, V3, V4 and V5. V5 is also referred to as the Middle Temporal area (MT). Top left, a brain section processed with dyes to visualize the stratification of the cortex. This allows the boundaries between areas to be determined.
Source: Zeki (2005). Reprinted with permission of The Royal Society (United Kingdom).

unknown country to a final destination without knowing the road network or carrying a GPS. In reality, the anatomical connections in the cortex form an even more complex network: Figure 8.4 shows only the main connections in the visual system. The higher and lower areas have connections to many more brain systems, such as those for hearing, touch, smell and taste, and sensations from the body. Based on the myriads of connections, other wiring diagrams of the cortex have been proposed since Felleman and Van Essen published their scheme, but they retain the essential feature that there is a kind of hierarchical organization to it.

But that is not all. The sensory stations of the cortex connect to areas controlling motor activity, memory, planning, decision-making, emotion, attention and other forms of cognition. Some of these areas are hidden deep under the cortex, for example in the basal ganglia, which represent very 'old' brain

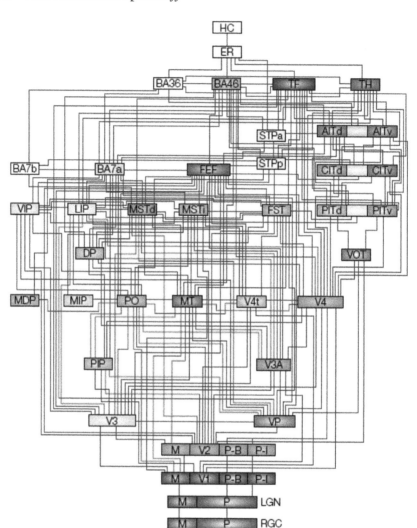

Figure 8.4 Roadmap of the visual system in the cerebral cortex. This diagram shows
the pathways over which information is transported from the retina to the
primary visual cortex (V1) and areas higher up in the visual hierarchy. At
the very bottom are the cells in the retina (RGC), which transmit light
information to two different layers of cells ('M' and 'P') in the visual
thalamic nucleus (LGN). From V1 and V2, information fans out to higher
regions such as the Middle Temporal area (MT) and V4. Above the visual
structures are areas in the parietal lobe (identified by the 'P' as the third
letter in an abbreviation) and temporal lobe (with a 'T'). At the top is the
hippocampus (HC).

Source: Felleman and Van Essen (1991). Reprinted with permission of
Oxford University Press.

structures on the time scale of evolution. The two-dimensional, 'flattened' road map of Figure 8.4 is a simplified reflection of a 3D labyrinth in which one, in greatly shrunken form, could roam around endlessly. It is like wandering through Giovanni Battista Piranesi's eighteenth-century imaginary dungeon landscapes (*Carceri*). If you zoom in on the six layers that make up the cortical layer cake, you can follow the fibre connections that cells in the superficial layers send out to their partners in deeper layers, and vice versa. If you reduce yourself to the size of one thousandth of a millimetre (one micrometre), you would find yourself in the deep layers of the cortex walking among forest giants: neurons with a pyramid-shaped cell body from which a thick trunk rises up to the surface (layer 1) of the cortex. This trunk branches into a few dendrites, which stick up with ever finer shoots (Figures 4.1 and 8.5).

Spikes travel up and down between the layers, but also horizontally through the layers. Played in slow motion, this process is reminiscent of M. C. Escher's closed worlds, in which blank-faced men ascend and descend stairs in an endless loop.[4] Occasionally, a cell is stimulated strongly enough by synaptic inputs from other cells to fire itself. From that cell, the spikes are transported along an axon included in a long slide, for example from area V1 to V4. This is anything but dull and dusty. It is a breathtaking process that is anything but vacuous: these cells are collectively engaged in processes that determine how we experience the world around us.

Comparisons with little men on subways hold only to a limited extent. An important difference between a transport network and a brain network is that travellers in the underground remain the same, even if they have passed one station or transferred to another line. Intuitively, you might think that 'information' remains constant as it passes through brain stations – after all, isn't the information an image or 'picture' that is transmitted from one station to another (Figure 8.6)? But this intuition is based on a misunderstanding. If only it were that simple! The only thing that physically travels across the fibre tracts, *at the level of brain cells*, are electrical pulse patterns. It is true that those patterns represent a certain amount of information, and it is not crazy to suppose that the patterns symbolize or represent something of the image that originally fell on the retina – but it is not a 'picture' that is literally speeding away over the axon bundles.

Once the patterns arrive at the next station, the electrical pulses are converted via synapses into electrical responses that the receiving cell generates in response to all the incoming inputs. A cell in the cortex can easily be fed by ten thousand incoming synaptic contacts. These do not all come from one 'sending' area (e.g. V1), but from dozens of others as well. On the receiving dendrites of a brain cell, all inputs are integrated (Figure 8.7). This integration is roughly done by adding up all the incoming inputs, many of which excite the cell and some of which inhibit it. The crucial difference with metro passengers is that the incoming pattern is not the same as the outgoing pattern, because the output of the cell is the result of the integration of inputs coming from various brain areas. The output of one neuron is thus processed

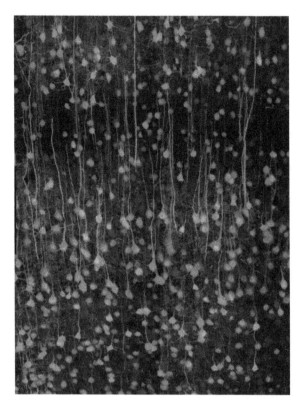

Figure 8.5 Neurons in the cerebral cortex. These cells have a more or less pyramid-shaped cell body, from which a spur (dendrite) emerges, extending upwards towards the surface of the cortex. The finer dendrites and axons are hardly visible in this picture. The technique used here to visualize neurons was developed by Joshua R. Sanes and colleagues (Cai, Cohen, Luo, Lichtman & Sanes, 2013).

Source: Jeff Lichtman, Harvard University (provided as courtesy). Reproduced with permission of J. Lichtman.

and transformed into a different piece of information when it reaches the next.

The inference that there is a hierarchy of lower and higher regions in the cerebral cortex is somewhat prejudiced. Naming an area as 'higher' carries the implicit message that the function of that area should also be 'higher', such as thinking or visual perception itself. It is tacitly assumed that, although V1 is important for seeing, this is only because it is a transit station for visual information, of which we only become aware higher up, in areas such as V4. In advance, this assumption might be correct, but it would mean we have to divide the cerebral cortex: there would be areas of the brain that make up the

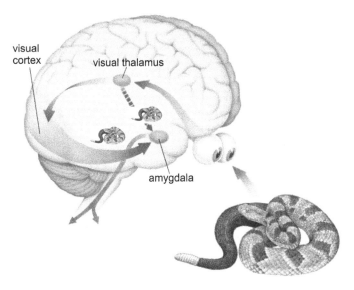

visual
cortex

visual thalamus

amygdala

Figure 8.6 Do images of snakes travel from the eyes through the brain? This image
illustrates the misconception holding that this would be the case. Neurons
in successive brain regions such as the visual thalamic nucleus, visual cortex
and amygdala (involved in evoking a fear response) signal patterns of
electrical pulses to each other, but at this level of organization there is no
'picture' being transported across bundles of nerve fibres.
Source: Adapted from LeDoux (1994). LeDoux used the original for a
different purpose than that intended here, namely to illustrate pathways in
the brain that regulate fear responses.

'realm of consciousness', whereas lower areas do not belong to this elite club.
They would be condemned to the 'realm of the unconscious'.

For the moment, it is important to have this assumption clearly in sight.
The implication is that somewhere in the brain, there should be a hard boundary between the conscious and the unconscious. If a stream of information
crosses that boundary, it would suddenly change from 'unconscious' to 'conscious'. Information would then 'enter' our consciousness, as if it were acced-
ing to a well-defined, privileged space. It seems as if this special space has a
magical quality, or possesses a soul that watches what enters. Here we stumble
upon the age-old problem of the *homunculus* – the idea that there is a little
man somewhere in the brain, who, alongside all the cells and fibre tracts, is
doing the actual watching and listening. This special 'space of consciousness'
is akin to the idea of a 'Cartesian Theatre', which we can imagine as a high,
domed hall with graceful, undulating balconies, where somewhere there is a
dressed-up soul gazing at the world stage.[5] This magical transformation from
'unconscious' to 'conscious' raises similar problems to those encountered by
Descartes, and is therefore an extremely risky assumption.

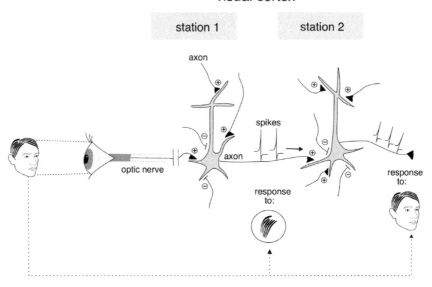

Figure 8.7 Information does not travel through the brain like a traveller through a metro system. Through the lens of the eye, the image of a person falls on the retina, after which cells send electrical pulses to the visual cortex (station 1). Arriving at a neuron of station 1, the optical information is integrated with other inputs (plus means: excitatory; minus: inhibitory) in such a way that this neuron generates a response (spikes) to a small part of the image (the person's obliquely oriented patch of hair). The next neuron (station 2) integrates the output of station 1 with inputs from other brain areas. This cell does not react strongly to the piece of hair, but to the whole head of the person.

What does the visual system's roadmap tell us about consciousness? If we think of consciousness as the brain's end station of information processing – the 'place' where all information comes together in one concentrated, grandiose experience – its seat should be found at the top of the hierarchy. The diagram of Figure 8.4 shows how all information flows upwards into one area – the hippocampus ('HC'). But in patients such as Henry Molaison, it already became clear that damage to the hippocampus does not lead to loss of consciousness. So the top of the roadmap does not lead us to the seat of the soul, but to narrative memory. So where is consciousness then? Fortunately, returning to the hippocampus, we have not completely lost track. For the hippocampus, with its neighbours in the temporal lobe, does provide us with a clue: narrative memory is needed to retrieve memories of events we once consciously experienced, and of which we can become conscious again. It does not provide us with a literal repetition of our original experience, but rather a reconstruction that we experience consciously.

This distinguishes the hippocampus from other memory systems. Henry Molaison showed that there is also a procedural memory, and this remains intact after the hippocampus has been lost. It is the motor cortex (located in the frontal lobe, just in front of the primary somatosensory cortex; Figures 7.1 and 12.1) and the basal ganglia that we need for this capacity to store habits and other motor skills. The moment you get on your bike and lift your supporting leg off the ground to ride away, sensory signals from your muscles and your balance organ – the vestibular system – evoke memories that rapidly trigger your motor brain systems to keep your body and bike upright. They enable you to effortlessly bring your supporting leg above the foot pedal and to gain speed by coherent pedal movements of both feet. When a child does this for the thousandth time, it happens automatically – it doesn't have to think about it anymore. If you are aware at all of your learned habits, then this applies to the global action: "I am riding away now" – but not to the hundreds of subtle muscle movements that make your bike go faster.

Nevertheless, through its differences with procedural memory, the hippocampus does show us a gateway to brain systems for consciousness. The hippocampus not only receives signals from the cortex but also sends information back. This hippocampal output first reaches higher regions of the temporal lobe that are primarily concerned with memory. From there, information retrieved from memory networks, aided by the hippocampus, excites the higher visual areas in the temporal and occipital lobes. It is these higher visual areas that show a relationship with conscious visual experience. This connection becomes clear first of all by looking at studies of brain damage. In Mr S.'s case, the damage was widespread and scattered, but other cases have shown that areas associated with shape perception extend from the higher regions of the occipital lobe to nearby areas in the temporal lobe. In both lobes, these territories lie on the ventral side (i.e. on the side facing the stomach, and being closer to the mouth and throat).[6] If these areas are lost, we lose the ability to consciously see shapes, while other aspects of vision (movement, colour, size or texture) may remain intact. In addition to complete form blindness, patients may suffer an even more specific type of loss: they can no longer recognize faces, even if they are of familiar people. They can, however, distinguish shapes of non-living objects, animals or plants. The patient still knows what a face is, but when he sees one, he cannot remember the name or the person that goes with it. This selective deficiency – prosopagnosia (face blindness) – can also be traced back to damage to higher visual areas on the ventral side of the cortex, including the fusiform face area (FFA).

Pursuing this lead, could there be separate areas for movement, colour, texture and other visual attributes in other higher regions of the visual cortex? Indeed there are indications for this. For example, in 1983, the rare phenomenon of akinetopsia (blindness to movement) was found in a female patient.[7] Due to cortical damage in both hemispheres, she could hardly see any movement at all, while her ability to see shapes, colours and texture was intact. She could also deduce movement from the sounds of passing objects or through her sense of touch. But the visual world appeared 'frozen' to her. When someone poured her a cup of tea, the stream of liquid appeared to stand still before her eyes, like a glacier. When she poured herself a cup of tea, she realized too late that the cup began to overflow and a puddle was forming on the table. In akinetopsia, a moving stimulus looks stationary, and a continuously moving dot is experienced as a stimulus that appears at successive positions in the field of vision, but is stationary at each position. Between those positions, there is nothing to see, as if a visual glue is missing between the stills. Brain scans showed that, within the woman's visual system, only a limited area was damaged. Based on studies in animals, it can be said that this area probably comprised the Middle Temporal (MT) region (Figure 8.4).

Essential nodes in the network

At last, a pattern seems to be emerging in the anatomy of visual consciousness. Based on the lesion studies, the idea that the visual system consists of nodes that are each essential to one specific property (or attribute) of visual experience was gaining ground in the 1990s.[8] Thus, there is no one particular end station in the brain where all visual information is forged together into a percept. Instead, we should think of a system composed of modules, each of which encodes a sub-modality or attribute (colour, shape, movement) that continues to function if another module fails. A strong example of a node is area MT, as already mentioned, being crucial for seeing movement. For the perception of form, it is hard to pinpoint one central node, but there is a group or network of areas that in humans are located in the area where the occipital and temporal lobes meet, on the ventral side. However, even if we talk about a 'network' rather than a nodal point for shape, it remains true that patients like Mr S. may suffer selectively from shape blindness, not from blindness to movement or other visual features.

In this transition zone from occipital to temporal lobe, there also appears to be a group of areas that are selectively linked to colour perception. Damage to this network in both hemispheres leads to total colour blindness, whereas the perception of movement, texture and shape can remain intact.[9] If this network fails in either hemisphere, the patient often only sees colour in the left or right part of her visual field, while the other half is grey or colourless. The networks for shape (including faces) and colour lie close together in the occipital-temporal zone, so that a stroke often – but not always – affects both visual properties.

However revealing lesion studies may be, in neuroscience they provide only impure evidence. Strokes, carbon monoxide poisoning and meningitis are tragedies in which misfortune throws punches at will. They are not limited to a single, well-defined brain region. To demonstrate functions of an anatomical structure, researchers need a lesion of exactly that one area. A clot in a cerebral blood vessel does not take into account the one area that a neuropsychologist is interested in. All the tissue downstream in the circulatory system is affected. Moreover, that one area may be criss-crossed by fibre tracts that connect entirely different functional systems. Loss of motion vision is usually linked not only to damage to area MT, but also to other areas. For example, the woman with akinetopsia also suffered from aphasia and a relapse in mental arithmetic. Large-scale degeneration is visible on brain scans, but subtle damage is difficult to visualize.

Solid evidence for the idea of nodes or modules for specific visual properties thus came not only from lesion studies in patients. It is more heavily supported by studies in animals, where one particular brain region is switched off in a controlled manner, or electrodes are implanted into the area. These electrodes consist of very fine wires and cause only minimal damage to the tissue. An additional advantage is that the brain does not contain any pain senses, so that the implantation involves relatively little discomfort. In 1990, Bill Newsome and his colleagues at Stanford University published a groundbreaking study in monkeys in which they demonstrated the relationship between motion vision and electrical activity in area MT.[10] Brain cells in MT show preferences in their electrical pulse behaviour for the direction of movement of stimuli displayed on a screen in front of the animal. One cell is strongly active when a pattern of dots in the field of vision moves from left to right, the other cell when it moves from bottom to top. All MT cells together cover the whole palette of movement directions and are also sensitive to different speeds of movement. Neurons that respond to the same direction of movement are not muddled up higgledy-piggledy, but neatly grouped together in columns. A column forms a functional unit of cells that are organized vertically, through all the layers of the cortex, as if you were poking through the layer cake of the cortex with an apple corer. A column is the cylindrical part that a very thin drill (1 to 2 millimetres in diameter) would cut out. If you zoom in on the core of the drill with a special microscope, you will see neurons extending their long dendrites towards the surface of the cortex (Figure 8.5).

Things in the outside world rarely all move in exactly the same direction. A flock of birds taking off in the air shows cohesion, but there are always individuals flitting in a different direction. In their experiment, Newsome and his colleagues made dots move through the visual field with varying degrees of coherence, ranging from all moving in the same direction to a chaotic jumble of different directions. The monkey was trained to judge the 'net movement' of all the dots together and to move its eyes in the same direction at the end of the compound stimulus. Humans and animals are extremely good at this task: only a few per cent of the dots need to move coherently to make a correct assessment. Newsome discovered that individual neurons in MT are often as sensitive at detecting net movement as the animal itself. In fact, some neurons were even more sensitive than could be inferred from the monkey's eye movements. All in all, there was a strong statistical relationship – a correlation – between the animal's motion vision (deduced from its eye movements) and the electrical activity of groups of MT cells.

But here the study did not end. Although Newsome found a correlation, this does not mean that the cells in MT are *causally* involved in motion perception. It is possible that seeing movement is mediated by other cells, elsewhere in the brain, and that MT cells only respond to that activity, which is the actual cause. The icing on the cake was investigating the causal role of MT cells. Instead of recording electrical activity, the researchers now administered electrical current pulses to MT tissue via electrodes. They artificially increased the firing of spikes by the cells by electrically stimulating them during the period the animal was looking at the moving dots. If the coherence of the movement pattern was weak, the animal often did not see it or only hesitantly responded. But when the cells with a specific movement preference (e.g. 'from left to right') were artificially stimulated, the monkey more quickly indicated the perceptual judgement 'from left to right' with its eye movements. The perception of movement was thus manipulated by making groups of MT cells more electrically active. This is a strong indication for a causal role of cells in the cerebral cortex in visual perception. The experiment has been widely followed up and was only possible thanks to detailed anatomical knowledge of the system: without the presence of columns of 'like-minded' cells, local electrical stimulation would have had no effect. The implications of Newsome's research are spectacular. If you manipulate a large group of cells by electrically stimulating them, you change the animal's perception – its perception of movement – as the animal expresses this through its behaviour.

Back to Mr S. and his form blindness. Did his accident lead to the loss of cells that selectively respond to shape but not to other visual properties such as movement or colour? This cannot be determined in him or other patients with form blindness, but studies in monkeys have yielded clear indications. In the road map of Figure 8.4, a group of small areas can be seen in the upper right-hand corner, the last letters of which are 'IT', the inferotemporal cortex. These are areas on the ventral side of the temporal lobe that are very similar to the shape regions in humans. When electrodes are lowered into these areas of the brain and the electrical voltage differences they measure are converted into sound via a loudspeaker, you will occasionally hear a distinctive crackling of spikes. A cell responds to one particular shape, such as the face of a fellow monkey. If this face is partly covered by a white or black bar, the cell still responds quite strongly. The cell tolerates deviations and empty spaces in its favourite stimulus. If a face is rotated so that it is not in frontal view but in profile, the cell continues to produce a strong response. Even if the stimulus is not shown centrally in the monkey's field of vision, but somewhere along the edges, the cell still responds.[11] It is likely that Mr S.'s brain also contained areas with cells that responded very selectively to shapes and were destroyed by his accident, while areas for other visual properties continued to function. But where do these shape-selective cells get their information from?

To answer this question, we need to go back to the primary visual cortex, V1, where research into the properties of visual cortical cells began. With the knowledge of areas MT, V4 and the inferotemporal cortex, one would think that V1 must encode all visual properties together and contain cells that respond to shape, colour, movement and all other sub-modalities. After all, the earlier studies by Holmes and Riddoch had shown that V1 is important for all our vision. When, in the late 1950s, David Hubel and Torsten Wiesel at Johns Hopkins University in Baltimore inserted electrodes into area V1 and stimulated the retina with a variety of visual stimuli, the loudspeaker initially remained eerily silent. To project light or dark stimuli onto the retina, they used metal and glass plates with round holes or black dots. Such dark or light dots were a tried and tested recipe for eliciting strong responses from cells in the retina, which had already been subjected to some more research at the time. The pictures were inserted by hand into their projection apparatus like a slide. But upon presentation of these circles or rings of light or darkness, the cells in V1 refused to fire spikes. Hubel and Wiesel scratched their heads. The stagnation of their research led to a feeling of crisis, the abrasive discomfort that they could not get out of it.

There is a nice story to tell about the creative way in which Hubel and Wiesel's deadlock was broken. After the Second World War, the east coast of the United States had become a vibrant art scene in which abstract painting made its appearance. Piet Mondrian died in New York in 1944, leaving behind his unfinished work *Victory Boogie Woogie*. Squares, black lines and primary colours. Before that, Cubism had already dissected complex forms into primitive elements. It would not be the first time that a breakthrough in one cultural segment gave rise to innovations in another. Instead of light and dark circles, Hubel and Wiesel, entirely in the spirit of Mondrian, started working with black rectangles and straight lines, and suddenly found cells that went off 'like a machine gun'.

There is only one problem with this story: it is not true. Hubel and Wiesel discovered by chance to which stimuli V1 cells reacted strongly. When, at a lucky moment, they slid a glass slide into their projector, they noticed that some cells precipitously started firing violently. They understood that the reaction was triggered by the moving edge of the plate, which cast a straight, dark shadow on the retina. The electrical response had nothing to do with the black or light spot on the picture.[12] V1 turned out to contain a treasure trove of cells that responded to a variety of rectangular bars of different sizes and orientations – but not to complex stimuli that humans or animals encounter every day, such as cars, chairs or conspecifics. Remarkably, V1 cells only responded to a straight bar if it was projected into, or moved through, a small part of the visual field. This part of our visual field can be imagined as a roughly circular segment that you would see when looking at the outside world through a toilet roll and is called the cell's 'receptive field': the part from which the cell receives its information. Cells in the higher, shape-coding regions work differently: they respond strongly to the stimulus itself, regardless of where it is presented in the field of vision. Hubel and Wiesel paved the way for mapping the entire visual system of the cerebral cortex, but it remained a mystery why their V1 cells had a strong preference for 'unnatural' stimuli such as black bars, and not at all for what animals and humans are used to seeing.

When the properties of cells in the higher regions of the cortex were clarified, it became interesting to compare them with the primary visual cortex. The idea took hold that the lower regions in the hierarchical organization of the cortex would encode the visual image as a set of simple, local features (such as 'black' and 'bar'). These lower regions would transmit their information to higher regions, which would then assemble this simple visual information into a larger whole, such as a face or a street scene in the case of shape perception. At the same time, we also know that the shape perception network is not strictly necessary for other properties such as colour, movement, size or texture. For the time being, it remains a mystery how shape information is interwoven with other properties into the total, integrated image we experience.

Following Newsome's experiments, has any evidence been found for the causal involvement of areas of the occipital and temporal ventral sides of the cortex in shape perception? Area MT consists of vertical columns of cells with the same directional preference, and this type of anatomical organization has also been found in the inferotemporal region, which includes the fusiform face area. A group of epilepsy patients, who were to receive electrode implants to locate the source of their seizures, were asked for permission to administer mild current shocks to their fusiform facial area via the same electrodes. When the patients were asked to look at the face of a person in front of them, first without electrical stimulation, they perceived the face as one would expect. When the electric stimuli intervened, they perceived distortions or even transformations of this face. "You turned into someone else. Your face metamorphosed... your nose got saggy and went to the left", said one patient. Another patient also reported that something perceivable changed about the face: "It was almost as if you were a cat." Others found that the face became more masculine, or rounder, or that a grimace appeared – or that the right eye ball looked like stone.[13]

This provides another strong indication that specific brain regions form a causal link in a variant of shape perception that is important for humans – and how crucial electricity is for that link. Faces are crucial to our social functioning. It is by way of faces that we recognize people, and their expressions show us the way to their emotions and feelings. Following the discovery of the fusiform face area, a brain region was identified in humans that is sensitive to spatial scenes, such as images of a domestic interior or a wooded landscape. This *parahippocampal place area* is also located in the border region of the temporal and occipital lobes, but lies closer to the hippocampus. When a patient receives electrical stimulation at this location, he or she experiences the illusion of a scene, which could be situated, for example, indoors or in the surrounding neighbourhood.

From local to global damage to the cerebral cortex

What happens to our consciousness when other parts of the cerebral cortex, in addition to the visual system, are lost? Massive damage to the entire cerebral cortex leads to coma or – in a somewhat less destructive scenario – to a vegetative state, as happened to Terri Schiavo. While a vegetative patient does show a day-night rhythm and simple, reflexive behaviour (such as opening and closing his eyes), a comatose patient no longer responds to any stimulus, not even a painful one. In a coma, electrical EEG recordings on the scalp mostly show a quiet, flat signal, occasionally interspersed with brief flashes of activity. There are no indications that conscious sensations or feelings are still present; neither can the patient stimulate his muscles to contract. Yet, during a coma a number of vital functions in the brain continue to run. The hypothalamus (Figure 2.1) contains centres for keeping up body temperature, internal hydration and blood salinity, and these nuclei will continue to function unless brain death occurs and tissue begins to die en masse. When patients come out of a coma and recover sufficiently to be able to talk, they say that they remember nothing from the previous period. Apparently, these people did not have conscious experiences that remained hidden or invisible to the outside world.

Disorders of consciousness also occur with damage to cell groups located deep in the brain: in the brainstem. The brainstem houses the dark basements of the brain that we already find in the oldest vertebrates of our evolutionary tree, like sharks, rays and the jawless lampreys. At the lower end of the brainstem we find the medulla oblongata, a rounded bulge that forms the bridge between the spinal cord and the higher parts of the brain. This bulge contains several groups of cells that send their axons to the cerebral cortex and thalamus (Figure 8.8). The endings of these fibres release chemical signalling substances that prompt the cortex and thalamus to increase their electrical activity. Two

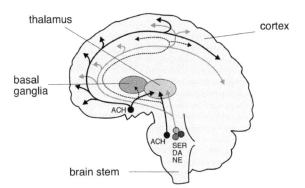

Figure 8.8 The lower end of the brainstem contains small nuclei of cells that project their axons to higher regions such as the cortex, basal ganglia and thalamus. These cell groups are essential for bringing the brain into a state where conscious experiences are possible. Transmitters are secreted from the endings of active axons that exert a slow effect on the excitability of the target areas (ACH: acetylcholine; SER: serotonin; DA: dopamine; NE: norepinephrine). Higher-order nuclei producing acetylcholine also contribute to increased excitability of the cortex.
Source: Adapted from Mesulam (2013).

of the messenger molecules are acetylcholine and serotonin, best known as a signalling agent affected by antidepressants such as Prozac. When these tiny cell groups are damaged by an accident or a stroke, consciousness is lost.

These brainstem nuclei fundamentally differ from the cortical areas on one point. Their activity is essential to get the cortex and thalamus in the right condition to sustain conscious experiences, but they do not determine the content of our experiences – the 'what' in what we experience. Their role is similar to that of the facility services to run a business, but they do not interfere with what that business is about. This contrasts with the cortical areas that – together with the thalamic nuclei to which they are mutually connected – do determine the content of our experience. The brainstem nuclei can be compared to the electricity grid, which powers studio equipment and broadcast towers. It is the cerebral cortex and thalamus that act as the broadcasters: they determine what will go on air.

Let us take a step back and consider where we are in the labyrinth of visual consciousness. Massive damage to the primary visual cortex leads to blindness: loss of visual awareness. In the case of specific damage to an upper cortical module, the patient does not become blind except for one attribute of vision: colour or movement or shape is lost – but not all attributes vanish at once. Together, the low and high visual cortical areas form a hierarchically ordered system, in which the primary cortex appears to provide the raw visual information from which the higher areas pick out one particular element to make head or tail of it: a specific property or sub-modality for which they alone are needed. This hierarchy works not only with signals sent from low to high levels ('bottom-up'), but also back from high to low ('top-down') and has a dispersed or distributed character: from the primary station V1, the information fans out to a wide range of areas that are also connected laterally (Figure 8.4). A hierarchy of areas has also been mapped in the cortex for hearing, touch and smell, while our knowledge of other sensory modalities is still insufficient to make any definitive claims.

What remains puzzling is: how do MT cells manage to give us a conscious experience of movement? While there are certainly circuits of cells in the cortex that explain why a cell responds to visual movement to the left and not to the right, this seems to be no more than a convenient mechanism by which the cell signals movement – a way of ensuring that a particular change in light patterns on our retina is detected. This may not be a lot more complicated than the way a light sensor in someone's backyard responds to the movement of a burglar or a cat.

But how is it that this mechanism in MT results in conscious perception? Is the signal transmitted to an even higher brain region, where the final 'interpretation' takes place that results in a percept? Some researchers try to approach the matter pragmatically: surely it is enough to know that there are motion-sensitive cells in MT that control other brain areas in such a way that we respond to that motion in our behaviour? But where does that leave perception itself? Like the little device in the backyard, a motion cell does not produce perception on its own. Perception normally consists not only of seeing motion, but also of an object moving against a background, within a situation characterized by sound, colour, texture, wind and the posture you adopt. The example of blindness already testified that people can respond in their motor behaviour to all sorts of stimuli that they nevertheless do not consciously perceive.

So, to be honest, the story about MT and the form regions awakens all kinds of phrenological discontent in me. It seems that, after an initially ignominious retreat, the one-to-one coupling between brain area and function has made a spectacular comeback. To some extent, the brain is equated with a wardrobe with dozens of separate drawers or modules – or with a large power station filled with devices that you can unplug without affecting the power supply. Compare it to someone listening to the radio and trying to find the source of the voice by pulling out all the parts from the device. The speaker as the 'cause' of the voice from the radio. Taking all the studies together, there is still good reason to believe that the visual system is made up of modules. But it would be too short-sighted to think that these modules work independently of each other. In patients, MT turned out to be a nodal point for motion vision, but this does not mean that the other intact visual properties these people experience – shape, size, colour – are exclusively coded by separate, standalone modules. So the question remains: is consciousness dependent on a large network of brain areas that constantly exchange information, or on separate units that each individually control our behaviour?

For the sake of convenience, I compared cortex and thalamus to a TV station for the production of experiential content. On second thought, this metaphor is misleading, because with radio and TV there are always viewers and listeners around: in the brain, information is only transmitted by neurons. And there it is again: the homunculus. How do you explain that this little man-in-the-brain could see and hear for himself? What is going on in *his* head? The consistent implementation of this idea leads to the conclusion that in the brain of the homunculus there must be another, yet smaller man, and so on ad infinitum: a regression of Russian Matryoshka dolls that ultimately explains nothing. In 1994, Francis Crick published *The Astonishing Hypothesis*, a book in which he put forward an alternative to the fallacy of the homunculus. His hypothesis holds that each of us is equivalent to the behaviour of a huge, interacting group of neurons.[14] Within the field of brain research, he thus articulated a tendency that many researchers, including Hubel, Wiesel, Newsome and many others before them, had come up with for a long time and supported with years of experiments. It is the idea that everything we experience, undertake, think, remember and imagine – really everything in our minds, including ourselves – can be traced back directly to the behaviour and interaction of the billions of cells in our brains.

Crick's 'astonishing hypothesis' was thus not that astonishing, and is in fact a reformulation of materialism. This philosophical movement emerged in the eighteenth century and holds that it is physical matter that forms the ultimate basis of the reality that surrounds us and that we experience. It breaks with

Descartes' dualism, which stuck to the mind as a separate substance that exists alongside matter. Materialism explains our mental states from principles that go back to physical laws, such as Isaac Newton's law describing the relationship between gravity and mass. If we try to capture the 'I' with its subjective experiences entirely in the collective electrical behaviour of neurons, we are working in a materialistic framework. According to materialism, consciousness can be conceived as a by-product of material processes and interactions, just as heat is a by-product of chemical reactions. If we were to hold Madonna, with her song 'Material Girl', strictly to a materialist account, the verse "Boys may come and boys may go / And that's all right you see / Experience has made me rich / And now they're after me", for example, would imply that the recording of her experiences with boys is nothing more or less than the rearrangement of molecules and synapses in her brain.

Materialism comes in different flavours and is often combined with reductionism. This movement goes further than just stating that our consciousness ultimately has a material basis: it states that our consciousness, a phenomenon of a higher order, can be fully reduced to physical phenomena that are of a lower order and take place on a micro level. The ice on which we skate in a severe period of frost can be reduced to the rigid crystal structure of water molecules. The ice is nothing but this rigidly ordered structure of molecules, even if they do not immediately appear so to us, ordinary mortals susceptible to illusion and deception. And so it goes with our minds, according to the reductionist: ultimately our minds – and with them our own 'self' – are nothing but a complex interplay of cells, spikes and molecules.

With the growth of neuroscience over the last 60 years, reductionism has become popular. Among its fervent adherents are philosophers such as Daniel Dennett, who in his book *Consciousness Explained* reduces the brain to a kind of computer and dismisses the qualitative properties of our experience (such as seeing colour instead of light waves of a certain length) as an illusion – an insidious trap we should avoid at all costs.[15] Not long ago, the institution where I work – the University of Amsterdam – launched a poster campaign in which its rising stars were allowed to put forward challenging propositions. One of those statements was that falling in love is nothing more than a dance of molecules. I felt this was funny and thought-provoking, and there is little to dispute that all sorts of chemical reactions are indeed taking place in our brain cells, culminating in patterns of electrical activity. But how does love arise from this story? Why should this dance of molecules give rise to any feeling at all? This is where reductionism, at least until now, has failed: it does not manage to bridge the gap between what we experience and the micro-processes taking place in brain cells. The Hard Problem persists. There is work to be done.

9 Suspended in the primeval sea

What zombies and the first animals on Earth reveal about the biological function of consciousness

I wake up and find myself submerged in murky, shallow water, several metres deep. Under water, there is a turbulent sea current and in this turmoil I try to find a passage to greater depths. On the seabed, I can see tubular plants, green blades and, in the distance, sponges and corals. I wriggle closer to the seabed, hoping to devour some algae and small creatures that look like sea fleas. On the way, I come across a wandering squid-like creature hiding in a flat, spiral shell with tentacles sticking out of its mantle opening. On the sea bed, a *Wiwaxia* shuffles around, a snail-like creature covered in scales and hard spines – too risky to attack and eat. I zigzag to get deeper, use my head protrusions to probe the bottom, covered with dead leaves. There I smell something interesting. Rooting around in the ground, I uncover a group of larvae, which I consume with relish. After the meal, I twist my body into a loop to check for parasites. With my body a few centimetres long, slender like an agave leaf, a strand in my back that gives my body firmness, and something resembling flapping tail fins, I am one of the larger creatures of this primeval sea. I may not have eyes worth mentioning, but my protrusions and sensors spread all over my body allow me to sense the world, explore and survive.

So far, things aren't going so bad. Further on, clear water shades into green-blue hues and I discover a forest of seaweed-like creatures, waving their long thin strands in the sea current. Above me, a spectacle of light breaking through the surface of the water and bursting into sparkling rays. Then, above me, a dark shadow emerges and quickly grows in size. Is it an *Opabinia* – much bigger than I am, with five eyes and a fearsome grasping trunk? Or is it an *Anomalocaris*, a predator with two gripper arms and a square, tooth-strewn mouth? Whatever it is, I only stand a chance by ducking away as fast as I can. I take cover behind a group of *Hallucigenias*, slow crawling creatures that are inedible because of the spikes they point outwards. But it is too late, the predator has seen me. I feel a stabbing and burning pain in the middle of my body. My spinal cord breaks in two and I lose all feeling in my tail. The light goes out. *Game over.*

About 541 million years ago the Cambrian explosion unfolded, when the number of living species on Earth increased rapidly in a relatively short period of time. Strong evidence for this burst of life is provided by the fossils of the

DOI: 10.4324/9781003429555-9

Burgess Shale, a soft shale formation in the Canadian Rocky Mountains that is 36 million years younger than the beginning of the explosion and holds a treasure trove of remains of bizarre life forms. On 30 August 1909, geologist Charles Doolittle Walcott set out on horseback to explore the area, now part of Yoho National Park in British Columbia, Canada. It was already near the end of the season, but he still hoped to find something nice. At an altitude of 2,286 metres, he drove along a path on a ridge and looked at a bunch of shale slabs scattered across the slope. There he came across 'many interesting fossils', as he wrote in his diary. In the 15 years that followed, Walcott collected 65,000 specimens with his family and assistants, revealing an unprecedented wealth of forms and species. Most of the species had been totally unknown until then, and often did not even faintly resemble the species of today, or even fossils of more recent date. *Hallucigenia* was so strange that people did not know what the top and bottom of the creature should be. The protagonist of the story is *Pikaia gracilens*, a little eel-like creature.

In his day, Walcott was famous among palaeontologists and geologists, but he only became known to the general public through Stephen Jay Gould's 1989 book, *Wonderful Life*. Gould argues that Walcott was trying to squeeze the Burgess Shale's extraordinary biodiversity into the straitjacket of our current animal kingdom classification. The Cambrian explosion was a testing ground for evolution in which all kinds of new animal species manifested themselves in a life-and-death struggle with each other – a colossal biological experiment resulting in the survival of the best-adapted species and the extinction of less 'successful' life forms (Figure 9.1). Because little was known in Walcott's time about species formation during that mid-Cambrian period, Gould's criticism of him is not entirely justified. Moreover, the 'modern' animal species, such as vertebrates and arthropods, do have their origins in the jumble of bizarre creatures that populated the Cambrian primeval seas. The most remarkable thing about the Burgess Shale fossils is not their incredible age: it is that they are the remains of soft-bodied creatures, animals without skeletons or other calcareous reinforcements.

A few years ago, my wife and I joined a mountain hike through Yoho National Park that took us to Walcott's quarry. We struggled up around Wapta Mountain, taking in views of vast coniferous forests that fringe the base of pristine mountains, and glaciers with waterfalls springing from them. From a rocky outcrop of schist, we caught a glimpse of Emerald Lake in the depths. Higher up on the mountainside, it started to snow lightly and a cold breeze quickened. The air smelled fresh and was tingling, clear and sharp as crystal. Our Russian guide announced a break, it was time for a sip of water and a Wonderbread sandwich with Provolone. Sitting on a rock, we felt our muscles and joints. Once again, I realized how rich this conscious experience was, filled with all the sensory modalities available to our brains: sight, smell, taste and bodily sensations. There was sound in the rustling of the wind, until the guide began a mini-lecture on the local geology. An hour later, arriving at Walcott Quarry, she handed me an authentic *Pikaia* fossil. If the shifts in

Figure 9.1 Impression of life in a primordial sea about 506 million years ago. This image is inspired by fossils of the Burgess Shale. The animal moving from the top left towards the centre is an *Anomalocaris*. The grey, flat worm-like creature at the lower right is *Pikaia gracilens*.
Source: Image credit: Karen Carr, © Smithsonian Institution (reproduced with permission).

the Earth's crust that led to the formation of the Rocky Mountains had never taken place, this specimen would have remained hidden from us at a depth of eight kilometres below the surface. What would it be like if the remains of ourselves were to reappear on the surface here, 500 million years from now, and our distant descendants – in a completely unforeseen guise – were to carve our fossil remains out of the bedrock?

Returning to life in the Cambrian, how realistic is the perspective I just presented of a primitive animal scavenging in the primordial sea? We know that *Pikaia gracilens* had a head-like extremity with frayed ends that resembled external gills, and a tail with a fin. The creature lacked a skull or spine, but its protrusions or antennae indicate that the head-like bulge harboured an array of sensory organs, such as for touch and smell. The fossils do not disclose whether *Pikaia* had eyes, brains or hearing organs. Prints of their musculature indicate that it was not a roving slug or a worm, but possibly a primitive ancestor of vertebrates – a distant ancestor of humans.

Is it realistic to think that *Pikaia*, as described, experienced all sorts of things? If you were to step into its shoes, would you actually smell something interesting, eat larvae with relish, inspect your own body – and even survey your entire environment? It seems we can imagine what it is like to be a *Pikaia*, but how would this animal see its surroundings if it has no eyes? If it had an olfactory organ, would it experience smells consciously? Sensors that respond to chemical substances are abundant throughout the animal kingdom, and are so essential for distinguishing edible food from junk, that it is not unreasonable to assume that *Pikaia* must have had such sensors. These sensors consist of cells that bind certain molecules floating around in their environment and then send a signal to the rest of the nervous system, allowing the animal to initiate a motor response, for example by moving towards the highest concentration of a nutritious substance. But does this also mean that *Pikaia* could smell consciously, or that it simply had sensors on its head which – like a smoke detector – were triggered when nutrients were detected, sending a signal to the muscles to start digging deeper in the soil?

We can easily dismiss the story of *Pikaia* as wild speculation without any hard facts. Yet this thought experiment brings to our attention an interesting fact. It is all too easy to assume that we can actually put ourselves in another creature's shoes – that we can empathize and 'feel' what it is like to be this eel-like, eyeless creature. But what we are actually imagining here is what it would be like to swim around in that primordial sea ourselves – how *we* would experience that submarine world. When we try to predict what a completely different being is experiencing, we build on our own imagination. This is the only capacity to picture things outside the concrete sensory world of the here and now that we have. Imagination is a powerful and creative tool, but it is always fed by our own past experiences. Our imagination is inevitably burdened with 'egocentrism'. We do not know exactly what an earthworm or a glass eel might experience, or what a *Pikaia* once experienced. We are not absolutely sure whether they could experience anything at all – whether they could rise above the level of a smoke detector.

What we can do, however – if we are prepared to look at an animal species in detail – is to examine what senses and nervous systems it has, and what possibilities these provide for producing a representation of the world through its sensory information. If an animal has never had eyes, or anything like them, since birth, it is reasonable to assume that it cannot see either. Here, 'seeing' means nothing more or less than that we have a visual image of the world around us, one that is rich in form, colour, depth, movement and texture. It could well be that *Pikaia* had one or more light sensors or light-sensitive pigments on its body, just as some jellyfish have small organs for capturing light. These organs contain light-sensitive cells that enable the jellyfish to move towards places with little or a lot of sunlight. But jellyfish are not endowed with lenses and the cells are not organized in such a way that they can provide an image of the environment. They do not form a retina onto which a light pattern from the outside world is projected.

Is it not chauvinistic to deny jellyfish and other primitive animals any visual experience? Are we not placing too much emphasis on human consciousness? It may seem a matter of empathy or intuition to attribute or deny conscious experiences to other organisms. But imagine if we were to look at a worm from the Burgess Shale fauna that had only one light sensor – one little sensor organ that measured how many light particles were entering per second. What could it do with that? Intuitively, one would think that this primitive organism could see something similar to the image in Figure 9.2: a faint spot of light surrounded by rapidly increasing darkness. This could be the sunlight breaking through the surface of the primordial sea. If the sensor is within range of incident light rays, you might think that the animal sees a spot of light; if the animal moves so that the sensor turns away from the light, it looks into the darkness of the sea.

But it is a misunderstanding to let the ability to perceive be determined by the physical environment in which a sensor does its work. The only signal this sensor can pass on to other cells in the organism is whether there is a lot of light or not – there is no information about where the light is coming

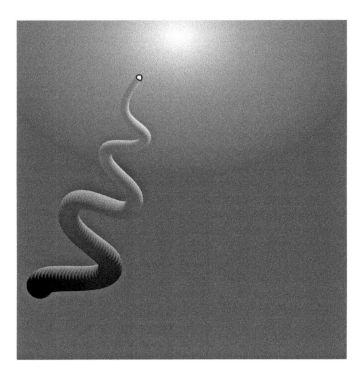

Figure 9.2 Worm with a light sensor at the end of its body. We assume that this sensor is the only sense the worm has. When the animal squirms towards the spot of light, there is a tendency to think that the worm could be able to see – but this is a misunderstanding.

from. Let us list the readings of the light sensor, one number per second at a time:

8, 5, 6, 1, 2, 4, 7, 7, 4, 5, 6, 6, 8, 9, 10, 9, 7, 5, 3, 1, ...

The nervous system of our Cambrian animal has the task of reading this sensor information and doing something useful with it. What can you make of this string of numbers if it is the *only* information you have? In fact, the only thing you can tell is that the sensor values go up or down from one measurement to the next. The sensor transmits so little information that it cannot possibly provide rapid updates of the entire visual environment. It does not code whether the light comes from the left or the right, from above or below. In fact, the sensor signal can only tell if there is a lot or a little of 'something' – but not that it is light! In other words, only the intensity of the signal is transmitted, not the identity of the stimulus. With this one sensor, the animal will not even be able to figure out whether it is light, smell, sound or touch. As a human observer, I told you in advance that the sensor transmits information about light, but the animal itself cannot deduce this from the numbers it receives.

The situation in which the animal's nervous system finds itself can be contrasted with a telegrapher receiving Morse code signals from a sinking *Titanic*. The telegraphist effortlessly decodes the series of short and long beeps into letters and the meaning of S.O.S. is immediately clear to him. But the nerve cells that are supposed to read the signals from the light sensor in the Cambrian animal do not have a key for deciphering the message: there is no translation available to turn electrical pulses into a visual image or other percept. The animal would need a special, as yet mysterious neural machinery to distil a meaningful sensation from the inputs.

A conscious being distinguishes between its sensory qualities: therefore it is logical that that one light sensor cannot produce consciousness. The same applies to an animal with several light sensors that would be scattered across its body. This scattering does make the sensory cells spatially ordered, but if they are not interconnected, there is no way to determine which signal is 'left' or 'right' in relation to any other sensor. Again, the animal has no way of determining which sensory quality or modality is involved. As much as we would like to grant a rich emotional life to an animal without a network of nerve cells, it is nonsensical to ascribe to it a consciousness that would even remotely resemble what humans experience. This is a question of logic, and has nothing to do with chauvinism or a sense of superiority.

The same logic leads to another inescapable conclusion: the absence of consciousness (derived from the inability to specify what the single sensor's output is about) may very well go together with adaptive motor behaviour, such as swimming towards the light. In fact, we need not speculate about life in the Cambrian seas to find an example of such behaviour: many single-cell organisms such as some species of bacteria and algae are able to move towards a light source based on a tiny, flagellar propulsion engine that is activated by absorption of light particles (photons). Again, we see how motor activity can be decoupled from consciousness. This might not seem spectacular at first sight, but in fact the tendency to equate 'sentience' in animals with 'behavioural responsiveness to stimuli' has become more popular in recent years. If sentience has anything to do with 'feeling' or 'consciousness' however, it must be kept separate from motor reactivity in general.

Does it make sense to assume that *Pikaia*'s 'light goes out' when he is bitten in half? Our subject – the 'I' of the story – would then be plunged into a pitch-black darkness – a conscious experience of a situation where light is totally absent. But when death occurs, all brain function grinds to a halt, and with it the possibility of maintaining consciousness – even a conscious experience of darkness – ceases. If we assume – against all contemporary knowledge of the brain – that there would be a soul that can continue to exist independently of the body, the question arises as to how this soul would be able to perceive, feel or communicate with other souls. After all, all senses, vocal chords and muscles are left behind in the deceased body.

Is consciousness good for anything?

All these considerations lead to one key question: what is the function of consciousness? Does it have any function at all? The cerebral cortex is made up of hundreds of areas. At least some of these areas are important for conscious perception: the Middle Temporal area, for example, is essential for motion perception. It would be strange if, during the development of the mammalian brain, a lot of energy was spent on areas that are essential for consciousness if this had no function at all. The brain uses about as much energy as a 13-Watt light bulb. This makes it incredibly economical compared to a supercomputer, which consumes roughly 2,000 million Watts of power, comparable to what the Hoover Dam in the United States supplies. Yet those 13 Watts represent no less than 30 per cent of the total energy required by our entire body, and much of this power is consumed by the cortex. Human evolution has apparently involved a considerable investment in the cortex, and together with the thalamus this happens to be the area that is strongly and uniquely linked to consciousness. Theodosius Dobzhansky (1900–1975), a geneticist from the Ukraine, famously said: "Nothing in biology has meaning, except in the light of evolution." Consciousness is a phenomenon found in living nature – at least in humans and most probably in other species including monkeys – and is therefore a biological phenomenon. But what use is it for survival and reproduction?

From jellyfish and *Pikaia* we jump back to the one species in which humans are so immensely interested: humans themselves. We are constantly trying to ensure our survival and reproduction by way of actions: gathering food and drink, defending ourselves against natural or human enemies, and sooner or later in life we engage in sex. If we have a home in a pleasant neighbourhood, with a supermarket around the corner, a primary survival scenario seems far away, but under the thin skin of our daily security, war, hunger, thirst and disease secretly wait their chance. But even in the relative luxury of a modern, western country, we must act to survive. As I write this, we are at the beginning of the Corona crisis and are witnessing people who despite government advice are hoarding food and toilet paper.

Actions come in different forms. Thanks to our procedural memory, actions such as walking, typing and chewing are so highly automated that we are hardly aware of them in practice. It is very convenient to let these habits run their course unconsciously, on autopilot. This leaves you room for more interesting stuff to do in the meantime: think about an important appointment, a job application or a journey you want to make. How handy this automation is, becomes clear when behaviour can no longer be completed on automatic pilot, as is the case with people with a specific kind of damage to the cerebellum. This brain complex is located at the bottom of the back of the head (Figure 3.2) and contains more cells than all the other parts of the brain put together. It is involved in linking sensory information to body movement and in learning and automating behaviour. Gordon Holmes, the British army doctor we met earlier, described in 1939 how, after damage to their cerebellum, patients suddenly had to think about every movement they wanted to make with their limbs. When coping with this damage, their conscious brain systems had to make room for figuring out movements that they had originally learned to execute self-evidently during their childhood. In addition to the cerebellum, there are other systems that prevent our consciousness from being overloaded with information – systems that regulate our habits 'under the radar', without us even noticing.

While habits are actions that we have often taught ourselves as children, reflexes are different: we are born with them. Reflexes often happen faster than our consciousness can keep up with. Your eyelid already closes before you become aware of an approaching mosquito. Reflexes are such basic protection mechanisms that it would be too risky to learn them late after birth. Much of our behaviour that is of primary importance for survival can be handled by habits and reflexes: actions that essentially do not require consciousness. This makes the question of what consciousness is good for even more pressing.

What helps in finding an answer is that reflexes and habits are relatively simple stimulus-response behaviours: "if *this* stimulus occurs, perform *that* action". If you lean too far to the left on your bicycle, turn your handlebars to restore your balance. The brain does not need to reflect or dub: the outcome is already determined. But your routine is broken when an unexpected, special situation arises: suddenly, a car appears in front of your bicycle and speeds off into the road right in front of you. It is in these complex, unexpected situations that the function of consciousness comes into play. You are startled out of your reverie. In the blink of an eye, you jerk your handlebars, but suddenly you also have to think hard about what to do. The aim of your action is clear: avoid a collision with the car and make sure you don't fall off your bike. But how do you achieve this so quickly? To solve the problem, your brain has to make sure that it has all kinds of information rapidly at its disposal: where is the car in relation to yourself? Is there more traffic on the street? Are your body and bike in a suitable position to swerve for the car? To the left or right? It is our consciousness that provides us, fairly quickly but not at lightning speed, with an overview we need to make a decision. This overview is multisensory: our conscious brain system shows us what is going on in the world at that moment, including the state of our own body. It is not that consciousness makes decisions for us; we have already seen how consciousness is independent of motor skills and language, and how the stream of consciousness continues tirelessly, even when we do not have to make decisions. Instead, consciousness *enables* us to make informed decisions – by giving us a survey of our own situation in the world.

Take 4 July 1998. The World Cup football tournament is under way and, on that day in Marseille, the Netherlands is playing the quarter-final against Argentina. With the score tied at 1-1 in the 89th minute, both sides are hankering for an extension. Defender Frank de Boer tries something crazy: he gives an improbably long pass, diagonally across midfield, to Dennis Bergkamp, who has to run to catch the ball. Miraculously he succeeds in doing so with his right foot – a silky first touch that immediately slows down the ball. Bergkamp outmanoeuvres Roberto Ayala, the defender who is right on his heels, passes him and shoots the ball with his right over keeper Carlos Roa into the goal. The Argentineans look on in amazement. What exactly was Bergkamp aware of during this action? We can't get under his skin, but we can imagine what it's like to be there on the pitch. I would hardly be aware of all the muscular tensions and contractions in my body – and even less of all the motor routines to adjust my posture and maintain my balance. What I would experience has everything to do with the main elements of this scene: Where is the ball? Where is my opponent? How do I get around him to get the ball into the goal? It is all about the survey of the situation – a sensory 'summary' of the most important data you receive – while the details of stretching and bending my legs and arms are handled on autopilot.

One of the key points about constructing a 'this-is-my-world-view' is that it is *rich* in information – information, moreover, that can be immediately absorbed and grasped. This wealth comes from very different senses: hearing, seeing, touch, physical sensations such as muscle tone, balance, smell and taste. For consciousness, the important thing is not that there are so many signals, but that we experience these inputs as qualitatively different. You experience a song by The Beatles in a fundamentally different way than you experience the taste of apple pie. This makes conscious experience radically different from the information processing we know from traditional robots and computers: they process all kinds of sensor inputs in the form of totally uniform series of zeros and ones. Whether a digital device processes visual or auditory information is irrelevant to how that information is represented within the device: it is a uniform – and to our perception very boring – language of binary numbers (zeros and ones). Our conscious experience is different: the confluence of many types of senses (modalities) makes the overview we experience multisensory or multimodal. People experience different types of information, a fact that is actually not explained within traditional computer science. Admittedly, we still face the question how the brain pulls off the trick.

Back to the car that shoots into the road in front of you. From your eyes and ears, the information of this scene becomes available, but let's assume this occurs exclusively in the form of zeros and ones. You cannot see the shape and colour of the car, as these are represented by numbers such as 010010100 and 1010101010. Also your own body posture, muscle tensions and internal feelings are digitally coded. With this kind of representation, your brain would be overwhelmed by a mishmash of millions of zeros and ones, spread over a plethora of data streams. There are two ways of dealing with these strings of numbers. The first, purely digital, option is for a computer to work with the numbers and calculate the motor output most likely to be best: tipping your handlebars to avoid being hit by the car and accepting the possibility of falling down. This scenario is devoid of any sensation: you feel, see and hear nothing. This means that the information is not directly graspable or knowable: the computer does not know what all those numbers are about. They would need a separate label for each data stream to determine which inputs relate to colour, shape, sound or whatever.

This strategy can work very well if the computer is fast enough. Computers that control self-driving cars can now more or less handle this. A recent Tesla model, for example, has a computer that can process 2,100 images per second from eight on-board cameras. This corresponds to 2.5 billion picture dots (pixels) per second, a fabulous speed that in computer jargon translates into 68 billion information units (bytes) per second. Although Tesla's system is inspired by the functioning of neural networks in the brain, a drawback of the brain crops up here: compared to these computers, neurons work very sluggishly. If living neurons were to imitate Tesla's on-board computer with the temporal characteristics they are known to have, they would need an insane amount of time to process all those data streams: by the time they had finished calculating, the self-driving car would already have collided with another vehicle.

The second option is to find a qualitative solution: find a way to make the information graspable or knowable at bullet train speed by transforming it through a mechanism that is peculiar to the brain and not used in laptops or PCs. The brain possesses a special kind of machinery that differs from ordinary computers and the classical artificial intelligence techniques that Tesla uses. This machinery is capable of making sense of the mash of sensory inputs: we see a 'blue car' instead of the sequence 011010101010. Colour is one of those special qualities that make conscious experience so different from series of numbers. When a car appears blue to us, we immediately know what colour we are dealing with. We no longer need a separate label. Without that special machinery in our brains, the piece-by-piece reading of the signals would go much too slowly and the information about scenes around us would not be instantly relatable to reach complex decisions quickly. We would be condemned to scan endless, soporific sequences of numbers and, like numb zombies, only respond to them motorically. Thank goodness our brains have developed in such a way that our consciousness is indeed characterized by an inexhaustible wealth of qualities.

All well and good: consciousness offers us a richly varied overview of yourself and your world. Is it the case that we look at that overview like we look at a painting? I have to admit that the word 'overview' has surfaced here for lack of a better word. It suggests that it is about having a synopsis or 'view' – a way of seeing – whereas it is the multiplicity of very different sensory experiences that is inherent to consciousness. Taste is not a matter of 'sight'. And the suggestion that we are watching an overview from a distance is also wrong: we experience a scene consciously by being in the middle of it, in three dimensions plus time. Consciousness immerses us in the scene we are witnessing. It's not that we 'watch' this scene as if we were playing a video game. What we are experiencing is an immersive experience of the situation. We are part of a very realistic 'video game' that unfolds around us in three dimensions, enriched with all kinds of qualities other than purely visual ones. This immersion is something that imperceptibly forces itself on us when we wake up in the morning: we not only *see* something, but we also *are* somewhere. We are in a spatial situation. We have a body lying horizontally in a warm bed, in a bedroom where the morning light enters through the window. Sleepily we look around us and gauge what is going on. All this offers a sufficient foothold, after our previous detours, to give a definition of consciousness: the phenomenon by which we have a rich, multisensory overview of our situation in the world – how the world feels and looks, and how our body is positioned in it.

Reflexes, habits and complex behaviour

There is good evidence that not all animal species have this kind of experience. It is simply not enough to face the world armed with a set of senses. The brain also needs to be able to forge all that sensory information into a meaningful whole – a 'scene' or situation sketch in which all kinds of sources of visual information, sounds, smells and tactile sensations have their place, in space and time. A funny example of a lack of situational awareness can be found on YouTube, where an African bullfrog is confronted with a smartphone.[1] The smartphone is held by a boy who starts a computer game in which digital ants or insects crawl across the screen from top to bottom. Each time an ant passes by, the frog jumps forward and sticks out its tongue. The victim is virtually crushed, but of course the frog does not get any food. The animal cannot help itself and continues to attack. It does not realize that its actions bring no reward, and that it is being taken for a ride by a kid with a smartphone. Finally, the boy moves his own thumb in the direction of the frog: the animal eagerly takes a bite of the thumb. Cries of pain follow, the deceived takes revenge.

The frog was deliberately placed in an artificial situation, so is it not logical that it has no overview of the game situation? The behaviour of the frog is consistent with what we know from many studies on amphibians in more natural situations. When detecting a teeming, small thing, a circuit of neurons is activated via a particular nucleus in the frog's brain – the optic tectum – that causes the animal to orient itself to the stimulus, so it gets ready to catch the prey. This happens without the animal paying attention to the wider environment.[2] The animal reacts to one conspicuous stimulus without taking the context into account. As early as 1953, experiments led to the conclusion that the tectum of the frog's brain contains 'bug detectors', cells that become electrically active when a beetle appears before the frog's eyes, and trigger the attacking behaviour. For the frog to be able to catch beetles in its natural environment, no consciousness or overview of the situation is needed. The experiments indicate that the orientation behaviour of the frog is triggered by local movements of the prey itself (and a limited part of the background around it), but not by the wider context.

Cognitive neuroscientist Victor Lamme, affiliated with the University of Amsterdam, has argued that human behaviour is essentially similar to that of the frog and can be explained globally by brain systems that each activate their own reflex, and compete with each other.[3] One system stimulates the execution of a tongue reflex, while another system counteracts this by commanding the animal to first walk forward a little bit, to get closer to the beetle. The strongest and most active brain area wins, after which the corresponding reflex is inevitably unleashed.

This view can be traced back more than a hundred years, to a book written by the British neurophysiologist Charles Sherrington (1857–1952), who was awarded the Nobel Prize in 1932 for his research on muscle reflexes depending on neurons in the spinal cord.[4] He notes that human behaviour is coordinated and consists of one piece. If you are given two stimuli at the same time, each of which would evoke a different reflex, then the result is a behaviour that does not consist of two – sometimes conflicting – reflexes but of only one reflex, which turns out to dominate the other. One of the reflexes is dominant and the other is subordinate. In line with Sherrington's view, you can think of the nervous system as an accumulation of lower and higher areas, in which the lower areas regulate simple stimulus-response behaviour, such as the patellar reflex. When the doctor taps the tendon just below your knee with a hammer, your lower leg shoots forward – a response that is crucial to keeping your body balanced while walking. This reflex is regulated by circuits of neurons in the spinal cord, which are in turn controlled by areas higher up in the pecking order. These higher circuits can keep the reflex under their thumb when it is undesirable to slip your lower leg, for instance when the doctor is standing right in front of you. This superimposition of control mechanisms forms a hierarchy in which the higher circuits rule the lower ones – a 'hierarchy of reflexes'. Whether these higher circuits embody our 'will' remains to be seen: the will is a rather vague concept that will demand further exploration later on.

But human behaviour is more complex than this. Far from all our behaviour is driven by external stimuli that are automatically linked to pre-established, stereotypical actions. Behaviour can emerge spontaneously, on impulse or because a memory comes to mind that indicates that you will have guests for dinner tonight. A spontaneous hunch can lead you to plan your behaviour – a cognitive activity that goes beyond the level of simple stimulus-response sequences. Rolling out a stimulus-response doesn't require a prearranged plan; you don't have to think about the possible outcomes of your action. With planned behaviour, on the other hand, there is a concrete expectation about the outcome you want to work towards: you try to anticipate the consequences of your behaviour even before the action takes place.[5] For example, there are two ways to go shopping. You can enter a shopping centre with an open mind, without a plan in advance, and then react impulsively to the billboards that force themselves brutally upon you. The other way is to think beforehand about exactly what you want to buy and navigate purposefully from one shop to another, with a shopping list in your hand or head.

Complex decisions are made after lengthy processes that take place internally, within your brain. How this internal 'hemming and hawing' works will be discussed later. These internal decision processes, which also take place without external stimuli, are flexible and work very differently from a rigid stimulus-response reflex. This is because the exact consequences of a complex behavioural choice are often unknown. Outcomes are uncertain, and through a subtle interplay of brain systems for planning, memory and conscious representation, the brain determines which choice option offers the best chance of survival or reproduction. Frogs are not known to sit for long periods brooding over decisions. Here, the lack of a well-developed cerebral cortex in amphibians is significant. Not only must frogs do without a visual cortex – which in monkeys and humans is essential for conscious visual perception – but frogs also lack a well-developed frontal lobe.[6] The case of Phineas Gage already showed that this lobe is important for planning behaviour and making balanced decisions. This is not conclusive evidence that frogs could never be aware of anything. But if they are, it should happen in a completely different way than in humans.

The idea that consciousness has a function is not uncontroversial. One school of materialism argues that consciousness is nothing more than a psychological concept, useful in our dealings with other people, when in fact it is the cells in our brain that take care of everything for us.[7] It is purely and simply the neurons that process sensory inputs, make decisions and control our muscles and internal organs. Consciousness would just be a side effect – a useless epiphenomenon that plays no role in our chances of survival, a figment of our imagination designed to explain our own behaviour. This would deprive consciousness of its raison d'être as something that can influence our behaviour. If this were true, it should be possible to go trouble-free through life without consciousness. In this scenario, we would behave exactly as we normally do, but have no conscious experience whatsoever. We would be zombies.[8]

The idea that we would continue to behave in the same way as we do now, but without a rich, spatial worldview, seems highly improbable to me. It is quite conceivable that our reflexes and habits would continue to work if we were zombies: the little hammer under the knee still triggers a movement. Habits can be executed without necessarily being linked to conscious experience. But if you arrive at a beach, totally unconscious, and are faced with the choice of swimming in the sea or eating an ice cream, how do you decide? There is no experience of seeing and hearing waves crashing in the surf. You feel no wind in your hair. You have no idea whether there is an ice-cream stall for miles around. You do not feel whether it is hot or cold. There is nothing. At best, you reflexively withdraw your foot from the burning hot sand you have just touched, but you do not feel that either. This makes zombies seem possible or conceivable in principle, but unrealizable in practice: our complex behaviour, accompanied by a never-ending stream of words describing our feelings, is at odds with an absence of consciousness. By 'us', I mean humans and animals that closely resemble humans; robots are a special case. Epilepsy patients suffering from an absence seizure are likely to lose consciousness temporarily, but may continue to exhibit particular behaviours. Does this not suggest the possibility of zombies? It is illuminating that they do not exhibit complex behaviour but *automatisms*: simple, stereotypical actions the patient can perform even when unconscious.

There is at least one other argument that could speak against a function of consciousness. In the case of very quick actions, our consciousness seems to be playing catch-up. Much of our behaviour appears to be determined unconsciously and irrationally. Our consciousness does not seem to have much grip on the deeper motives that actually direct our behaviour. Consciousness has been characterized as a 'chatterbox' that only tells us a story after a decision has already been made, a piece of fiction that has no eye for the hidden mechanisms that arrange our behaviour and that especially fits in well with our self-image as a rational, social being that lives in harmony with its environment.[9] Even in a relatively 'simple' behaviour like the reflex action of pulling your hand back from a hot burner on your electric stove, the movement takes place faster than you become aware of the pain. This confronts us with a paradox: why should you become aware of that dreadful pain if your hand has already been brought to safety? Is it a punishment from God? And why, when we grow up, should we spend so much energy on the development of a cortex and thalamus, if all we get in return is a jabber-jaw that is behind the times?

Generating a conscious experience does indeed take time: an image must be displayed for at least about six hundredths of a second in order to give rise to a recognizable percept.[10] This relates to the time it takes for our brains to concoct an integrated sensation from the jumble of inputs that reach them – a process that continues even after that six hundredths of a second has passed. This may seem a minuscule amount of time, but it must be said that the neural loop that triggers a reflex is even faster (in the case of the patellar reflex, it is about two hundredths of a second). And yet, when you consider that six hundredths of a second is enough to trigger a complete update of a visual overview, and that pondering over complex decisions takes even longer, this time span is not so bad.

So why that prolonged pain, as a seemingly useless punishment afterwards? First of all, your conscious experience enables you to consider and plan your next action, such as looking for a water tap to prevent a worse burn. For this search, an overview of your current situation comes in extremely handy. But there is another function, however painful its exercise may be. You feel the pain as you survey your situation and can thus better identify the cause. You see the glass-ceramic cooktop with a barely visible, red glow in the front right-hand corner. That is the direct culprit. But why did your hand come too close to it? To figure out what happened before the pain started, your brain's systems of consciousness and memory exchange information.[11] You see your phone next to the heating coil and realize that you were distracted by a phone call while you were cooking. You overlooked the red glow. In the process of determining cause and effect, your brain is simultaneously busy learning, with that persistent pain as a punitive signal. Telephone away while cooking, or else! Turn off the cooker when you are not using it!

But can't we learn without that pain? Why must pain be so damned painful? Can't we just say a few stern words to ourselves? Why did evolution not give us a 'learning signal' that does not hurt so terribly? Here is the catch about consciousness: it signals a risky damage to our skin and it is, for our own survival, much more useful to experience the pain because, by doing so, we will learn more intensively how to avoid the causes of pain. A stern word is easily ignored. The same applies to pleasure or euphoric delight. If the feeling of an orgasm were replaced by information such as: 'I should really like this', sex would hardly be interesting for many people.

"Hey, but wait a minute!" Matt the Materialist, fan of consciousness as epiphenomenon, shouts. "This is not what we had agreed on. The deal was that our brain cells do all the work to translate sensory stimuli into behaviour. So they also make the supposedly complicated choice between swimming or eating ice cream. The neurons fix up all the steering of behaviour for us, no separate thing like consciousness is needed." Even if we assume that a zombie copy of yourself is capable of exactly the same behaviour as you are, the problem remains that the zombie would lack conscious experience. In all its doings, the zombie has to sail blind; in practice the lack of consciousness would make the performance of complex behaviour impossible. The multifaceted overview that we experience does exist. Without that experience, we would not know that we are somewhere, in space and time – or even that we exist ourselves. This fundamental reality of our experience again raises the question of what happens to those industrious neurons on the one hand and consciousness on the other.

Here the ghost of dualism that Descartes struggled so much with, looms large again. If body and soul are two radically different substances – one material, the other immaterial – then a connection between them is not possible. If the connection were purely material, it would not be capable of communicating with the immaterial (think, for example, of a telephone cable that, operating with electrical signals, would have to make contact with something immaterial – a 'mind' or 'spirit' – which, by definition, is not receptive to a physical phenomenon like electricity). If, on the other hand, the connection were purely immaterial, this would mean that signals from the 'mind' would have an effect on material reality as described by physics. But one of the fundamental principles in physics is the law of conservation of energy, which implies that the causes of material changes must lie in matter itself: there is no place for mysterious forces or energies from outside (or beyond) material reality. Fortunately, dualism is not the only possible answer to materialism. It is also possible to disagree with a 'hard' materialist like Matt. This is because there is room for a third possible view, which on the one hand attributes an essential role to brain networks in generating consciousness, and on the other hand recognizes that consciousness really exists, as a result of brain activity. The time to explore this 'third way' is approaching.

But first back to those wretched zombies. The zombie argument is a philosophical thought experiment that asks us to imagine that there are beings that behave just like us, but have no consciousness. We can imagine quite well how neurons are interconnected, how they produce electrical pulses in the blink of an eye and transmit them to each other – like a gigantic network of optical fibres transferring flashes of light. But if those hard-working neurons are busy processing sensory stimuli, can we really imagine that consciousness is absent? Or that it is actually present? This is where our imagination fails us, because consciousness is not a 'thing' that goes on underneath those little brain cells, or hovers over them. It is not a 'thing' that we can imagine at all. It belongs in a different category. This is an insight put forward by philosopher Gilbert Ryle in his book *The Concept of Mind* from 1949. Let us imagine someone visiting Oxford University for the first time in his life. The guest is shown around the lecture and dining halls, the libraries, the laboratories and the perfectly trimmed lawns that adorn the courtyards. At the end of the tour, the visitor says to his host: "All of this is very nice, but where is the university?"

The concepts of 'hall' and 'lawn' cannot be forced to function on the same level of understanding as 'university', and so it is also a mistake to think that when we see a network of living neurons we can imagine that consciousness is present or absent in it. But this does not alter the significance of the existence of conscious experiences and of them being linked to our brains, even apart from our behaviour that is visible to others, and of the fact that they are absent during significant periods of our lives, as we realize when we wake up from a long, dreamless sleep. The zombie argument tries to seduce us into believing a certain intuition that, on closer inspection, is completely unsubstantiated and even false. I can open a wristwatch and show you the timepiece: "Look, there is no consciousness here." But why would you believe this if you leave out all the detailed knowledge about brains, psychology and watches?

An alternative to the 'hard', purely reductive variant of materialism is to accept that all those hard-working neurons in our brains together can apparently – under appropriate circumstances – generate or induce conscious experiences. This is not an ability that neurons simply have, as given by God. A culture of brain cells in a petri dish does not need to have conscious experiences at all, and the chance of this happening is negligible. Cells in a culture dish connect spontaneously and haphazardly, and it would be an extreme coincidence if a structured network were to form in this way, producing experiences of smells, colours or melodies. But if the wiring and activity of neurons within a normal brain is in order – after a long process of embryonic development and learning experiences in childhood – and they are part of a healthy functioning network that integrates sensory stimuli in just the right way, then those cells can contribute to producing a conscious experience. Admittedly, this still sounds a bit like Aladdin conjuring a djinn out of his magic lamp. Nevertheless, I will try to make the case that this is a suitable route to do justice both to our grey brain mass and to the existence of a rich, qualitatively varied world of experience. The greatest challenge on this path is not to fall into the same trap that caught Descartes: the idea that body and mind are separate yet mysteriously influence each other.

How does all of this lead us further in our quest? In previous chapters it was shown that consciousness is not acutely dependent on cognitive abilities such as memory, emotion or direct control of motor activity. The importance of our senses for conscious perception is clear, but having separate sensory cells is not enough: organisms with only a few light sensors are not able to form an image of their environment. When a light sensor is active and transmits its electrical pulses to the nervous system, the signal itself does not reveal that it is about light: to the nervous system, an arbitrary signal can just as easily mean 'sound' or 'taste'. The enigma of conscious experience may become a little less mysterious if we conceive of it as the qualitatively rich overview of the situation in which we find ourselves: we are 'immersed' in a world including a body. If we accept that reflexes and other automatically performed actions have little to do with consciousness, the possibility emphatically opens up that it has a function in weighing our worldview against what we want: in making complex decisions and planning our behaviour. The more we try to insist that our consciousness is behind the times and that zombies should be able to go through life just fine, the harder we are confronted with the fact that they would not see or feel their world – and are thus condemned to a limited behavioural repertoire.

But the titanic struggle between matter and mind does not end in a draw so easily. Helen, the monkey, went through life without a primary visual cortex (V1) and, despite several indications of blindness, still displayed interesting behaviour that required light information. She could locate and pick up objects such as nuts on the floor of a test chamber and could distinguish between objects. She could even pick a passing fly out of the air. Is this not strong evidence against the idea that consciousness is necessary for complex behaviour? First of all, Helen only had area V1 removed, so her vision was affected, but not her hearing, touch, smell, taste, balance or proprioception (sensory information about body position and movement). She was thus far from being a zombie monkey. During the eight years that Nicholas Humphrey examined Helen, he discovered some remarkable things. Helen could indeed pick up currants from the floor, but she was easily enticed to pick up pieces of tape as well – black, red or green, it didn't matter. It gradually became clear that she could not recognize objects based on their shape or colour, but only by means of very conspicuous features such as a bright versus a dark hue. She did not grasp an object between two fingers, but brought her whole palm over the object before putting it in her mouth.

Even more striking was the fact that, although Helen could manage well in familiar surroundings, she would blunder hopelessly when entering a new, unfamiliar space. Even when she was in her own room, she lost her head completely when she was startled, for example by a door slamming unexpectedly. When she got scared, the capacity for spatial vision seemed to desert her. This is significant: within a familiar environment, we can rely much more strongly on automated behaviour.

But Humphrey's most important discovery was that Helen could not do something that is quite normal for other apes, or humans. When we want to grasp an object within reach, we normally look at it first, so that we can get a precise image of it and make an accurate grasping movement. This grasping was within Helen's capabilities. But we can also grab a cup of coffee while our eyes are fixed on something else, such as a newspaper or a smartphone. This type of behaviour was not mastered by Helen. She was unable to grasp objects outside the area on which her eyes were focusing – something for which we need a visual overview of our surroundings, fuelled by light information reaching our retina from the edges of our field of vision. 'Tunnel vision' is probably out of the question here, as Helen was blind on multiple tests. Her brain still had lower visual areas at her disposal, hidden under the cortex, that gave her the ability to respond to coarse light information without visual awareness.

A particularly revealing experiment was one in which Humphrey stuck a piece of black tape to the floor amidst a number of obstacles. Helen discovered the object, tried to pick it up, walked around the room and then tried again and again to pick up the tape and put it in her mouth. Why did her interest in this unappetizing object not gradually fade? Humphrey notes that, as soon as the piece of tape landed directly in front of Helen's eyes once again, she treated it as a new discovery. As she walked around, she could not keep track of the tape's position in the room. She 'forgot' its position the moment the light information disappeared from her field of vision. Occasionally, the tape caught her eye again, which brought the right light information back to her retina to prompt her to grab it, but this did not lead to a spatial overview in which the tape had a stable position in the room, something that healthy apes and humans find quite normal despite their body movements. You walk around your dining table and see that the dining table remains in the same place in the room. Of course! But how is this possible when you know that your body is moving forward and your eyes are darting in all directions, so that the table has no fixed position at all on your retina? This brings us back to the function of consciousness. In terms of visual information, Helen lived in a totally 'egocentric' world where she could respond to objects that happened to be projected on her retina when she looked in their direction, but there was no question of having a stable 'this-is-my-world-view'. Very difficult to work with, unless you are a creature of habit.

10 A code in cuneiform script

On the simulacrum our brain creates

Over the past 20 years, there have been many science fiction movies about artificial intelligence and brain manipulation to enjoy in the cinemas. In *Ex Machina* (2014), Alicia Vikander plays a robot who seduces a software programmer into believing she has a consciousness. *Transcendence* (2014) shows how the body of AI researcher Will Caster (Johnny Depp) slowly dies, but his consciousness is uploaded into a quantum computer. My old favourite remains *The Matrix* (1999), in which a computer hacker – 'Neo', played by Keanu Reeves – discovers that the world he lives in and experiences as real is actually a computer simulation. If you set aside the kung fu ballet of rattling machine guns, men with reflective sunglasses and women in tight leather suits, this is an evocative film. Neo meets Morpheus, the leader of rebels who rise up against the ruling regime and manage to stay out of the overarching computer simulation. Morpheus instructs Neo to choose between two pills: a blue pill that will make Neo return to his ordinary, old life, or a red pill that will reveal the truth about the sham world of computer simulation, the Matrix. Neo takes the red pill and undergoes the collapse of the world he has hitherto experienced as normal and comfortable. He wakes up in a large vessel, filled with a liquid that is similar to amniotic fluid, with an array of cables plugged into his head. He is surrounded by an endless number of barrels containing people who are also plugged in, but unable to free themselves. Neo is picked up by the group around Morpheus and taken aboard the rebel ship.

In the course of the twenty-first century, Morpheus explains, humans built intelligent machines that became so smart that they revolted against their creators. The human race tried to cut the machines off from their source of energy – the sun – but the machines managed to control the humans and put them in those barrels of liquid, tapping bioelectric energy from their brains. Ignorant of their actual fate as slaves in a power plant that supplies the supercomputers with electricity, the people live within a giant simulation that pacifies them and keeps them happy within a realistic and acceptable mock world.

Is it possible that our brain, fed with information streams from a supercomputer, sees and feels a world that is perceived as real? Could the brain figure out whether the information it receives through those cables is real or

DOI: 10.4324/9781003429555-10

not? This question was already asked by philosopher Hilary Putnam in his 1981 article 'Brains in a Vat'.[1] He proposes the following thought experiment:

> Imagine that a human being (you can imagine this to be yourself) has been subjected to an operation by an evil scientist. The person's brain (your brain) has been removed from the body and placed in a vat of nutrients which keeps the brain alive. The nerve endings have been connected to a super-scientific computer which causes the person whose brain it is to have the illusion that everything is perfectly normal. There seem to be people, objects, the sky, etc.; but really all the person (you) is experiencing is the result of electronic impulses travelling from the computer to the nerve endings. The computer is so clever that if the person tries to raise his hand, the feedback from the computer will cause him to 'see' and 'feel' the hand being raised. Moreover, by varying the program, the evil scientist can cause the victim to 'experience' (or hallucinate) any situation or environment the evil scientist wishes.

Strikingly, with this idea Putnam is building on the work of Descartes, who in his 1641 *Meditations*, unaware of the supercomputers of more than three centuries later, also spoke of an 'evil demon' who floats us illusions that we, poor and naive people, would experience as our reality. Descartes used this demon to support his motto: "I think, therefore I am": even if illusions were the only thing you could experience, there must be something or someone who undergoes them – something is happening in or to you.

Putnam's version of the demon argument makes a number of assumptions, such as the ability of supercomputers to continuously provide our brains with just the right feedback to dish up a world to us that we can move through smoothly and yet appears stable and reliable. Moreover, these supercomputers must have the fabulous ability to give us – as a group of 'slaves' in vats – the collective hallucination that we can talk to each other directly. If I wanted to talk to you, I could not do so using my vocal cords, tongue and lungs (for I, as a separate brain, have none), and you are lacking the ears to hear me directly. Speech signals would be sent from my brain via electronic links to the computer, which then emits feedback to your auditory nerves and brain areas to create the illusion that you can hear me talk directly. We also assume that our brains can be kept alive in the vat without having connections to the rest of our bodies. This last assumption is not too bizarre, since experimental researchers already showed in 1991 that the brain of a guinea pig could be kept alive in its entirety in an artificial environment – *in vitro* – for hours. They achieved this in a surgical tour de force, in which all the major blood vessels that go in and out of the brain were connected to tubes transporting a fluid rich in oxygen and nutrients, having a composition very similar to the fluid that normally flushes our brain cells.[2]

But let's return to our key question: could the brain-in-a-vat actually be aware of a world like that experienced by normal people? Putnam adds: could those brains say or think that they are a bunch of brains-in-a-barrel? His answer is: "No, they could not." Brains floating 'disembodied' in a container, he argues, might in principle be able to think or utter words, but that would not enable them to refer to real things in the outside world in the way that we – people with normal connections between brain, senses and body – can. The problem of the brain-in-a-vat, Putnam argues, is that it is locked up in a fictitious world where words or brain signals have no meaning: they do not connect to anything that in fact exists in the outside world – the world outside the brain-plus-computer. With its vicious signals, the computer does trigger all sorts of sensory inputs in the brain, but these produce little more than gibberish, devoid of meaning because there is no reality behind it. If a computer is fed electrical inputs by the brain to utter the word 'tree', it has no meaningful representation or display of this concept, because it does not refer to any actual tree in our environment. The real tree is missing from the story. In a similar vein, the brain-in-a-vat cannot really think that it is a brain-in-a-vat: within its confined, simulated world, the words 'brain-in-a-vat' do not refer to actual brains or vats (they cannot 'see' either of them in real life).

At first sight, Putnam's argument seems to cut ice. It has found much support among philosophers. But does it also fit with knowledge from contemporary neuroscience?

We travel to the beginning of the nineteenth century. At that time, the fledgling science of sense and brain physiology was dominated by such greats as Johannes Müller (1801–1858) in Germany. In the portrait (Figure 10.1), Müller poses as a classic, bearded statesman, accompanied by a jar of brains in alcohol. With his voluminous books such as *Handbuch der Physiologie des Menschen*, he was considered a giant authority in his field.[3] One of the most important physiological laws he laid down is known as the 'doctrine of specific nerve energies'. This doctrine deals with a simple but puzzling phenomenon that we all know. If you accidentally get a push against your eye, you not only experience this as a sensation of touch (possibly with pain), but you also *see* something (little stars or a flash of light). In the third law of his doctrine, Müller therefore states that one and the same external cause affecting each sense (such as the push against your eye) can give rise to different sensations (touch and vision). These sensations are enabled by the special endowments (properties) of the nerve connected to the sense organ. For each sensory cell, plus the connected nerve fibre that runs from it to the brain, a type of stimulus can be identified that best stimulates that sense. For example, the auditory organ in your inner ear is maximally sensitive to sound waves. But the 'wrong' type of stimulus, such as a powerful slap in the face, is also capable of producing a sound sensation – 'it hurt so much that my ears were ringing'.

With today's knowledge, it is not surprising that senses are sensitive to several types of physical stimuli. In the cochlea of our inner ear, we find countless cells with tiny hairs on their membranes, which are sensitive to the vibrations propagated by the fluid in this organ, generated as they are by sound waves in the air that make our eardrum oscillate. The cells transmit their signals to

Figure 10.1 Portrait of Johannes Müller (1801–1858).

the fibres of the auditory nerve, which enters the brain. No wonder that these hairs are also agitated by a slap on the ear and promptly pass on signals to the brain. But even without this contemporary insight, Müller realized that the nature of the sensation (or modality: seeing, hearing, etc.) we experience is anchored in the structure of the senses and the nerve tracts that carry the pattern of stimulation to the brain.[4] Nowadays this seems self-evident, but in the early nineteenth century there was an alternative way of thinking about this. This other possibility held that the nature of a sensation is determined by using the same sense organ in multiple ways. A single sensory cell somewhere in the body could, in principle, be used to produce two different sensations, depending on the pattern of electrical pulses it delivers. For example, 'strong and regular pulsing' for a hearing experience and 'weak and irregular' for a tactile experience. This way of shaping a specific sensation is called 'pattern coding': the code that determines which sensation you will feel depends on the pattern of electrical activity sent from your sensory cells to the brain. In contrast, the way that Müller proposed – and which is widely accepted today – is called 'labelled lines coding'. Here, the sensory modality is determined by which sensory cell (and corresponding nerve fibre) is stimulated, while the pattern of pulses is not essential. The lines that run from the sensory cells to the brain are, as it were, labelled to indicate what kind of sensation you will experience, given the stimulation of your sense organs.

Müller and his contemporaries got onto another crucial fact. They discovered that the stimulation of a sense organ is not necessary per se to elicit a conscious sensation. To obtain a visual sensation, it was sufficient to stimulate the optic nerve. For someone to experience some sort of sound, it was enough to stimulate the auditory nerve. The sense organ itself can be bypassed, as long as you hit the right nerve. When this notion dawned on Müller, he began to focus on the special properties of the nerves and less on the sense organs themselves. Hence his thesis about 'specific nerve energies' arose: the optic nerve harbours a special form of energy that gives rise to seeing things, while the nerve originating from the inner ear is a carrier of another form of energy that gives rise to hearing.

However, this idea turned out to create a fundamental problem. In physics, it is quite normal to work with different forms of energy: light is a form of electromagnetic energy and sound waves are a form of kinetic energy. A blow to the eye falls under the heading of 'kinetic energy'. But in the nervous system, after such a blow, the peculiar situation occurs that different kinds of physical energy can give rise to only one kind of sensation (you see something, either because light falls on your retina or because of a blow on the eye). Even if we assume one kind of physical energy, there is no unambiguous relationship with the sensations it produces: the kinetic energy of the blow produces a visual sensation via the eye, a sound sensation via the ear and the experience of a brief but painful body contact via the skin. Apparently, there is no one-to-one relationship between the forms of energy recognized by physics and Müller's nerve energies. That doesn't feel good.

But now all joking aside. Later research in the nineteenth and twentieth centuries made it clear that there could be no question at all of the different nerve energies Müller was talking about. His pupil Hermann von Helmholtz, whose fame was soon to exceed that of his teacher, and generations of researchers after him, showed that all nerves transmitting sensory information to the brain work in roughly the same way. For all modalities, there is only one type of electrical pulse that transmits information from sensory cells to the central nervous system. This is just as true for the nerves that emerge from the brain and spinal cord and carry signals to our muscles and inner organs, such as the heart and intestines. There is only one kind of 'nerve energy': the energy involved in sending electrical spikes across all our nerve fibres.

It is therefore no surprise that Müller's doctrine of specific nerve energies has fallen into disuse. In itself, this is not a disaster. But what has not fallen into disuse is the idea of 'labelled lines' coding. This is understandable, because our knowledge of the brain still suggests that it is the identity of the sensory cells, with their thin and long lines to the brain, that determines what kind of sensation we will experience. Now it turns out that all those little lines work in the same way: without exception they pass on the information in the form of spikes. From the body, sensory information first penetrates into an array of lower brain nuclei, and then rushes to higher stations in the thalamus and cortex – the brain areas especially needed for conscious content. The big remaining problem is that the cells in these receiving brain areas cannot 'read' the pulses to see what they are about. The cells do not know the anatomical source of the pulses, and the pulses themselves are not labelled as to which sense they come from. This means that it cannot be the electrical pulse travelling along a nerve fibre alone that determines which sensory modality is involved: it is the brain that must provide an *interpretation* of these pulse patterns.[5] So the question is: how can the brain make any sense of the gobbledygook made up by the millions of pulses it receives every second?

Let's imagine a random neuron lying in the cerebral cortex, as part of a system that produces conscious sensations in a modality we do not know beforehand. The neuron lies there relaxed and comfortably luxuriating in a bath of warm, revitalizing fluid, emitting electrical pulses at its leisure as inputs come in from other neurons that make contact (Figure 10.2). One input triggers the neuron to become more active, another inhibits it. What on earth are all these inputs about? Is it visual or auditory information, or tactile information that originates from the skin? All those neurons with their fibres and synaptic endings work in pretty much the same way, and that one neuron, bathing in blissful ignorance, responds to all those inputs in a similar way: with a fluctuation in the rate at which it fires pulses. Even if we scrutinize a group of cells in one area, this group has no knowledge about the anatomical origin of the information it receives. The cells in the group do not 'know' what kind of information they are processing. They know not what they do. They are totally clueless. They are too small a unit within the brain to be attributed any 'knowledge' at all.

Figure 10.2 The neuron bathing in blissful ignorance.

When the brain gets started with processing all those millions of inputs from the body, it is on its own when it comes to interpreting the information. There is no separate code that travels along with the sensory input and tells the cells in the cortex, "Hey, pay attention, this is visual information!" When streams of information travel from the retina to the brain and, via a way station in the thalamus, reach the cerebral cortex, the spike-shaped electrical pulses do not suddenly change from purely electrical activity into 'visual information'. There is no sign at the border of the visual cortex greeting incoming spikes with the text: "Welcome to the visual cortex!" (Figure 10.3). Nonetheless it is still true that we, as outsiders who can look at other people's brains, can refer unencumbered to the area of the cortex in the occipital lobe as 'visual cortex'. After all, selective damage to this area leads to blindness (while other sensory modalities remain intact), and in addition, this lobe is the first area of the cortex to receive information originating from the retina. But it is a misunderstanding to think that this area is *intrinsically* visual: it would be pure witchcraft to say that all the pulses coming in here became 'visual' – as if by magic.

Back to Putnam's thought experiment. That it is the brain that must interpret 'anonymized' inputs means that his brain-in-a-vat faces exactly the same problem as a normal brain, connected to the rest of the body with all the senses it has on offer. Brains fed purely by information from a supercomputer would be condemned to meaningless gibberish, Putnam says, because their word for 'tree' cannot refer to a real tree – a tree in the outside world – but only to a fictitious tree that has been fostered by a computer simulation. But this view is now counterbalanced by a solid chunk of neuroscience that shows

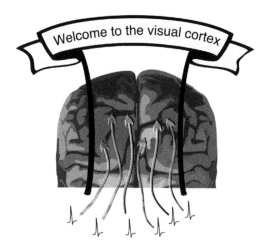

Figure 10.3 When electrical pulses from sensory organs are transmitted to the cortex via intermediate stations, there is no sign at the entrance that suddenly labels the incoming information as 'visual'. This cartoon illustrates the misconception that electrical pulse patterns suddenly start to represent 'visual' information on arrival in the occipital cortex, the piece of cortex located in the back of the head.

that even a healthy brain, encased in a normal body, has to make do with the same spikes that provide it with information in an identical way to Putnam's *in vitro* brain. Even in our own brains, there is no label glued to those pulses that says: "Hey, but *this* is information from the *real* outside world."

Imagine that your own brain is immersed and kept alive in a vessel, and stays connected for a while to the sensory cells in your own body, and that the motor outputs from your brain continue to have effects on your muscles and internal organs. Your body-without-brain is placed right next to the vessel, so the connecting lines are somewhat longer than usual. Despite the physical separation, we assume that your body-brain combination can just do its job. You open the fridge, take out a can of cola and drink it. Deliciously tingly and cool, as always. What you experience and put into words really refers to the drink in front of you. This is exactly what you understand by cola, this is what cola means to you. But then, in the blink of an eye, all the inputs and outputs are taken over by the supercomputer, which according to Putnam simulates everything flawlessly. The computer triggers electrical pulses in your nervous pathways just as your own normal sensory cells would do. You want to open the fridge and take out a piece of cheese. This works out, as far as you know, because the computer effortlessly and without noticeable delay mimics the sensory inputs that match the motor commands your own brain sends to the computer. You perceive that the door opens, that your hand grabs a piece of cheese, that you have to apply pressure to the knife to cut a slice. The slice tastes deliciously creamy and sharp, just as aged cheese should. The supercomputer does its job perfectly: your brain has no way of determining what is real and what is fake. As long as all inputs and outputs are correct, the feedback the computer provides is experienced as real and meaningful as the signals from your own body.

The Matrix reflects a scenario that is possible in principle and that stimulates us to question our own assumptions about knowing reality. If a supercomputer can trick our brains into experiencing an alternative reality, and believing in it, is there a chance that this is actually happening to us? Recently, I visited a gaming centre in the heart of Amsterdam with my research group and, wearing a virtual reality headset, I noticed how easy it is to be fooled by the simulated world presented to me by these oversized glasses. The illusion became more powerful when I turned my head to the left or right and the computer presented me with exactly the right field of vision to match my head movements. It wasn't long before the simulation took me up to the roof of a skyscraper and a voice from the headphones instructed me to walk a narrow wooden plank that led from the roof to a virtual abyss. I overlooked a cheaply designed city that was obviously fake. I repeatedly told myself that I could easily step off the plank and begin a blissful gliding flight, but the sensory illusions, conspiring with vertigo, prevented me from doing so. The hallucination had already become too powerful. Even the modest computing power of these VR glasses is convincing enough to make us believe in an alternative reality, complete with gut feelings.

The *Matrix* scenario goes further than this: it assumes that an illusory reality can be conjured up collectively in a large group of people, and that this simulation runs continuously, with the same smooth dynamics in optical flow that we experience every day. Based on the increasing computing power of future supercomputers, a select group of philosophers and entrepreneurs in Silicon Valley – including Tesla boss Elon Musk – are seriously considering that in the future, supercomputers will be able to present us with simulations that are indistinguishable from reality.[6] They believe artificial intelligence will grow so rapidly that supercomputers will come to dominate us in a post-human civilization and will be able to create simulations in which we – as the 'ancestors' of these superior beings – will experience a virtual world that we regard as real. What we experience as the here and now, at the time of reading this book, would even be the result of a projection calculated retroactively by the supercomputer, running in the future. That we currently would be nothing more than a projection of a supercomputer mimicking the world of its primitive ancestors, might be amusing and even humbling – yet is also extremely improbable. Why would the supercomputers of the future do this if they are already in charge of planet Earth? Why would they spend an incredible amount of energy on a virtual reality game that they do not need for their own survival? In *The Matrix*, supercomputers are supposed to harvest energy from human brains in vats, but in fact the brains guzzle energy instead of delivering it. Similarly, the computer simulations needed to maintain an illusory reality only drain energy.

Moreover, even the supercomputers of the future will occasionally have flaws: an error in the programming code, a crash, a simulation that does not run as perfectly as the seamless transitions that characterize our daily lives. When, in the year 2119, Microsoft's Windows 167 comes on the market, who may hope that it will be entirely free of bugs? I imagine that your virtual life will suddenly be interrupted by the message: 'Downloading updates...', or that your virtual lover will suddenly 'freeze' because her simulation crashes while yours continues. There is also an ethical objection to this scenario. If the computers of the future are smart enough to make their human ancestors believe in a simulation, they should also understand that it is immoral to do so. They would understand that one cannot do it to people, making them believe they live in a grandiose illusion and thus depriving them of their right to truth-finding. It also becomes painfully clear that the computers would have presented us with all sorts of natural disasters, wars and the Holocaust. This is downright sadistic, because the computers understand that their ancestors experience the simulations as 'real'. The pain and grief we feel are real. But what if these supercomputers were evil, malicious machines? If they would in fact be as intelligent as assumed, they would start arguing with each other in no time about the content they are allowed to simulate. A transhuman society could only remain stable if it keeps up a certain level of ethics.

Apart from all science fiction, something essential emerges from this mix of philosophy and neuroscience. Out of the sensory jambalaya the brain receives, it has to synthesize something sensible. The information it gets delivered consists of nothing more or less than electrical pulses – spikes – and is thus encoded in cuneiform script. There is nothing or no one to provide your brain with a key to decipher this code before it enters your brain. Our brains are faced with the almost impossible task of making sense of all the inputs they receive – of interpreting the objects and events that the inputs cause. It is no exaggeration to say that we ourselves live in a brain-created simulation: a simulacrum. This is not a simulation that grants us a means to play 3D video games, but to mimic or model as closely as possible what is going on around us. To make complex decisions, we need a reliable overview of our situation and our body, an update of our sensory modalities in the here and now.

For some people, this message will be a foregone conclusion. It finds its roots in the work of the philosopher Immanuel Kant (1724–1804) and even the philosophers before him, such as Plato. In his *Prolegomena zu einer jeden künftigen Metaphysik* (*Prolegomena To Any Future Metaphysics* 1783) Kant said:

> And we indeed, rightly consider objects of sense as mere appearances, confess thereby that they are based upon a thing in itself, though we know not this thing as it is in itself, but only know its appearances, viz., the way in which our senses are affected by this unknown something.

The idea that we live in a brain-generated simulacrum has been strongly bolstered by evidence from brain research, not only by myself but also, for instance, by Anil Seth and Steven Lehar.[7]

With illusions such as the 'rotating snakes' by the Japanese psychologist Akiyoshi Kitaoka (Figure 10.4), the realization dawns on us that we do not experience the outside world in an objective manner, but that we are dealing with an interpretation or reconstruction of it. In the case of an illusion, there is, as it were, a crack in the wallpaper of our reconstruction of reality, which leaves room for multiple interpretations. This lack of objectivity is also manifested in illusions or pictures that you can 'see' in two ways. In each of the four images in Figure 10.5, two different perceptual interpretations are possible. Which of the two interpretations is chosen by the brain depends, amongst others, on visual cues in the image (as in the Kanizsa triangle), on the spatial resolution the brain has on offer to interpret the sensory information (Einstein-Monroe) or on the part of the image where you focus your attention and which is kept in your working memory (duck-rabbit). But apart from these obvious, striking cases, the lack of objectivity is something that our brains constantly have to deal with as long as we are awake or dreaming. As Kant already recognized, the *Ding an Sich* – the thing as it is in the external world – cannot be directly known or perceived.

For other people, the idea of a simulacrum created by the brain itself is new, shocking or controversial. There is something in us that intensely and emotionally resists the idea that we cannot see the outside world directly, but only experience a representation of it. The realization that we live in a

Figure 10.4 The 'rotating snakes' illusion by the Japanese psychologist Akiyoshi Kitaoka. The illusion of rotating movement is strongest in the periphery of your field of vision – where your gaze is not directed.
Source: Reproduced with permission of A. Kitaoka, Department of Psychology, Ritsuymikan University, Japan.

simulacrum is upsetting and repugnant to us. The world presents itself to us as 'real' and completely transparent; it is beautifully clear and obvious. In Kant's era, the Scottish philosopher Thomas Reid wrote that there is no 'veil' between us and reality.[8] We do not experience things around us as a product of our fantasy or imagination at all – they are real things that we can see, feel and pick up. Things have a stable presence in our surroundings and are not just conjured up by our imagination. Of course we feel this way. But the reason we experience all perceived things as real and stable is that the constructs our brain produces are designed to make our representation of the world as direct and useful as possible. There is a biological function behind all of this. Moreover, perception is a different form of consciousness than imagination.

Suppose you were to have an experience that reflected all the delays with which sensory signals are transmitted from the farthest corners of your body

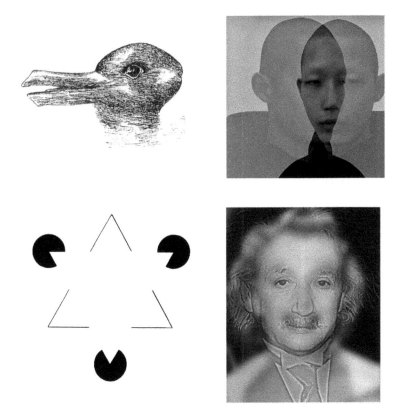

Figure 10.5 Ambiguous images: images that can be seen in two ways. Clockwise from top left: the duck-rabbit figure by Jastrow (1900); a Buddhist monk who looks both to the right and straight ahead (credits: Alain Pichon); portrait that up close is perceived as Albert Einstein, but from afar as Marilyn Monroe; the Kanizsa triangle. For each of the four images, two different perceptual interpretations of the image are possible. The technique of producing 'hybrid images' such as those of Einstein and Monroe was described by Oliva et al. (2006).

to your head. If you bring your foot close to a pleasantly crackling wood fire, it takes about two seconds to transport the mild heat signal from your big toe to your brain,[9] but you seem to feel that snug warmth immediately. Is it convenient or useful to make that delay part of your experience? Would you rather see a tree as the best possible estimate your brain can deliver of it, or as a complicated sum of all kinds of imperfections and noise in your eye lenses, the vitreous body in your eyeballs, your retina and the onward route into your cerebral cortex? For your survival it is more convenient to have a view that corrects for all that junk and clutter along the way, and thus provides a view of what, in our best estimation, is going on around us. The debate between the 'direct realists'[10] and the 'representationalists', who argue that it is a brain-generated representation that we experience, has raged for centuries and flares up from time to time.

What is special about the times we live in is that neuroscience has advanced far enough to show that direct realism is based on a misunderstanding. It is a hard, anatomical and physiological fact that we cannot perceive things in the outside world directly: perception cannot come about by somehow bypassing our senses and nerves (unless we stimulate the brain directly, for example with electrodes). When we stick a bar of chocolate into our mouth, our brain, working with the electrical pulses from the taste buds on our tongue, almost literally makes chocolate out of them. Fortunately, the result is that the chocolate is in fact experienced as direct and real, as opposed to a fantasy or daydream about chocolate. That feels a lot better than tasting a bunch of electric pulses. Perhaps surprisingly, this conclusion is in line with a parable from Buddhism. Two monks are quibbling about a flag waving in the wind. "What is moving here is the flag", says the first. "No", objects the second, "it is the wind that moves". At that moment, a Zen master walks by. "It is neither the flag that moves, nor the wind", he interjects, "it is the mind that moves".[11] Finally, another commenter says, "It all comes down to the same thing – as soon as the mouth opens, it's all false."

Of course, you may now ask: what is the point of all this? If our brains produce a simulation of reality that is so good that we experience it as real, why is it important to tell that there is a difference? Life goes on as it is – business as usual. Later, I will make the case that it is important to make this distinction – not always, but especially in exceptional situations that make a vital difference to people with brain disorders. But first it is time to look more closely at another question: how does the brain manage to build a construct of reality?

11 Predicting the present

How does the brain construct a model of the world and your body?

Before S. K. was treated, he ran an overcrowded shelter for blind youth in a suburb of New Delhi. He was 29 years old and had been practically blind all his life. He managed to get around on the street with a blind cane, and could read written text in Braille. He had learned to understand shapes such as circles and squares through his sense of touch. Could anything ever be done about his handicap? If his eyesight could be restored, would he suddenly see the world as crisply and clearly as a healthy person who opens his eyes when he wakes up?

There are probably as many as 400,000 blind and extremely visually impaired people in India. Many blind children suffer from a congenital form of cataract; a majority of them do not live to see their first birthday. What makes this situation particularly distressing is that blindness is treatable in at least 40 per cent of these children. For about three hundred dollars, the hard, opaque eye lenses that a child is born with can be removed. An artificial lens can be placed in the space freed up under the cornea. One of the initiatives that is slowly improving the fate of these young people is Project Prakash, led by Pawan Sinha and his colleagues at the Massachusetts Institute of Technology (MIT).[1] 'Prakash' is Sanskrit for 'light'.

Apart from the enormous gains to be made for the eyesight of these children, the eye surgeries shed light on the development of visual consciousness in humans. When a newborn baby opens her eyes, does she immediately see the world as it is, or does she have to learn to see? As early as 1890, William James speculated that a baby's experiences would be "one great blooming, buzzing confusion",[2] but he had little to back up his claim. If perception comes down to constructing a representation of the outside world, one expects the brain to learn to distil something recognizable and stable from all the sensory inputs it receives. If someone has been blind from birth, can she dream in visual images and colours? Isn't there something ingrained in our brains that enables us to imagine colours and shapes anyway, even if we have never seen them in the world around us before? If a blind person starts to see later in life, does she automatically understand that a shape she could only grasp by touch (such as a doorknob) corresponds to the newly acquired visual image of the same shape?

DOI: 10.4324/9781003429555-11

Unlike most patients of Project Prakash, S. K. did not suffer from congenital cataract, but from a rare defect called aphakia: the child is born without lenses in both eyes. Otherwise, the eyes are complete. With this defect, a lot of light does reach the retina, but because of the absence of eye lenses, no sharp image of the outside world can be projected onto it (Figure 11.1). In S. K.'s case, this defect could largely be remedied with glasses that correct for the lack of natural eye lenses. The glasses cost less than twenty-five dollars and could be purchased for him thanks to Project Prakash.

What did S. K. see when images from the outside world were sharply focused on his retina for the first time in his life? This turned into a big disappointment. S. K. described his new visual world as a tangle of colours and bright or dark spots with no clear organization or coherence. From the confusing images that came to him, he could distil no objects, no things with a clear outline and 'solidity' or permanence. When he looked at an object such as a chair from different angles or places in a room, he did not see the same object. A picture with a circle overlapping a square produced an inextricable interplay of lines rather than two separate, distinct shapes. If he looked at a picture of several objects in an everyday environment, such as a bicycle parked in the street, he could not make heads or tails out of all the shadow patterns, colour shadings or occlusions – patterns in which part of an object is hidden from view by another thing standing in front of it. Each piece with a slightly different colour or brightness seemed to be a separate 'object' and did not string itself together with another puzzle piece to form a coherent object.

So his newly acquired eyesight was rather underwhelming, at least at first sight. For the team of ophthalmologists there was no point in acting surprised. Older literature on congenital blindness had already indicated that patients do not immediately see well after an operation, as if a veil that was blocking their view of reality were suddenly pulled away. As early as the nineteenth century, a doctor wrote: "The newly operated patients do not localise their visual impressions [...]. They see colours much as we smell an odour of peat or varnish

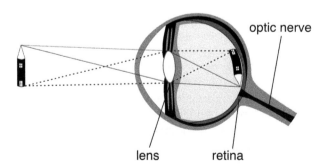

Figure 11.1 The eye as a camera obscura. Due to the curvature of the eye lens, light rays from objects in the outside world are deflected in such a way that the image is projected upside down and sharp on the retina.

[…] but without occupying any specific form of extension in a more exactly definable way."[3]

A few months after S. K. put on his glasses, it became clear that his vision was in fact improving. Whenever a thing began to move within his field of vision – like a car first idling at the side of the road and then starting to move – he could interpret it as a coherent object. Movement acted as a guide to learn to distinguish things. Seemingly separate areas of colour and shiny or dark spots suddenly all moved in the same direction, but remained grouped in space: they joined together to form a coherent thing. It is as if someone with normal vision faces a chameleon, which at first sits still and is totally at one with its surroundings due to its camouflage pattern – and is not noticed to begin with. As soon as the animal jumps forward to catch a grasshopper, the observer suddenly recognizes it. Apart from coherent movement, S. K. also learned to use other visual properties to distinguish things from their surroundings.[4] Think of the spotting pattern of a leopard hiding behind tall savannah grass, helping you to distinguish the outline of the animal despite the interruptions the grass plumes provide in the continuity of its silhouette. An illusion like the Kanizsa triangle (Figure 10.5) shows how our visual system tends to attribute contours that are exactly in line with each other to one and the same thing: a seemingly white triangle that seems to float bright and light above the surface of the three Pac-Man shapes. In the 18 months since S. K. got his glasses, his brain learned to make use of these hints or cues inherent in our natural visual world, and gradually improved its ability to deconstruct scenes into compositions of objects. After his initial disappointment, S. K. became a happier person, no longer confused by a cacophony of impressions, but able to enjoy his visual environment.

That a 29-year-old man can still learn to see with a simple pair of glasses is remarkable. After Torsten Wiesel and David Hubel had completed their research on the electrical responses of cells in the primary visual cortex, they carried out experiments supporting the predominant view that the visual system in our brains goes through a 'critical period' in its development shortly after birth. In humans, the duration of this critical period is estimated to be several months, and during this period there is an increased degree of synaptic plasticity and associated learning capacity of the visual system. In other words, during this period, synaptic connections can easily be made stronger or weaker, often for longer periods of time. A strong synapse exerts more influence on the excitability of the recipient cell than a weak synapse. If the retina is deprived of normal, sharply delineated light patterns in those first months, the system will miss out on an essential link in its development. It will not be able to make up for the damage through later life experiences. Project Prakash, however, showed that the visual system retains some of its ability to learn to perceive even in later life.

What about the ability to jump from one sensory modality to another? Does a patient who is largely cured from his congenital cataract understand that the image of a doorknob corresponds to the shape he feels in his hand when he opens the door? This question was already raised in the seventeenth century by William Molyneux, who was married to a blind woman and is mentioned in *An Essay Concerning Human Understanding* (1689) by the British philosopher John Locke. Molyneux's question is: If a man born blind can feel the differences between various shapes (such as spheres and cubes), would he – if he acquired vision – be able to tell the same objects apart purely by sight, before he was allowed to use his sense of touch? Philosophers have pondered this question for centuries. Some have argued that the sense of touch can be utilized to construct an abstract 'schema' of an object that can be evoked by a new experience (such as newly acquired sight) without having to go through a laborious learning process. Seeing the cube would be enough to recall the abstract scheme and recognize the object immediately. Others thought that humans and animals have no innate ability to directly extract from new visual experiences a three-dimensional model of an object that seamlessly connects to the knowledge gained earlier through feeling the object.

After this bickering had gone on for centuries, Project Prakash provided an answer. When children with congenital cataracts recovered from surgery and were given the opportunity to feel objects with their hands, they were unable to subsequently recognize the same objects visually. There was no ingrained capacity to transfer knowledge from one modality to another. Molyneux's question could finally be answered with a clear 'no'. Yet after a week of visual experience, this answer had to be nuanced: the children became increasingly better at visually recognizing things that had previously passed through their hands. Their recognition scores went from the level of pure guesswork to a percentage of correct scores that was significantly better than could be attributed to chance. Thus, even after early childhood, brain networks appear to remain plastic: they adapt to changing inputs from the outside world and learn to determine whether one input fits another. They remain malleable and capable of learning. It is true that not all visual capacities are amenable to improvement, such as the ability to distinguish very fine visual details. But Project Prakash also demonstrates the power of empirical research: where philosophical arguments remained diametrically opposed through the ages, empirical observations can sometimes, with a bit of luck, bring clarity.

Helmholtz: trimming away time

When we learn to see the world as babies and toddlers, how does this work? This question requires us to delve deeper into the workings of our brains. For conscious perception we may assume that the brain constructs a representation of our situation – that is, of the world around us and of our own bodies – but that does not tell us how this constructive activity is structured. For this we must first consult Johannes Müller's most brilliant pupil: Hermann von Helmholtz (1821–1894).

It is 1849 when Helmholtz (Figure 11.2) and his newly wed wife Olga move from Berlin to the old and distinguished Königsberg in East Prussia. As

Figure 11.2 Portrait of Hermann von Helmholtz (around 1842).

a result of the defeat of Hitler's armies against the Soviets in the Second World War, this city was transformed into the Russian exclave of Kaliningrad, a place full of military activity and rich in Stalinist concrete buildings. But at the time, Königsberg was a thriving, German-speaking trading centre, famous for its stately buildings along the River Pregel and its seven bridges. The university, the Albertina, was founded in 1554 by the Duke of Prussia to spread Lutheran faith and boasted a string of great names. Immanuel Kant was hooked to the city and spent most of his life there, and Helmholtz arrived in the city only decades after his death in 1804. From Königsberg, Kant's philosophy penetrated into the pores of the European natural sciences as practised by Helmholtz and Müller. For Hermann and Olga, the biggest drawbacks of East Prussia were the winter cold and the fog. At Kant's funeral it had been so cold that the ground was frozen stiff and the earth at first refused to take the corpse: it was almost impossible to dig a grave.

Hermann had met Olga in 1847 and instantly fell in love with her. The daughter of a widow in the circle of the philosopher-king Frederick II of Prussia, she met Hermann at a musical soirée of Potsdam's elite. Olga's sister Betty describes Hermann as "very serious and introverted, a little awkward and uncomfortable among all the lively and worldly young men". She character-izes Olga as "not beautiful but finely honed and charming", a good observer, astute to the point of being sarcastic.[5] The couple soon became engaged, but marriage had to wait until Hermann earned enough to support them. With his appointment in Königsberg that time had come.

Seen from the perspective of the twenty-first century, Helmholtz mastered an unlikely number of fields. He did pioneering research into the functioning of the nervous system, hearing and vision. At the same time, he laid the foundations of modern psychophysics, the branch of science that investigates exact connections between physical phenomena such as light and air pressure, the sensitivity of sense organs and brains, and the speed of our motor system reacting to sensory stimuli. But he also revolutionized physics, for instance by formulating the law of energy conservation. En passant, he invented new devices such as the ophthalmoscope, an instrument to look into the eye from the outside and examine its internal tissues. Helmholtz's nearly universal overview of the natural sciences has become virtually impossible in our times because each of its sub-fields has become highly specialized and the professional literature has expanded enormously.

In 1849 Helmholtz concentrates on a specific problem: what is the speed of signals travelling along a nerve? It was already known that nerves could be stimulated electrically and that the excitation of a nerve running to a muscle could cause a contraction. Conversely, it was also discovered that electrical stimulation of a sense organ, such as an ear, can cause a conscious sensation. Johannes Müller had insisted to the young Hermann that it must be practically impossible to measure the speed of nerve conduction, because it would almost certainly approach the speed of light. In Berlin, Helmholtz had gained experience in measuring contractions in the calf muscle of frogs, but this was done with devices that were too inaccurate to record the time differences between excitation and contraction. In the Albertina of Königsberg, Helmholtz and Olga set about building a new laboratory, full of the latest electrical gadgets: current generators, capacitors to store electrical charge and soot-covered, rotating drums on which a metal pen scratches to record the course of muscle contractions in time. Olga, too, throws herself into the new measurements and helps operate the fragile and sensitive instruments. Helmholtz awards her the title of 'Director of Protocol for Observed Measurements', which at the time was about the highest possible status for a woman in science.

The result of the measurements is nothing short of spectacular. Hermann and Olga find an unexpectedly low speed in the propagation of nerve signals: only 25 to 43 metres per second, incredibly more protracted than the speed of light (300,000 kilometres per second), but also much slower than the speed at which an electric current travels through the watery salt solution in which the cells of our body tissues are immersed (about 33,000 kilometres per second). Müller is proved wrong: there appears to be a 'lost time' between the nerve stimulus and the onset of muscle shock – a time reminiscent of Marcel Proust's later magnum opus *À la recherche du temps perdu*.[6] The couple also discovers that there is a short time interval between the arrival of the nerve impulse at the muscle and the moment the contraction starts: about one hundredth of a second. Nowadays it seems only logical that electrical signals need time to dash to and fro in our nervous system, but in the mid-nineteenth century this discovery sparked a revolution. Descartes' idea of brain-mind communication by means of an 'animal spirit' was definitively discarded. The functioning of nerves turned out not to depend on an immaterial substance or mysterious form of energy, but revolves around the conduction of electrical pulses, which happens relatively slowly and neatly obeys the laws of physics. Just as the propagation of sound waves through the air can be understood in terms of physical principles, nerve pulses can be understood in terms of the operation of molecular and electrical processes in the tiny fibres that make up nerves.

However, even in this physics story, questions pop up. If an electrical impulse, generated directly in a nerve, needs time to travel to a muscle, it will take an even longer time for the brain to send an impulse that reaches the muscle. This is because the nerve that excites the calf muscle originates in the spinal cord, which contains intermediate cells controlled by the brain. If the brain is the source of the command that gets our muscles moving, time would have to pass between this command and the actual physical movement. Helmholtz's father was a philosopher, and in a letter to his son he remarks: "Concerning your experiments, the results seemed to me from the outset a little strange, for I do not feel my thoughts and bodily reactions as taking place successively, but rather simultaneously."[7] Helmholtz replies that he had no doubt that

> the interactions between spiritual and corporeal acts always originate in the brain, and that consciousness and spiritual activity have nothing to do with the time taken for information to come from the skin, the retina or the ear, and that for the soul this nervous conduction inside the body is just as good as outside like the conduction of a sound from its place of origin to the ear.

This answer may have reassured his father, but it still leaves us with the feeling that we are stuck in the same quandary as Descartes. How do interactions between mental and physical activity take shape? Is this not more of the same dualism from which Descartes could not escape? Even if we take the 'lost time' between nerve impulse and perception for granted, what happens between the arrival of that nerve impulse in the brain and the moment we perceive the stimulus as something that happens outside of ourselves? The 'solution' Helmholtz presents to his father must have been unsatisfactory to him as well, for in his later years he comes up with a more substantiated story.

Hermann and Olga have since had two children, but Olga finds it increasingly difficult to bear the bleak Baltic climate and suffers from a lung disease. Via Bonn, the family ends up in Heidelberg, where Hermann sets about writing a monumental anthology of more than a thousand pages – the *Handbook of Physiological Optics* – in which he condenses all the knowledge about vision gathered to date.[8] Helmholtz picks up the thread that Müller had rolled out: the relationship between natural, external stimuli and sensations.

Helmholtz argues that sensations are something quite different from the physical phenomena that cause them. Müller had already recognized that we can experience light sensations without our eyes being physically stimulated by light, for example by a brief distortion of an eyeball. However, we also recognize that there is a kind of radiation that harnesses too little energy per particle (photon) to be able to cause a sensation of light: infrared light, which can cause a sensation of warmth but does not sufficiently excite the light-sensitive cells (cones and rods) in our retina. Thus, there is no unambiguous relationship between radiation as a physical phenomenon and the sensation of light.

At this point Helmholtz goes a step further than Müller. Percepts of objects outside ourselves, he says, are representations resulting from psychic activity. This activity enables us to recognize an object, and this recognition amounts to making a judgement about the cause of the sensory stimulation. Our psyche makes an inference about something in the outside world that triggers the sensory inputs. When we see a candle flame, we are not literally seeing the particles of light impinging on our retina, but a representation of what we judge to be causing that particle pattern: a burning candle. When we listen to music, we do not hear a mixture of waves in air pressure in all kinds of frequencies, but a clear and vivacious melody coming from a violin. Sniffing at a glass of wine, it is not the chemical bonding of all kinds of molecules to the membrane of cells in our nasal cavity that we experience, but we are subject to a deliciously wood-ripened aroma rising from the glass.

Sensory inference is a process that can be interpreted as your 'best estimate' of what is going on. This does not happen for free, but is the result of a learning process. By positing this, Helmholtz contradicts many of his contemporaries, who believed that our perceptual capacities are predetermined before we are born and are 'ready' to grant us a full view of the world as soon as we see the first light of day. Helmholtz ripostes that infants and toddlers must first learn to distil a meaningful representation of their environment from the jumble of sensory inputs their brains receive. Even if vision is acquired later in life, the brain has retained some capacity to learn to see and recognize complex objects. The patients of Project Prakash frankly prove Helmholtz right.

With his thesis on sensory inference, Helmholtz takes perception away from physics and places it downright in the realm of psychology. What we perceive is different from the thing in the outside world that causes that percept. By consequence, our conscious experience of colours, smells and shapes can consist of no more than symbols or signs. If we see a blue sea before us, the colour blue refers to a physical property of the light reflected from the sea into our eyes. 'Blue' is merely a symbol that typifies the light of the sea in a certain way, and so it may well be a rather arbitrary sign – a sign that something is going on in our world, in this case the water taking on a particular tint of blue as it waves towards the surf. This sign can be just as arbitrary as the symbols of which language is composed and which we learn to write and spell one by one at school. If symbols or representations were completely arbitrary, then you might perceive the colour of a tomato as red where I see green – even though we would both speak of the same tomato as being red.

That perception essentially consists of forming a belief or conviction about something in the outside world that causes patterns of sensory stimulation can be seen as a leap forward. This belief or estimate is not initially expressed in words, but in what we perceive: shape, colour, sound, taste, a sense of turning or speeding up. An advantage of the idea of sensory inference is that it does not need to produce an 'internal picture' in the brain – a need to which the supporters of the motor-sensory theory object – but places the cause of the sensory inputs in the outside world: *what* we perceive happens outside our brain. The information carriers that produce the belief may reside in our brains, but the content of that belief is located in the world outside them. Returning to the discontent Helmholtz's father felt when he wrote to his son that his thoughts and bodily reactions are experienced simultaneously, it can now be argued that this is part of our belief or set of assumptions that shape our perceptions. If, on a summer's day, I suddenly find myself with my foot on a hot stretch of beach, my brain constructs my experience of the situation in such a way that it seems as if I am withdrawing my foot at the same moment. 'I pull back my foot as soon as it touches the sand' – but this is only an appearance of a state of affairs. The time it takes for the heat stimulus on my foot to travel to my brain is not part of the end result of the construction. My brain apparatus 'trims away' a piece of time from the actual sequence of events in my body. It only seems that I become aware of the heat at the same moment as my foot touches the sand. That a piece of time gets 'lost' is thus the consequence of an active brain process, by which sensory inputs are, as it were, edited. Another powerful way of illustrating this process is by illusions (Figures 10.4 and 10.5) that derive their power from the conflicting information they offer, so that we are forced to switch back and forth between one hypothesis ('the snakes are rotating') and another ('the snakes are standing still').

At the same time, Helmholtz's move is a caper from biology to psychology that raises new questions. Who or what makes all these judgements? How does the brain spin a sensory inference out of electrical stimuli? These questions keep recurring regularly, but we need to keep courage. If only there were a simple answer! In my experience, it is precisely these moments of 'being stuck', unfulfilled curiosity and the abrasive mental itch of just-not-knowing, that lead to new discoveries and insights. Helmholtz did not get around to elaborating on his buck jump; he died in 1894. Shortly before his death, he could look back on a gigantic career, laden as he was with medals and other badges of honour. He knew the great minds of Europe, who all recognized the importance of his discoveries and inventions, and had founded a new research institute with his friend Werner von Siemens, founder of the industrial empire bearing the same name. He was a member of the privy council of the German emperor, Kaiser Wilhelm II, an honorary post he was delighted with.

By then, it had been 35 years since the inclement Baltic climate had finally taken its revenge on the couple and Olga had died. Their move to the milder environment of Heidelberg had been to no avail. Hermann had dealt with the shock through hard work and fanatically playing music. In one of his last photos, he poses in a lecture hall with all kinds of formulas chalked on the blackboard – but he looks a bit tired and sad. In his later years, his views on psychology were increasingly questioned, and even William James – by no means an opponent of the study of brain and consciousness – launched painful attacks on him. With the rise of Charles Sherrington, the climate shifted to the study of reflexes as the basis for all our behaviour. Helmholtz's psychological legacy, which emphasized the adaptive and creative capacities of brain systems, had to prepare for a long hibernation.

And so it happened that early psychology, which had an eye for consciousness as a subjective given, gradually gave way to behaviourism. This movement grew under the wings of Ivan Pavlov and John Watson, who tried to explain human and animal behaviour as a result of reflexes and simple learning processes. They focused on learning the link between sensory inputs and reward or punishment, modifying motor or involuntary (autonomous) output, such as salivation in Pavlov's dogs upon hearing a bell that predicts a slab of meat. Watson rejected introspection as a method of ascertaining psychological processes or 'psychic activity' and conceived the brain more or less as a 'black box' whose precise workings could not be unravelled. The psyche was a subjective entity that by definition fell outside the realm of scientific, objective study. Infamous is Watson and his student Rosalie Rayner's experiment with a nine-month-old baby (known as 'Albert') in which Pavlov's learning method was used to induce a phobia in the child by having it play with a white laboratory rat and linking each touch of the animal to a terrifying noise.[9] As expected, little Albert was indeed frightened by the rat but also by other hairy white things, such as a Santa Claus with a white beard. No attempt was made to cure Albert of his fear.

Influenced by black box thinking in the early twentieth century, the new generation of psychologists came to regard Helmholtz as a symbol of the old, established order, unpopular with some politicians and thinkers such as Lenin, who felt that he placed too much emphasis on the subjective in humans and therefore dismissed his views as 'bourgeois'. What also didn't help was that the old German order was turned upside down in this period: on 10 November 1918, Kaiser Wilhelm II, faithfully served by Helmholtz but now considered by many to be a key figure in unleashing the First World War, sought asylum in the Netherlands upon his arrival at the small station of Eijsden, near Maastricht. It was not until deep into the twentieth century that a modern psychology emerged with an eye to the cognitive and constructive properties of the brain.[10] The realization that the human mind is more complex than a collection of stimulus-response reflexes slowly began to flare up again.

How could the complex organization of cognitive processes be made more tangible? By 1970, there was still a huge gap between all the forms of cognition that psychologists were interested in and the basic knowledge about neurons that neuroanatomists and physiologists had accumulated. For psychologists it was nice to know that Hubel and Wiesel had found cells in the visual cortex which respond electrically to moving rods, but this gave little clue as to how our brains perceive an entire visual scene. The highest achievement in brain research, leading physiologists felt at the time, was to describe how brain cells work, how they are synaptically connected and what chemical messengers they use to influence each other.[11]

Mental arithmetic with brain cells: the discovery of neural networks

To move on from the questions left by Helmholtz, we turn to a younger field within brain research: computational neuroscience. This may sound a bit intimidating, but it is less complicated than it seems at first glance. This branch of neuroscience has grown out of the insight that brain cells do more than just produce electrical pulses and release transmitter molecules onto each other. Computational neuroscience understands the brain as a special kind of computer: a complex and versatile calculator. It does not take the brain to be an ordinary home computer with one very fast, information-processing unit, but a computer that consists of a huge number of information-processing units: the neurons.

During the Second World War, Warren McCulloch, a neurophysiologist in Chicago, came to suspect that brain cells could function at a different conceptual level than the pure, wet anatomy and physiology of material synapses, axons and cell bodies: the level at which neurons perform calculations. As brain cells fire pulses, they are also calculating – with, and by virtue of, those pulses. If you feed a network of neurons with sensory, electrically encoded information, the network – if properly constructed – can perform calculations on those inputs to control our eyes, arms or fingers. The light patterns reflected from an apple into our eyes are converted by an elaborate brain network into motor signals for executing a grasping motion. Around 1942, McCulloch met Walter Pitts, who at the time had no income and was homeless. Walter had grown up in a family with a father and brothers who treated him roughly and regarded him as a freak, but at the same time he emerged as a child prodigy. At the age of 12, he was already making critical notes on the work of the British philosopher and logician Bertrand Russell, with whom he corresponded. Walter was extremely timid, shy of people and introverted, and with his thick glasses, bad teeth and habit of twisting his hair into curls, he was not an attractive boy to make contact with. At parties, he felt like a 'mutant', unable to ask anyone to dance. He had an enormous aversion to revealing his name and refused to sign forms and papers. Later in life, this led to his being denied access to prestigious positions at the Massachusetts Institute of Technology. Eccentric as Pitts may have been, he remains one of the great heroes of this story. Together with McCulloch he built a mathematical proof demonstrating that networks of brain cells can perform the same calculations as the kind of computers we use in our everyday lives (quantum computers, because of their unique computing capabilities, fall outside this domain). McCulloch and Pitts' work formed the very basis on which artificial intelligence researchers in the 1960s, such as Marvin Minsky, developed computer models of neural networks.

An essential ingredient of McCulloch and Pitts' brilliant work is that a brain cell is conceived as an abstract, mathematical computational unit, which as such is stripped of its biological details such as a membrane of fatty molecules and the production of transmitter molecules. The brain is transformed from a blubbery mass into a gigantic calculating machine, without looking like the calculating machine we all know. The living neuron is abstracted into a mathematical model neuron. This contains, first of all, a component on which synaptic inputs from other cells are received (this represents the dendrites of the neuron, which receive inputs from other cells). These inputs are added up and passed on to the next component, which represents the cell body where all the dendrites come together (Figure 11.3). The cell body model uses a threshold to determine whether the sum of synaptic inputs is strong enough to cause the cell to fire spikes or not. This 'decision' is summarized in a number that represents the output of the neuron and this is immediately sent to all the cells that the model neuron projects to. These are the cells to which the spike-emitting neuron sends its axons and with which it has established synaptic connections. So the model neuron essentially works as before, except that the slimy and greasy details are left out.

With these abstract neuronal units, small networks can be constructed that can perform cognitive functions such as sorting apples and pears according to their sensory characteristics, fed into a first layer of cells. The bottom part of Figure 11.3 shows what is needed for this task: a network consisting of one layer of cells that all project, with their axons and synaptic endings, to a next layer of cells. The first layer of cells processes sensory inputs such as the colour or brightness of image dots that are presented to the network via camera images in the form of series of numbers. The connections between the first- and second-layer cells are plastic: this allows the network to learn to translate the sensory inputs into an output that is produced by the cells of the second layer. This output encodes the category or class to which the presented image belongs: apple or pear. To learn properly, the network needs to be trained on a lot of example images of apples and pears, each supplied with the correct answer: based on the mistakes that the network makes while learning, it receives feedback that can be used to adjust the strengths of the synapses. But after this learning process you get something worth every penny: a simple network that can nevertheless do interesting cognitive work. The deep learning networks that are currently making headlines in artificial intelligence are much more elaborate than this two-layer network, but they are based on the same principles.

The classical neural networks of yesteryear, as well as many modern deep learning networks, use one-way communication: inputs are always passed from a first layer of neurons to the next layer, and so on to subsequent layers. The later, higher layers do not send information back to the earlier ones.[12] This

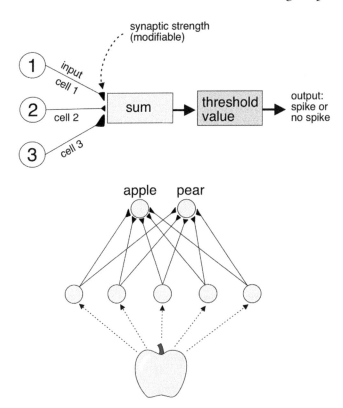

Figure 11.3 (Above) Abstract, mathematical representation of a neuron. The neuron adds up the inputs it receives from other cells (1, 2 and 3). The result of this summation shows whether the threshold for firing a spike is exceeded or not. (Below) These 'McCulloch-Pitts' neurons can be used to build a neural network that learns to sort images into apples and pears. The bottom layer of cells (circles) encodes sensory characteristics such as colour and shape of an apple. This layer projects to a higher layer of only two cells, where the synaptic connections coming in from the bottom layer (black triangles) are plastic. These two cells encode the category 'apple' (neuron on the left) or 'pear' (neuron on the right).

structure for propelling signals forward through the network (a 'feedforward' architecture) does not bode well for the idea Helmholtz had in mind: he conceived perception as the construction of a representation or hypothesis of what causes the sensory inputs. You might say: the cause of inputs is the apple or the pear in the presented image, and that distinction is exactly what the network spits out as output. But here the output consists of only two numbers: one cell fires at 'pear', for example, the other only at 'apple'. Something or someone is needed to interpret that firing of cells as something you can observe and or talk about: what does the activity actually mean? The network does not make a reconstruction or representation of the original image that causes the inputs to it. How could the brain do this? In this situation, the only material it has available to do this lies in the sensory inputs themselves. From this arises the idea that we need to build a different kind of architecture – a network that can construct from the sensory inputs a representation of their cause, and then allows the correctness of that representation to be tested against those same sensory inputs.

This culminates in a new design in which sensory inputs are first processed by a bottom layer that sends its signals to a middle layer and hence on to a top layer (Figure 11.4). The representation encoded by the joint electrical activity of cells in this top layer has the nature of a prediction. The functioning of this type of network is therefore called '*Predictive Coding*'. The prediction is not about gazing into the crystal ball of your future, but about the sensory inputs that are flowing into the brain at the same moment.[13] So prediction is about the present: what is happening in the outside world that explains the sensory inputs that are coming in *now*? With this, the prediction can also be described as a 'best guess' representation of the sensory causes or – to stay with Helmholtz – as an inference about them.[14]

With the activity in the top layer, the network is not yet complete. The cells of this layer send their axons back to the middle layer, which in turn projects

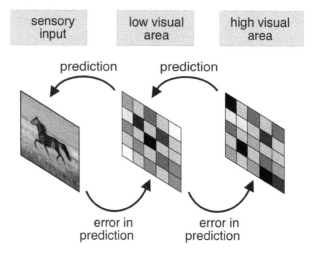

Figure 11.4 Network for Predictive Coding. Visual inputs derived from a horse are processed by the lower, sensory layer of the network (left). The network's function is to represent the horse, as the cause of the sensory inputs, in the best possible way. This is done in the middle and right-hand layers, which mimic a low and high visual area, respectively. The representation consists of a pattern in which some neurons are more active than others (indicated by shades of grey; each square is a neuron). At these two levels, the horse is not externally recognizable as such. Through an interplay of predictions and error messages, the network is able to improve and learn from its representations.

Source: Adapted from: Dora, Pennartz and Bohte (2018).

back to the bottom layer, so that the middle-layer prediction is transferred to the level where the sensory data comes in. A crucial step is to compare this prediction with the actual state of the sensory inputs. This comparison is accomplished using another mathematical operation that neurons can perform: subtraction.

While the addition of inputs can be explained as the convergence of excitatory (activity-enhancing) synapses on the dendritic trees of neurons (Figure 11.3), a subtraction can be performed using a combination of an excitatory and an inhibitory synapse. This way, cells in the lower layer can determine the difference between the prediction and the actual input. In other words, an error value is calculated in the accuracy of the prediction compared to the real sensory inputs. Like the apple-pear network of Figure 11.3, a network that learns to code predictively starts from a totally naive, untrained state – like a baby that still has to learn everything from scratch. The error signal determined by the cells in the bottom layer can be transmitted via their axons to cells in a higher layer, whose synapses can be altered to allow the network to make ever better predictions: its representations of what is happening in the outside world become ever more accurate. This reminds us of the children who were born blind and only started to see later in life: their 'seeing' is probably also the result of a learning process by which their brains are able to concoct better and better representations of their visual environment.

Even when a predictive coding network has finished learning, it still needs some time to make sense of an arbitrary sensory input coming in via the eyes. For example, if you input a totally new image into the bottom layer – say, the image of a pink-purple striped elephant you have never seen before – the network still needs several waves of activity backwards and forwards to converge to a good representation of it. Also in this process, the error signal is important. So even an accomplished network needs some time to arrive at a decent representation of the world. This is consistent with tests showing that the human brain needs a measurable amount of time to arrive at a perception it can tell something about.

In recent years, the interest in Predictive Coding has surged.[15] Researchers realize that the constructive and creative capacities of the brain cannot be ignored when it comes to perceiving and learning to perceive. This is good news for Helmholtz, even though this reappraisal is rather late in coming. But it is especially good news for anyone looking for connections between neuroscience and psychology: a fusion between these two traditionally separate disciplines is slowly but surely taking place. In a large European research project, the Human Brain Project, I have been doing research on Predictive Coding at the University of Amsterdam together with Sander Bohte from the Centre for Mathematics and Computer Science, Shirin Dora, Matthias Brucklacher, Kwangjun Lee and others. We examine the way Predictive Coding may work in the brain. Shirin expanded an older model with two network layers[16] into a deeper network – a network with many layers – that increasingly resembles the architecture of the visual system of the cerebral cortex (in Figure 11.4 this depth is symbolized by only three layers). Strikingly, during the learning process the model neurons start to behave more and more like cells in the living visual cortex. The activity in the lower layers looks much like what Hubel and Wiesel saw in the primary visual cortex, whereas the higher layers respond to whole objects and faces – just as is seen in the inferotemporal cortex, on the ventral side of the temporal lobe. Strikingly, Hubel and Wiesel saw hardly any responses to natural images in their V1 cells – which, according to Predictive Coding, can be explained by the fact that the structure of these images had already been learned during prior learning, so that they became increasingly predictable and thus produce minor errors.

Quite possibly, I am feverishly infected by enthusiasm for Predictive Coding as a paradigm for explaining perception. With a dose of healthy scepticism one might object: all well and good, but this is still about a network that only performs calculations on numbers – where is the conscious experience of colours and flavours? This makes us face the Hard Problem again: the rich, qualitative domain of our conscious experience is something other than a series of calculations, or the circuits of brain cells that perform them. It may seem like we are back to square one, but yet something has happened. The problem is not as hopeless as it seemed, but will still need our closest attention: I will argue later that Predictive Coding provides an important cornerstone to understand consciousness, but is not sufficient on its own to crack the Hard Problem. But let us stay positive for a pause: over almost two centuries, Helmholtz has given us the idea of sensory inference and we can convert this with today's supercomputers into network models that mimic this brain process. We now have tools in our hands to investigate how the brain constructs a representation or hypothesis about visual inputs received. A hypothesis, by definition, relates to something: it is about something. I expect research on Predictive Coding to soar: it will nestle in intelligent machines and robots[17] and develop into a basic standard model of perception and cognition, similar to the model physicists use to explain the behaviour of elementary particles. Before we delve deeper into the relationship between Predictive Coding and consciousness, it is necessary to address another question that can no longer be swept under the carpet: where in the brain is the 'I' that experiences all of these representations?

12 A strange encounter with the world, your body and yourself

A brief autobiography of self-awareness

In a room in the east London suburb of Hackney, Peter Chadwick is writing in his diary. It is 1979 and he has not had an easy time of it. He is 33 years old. His father died when he was eight years old and he grew up in a single-parent household, accompanied by his mother Edie and his mentally handicapped brother. As an adolescent and teenager, Peter presents himself as invulnerable and strong, is the apple of his mother's eye and feels insensitive to the social isolation of the little family. Beneath his firm exterior, a softer, feminine structure slowly develops, which manifests itself in travesty. He grows his nails and dons a feminine, cherubic garment. There is gossip at school and in the neighbourhood. He is bullied and ridiculed and, after leaving school, moves from town to town, haunted by scandals that make him a 'local celebrity'. At the same time, he tries to maintain his macho image through athletics and boxing.

While he sits writing in his little room, Peter notices something strange. It starts to rain, harder and harder, the drops hitting the windows. When the story he is writing takes a dramatic turn, it starts to rain harder. When his words soften, the rain calms down too. There seems to be a mystical connection between Peter's mind and the outside world. He has the idea that the outside world is addressing him; he has the feeling that the outside world was 'meant just for him'. This ties in with an experience he had recently, when he turned on the radio and started listening to a well-known DJ. The DJ was making mocking jokes about a cupid-like girl (*'cherub girl'*) and Peter strongly related this to himself, given his tendency to dress like a woman. It became clear to Peter that the DJ was talking about him: the slander and backbiting had reached national dimensions. The thought crept up on Peter that he was being watched by everyone and everything and that the outside world was totally preoccupied with him. This was not just annoying. It sometimes made his mood euphoric: from his socially isolated position he was now turning into a national celebrity. That he was constantly followed on the radar of the outside world gave him the grandiose feeling that he mattered. The outside world was constantly passing on 'signs' or signals to him: nothing happened by chance any more.

Of course there had to be a logical explanation for this state of affairs. Peter began to see the connection between the national media and the signs he

DOI: 10.4324/9781003429555-12

picked up on the street in the light of an all-encompassing Organization. The messages the Organization conveyed to him became increasingly unambiguous: "Change or die!" This reminded Peter of his mother, who had died in the meantime. She, too, had propagated this hard-line attitude during the tough times of Peter's youth. Peter suspected that his mother had some influence on the Organization, ruling from her grave. Through an accumulation of apparent coincidences, Peter came to realize that his death was imminent. The only question was how it should be accomplished. At that moment, Peter had a job in the accounting department of a company, and a man in the packaging department shouted something to a colleague about the way an order should be delivered: "He has to do it by bus!" For Peter it was clear that this man also belonged to the Organization, and he interpreted the message as an indication of how to commit suicide. Two days later Peter threw himself under a double-decker bus on New King's Road in Fulham. In his mind, this street referred to the Way of the New King (Jesus), a role that Peter could take on once the satanic forces would be driven out of him. From a pathetic, penniless outsider in Hackney, Peter was transformed into the grandiose Saviour of Mankind. Peter was pulled from under the wheels of the double-decker and taken by ambulance to Charing Cross Hospital. He survived his suicide attempt and was given medication for psychosis. From then on, he began to recover, physically and mentally.

Chadwick's brave, open account of his schizophrenia is remarkable because it is not limited to the dry, clinical symptoms of this devastating mental illness. It is mainly about what happens to a person in a world that is taken over by delusions.[1] A characteristic of schizophrenia is the blurring of boundaries between the 'self' and the outside world, as evidenced by Peter's account of the rain that lashes down intensely on the rhythm of thoughts he records. He loses control over what he thinks is the case in the world, and is unable to steer his own thinking properly. His delusions take control: he can no longer determine for himself which events attributed to the outside world originate from his own interpretations and imagination. He becomes a slave to an internal system that imposes a false belief on him – the conviction that he is at the centre of a global organization that is plotting on his life. When he is walking down the street and sees a man in the distance saying something to a passer-by, he takes it as a slanderous comment on himself, whereas it would be obvious to an outsider that the man is too far away for Chadwick to understand. The delusions dictate how Peter must think and how he perceives and interprets things. He must and will find out where all the signs lead.

In our search for the relationship between consciousness and brain, the 'self' is an important element that has been missing from the story so far. What is the 'self' and what takes place in our brains when the 'I' comes to the fore? Consciousness has emerged as a phenomenon that gives us a multimodal overview of our situation in the world. But this definition of consciousness will ultimately fail if we cannot explain how this overview relates to the subject having this overview: to ourselves. If we follow the thesis that conscious experiences arise from the constructive activity of our brain – whereby a large network of neurons generates an internal model or simulacrum of our current situation – then the question remains, who or what is undergoing these experiences? Who is the person who watches all this constructive activity, with its exuberant displays of colours, sounds, tastes, pleasures and other splendours?

The beginnings of an answer can be traced in that the 'self' is a layered concept – one with a number of different elements that are closely intertwined, but also have a structure and even a hierarchy between them. Let us return to the Cambrian primeval seas of Chapter 9 and see what challenges *Pikaia* and other primitive life forms faced as they began to move across the seabed in search of food and fleeing from predators such as *Anomalocaris*.

Where does this movement come from?

In the beginning was the Word, says the Bible, but the brain's evolution obeys the adage: in the beginning there was movement. Once an organism can detect movement, it is able to do interesting things. What does detection of movement mean to an animal? A movement means either that the animal itself moves, or that something other than the animal in the environment changes position. To survive in the primordial soup, it is absolutely essential to be able to make this distinction. You can detect movement with different senses: sight, touch (someone brushes your skin while you keep your eyes closed), hearing (in the street you are passed by an ambulance that races past with a loud siren) and the balance organ in your inner ear, which provides information about accelerations and rotations that your head undergoes in three dimensions. For all these senses, our evolutionary history has witnessed the development of matching circuits of neurons that are sensitive to the speed of movement: they measure the distance a stimulus travels in a given time period.

The fact that primeval animals must have had neural circuits to detect movement using light information marks a huge step forward in animal evolution. But how could the brain determine what was moving: the animal itself or a thing in the outside world? When an object approaches the animal, it has to work out at lightning speed whether it is a threatening predator or a source of food. It will either flee or attack. Even if the object is stationary and the animal itself moves, it must decide whether to stay on course or make a turn, but at least the situation is safer for the time being and the animal is more in control of its own fate.

To be able to make this distinction, the principle of *'efference copy'* developed in the early evolution of animals. If an animal itself moves actively – and thus not by passively drifting along on a sea current – this means that the motor centres of the primitive brain will send a command signal to the musculature to make the tail muscles beat. *'Efference'* means 'outgoing': it refers to signals that are sent from the motor parts of the brain to the body (Figure 12.1), as opposed to signals that are sent to the brain (afferent signals). Below I will use the more appropriate term 'command copy'.

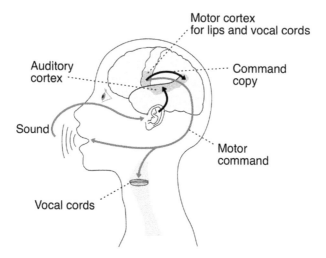

Figure 12.1 Principle of command copy. Movement of the lips and vocal cords are controlled by a part of the motor cortex (grey arrows). At the same time, a copy of this command is sent to the auditory cortex (upper black arrow). When physical speech is produced by movement of the lips and vocal chords, this sound information is processed via the inner ear and next by the auditory cortex. With the confluence and integration of the command copy with the sound information in the auditory cortex, the brain is able to determine that the cause of the sound lies within the person. For more information on brain control over the vocal cords, see Dichter, Breshears, Leonard and Chang (2018).

In addition to immediately sending motor commands to muscles, a copy of these signals is sent to sensory centres within the brain. If a visual centre of the brain detects a movement, but also receives information that a movement command is being sent, the conclusion can be drawn that the perceived movement is caused by its own motor activity. A fish wiggles its tail, so it is logical that visual movement is detected in its brain: self-induced movement in the visual scene. By the same token, the command copy acts as a predictive signal: when the brain sends out the command "tail move!", there will be a change in the visual world that is expected on the basis of the forward motion that is going to take place. This is consistent with the theory of Predictive Coding and the principle is supported by recent experimental research.[2] For the time being, this is purely and simply a cold calculation by nerve cells and says little about consciousness or self-awareness. We still seem light years away from the delusions that schizophrenic patients suffer from. Nevertheless, the principle of command copy lays a foundation for building a construction of the 'self' further down the line of evolution. En passant, the predictive effect of a command copy also explains why it is barely possible to tickle yourself: the funny feeling is much stronger when someone else runs their fingers over your skin than when you do it yourself, because the other person's movements – as opposed to your own – are hardly predictable.

How do we envision the transition from this motor, primitive 'self', as yet devoid of consciousness, to the subjective 'self' to which we attribute our mental faculties and which faces the world so proudly and intrepidly? Once again, we are tempted to seek a direct connection between a neuronal embodiment and a mental, spiritual form of the 'self'. But this leads us straight back into the trap of dualism. It is more fruitful to observe soberly that the principle of command copy only lays a basis of malleable dough for the layered cake of which our complete 'self' is composed. What will the next layer of the cake consist of?

Would the owner of this body part please come forward?

Early in the evolution of animals, the ability to gather information about who or what is moving was of colossal importance. Equally relevant is the ability to distinguish between your own body and the rest of the world. Elongated organisms such as moray eels or snakes have to discriminate in an instant whether something wriggling through their field of vision belongs to their own body or to someone else's: is it an edible morsel or something that needs protecting? Is damage to this meandering thing a reason to bite through or to tend to one's own wound? It seems obvious that we can automatically determine which objects in our environment belong to our own body and which do not, especially if we have knowledge of our own motor commands. If the tail-shaped thing obeys the motor command our brain sends out, it belongs to 'us', our own body. If not, it is not part of our body and becomes something to be investigated, feared or devoured. But this distinction is not so easy to make in all species: an octopus has eight long, writhing arms full of suction cups. Each of these arms has a certain autonomy – an ability to produce its own movements independently of the central brain in the head.[3] Despite this relative autonomy, the brain of this animal is able to distil, from the multitude of sensory signals, where each arm is globally located in space and how it moves. This way the octopus brain prevents the eight limbs from getting tangling up and enables coherent behaviour of all those arms at the same time, as is necessary for the capture of prey.

Apart from the primitive motor 'self', secured by the principle of command copy, the 'self' also exists as a bodily integrity. Our body normally consists of a torso, two legs, two arms, a head, with some odd appendages such as a coccyx, some body hair, auricles and lips that enclose a cavity which can be opened in all sorts of strange and wondrous ways. Anything outside your body, like the fingers of a loved one with whom one of your hands is entwined, does not belong to you, no matter how dear the other person is to you. You have feelings in your own fingers, not in those of your loved one – no matter how hard you try to empathize with this significant other. The feeling you can experience in all parts of your body is anchored in the body map of the somatosensory cortex (Figure 7.1). The patterns of neural activity in this area of the cortex – together with those in connected areas in the wider cortical network – are at least as important for the feeling of having an integral body as the physical parts of our body themselves. This was already underlined by the feeling that the woman with amelia, A. Z., had in the phantoms of limbs she had never possessed.

In rare cases, the sense of physical individuality – the feeling that we own a body – can be affected by brain damage. A stroke in the right hemisphere of the brain can damage areas of the parietal lobe and an area hidden beneath the surface (the insular cortex) to such an extent that the patient feels that a part of the body no longer belongs to her. Sometimes this involves a whole half of the body, but more often it is an arm or leg. These estranged limbs are located on the opposite side of the body relative to the brain hemisphere being affected: damage in the right hemisphere causes problems on the left side of the body. The loss of subjective 'ownership' (somatoparaphrenia) manifests itself when the patient, lying in a hospital bed, tries to push her leg out of bed: in her experience, this is a strange, external object that she wants nothing to do with.[4] To an outsider, this seems bizarre: after all, the patient can *see* that her leg is attached to the rest of her body. But when it comes to our very own physicality, vision is not as dominant as it is in experiencing the outside world – 'the world at a distance'. Often, somatoparaphrenia is accompanied by a loss of sensation in the part of the body that is experienced as alien, as well as by a half-sided or more limited paralysis of the body.

By consequence, the brain can no longer process sensory stimuli from the 'dispossessed' leg; the brain becomes sensorially cut off from it. To be more precise: higher regions of the cerebral cortex can no longer integrate the inputs from the leg into the conscious experience of the situation in which the patient finds himself. If, moreover, the leg no longer responds to motor commands that the brain would normally send to it via the spinal cord and thus remains paralyzed in bed, these higher areas draw the 'conclusion' that there is no reason to assume that the leg 'belongs'. Again, this is not a conclusion articulated in words, but a sensory inference: in reconstructing or assessing the state of the body, the brain lacks evidence that the leg is an integral part of the body, and so it is considered part of the outside world. Meanwhile, there is another leg in the bed, but this contains sense organs that do communicate with the brain. As soon as this leg comes into contact with the passive, communicatively isolated leg, the sensation of touching a strange, warm piece of meat arises – "Off with it, out of bed!"

Distortions of one's own body image can take even stranger forms. Some patients hit by stroke in the brain's right hemisphere said that they suffered from the illusion that they were not wanting to dispose of a limb, but rather that they were gaining something. One of these people could no longer see anything in the left half of his field of vision and was paralyzed in his left leg and arm without realizing it. He started complaining about a 'nest of hands' in his bed and asked the doctor to amputate these organs and put them in a bag. Six days later, when the man had become aware of his half-sided paralysis, he described how his left hand began to shrink and give way to a new hand, which became increasingly fleshy and bulky.[5] Upon further questioning, the man actually appeared to think that there were several extra hands on his body – hands without arms – two of which were located at the level of his left knee.

How exactly this case can be understood is an open question, but it is likely that the stroke led to a reorganization of the brain network underlying the representation of one's own body image. Possibly, the loss of conscious sensation in the left half of the body is linked to the construction of a representation of extra body parts (the nest of hands) because there are still residual sensory signals transmitted from the left body half that are internally explained as a set of extra appendages, as a substitute for body parts considered lost.[6] This also fits in well with the principle of Predictive Coding: the brain constructs a 'best guess' representation that attempts to predict the incoming signals. As this process succeeds better and better, the error in the prediction is reduced and the input is thus 'explained away'.

Apart from brain damage, our sense of body ownership is easily susceptible to other disturbances of brain function, for example by psychoactive substances. When users of ketamine enter a 'K-hole', psychedelic phenomena occur such as an *out-of-body* experience (the subjective experience of stepping outside your own body) or the feeling that your body is merging with your surroundings. The distinction between your own body and the outside world temporarily ceases to exist.[7] These (risky) trips rub the difference between consciousness and self-consciousness in our faces: ketamine induces an altered perception of the 'self', but the user remains conscious – he does not become unconscious.

What does this difference between consciousness and self-awareness come down to? By consciousness, I mean purely experiencing all sensory qualities of the situation around us and in our bodies – experiencing a multimodal overview of the world including our bodies. You can lie there daydreaming and, moments later, stare outside and be aware of roof-tiled houses, bicycles and cars across the street, silhouetted against a cloudy winter sky. To see this, you do not necessarily have to put into words what you are experiencing. During your experience, you need not be aware *that* you are seeing – while the seeing goes on without being bothered by reflections. Only later do you realize that it is *you* who are seeing all this, from the place where you are. Only now is there self-awareness. So when you wake up from sleep or when pausing your daily grind for a second, self-awareness usually follows, as a reflective step, upon your pure and basic perception or something you imagine, dream or perceive.

This difference between basic, sensory awareness and self-awareness is reflected in the development of young children. At the age of about 18 months to two years, toddlers go through a phase in which, in their behaviour and nascent speech, they refer to all kinds of things without distinguishing between themselves and their surroundings. When standing in front of a mirror, they try to approach the being they see in the mirror as if it were someone else. Only later do they express themselves in a way that points to self-awareness. Now, when they stand in front of the mirror and see a prominent spot on the face in the mirror image, they will touch the spot and examine it on their own body. This mirror test also works in some animal species and offers a glimpse into the spread of this capacity for self-recognition and reflection through-out the animal kingdom – and indirectly into the evolution of self-awareness. Behavioural scientist Frans de Waal and his American colleagues applied a white cross to elephants in the Bronx Zoo, diagonally above one of their eyes.[8] The animals not only investigated how the cross felt and how it could be removed from their skin, but also tried to reach the cross from inside by stick-ing their trunks into their own mouths. This suggests that elephants recognize themselves and their brains construct a model of their own body. Great apes and dolphins have also passed such mirror tests.

Russian filmmaker Viktor Kossakovsky took a mirror test from his two-year-old son, Svyato, and made a documentary about it. For the first two years of his son's life, Kossakovsky covered up all the mirrors in his house so that the child could not form a visual image of himself. Then Kossakovsky puts his son to the test and places him in front of a wide and tall mirror in his house. The child smiles and moves his head up and down. As soon as it starts to move, the other child starts to move as well. This discovery leads the toddler to palpate the mirror, to slap it and to investigate how his likeness reacts when he licks a plastic bowl. The viewer witnesses the genesis of a self-consciousness, or at least a part of it. An arm goes up and down: this is both felt and seen. At the same time, the boy in the mirror moves his arm. The physical sensation and the visual mirror image go exactly together and must therefore be related. There must inevitably be a common cause: himself.

A symphony of the senses: sight, touch, feeling and... lift-off!

At this point, we have identified two strata in the geology of self-awareness: the command copy (the signal that it is you who are moving) and the construc-tion of a coherent body image (the sense of having a body that is bounded relative to the outside world). At this point, I could conclude the story of self-awareness simply and comfortably, like a guru presenting you with the latest neurotherapy. Reality is more stubborn: the two layers we identified are only the most basic structures on which the evolution of self-awareness has stead-ily and diligently built. The interplay of motor commands from the brain and sensory signals from the body – from the tactile sensors in our skin and the proprioceptive senses in our muscles – is undeniably important for the sense of owning a body, but how do bodily sensations relate to sight and our other senses? What happens, for example, when bodily sensations become discon-nected from what we see of our own bodies? Which sense then best represents your own perspective?

Physical sensations usually take place in the background of what commands most attention in our daily lives: seeing and hearing. We perceive the world around us from a visual perspective that is determined by our own position in space – an 'egocentric' perspective. If you stand on a straight country road in a wide, flat landscape, the road seems to become narrower and narrower towards the horizon, and widens towards yourself. That seems obvious, but isn't it strange that you don't see this road as it really is? The road has the same width everywhere, and so it would be more accurate if you saw the road as having 'the same width everywhere'. But this would mean that you would have to see the road from above, from the perspective of a bird flying overhead. Why does our visual system choose the egocentric vanishing point, foisted on us by a bunch of Renaissance artists from the fifteenth century?

A view from above would not give a good picture of your situation, because your body is in fact on the ground and not high up in the sky. Throughout evolution, our brain's systems of consciousness have evolved to provide the best possible representation, that is, one that is as useful as possible to you and from which you derive maximum benefit – which is not necessarily the most objective representation. The bird's-eye view would create the illusion that you have a wealth of information about the total landscape you are overseeing, which does not fit with the ground position you actually have. In the end, the best way to deal with a car or a cheetah rushing towards you is from a self-centred perspective: it is this view that best represents the information you have at that moment, even though it is not true that the cheetah gets bigger and bigger as it approaches.

Normally, our brain systems for visual and somatosensory representation work together seamlessly. The way we look at the world is invariably linked to the position and orientation of our head and eyes, which determine how light impinges on the retina. There is no contradiction between our spatial position as experienced visually and the position of our body parts, containing senses in skin, muscles and internal organs that inform the brain. The fixed link between our visual perspective and our bodies seems so self-evident that one would suspect that no special brain mechanisms are needed to establish it. But appearances are deceptive.

With epilepsy, people can sometimes have out-of-body experiences. A patient who had a small area of the brain in the right parietal lobe (the *angular gyrus*[9]) electrically stimulated as part of her epilepsy treatment, described how she seemed to be rising above her body: "I see myself lying in bed, from above, but I only see my legs and lower trunk." Often an out-of-body experience is initiated by the sensation that the patient is beginning to feel 'light' and has the feeling of ascending.

A variant of these illusions of self-localization or self-awareness is the autoscopic hallucination.[10] It, too, usually occurs in patients with epilepsy, having a source in the parietal or occipital lobe and often caused by a tumour or lesion. Sometimes this type of hallucination occurs in migraine patients and even in healthy people, although the latter are suspected of having a mild form of epilepsy that has not yet been brought to light by clinical examination. Patients see themselves, usually in mirror image, appearing for a few seconds in the space around them. Often only their upper body is visible, in colour, and this self-image may be stationary or show gestures and facial expressions.

In rare cases, the patient sees herself reflected several times simultaneously, as if she were in a hall of mirrors. Unlike in an out-of-body experience, she continues to see the situation from her own body position and perspective: her perspective does not 'jump' to that of the mirror image or to another place, somewhere high up on the ceiling of the same room. The person remains 'in her body'.

A form that lies in between out-of-body experience and autoscopic halluci-nation is the heautoscopic experience. The patient sees the image of her body in a space outside herself, but now the place of the 'self' changes between the location of the physical body and that of the illusory body. At one moment the person identifies herself with the autoscopic image, at another she slips back into her physical body. While an autoscopic experience depends heavily on visual hallucination, in heautoscopy bodily sensation and the sense of balance come into play more strongly. Often a vertigo is experienced in heautoscopy. The patient feels her body becoming lighter and seems to break free from it; the body seems to be left behind as an empty shell, releasing a feeling of alienation. Now it is the doppelganger with whom the patient identifies. The doppelganger does not have to look the same as the patient: sometimes the doppelganger looks smaller and older or younger, and in a few cases the sex is different. Despite these differences, the illusory appearance really feels like one's own double. A patient says:

> I would sit at a table and have beside me or in front of me another 'me' sitting there and talking to me. That's my double. I have the impression of seeing him materialise before me; generally he would tell me that I had misguided my life … I do hear him, it's an auditory impression, it's a sensation. He has the same voice as me, maybe a little bit younger, he indeed seems to be a little bit younger than me. At these moments, I would have the impression of being in a state of as if I were an unreal piece which does not belong to my home. At these moments I really do believe in the reality of the double.[11]

A 15-year-old girl suffering from epilepsy experiences the onset of an attack as a feeling of disgust and the unpleasant sensation of having to vomit. It is as if her body is on fire and she can no longer breathe – as if someone wants to strangle her. She sees a transparent shape leaving her physical body, and it feels as if this translucent object is her 'soul' fleeing her flesh and bones. That soul is white and looks down on her from above. From this position she recognizes her own face and the top of her torso. However, she does realize that she is still lying in a hospital bed – something that distinguishes this heautoscopic experience from an out-of-body experience. Towards the end of the seizure, the 'soul' returns to her physical body.[12]

When I talk about such experiences in a presentation, I am sometimes approached afterwards by people who say that they too have experienced something like this – but then in *real life*, not as a hallucination. It is striking

how convinced and emotional they are about the truthfulness of their experiential adventure. They tell how they lie in bed and watch their souls rise
from their bodies to make a long journey high above a nocturnal landscape of
villages and cities. They *are* their souls, and they are really experiencing this.
How dare I say that this is actually a fake experience? I can feel pretty bad
when I try to make it clear to people that they are 'just' having a hallucination;
it almost feels like you are trying to deny or negate their 'soul' or intimate private experience. "Don't doubt my experience, because then you doubt me."
Can't we – following amongst others the cardiologist Pim van Lommel, who
wrote a book about near-death experiences[13] – turn the matter around and
ask: why shouldn't an out-of-body experience count as positive proof of a soul
that has become detached from the body? After all, the patient sees it happen
with his own eyes!

There is no ironclad evidence that there can *never* be a soul separating from
the body. In any case, no proof is possible to show that something does not
exist (unless it is in logical contradiction with something that exists with certainty). This is because the collection of observations that we have at present
may not be complete: in principle, new facts may come to light in the future
that could point to the existence of an independent soul. Here, I firmly stand
up for the existence of the 'mind' or psyche, but as something strictly and
inseparably connected to the body, particularly the brain in that very special
state we call 'conscious'. Our mind is nothing more or less than the collection
of cognitive and perceptual processes mediated by the brain, including our
consciousness. By consequence, it is not a far stretch to ascribe mental properties to the intact, awake brain ('the brain believes', 'the brain decides', etc.).

A foremost reason for doubting an independent soul is that subjective experience – no matter how 'real' we think it is – is no proof of objective truth: even
the sense of realness is encoded by brain cell activity, and any claim to objectivity must be supported by an observation that can be reproduced by other
people. Religions have a special tradition of claiming absolute truths based on
individual religious experiences, such as apparitions of Jesus, Mary or a host
of saints. Instead of actual appearances, these revelations – usually attributed
to one gifted individual – are likely based on hallucinations as induced by epilepsy. Not without reason, epilepsy was considered a sacred disease in ancient
Greece. Epileptics had access to a mystical world, a realm of hidden experiences from which it was deduced that there is a 'soul' that could rise above the
physical body, and must therefore be able to exist independently of it – even
after physical death.

A wonderful story, and fodder for centuries of wishful thinking. Let us not
forget that we are dealing here with patients with a serious brain disorder. That
the existence of an independent soul is highly improbable is demonstrated by
the stories told by the patients themselves. In an out-of-body experience, the
patient generally does not see herself in full, but the body image is incomplete
and rather sketchy – exactly as described in other forms of visual hallucination.
When the patient is asked to describe in detail what she saw apart from her

own body, when looking down from the ceiling of the room, she has little to say. She appears unable to describe what the top of a cupboard in the room looked like, or whether there were any items lying on it. This fits with the idea that during the attack the brain generates an illusory estimate of the situation based on the information the patient has at that moment, lying in bed.

The idea of an independent soul is also plagued by all kinds of logical inconsistencies. If the soul ascends from the body and looks down from above, is there not a set of eyes missing to help with the job of viewing? How would a bodiless soul be able to see anything at all? If, in a heautoscopic experience, the soul is detached from your own physical body, why should it take on your own form – the form you know of yourself from the mirror? Why do we not see the soul as a radiant ball of light? And finally, Descartes' great dilemma remains unsolved: how should a soul, as an immaterial thing, communicate with the matter of your body? Returning to the case of the 15-year-old girl, is it not strange that the child's soul would ascend while she herself is still in bed and sees it happen? Does this not indicate that she still has her 'soul' in the same place, namely where her body is?

There is an alternative explanation for out-of-body experiences that reconciles the clinical elements of self-hallucinations with the patients' own stories. It is no coincidence that many hallucinations begin with a feeling of lightening and rising. In the case of a person lying still on the bed, this indicates a hallucination in her sense of balance: it is not so much a false representation of the static body posture that comes to the fore here (e.g. the sensation of leaning forward too much), but rather a feeling of upward acceleration. Brain areas in the parietal lobe, plus adjacent areas in the occipital and temporal lobe, are involved in integrating this vestibular information with what you see and feel in your body. Taking these streams of information together, these networks calculate the best possible estimate of where you are in space and what position your body is in – a best guess that corresponds to the conscious representation of your body at that moment.

When these areas are hit by an epileptic seizure – rushing through the brain like an electrical storm, and striking down the subtle neural patterns that encode your experiences – the brain is no longer able to construct an unambiguous representation of where the patient is or how she moves. In an out-of-body experience, it is not our visual consciousness that dominates, but rather that other sense, our sense of balance and acceleration in three dimensions. Normally, this modality operates in the background of our experience, but it can boast a staggeringly long history of evolution. The sense of ascent is in control and the visual perspective must conform to this. This is almost unimaginable, but then it is our visual faculties that we usually rely on to imagine something.

In a famous experiment conducted in the late nineteenth century, healthy subjects were given glasses containing prisms that caused them to see the outside world upside down.[14] Everything that is normally at the top of our field of vision – clouds, birds, house roofs – is now projected downwards, and the pavement, manhole covers and the feet of passers-by suddenly appear at the top. After wearing the goggles for two confusing weeks, the test subjects report that their visual world has returned to normal: towers and houses that were upside down are now upright again. Between the start of the procedure and the normalization of the image, an interesting transition phase takes place: people report that some objects are seen as before in the good old times – upright – while other things are still upside down. The corrections the brain makes when updating its world model to make things look 'normal' again are related to the context and 'reality rules' to which our visual system is bound.

A candle that is initially seen upside down, flips upward as soon as it is lit: that flame must and will go up. When you pour a glass of milk, it cannot be the case that the milk flows upwards, so the glass tips over to its normal orientation. The pressure we experience on our feet comes from below, and this signal is transmitted by the tactile senses in the soles of our feet to the body map of the somatosensory cortex. This pressure from below matches the signals from our vestibular organ which indicate that we are standing upright – even though our visual system suggests we are upside down. If our visual system would insist that the ground we are standing on is situated above us, this visual representation is drowned out by the more powerful bodily sensation and balance systems. The visual system can stand on its head for as long as it wants; it will be dismissed as a faulty misfit by the larger cortical system and must adapt to the powers that be – the senses that keep our motor interactions with the outside world running smoothly.

Likewise, the visual impression of an out-of-body experience is something that is controlled by pathological sensations in body posture and movement. Without questioning the authenticity of people's out-of-body experiences, such experiences do not even provide a shred of evidence for an independent soul or a paranormal phenomenon such as an out-of-body soul or astral body. It can be explained as an attempt by our conscious brain system to provide a best estimate of a person's sensory state in which what we see conforms to a false sense of 'lift-off'. Similarly, the near-death experiences that patients talk about after surviving a cardiac arrest are very special, but do not point (as Pim van Lommel claims) to a cosmic consciousness outside of ourselves: they can be explained from the fact that our conscious brain system can continue to function for some time even in the event of a serious lack of oxygen, and in this state generates hallucinations.

Rising above rough sensations

At its core, as we have seen so far, the 'self' appears to have been built on three solid foundations: the command copy, the sense of bodily identity and the integration of bodily and other sensory signals, with vision and balance playing the key roles. At this point, the 'self' is still a very physical, sensory thing: a body with a brain that weaves together all kinds of sensory information into a big picture. It is a 'self' that fits well within the picture of raw sensory sensations that I have outlined until now. But precisely for self-awareness there are even more layers or pillars to be identified by which it towers as a brain-generated construct above the level of basic sensations. One of these layers is the 'acting self' – the sense of 'agency': through actions we devise and plan ourselves we can make a difference in the world.[15] Thus far, the 'I' has reluctantly emerged as a perceiving entity, as something that is able to distil a consistent, bodily self-image from streams of sensory inputs. There is little thirst for action here.

When sensors in our hypothalamus – deeply hidden in the basement of the brain – detect that our blood sugar levels are dropping too far, it is time to find food. We don't consciously taste our blood sugar levels, but sensor readings in the bloodstream indicate outside of conscious awareness that our energy balance is about to be disturbed. Higher regions of the brain are activated to initiate foraging behaviour. Yet higher regions are enabled to express ourselves consciously and audibly: "Time to go shopping and prepare food." A food-search plan is drawn up. We rush to the supermarket, fill up our trolley, give the shop financial satisfaction for the booty acquired and prepare the food to keep ourselves alive. In our foraging behaviour, we seem to be a slave to the brain systems that balance our water and nutrient supplies, but this does not mean that our environment dictates exactly what we should do. We have a sense of having some choice and options to act upon. We are fitted with a 'self' that not only observes passively but can also choose, plan and execute actions more or less independently of our environment. Even though our appetite drives us to acquire food, when we are on a plane we still have the choice of 'chicken or pasta'.

This is not the end of self-awareness: at least two more indispensable ingredients have been left out. The 'I' is about personal identity: who are we, really? If you are in a group and someone asks you who Matt is, you can of course refer to a body quite literally ("Matt is standing right over there"), but in a broader sense it is much more interesting to know who Matt is as a person: where he comes from, what family and friends he has, what he does for a living and what his character is like. Whenever Matt gets the chance to tell his story, he will heavily rely on his episodic memory: his personal, autobiographical memories, which he is able to put into words thanks to his general knowledge of facts and vocabulary. As Henry Molaison showed in Chapter 3, episodic memory strongly depends on the hippocampus and surrounding areas in the temporal lobe. This system gives us a 'historical self', endowing the larger system of self-representation a deep temporal dimension not found in raw sensations. Another component of our identity is 'personality'. This too is dependent on past life experiences, but relates more directly to traits such as temperament, extroversion or introversion, impulsivity or thoughtfulness – traits that are generally more strongly associated with the prefrontal cortex and basal ganglia than with the hippocampus.

Over all these slices of the cake lies a thick, shiny icing: the 'social self'. This comes to the fore when we start interacting with others and distinguish ourselves from the group we are in by having a quirky opinion or a crazy remark.

When you meet someone new at school or in your working environment, your brain consciously or unconsciously tries to build a model of his character and intentions – a mini theory of how the mind of this individual works: an estimate of what it is like to be this other person (also referred to as 'Theory of Mind').[16] This may result in empathy, other kinds of social sensitivity and morality, but during early development this process primarily revolves around attributing wishes, intentions and knowledge to other beings that may differ from your own. A characteristic example is a situation in which a young boy watches a girl receive a piece of chocolate. She puts it on a shelf and leaves the room, while her mother remains present and puts the chocolate in a refrigerator. What happens when the girl enters the room again? If the boy expects the girl to walk to the shelf first, he understands that she does not have the knowledge he has acquired in the meantime. Such Theory of Mind capabilities are probably not unique to humans or great apes: the behaviour of ravens, dogs and scrub jays (mainly found in North America) suggests that they, when storing or digging up food, are able to keep conspecifics from plundering their food supply.[17]

When we put together a detailed model of the other, we can hardly escape attributing a mind or 'self' to the other. This also has consequences for ourselves. For a correct model of the other also includes a model of yourself: you try to predict how the other will react to you as soon as *you* enter the picture. The other person will also have to create a model of you, so that a game of ping-ponging internal models arises.

This results in the social layer of our self-consciousness: the image we have of ourselves as derived from the behaviour of others. I attribute a 'self' to you and at the same time you treat me the same way: the impression emerges that every other individual is more than just a physical body. Take a person who is very close to your heart – your lover, one of your children or another precious family member. Now try to join the somewhat macabre thought-experiment that this person is nothing but a collection of flesh, bones, blood, organs wrapped in adipose tissue and a smooth layer of skin on top. No personality, no character, no 'self' – just warm-blooded matter. When you see your loved one walking through the house, imagine that he or she is half translucent and offers a glimpse of all the bones and organs swaying to the cadence of the walking skeleton. This exercise has a morbid quality and I can only tolerate it because it is a thought-experiment. As soon as we start interacting with our loved one by talking to her, exchanging glances or having warm and physical contact, a *person* inevitably appears, an individual that we recognize and that evokes emotions in us. In the same way, others ascribe a 'self' to us – even though the image of that collection of bones and organs is, physically speaking, not untrue.

The complexity of self-awareness is staggering. What solid ground do we have under our feet? Self-awareness is rooted in evolutionarily ancient principles available to animals that can move independently throughout their world: the principles of command copy and of body ownership. These are not yet sufficient to guarantee self-awareness: they work quietly in the background, without our needing to be aware of it. Consciousness only comes into play when we experience an overview of our situation in the world that includes our body. The situational survey produced by the brain actually includes everything except the brain itself – it includes everything outside the organ that produces the overview. If a surgeon sticks a needle into our brain, we do not feel it. We do not feel and locate pain in the brain, but in a place in our body.

Spatial position, posture and movement: they provide essential information for constructing our conscious experience, and this experience helps us choose what we can take or leave given our position in the world. If we bring the 'self' into this world view, it is first of all a physical thing that we introduce, composed of different modalities. The simulacrum that our brains produce about how our bodies relate to the world is based on a subtle, subcutaneous conspiracy between sight, touch, internal bodily sensations and sense of balance (with hearing, taste and smell also occasionally taking part in the conspiracy). What we see is rarely the only content of what we are aware of – seeing is contained within a richer situation in which our body, with all its other senses, assumes a leading role, although we are not always attentive to it.

If we accept that conscious experience is grounded in brain mechanisms that produce sensory inferences, the question of who is watching or experiencing all this inevitably arises. After examining the drilling samples taken from the layers of our self-consciousness, the answer seems obvious: it must be us, our 'I', which has so many facets, but undeniably claims the right to exist. And yet, when it comes to our primary, sensory consciousness – the thoughtless staring at the blue sky or the roof tiles across the street I live in – the answer must be negative: no one is watching at all. I say this so confidently because a model in which, on the one hand, we have a conscious representation of our world and, on the other, an 'I' that looks on, takes us right back to dualism. It takes us back to the Cartesian theatre where the spectacle of the 'conscious content' appears on stage and the 'I' watches it from a balcony. Also Daniel Dennett has fervently argued that this is the wrong way to think about consciousness. It brings the 'I' as homunculus back into our thinking – and with it the question of what happens in the homunculus that makes *it* see, and so on ad infinitum.

The 'self', in short, can be understood as a higher-order construct, which is better left aside when we talk about primary conscious sensations. To see the colour red, it is not necessary for there to be a separate 'I' that perceives it. The 'I' as body or personality only appears much later in the circus programme of the mind. Returning to the idea of sensory inference, it may feel awkward that there is no one around in this process to do the watching, or experience representations of the outside world. There is, however, active brain tissue that does this. Helmholtz made a big step forward with his idea that the brain draws inferences from its sensory inputs, but also insisted that our conscious sensing must depend on a separate, *psychological* activity. We have now come far enough to take the next radical step. When it comes to conscious experience, this 'psychic' activity is *the same* as the brain activity generating a representation of the situation. No 'psyche' or 'I' is needed to get going separately with these representations, to 'make' them conscious or to take the next step in interpretation. The producer of representations is observer at the same time. This does not diminish the fact that the 'self' is an important construct, which we also need in our language to express who we are talking about. Within the spectrum of cognitive functions, language forms a separate category that strongly coheres with the functioning of our left-brain hemisphere. But this does not alter the fact that we do not need an 'I' or language for our basic sensory awareness.

Does this cocktail of neuroscience and philosophy have more to offer than chitchat about the bizarre excesses of brain damage? The fate that befell Peter Chadwick is not unique: in the West, schizophrenia affects about 2 to 3 per cent of the population at some point in people's lives. This mentally devastating brain disorder, starting as a disturbance in the relationship between the 'self' and the outside world, is now becoming increasingly better understood.[18] Chadwick perceived the fluctuating intensity of the clattering rain on the window as something that happened outside himself, whereas the source of this fluctuation was in his brain. This misattribution to an external source is characteristic of schizophrenia. Chadwick's brain generated a deceptive simulacrum in which sensations were attributed to the wrong causes. When patients start hearing voices, they do not attribute them to their own imagination and fantasy, but locate the cause outside themselves – with the CIA or some other supreme organization. The list of brain disorders that result in disturbed self-awareness or self-image is frighteningly long. Next to schizophrenia and the collection of brain lesions we already encountered, we find autism and anorexia. Autistic people often have a disturbed delineation between the self (their own body) and the outside world, possibly because the sensory inputs required for making this distinction are confused.[19] Anorexia is known as an eating disorder, but especially girls and women with this condition may also have a distorted view of their own bodies.[20] Chadwick has aptly expressed the importance of a good mix of neuroscience, philosophy and other disciplines: "The qualities of consciousness, which are not simply an irrelevant by-product of cerebral and cognitive processes in hardware, do play a critical role in the establishment, maintenance and recovery of the psychotic state."[21]

13 The free will of Tolman's rats

On the hidden mental life of rodents, imaginary actions and independent decisions

Rats are wonderful, clever and social animals. Their versatile and adaptive behaviour contradicts the image of the filthy rat running down a dark alley or crawling into a sewer. The rat that works its way through the cracks of an old house and suddenly finds itself face to face with a bewildered occupant. The rat as a pest – a source of nuisance and pathogens we want to get rid of as quickly as possible. We take in a cat, or even use rat poison – a toxin that causes the animal to bleed internally and die slowly. Get rid of those filthy animals. Zero tolerance.

A few years ago, I used to let rats run over my arms and shoulders. Not dirty sewer rats, but specimens with a shiny, clean, white fur. They planted their little claws firmly in the cotton fibres of my lab coat, uncomfortably at first, but later with certainty and confidence. They sniffed around, exploring possible routes across my limbs and torso, probing this curved landscape with their oscillating whiskers. The animals made me cheerful. They are playful, inquisitive and courageous – knowing how to find their way from one shoulder to the other, via the isthmus of the neck, which they tickle with their little paws and primordial, scaly tail. Despite their limited brain size, their entire behaviour is characterized by adaptability and intelligence. Once accustomed to a caretaker, rats become affectionate. They are amiable creatures that cuddle up together when in a group. This behaviour contrasts with the image of the aggressive rodent scavenging through piles of rubbish in the street – a contrast that has been just as sharply marked in the history of animal psychology over the past hundred years.

In the mid-1930s, Edward Chace Tolman (1886–1959; Figure 13.1) was working out a set-up for studying rat behaviour in his laboratory at the University of California, Berkeley. There is still a lot of sawing and hammering to be done, but also in his mind Tolman is struggling with something. He has been trained in the American tradition of behaviourism. An animal learns something, so the idea goes, because connections are changed in the brain, on the one hand between neurons that process sensory stimuli, and on the other hand between neurons that steer its behaviour in response to those stimuli (see also Figure 5.1). If a rat catches the scent of bratwurst, it learns to follow the scent trail and locate the food source. If the rat is confronted with a maze

DOI: 10.4324/9781003429555-13

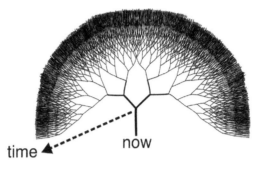

Figure 13.1 (Left) Portrait of Edward Chace Tolman (1886–1959). (Right) The choice options we have in determining our future actions can be represented by a tree branching ever more finely into the future. The present corresponds to the tree trunk.
Source: University Archives, The Bancroft Library, University of California at Berkeley. Photograph by Dorothy Moore.

that contains a place with food somewhere inside, it will explore this environment until it finds that place, and will remember that a left turn at the first T-junction does not lead to a reward, but a right turn does. Intelligent behaviour arises because animals and humans learn a chain of stimulus-response connections or associations. The longer the chain of associations, the smarter the behaviour appears to us.

A learning process is more than stimulus-response coupling: getting a reward is also essential. An animal will often be hungry or thirsty to enter a completely unknown labyrinth at all. The behaviourist Edward Thorndike argued that it is the reward that ultimately ensures that the animal learns to respond to the stimulus in its behaviour. At the end of the road, a piece of food awaits the animal, which will reinforce its tendency to take the first right turn. The learning process is controlled by reward or punishment. When Tolman enters the scene of animal psychology, this stimulus-response-reward story is cut-and-dried for him. But now, in the thirties, the matter does not sit well with him.

Tolman grew up in a Quaker family in the small town community of West Newton, Massachusetts. His mother was a Puritan follower of this evangelical Christian movement, which held distinctly pacifist views. During the First World War, Tolman got a research job at Northwestern University in Chicago and was faced with an important choice – one of the many T-junctions of his life. Should he speak out for or against the war? He found himself to be in emotional conflict, but decided to add his name to a pacifist publication in a student magazine. He was fired by the Dean. Tolman defined himself as a dissident and obstructionist: brave but lonely. Later, he also increasingly opposed the behaviourist zeitgeist, impressed as he was by William James, whose frank description of the phenomena of consciousness ran counter to the straightforward views on stimulus-response coupling.

Also in his later years, Tolman dares to go against the mainstream. During Senator Joseph McCarthy's anti-Communist witch hunt in the 1950s, the University of California tries to fire Tolman because he refuses to sign an oath of allegiance. Tolman refuses not because he would be disloyal to the United States, but because the demand to sign infringes on academic freedom. Tolman wins the ensuing court case with flying colours, and the Supreme Court of California rules that all those who refused must be given their jobs back. Looking at Tolman's portrait, it is hard to tell that he was rebellious in a refreshing way. No wild hair like Albert Einstein had, but a neatly trimmed triangular moustache in a decent, somewhat dull appearance. Yet this man deserves eternal fame.

What Tolman observes in his rats is not a jerky succession of stimulus-response reactions ('twitchism') but a fluent behaviour that is tailored to their environment even without rewards, and that even seems to anticipate what is coming further down the line, out of sight. When Tolman allows a rat to freely roam a maze, it turns out that the rat finds the way better and better even *without* reward. Animals learn spontaneously – not just because they expect to be rewarded in the near future, but because it is in their general interest to get to know their environment. This 'hidden learning' leads Tolman to believe that the brain must be more than a simple switch box, as used in his time to enable conversations between widely separated telephones.[1] There is more to it than the fact that a stimulus (the sight of a pedal) must be coupled to a response (the pressing of the pedal). It dawns on Tolman that there are mental processes going on in the rat's brain that are more complex than what can be deduced from the animal's visible behaviour.

Within the behaviourist zeitgeist, this is a crazy and dangerous idea. Is it possible to find evidence for it? After much hemming and hawing, Tolman comes up with a simple test set-up. He cobbles together a platform on which a rat is placed about 70 centimetres above the floor. From this platform, the rat has to jump to the other side – over a gap of 20 centimetres wide – and choose whether it will land on the left or right side of the plank on that other side. On both the left and right side, there is a small door that the rat must push open for a chance at a reward. While practising this behavioural task, the rat learns that a choice for the white door always leads to a reward, but a choice for a black or grey-coloured door does not (whether it is on the left or right does not matter for his odds). In Tolman's time, this experimental plan was considered low risk, but in our time, it would probably be rejected by an ethical review committee. An unfortunate jump could cause the rat to hit the ground and injure itself: a form of avoidable distress. But that is beside the point. Tolman's rats appeared to learn to choose the correct door more quickly if the contrast between the two doors was maximum (black versus white) and to have difficulty with a weak contrast (light grey versus white). This was completely as expected and posed no challenge whatsoever to the classical behaviourists.

Fictitious actions

Then Tolman takes a closer look at his rats' behaviour. Before a rat takes the plunge, he observes a 'hesitation': the animal turns its head from left to right a few times. The animal looks back and forth, and then again, as if it is weighing up its options. Shortly before Tolman, the term 'vicarious trial and error' (VTE) had been coined for this behaviour.[2] This means that the animal is internally and virtually trying out one or more actions – either consciously or unconsciously. The animal performs fictitious actions ('trials'), estimates what the result will be ('error' or else reward) and does this in a way that replaces the normal physical action ('vicarious'). Tolman observes that the amount of VTE behaviour of the rat keeps pace with the learning behaviour of the animal. If a rat shows a rapid increase in its number of correct choices, its left-right head movements also increase. Once the animal has learned the trick of choosing the white door, the number of VTE movements decreases. If the animal learns little, it also shows little VTE behaviour.

What could this VTE behaviour mean? Within behaviourism, there was little room for concepts such as 'hesitation' or 'doubt'. Above all, this school of thought is about learning stimulus-response associations – seeing the white door and jumping to the corresponding part of the shelf, be it left or right. The strength of the learned link determines whether and how the rat jumps, but leaves no room for an internal process such as doubting (you can feel here how Descartes' grave begins to shake: the old man starts tossing and turning). Without treading on thin ice by arguing that rats can imagine things the way humans do, Tolman proposes that a *hypothesis* forms in the rat's brain. If I do this, then what happens? If I jump towards the white door, do I get rewarded? If I jump to the left side each time and don't pay attention to the colour of the door, am I more likely to get rewarded? In a rat brain, there will be no language to formulate a hypothesis, but recent neurophysiological research indicates that hypotheses and expectations can in fact be encoded in the firing behaviour of neurons, even without language.

The formation and testing of hypotheses may seem an abstract, theoretical hobby that we especially ascribe to humans, but it is an activity that is just as important in the evolution of animals as it is for humans. Suppose you find yourself in an unfamiliar forest and are confronted by a huge, untethered dog blocking your path. What are you going to do? Without realizing it, you dig into your memory to see if you know this breed of dog and what your experiences with it are. Is the animal a dangerous biter or a bluffing barker? Do you try to sneak past it, or do you grab a stick to ward it off? Is its owner somewhere to be seen? You weigh up and observe how the animal behaves. From all the hypotheses or action options that present themselves, the most promising ones remain. You take the stick and carefully walk around the animal. Before we actually carry out complex or risky actions, we review our options to better assess the possible consequences. This is the stage of mental action that follows on our primary, conscious sensations, and draws upon them. Computer models show that the brain can indeed learn faster if it uses virtual exercises, or in other words: internal simulations. Moreover, they save energy and time because not all options have to be tried out physically.[3]

In a similar vein, the philosopher Karl Popper has pointed out the enormous evolutionary advantage to be gained from the internal formation and testing of hypotheses: this way it becomes possible for not ourselves but our hypotheses to die.[4] Hypotheses, especially in humans, go beyond the left-right choices of Tolman's rats. The more wide-ranging and life-defining the choices we face, the longer we think about them. Do you accept that job that will advance your career but is not as interesting as hoped? Do you keep the baby now that you are unexpectedly pregnant? Do you give up part of your job to assist your old and needy mother? When the uncertainty of the outcome remains high, we fret more than is good for us.

The Israeli historian and futurologist Yuval Harari has argued that the success of the human species, *homo sapiens*, is due to its ability to unite large groups under a common ideology: large-scale cooperation in the area of food supply and warfare is possible only once this is achieved. Using our knowledge of the brain, however, it can be argued that it is at least as important for the success of *sapiens* to predict as far into the future as possible what will happen to you and your group, and to run through as many optional scenarios as possible. If a boy likes a girl, he will first try to find out if she fancies him too. If she doesn't, the question arises as to what he should do to become attractive. What will his rivals do to get her attention? How will they react to him if he approaches her? Can he find an excuse to use her friends to force an opening? Who does the girl have her eye on? This culminates in a never-ending game that branches out further and further into the future – like a tree that is rooted in the past but branches out upwards into all the options that lie open for the future (Figure 13.1).

Long-term planning is a function associated with the prefrontal cortex (Figure 3.1), and it is understandable that the relative size of this structure has exploded in mammalian evolution from rodent to human. From this vantage point, it becomes clear why the enormous prefrontal damage in Phineas Gage – the explosives man at the Vermont railway – had little effect on his short-term behaviour, but had all the more consequences for his social behaviour. Inadequate social behaviour is not an immediate threat to your survival, but it does lower your status in the group to which you belong: less sympathy and help in the longer term will come your way. Prefrontal damage leads to a shrinking of one's 'cognitive horizon': the range for one's future behaviour is reduced.

The internal search for action options and the execution of simulations come at a price: it is computationally intensive work that requires time. This makes it understandable that Tolman saw the VTE behaviour in his rats decrease when the actual learning process was completed. Once the rat has learned that choosing the white door will certainly lead to a reward, it no longer needs to waste time weighing up the options: the behaviour can now be automated. A habit is born.

A brain map for cognition

It was no great surprise that Tolman's contemporaries did not line up to embrace his new ideas. His colleague Edwin Guthrie mockingly remarked that Tolman's rats would remain "buried in thought" in their maze, because there would be no decisive incentive to persuade them to move in this or that direction.[5] "*Buried in thought*" – laughing out loud, imagine – do you believe it? How can something like that ever be proved? Tolman is not put off by his critics. In 1948, again touching on the sore spot of behaviourism, he extends his ideas about mental processes in animals to the idea that, when exploring a new environment, they create a 'cognitive map'. In a physical maze, this internal map is of a spatial nature: the brain encodes the locations of paths, T-junctions and feeding sites relative to each other. But the map can also contain information about what the animal must do or not do at a certain place in order to reach its final destination: if you turn left at the central T-junction, you will enter a dead-end corridor.

The idea of a cognitive map is powerful and widely applicable: instead of a spatial representation, one can also think, at least in case of humans, of a cognitive structure that helps you with navigation on the internet: your surfing behaviour can be dissected into all kinds of small decisions to fill in search terms and click on hyperlinks. A game of chess can be seen as a quest through a cognitive maze of possible moves, with your opponent repeatedly closing or opening corridors for you. Actually, our entire living environment consists of a web of causal relationships between things that are only partially perceptible to us. From the stimuli we perceive in a context of space and time, runs an invisible web that connects these with potential actions and consequences. Through mental simulation, this web can be explored to choose the best path to the future. If this is successful, you have constructed a good cognitive map of the web you live in.

Who was the ultimate winner in the boxing ring of animal psychology? The theory of stimulus-response coupling has not been proved false: even today, it is still recognized as an important learning process. At the same time, it is a limited process because it mainly explains how simple forms of behaviour and habits are controlled. Tolman's influence went far beyond this and stimulated many novel developments in cognitive science, centred on the idea that our behaviour is not only governed by stimuli and hunger pangs but also by internal cognitive processes. His work fuelled the emergence of ideas about the irrational grounds on which human decisions are often based – including a framework of thinking awarded the Nobel Prize in Economics in 2002.[6]

Tolman's theory of the cognitive map received a spectacular follow-up when the London neurophysiologist John O'Keefe discovered how the firing behaviour of neurons in the hippocampus (Figure 3.1) is associated with an animal's place in its environment. I first met John when I picked him up from Amsterdam airport sometime in the late 1990s to accompany him to deliver a lecture for young Dutch researchers. John has been trained as an aeronautical engineer and makes a modest and understated impression. With his red cheeks and short white beard that runs from ear to ear across his jaw line, you would expect him to spend his life more in the open air rather than in laboratory spaces. John said that he had first adapted the technique used by Hubel and Wiesel to measure neurons in the visual cortex for use in free-ranging rats. He was then able to study how cells in the hippocampus became electrically active as they explored their spatial environment.

He observed that a hippocampal cell started firing strongly when the rat was in one particular place in its environment (the 'place field' of that cell, as illustrated on the T-shaped set-up in Figure 13.2), while that same cell remained silent in other places. Other cells, close by or further away in the hippocampus, fired strongly in other places, scattered over the same environment. Each place in the room that the animal visited appeared to be encoded by all these 'place

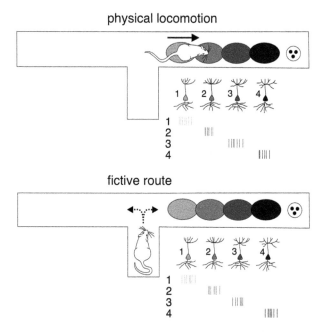

Figure 13.2 (Top) When a rat moves physically across a T-shaped set-up, neurons (place cells) in the hippocampus become sequentially active when the rat reaches specific locations on the set-up. Place cell 1 fires strongly when the rat is on the light grey spot, place cell 2 on the adjacent spot and so on. The arrow indicates the walking direction. To the right of the path is a reward spot with three pieces of food. (Bottom) If the rat is stationary on the T-junction and hesitates, place cells become active in the same order as they would be during physical walking movements. The hippocampus generates virtual routes without the animal actually walking down a path.

cells' together. When the rat was transferred to another, new environment (for example, a triangular runway somewhere further along in the laboratory), the places in this room also turned out to be coded by hippocampal cells. These were usually cells that were not active in the previous environment, but researchers also found neurons that fired in both environments. This indicates that a single cell cannot be enough to code which environment the rat is in: the code for each space is determined by a large collection of neurons. Later, this brain code for spatial location was also found in the human brain. Together with two Norwegian colleagues, O'Keefe received the Nobel Prize for Physiology or Medicine in 2014 for the discovery of this brain system for spatially mapping one's own location. One would wish that Edward Tolman could have shared in this honour. This was not to be, but at least his thinking has received support from countless studies and, in the struggles with behaviourism, gained the upper hand.

But what about Tolman's other idea – that VTE behaviour has to do with sifting through internal hypotheses about action options? Can any such 'mental activity' be found in the brain? So far, the hippocampus has been associated with two functions that at first glance seem very different from each other. In Henry Molaison's case, the hippocampus proved to be indispensable for narrative memory. But just now, I had the nerve to claim that the hippocampus is crucial for encoding your place in the spatial environment. Which of the two versions is correct?

Both versions make sense and are consistent. Our narrative memory consists mainly of a gigantic collection of personal memories, and a characteristic feature of these is that they are about concrete events in space and time. They are about a 'what' (an event), a 'where' (place in space) and a 'when' (moment in time). The electrical firing activity of hippocampal cells that occurs selectively when you are in a particular place provides a code that is not only useful for knowing where you are but is also an essential ingredient of personal memories. When we remember an important event – such as the attack on the Twin Towers in New York – we also remember where we were at that moment.[7] Perhaps surprisingly, when the hippocampus is damaged as in Henry Molaison's operation, patients are still able to find their way around their home or town. They lack the contribution of the hippocampus to the cognitive map of their brain, but retain the stimulus-response memory that the behaviourists had been harping on about: "When I see the birch tree, I must turn left, and then I will get home." In Alzheimer's disease, the decay of memory systems is so massive and widespread that this alternative mechanism for finding one's way is also gradually lost.

How does the process of recalling a memory work? It often starts with a *cue*: an irritating music tune that brings your primary school back to life in your imagination or a smell that takes you back to your childhood home. But memory traces can also emerge spontaneously, for example during sleep. This was shown when the electrical activity of hippocampal cells of rats was monitored during periods of sleep alternating with a waking period, during which the animal roamed freely through an environment.[8] As expected from O'Keefe's discovery, as the rat walked around, a variety of cells became active as soon as the rat visited the places that corresponded to their place fields (Figure 13.2). When the rat went to sleep after this behavioural experience, the cells spontaneously started firing again, without an external stimulus, in the same order as they had done during the animal's prior behaviour. It was particularly deep sleep – the sleep characterized by slow electrical waves in the cerebral cortex (Figure 6.2) – that showed this replay of electrical pulse patterns. Replay occurs 5 to 40 times faster than the rate at which the animal's pathway is encoded in the active behavioural state: a five-second behavioural period recurs offline in a burst of activity lasting less than half a second. The playback of information is not limited to the hippocampus: connected brain areas such as the nucleus accumbens, located in the basal ganglia (Figure 3.1), also participate. While the hippocampus plays back the animal's spatial route, the nucleus accumbens expresses information about the rewards along that route offline.[9] Because replay occurs most strongly during deep sleep and this type of sleep is hardly accompanied by consciousness, it is unlikely that replay equals conscious re-experience as driven by memory. Replay flies under the radar of consciousness. It is much more likely that replay has a function in retrieving and reinforcing memories of important events at the expense of irrelevant memory traces that are weakened – a process that does not require consciousness.

Back to the hemming and hawing of Tolman's rats. What happens in the brain when the rat is faced with a difficult choice? Thanks to the techniques developed by O'Keefe and colleagues to measure the electrical activity of large numbers of neurons simultaneously in an actively moving animal, it was possible to study what information the hippocampus encodes when the rat is faced with a T-junction. Here too, the rat hesitated between choosing left versus right in the initial phase of the learning process: at first, it was unclear where the most reward was to be found. As the animal approached the T-junction, the hippocampus appeared initially to represent its actual, physical position, exactly as you would expect on the basis of O'Keefe's earlier findings. Thus, a neuron became electrically active the moment the animal walked through that neuron's place field (Figure 13.2, top).

But when the animal arrived at the T-junction, during VTE behaviour, the hippocampus began to behave strangely. The cells now started to encode positions of the animal where it *might* go in the future, that is, to places in the maze that would only be reached if the rat turned left or right. Physically, the animal was at the T-junction, but its brain played a series of fictitious routes that would occur *if* the rat were to turn left or right (Figure 13.2, bottom). Unlike replay, this 'forward sweep' does not take place ten times as fast as during normal locomotion, but in the normal rhythm the hippocampus usually works with. While the rat is engaged in its hesitant back-and-forth behaviour at the junction, the hippocampus is encoding not only the option ultimately chosen, but both routes from which a choice can be made.[10]

What we see here is nothing more or less than a reflection of an internal cognitive process that takes place in the rat brain. The animal does not necessarily need to be aware of this. The representation forged by the hippocampus travels ahead of the animal, and is thus able to do more than code the animal's current position or the sensory stimuli occurring at that moment. As part of a larger network, the hippocampus plays different spatial paths that can be used for internal simulation of future behaviour. It is as if the hippocampus is painting a landscape of future options with forward brushstrokes, each brushstroke quickly fading away. This process, too, carries a profit motive: reward-sensitive cells in the nucleus accumbens appear to join in the forward sweep. Returning to Guthrie's sneer at Tolman, my American colleague David Redish remarked that Tolman's rats were indeed "lost in thought". On this point, too, history has vindicated Tolman.[11]

At this stage, it is tempting to ascribe 'thoughts' to rats, but beware. Rats are smart, cuddly and noble, but they are not miniature people on four legs. Neither animals nor humans are probably aware of the spatial representations produced by the hippocampus. Already with Henry Molaison we saw that the loss of the hippocampus in both hemispheres does not lead to a loss of consciousness – in any sensory modality. However, there is evidence that the fictitious pathways found in the rat hippocampus also occur in humans and are used for planning and imagination. When healthy subjects are shoved into a brain scanner, their global brain activity can be monitored on a slow time scale. When they are instructed to play a computer game in the scanner, and have to think about which spatial path to choose in order to reach a desired destination, increased activity is also seen in their hippocampus.[12]

Are there forms of internal simulation that we do become aware of? Two obvious candidates present themselves here: dreaming and imagination. Unlike perception, both can unfold without external stimuli and can be considered internal simulation. While imagination, as a cognitive process, can be adjusted quite easily from the inside or outside, the dream is its wilder sister that runs its course autonomously and unrestrainedly while you sleep – associative, emotional and hallucinatory. Neither has any obvious function in planning or teaching behaviour. We may fantasize or daydream for pleasure, or reminisce about a long, languid camping holiday. But even our imaginations and dreams have to get their information from somewhere, and past experiences are the appropriate source for this. In our imagination, we effortlessly assemble all kinds of elements into objects that we have never seen before – such as a yellow-purple-striped unicorn – but for this, the individual building blocks are indeed retrieved from our memory. Again, the hippocampus is indispensable for this. In a study with patients, Demis Hassabis and colleagues from University College London showed that imagining new spatial experiences was severely impoverished when the hippocampus was damaged and the brain could no longer call on narrative memory.[13] So while the forward sweep in the hippocampal representation of spatial location is linked to VTE behaviour and planning, the same hippocampus, at least in humans, also plays a role in feeding and fuelling our imagination – as a conscious form of internal simulation.

The freedom to deliberate

What does all this have to do with free will? The mystery of free will is about as old as the body-mind problem, but it is not always clear what is meant by it. The first question that comes to my mind is: free relative to what? Is our mind free to do what it wants in relation to the matter of which our body is composed? Or are we free relative to our environment? To other people? In ancient western civilization, free will is contrasted with the lack of freedom: slavery, submission, bondage and imprisonment. The Roman *liberi* were free persons facing *servi* (slaves), and also the children and lovers of a free person were called 'free', as people to be honoured and loved. The Proto-Germanic word 'Frijōną' lies at the basis of the old English word 'freen' and means to love, to free and to like. It gave rise to the similar term 'vrijen' in Dutch, which means to have consensual sex – as opposed to enforced sex. 'Free will' seems to have arisen as a concept to indicate the absence of coercion by others – a definition rooted in power relations between people. Insofar as people are free to want something in relation to others who feel they have control over their lives, free will does indeed exist. No problem. But this is a will that is free in relation to the environment.

Is our conscious mind also free in relation to our body – to the matter of which we are composed, and therefore to the natural laws to which matter obeys? Are we in charge of our own actions, and what part of our choices is already fixed in our brains before we have the feeling of making a conscious choice? That our 'mind' does not operate independently of the activity in our brains is underlined by a cartload of evidence, of which only a fraction is touched upon here, such as the blunting of spontaneous volition in lobotomy patients. Whether it is deep brain stimulation, manipulation of genetically altered brain cells with laser light, or measurements of electrical activity of large groups of brain cells, all point to the fact that the total collection of cognitive processes that make up your mind depends on brain activity. This is not to say that matter represents the sole, acknowledged reality, or that the 'mind' is merely an abstraction or fabrication. But when it comes to the question of whether our minds are free in relation to the matter of our bodies, the answer must be negative. Whether we like it or not, our minds are ultimately rooted in the laws of nature.

This form of physical despotism does not automatically mean that everything that happens in our lives, and which we decide for ourselves, is predetermined. Quantum mechanics has shown that the behaviour of elementary particles (such as electrons and quarks) contains fundamental uncertainties, even if their location, speed or mass can be measured individually. Sometimes this uncertainty is invoked to support the existence of free will, but this argument is countered by the fact that uncertainties in quantum behaviour occur on too small a scale to affect large-scale processes in the brain (such as perception, planning and decision-making). But even without quantum theory, free will – here understood as undetermined or undefined by the laws of nature – is not necessarily doomed.

The electrical excitability of brain cells depends on the interplay of different types of electrical activity in synapses, dendrites and cell bodies. If we zoom in on the molecular structure of the cell membrane – the envelope that regulates this excitability – then particular proteins become visible that form a channel right through the membrane (Figure 13.3; see also Figure 4.1). The proteins form a pore, comparable to a tube in the eardrum or a pipe used to run electrical cables through a wall. The pores are channels that can open and close and regulate which charged particles enter or leave the cell. These are not the elementary particles that make up atoms, but atoms that are positively or negatively charged (ions) because they have absorbed electrons from other atoms, or donated them: in practice, it is all about sodium, potassium, calcium and chloride ions. The opening and closing of ion channels depends on the electrical voltage across the membrane or on the binding of transmitter molecules to the proteins. Unimaginable scenes take place on this molecular scale: ten million ions can pass through one channel per second.

Each neuron harbours a fabulous zoo of ion channels: some let sodium ions into the cell, others let potassium ions out; still others let through a mixture of

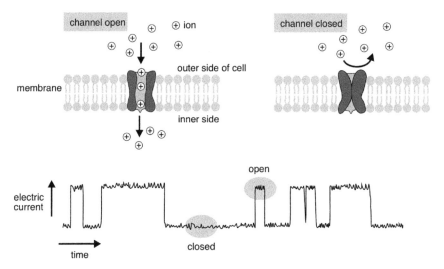

Figure 13.3 (Left) An ion channel consists of proteins that together form a pore through which charged atomic particles (ions) can flow into or out of the cell. Here, positive particles (for example sodium ions) flow in from the outside. (Right) Under the influence of a change in electrical voltage across the membrane or of the binding of a transmitter molecule, the channel can close. (Below) In a time span of thousandths of a second, the state of an ion channel can spontaneously and unpredictably 'flicker' back and forth between being open and closed.

ions. Each type of channel has its own dynamics that influences the electrical behaviour of a brain cell over time. When a cell is excited, a mixture of openings and closures of ion channels occurs whose net effect is to cause positively charged particles (usually sodium ions) to flow into the cell, increasing the likelihood that the cell will fire a spike. A fine glass electrode can be used to measure tiny electrical currents, on the basis of which the opening and closing of a single channel is measured. If you follow the opening and closing of an ion channel over a long time, the pattern of electric currents looks like a random flicker, jumping back and forth between the open and closed states, and this process is very much like an (undetermined) random process. With current knowledge, it is not possible to predict the precise behaviour of a single ion channel. One major difference with quantum mechanics is that a single ion channel can in fact have an effect on a 'large' object such as a brain cell that has to 'decide' whether to fire or not. Does this offer any relief to free will?

It is to be feared that even the innumerable ion channels, spread across billions of neurons, provide no guarantee against the dictatorship of physical determinism. There are two arguments in favour of this idea. The first is that the 'decision' of a neuron to fire a spike or not depends only to a very limited extent on an individual ion channel. A neuron has many thousands of ion channels, and ultimately the influence of all these channels is factored into a total sum that determines whether the neuron becomes active or not. But then we are talking about only one of tens of thousands to billions of neurons involved in a major brain decision: *chicken or pasta?* The influence of a flickering ion channel is therefore too small to carry any meaningful weight in directing behaviour. In other words, despite the chance processes at play at the micro level, the brain is bound by deterministic laws of nature as they apply to macro objects.

The second argument is akin to the philosophy of Arthur Schopenhauer (1788–1860), who followed in Immanuel Kant's footsteps and formulated his main ideas prior to Helmholtz. He saw the world as something driven by blind, lawless impulses, not in search of a goal and totally undirected. Imagine, in the spirit of Schopenhauer, that the random opening and closing of an ion channel did in fact determine your behaviour. If you find yourself at that all-important T-junction in your life – the choice between two jobs, two suitors, two world travels – then that single channel would make your brain switch back and forth between choosing one or the other. In the long run, this would start to look very strange. After all, what do you buy with random back-and-forth flickering? If your brain was ruled by a slot machine, it would be unpredictable and, in some sense, 'free', but it would not produce interesting, functional behaviour. At the mercy of the whims of chance, you would never arrive at the greengrocer's to do your shopping: at every street corner, your brain would keep randomly 'choosing' between left and right. You would move as erratically as a grain of ground coffee on a puddle of water. Schopenhauer judges: if you make choices according to the roulette ball, you will never really want anything. Your will will not be consistent or tenacious.

As 'free' and independent as you would be from your environment, your free will becomes empty and useless.

Free will only becomes an interesting thing to have if it can guide our actions – if behind our actions, gestures and words there is a plan motivated by drives of which we are sometimes, but not always, aware. Influenced by the behaviourist spasm to reduce behaviour to stimulus-response couplings, it has become mainstream to deny the existence of any form of free will. If the brain is presented as a simple switch box in which external stimuli are linked to corresponding actions, then you can predict the behaviour of the animal from a stimulus. Consciousness, well, it hobbles along uselessly and tries to play catch-up. Only in retrospect does it tell us a story that rationalizes what all sorts of unconscious processes in the brain had already determined for us a long time ago. Is it indeed the case that our will, chained to the determinism of the laws of nature, is governed by unconscious brain processes?

The idea that our actions – including decisions we think we are consciously making – are determined by unconscious brain processes, is illustrated by a well-known experiment by neurologist Benjamin Libet from 1983.[14] He asked test subjects to relax in a comfortable armchair and look at a screen that showed a dot of light describing a circle, like the path taken by the tip of a second hand across a dial. The subject was asked quite simply to decide when he wanted to flex the fingers or wrist of his right hand. He also had to determine the moment when he became aware that he wanted to make this movement, based on the clock position of the light spot. A few seconds later, he expressed this through words ("I wanted to move when the dot arrived at the seven o'clock position"). During the experiment, Libet recorded electroencephalographic (EEG) signals from the scalps of his subjects to gain insight into the course of brain activity in relation to the conscious moment of will.

For many brain scientists, the result came as a shock. Before a finger movement was initiated, Libet observed in the EEG an electrical voltage difference that was directly related to preparing the movement (a '*Bereitschaftspotential*' or *readiness potential*). He was able to localize the onset of this brain signal in time to about 0.6 seconds before the conscious moment of will was reported. The amazing thing was that the awareness of the decision – feeling the urge to move – was only 0.2 seconds before the moment of physical muscle movement. The time difference between the onset of the readiness potential and the moment of awareness was thus a staggering 0.4 seconds – an ocean of time for the brain to process information. Libet concluded that this difference corresponds to the time the brain unconsciously needs to prepare for action. The start of this slope, according to Libet, counts as the moment when the brain unconsciously determines whether a movement will be made, whereas the subject only becomes aware of the impending movement just before its onset. This would indeed mean that the action has already been determined before consciousness comes into play. Again, there seems to be no role for a conscious, free will. Libet did note, however, that consciousness could 'intervene' late in the process with a veto, to prevent the planned movement from going ahead.

The significance of Libet's test has been the subject of much debate, but only recently has a fundamental problem come to light. The result of the test is essentially an artefact – an artificial effect of the way Libet analyzed and interpreted the electrical brain signal. At rest, the EEG of the cerebral cortex shows spontaneous activity characterized by slow waves (Figure 13.4, bottom). Electrical voltage differences in the cortex fluctuate spontaneously over time, with the peak-to-peak time easily reaching 10 seconds, but it can also be shorter, depending on the subject's level of vigilance or alertness. When Libet's subjects relaxed in their easy chairs, these spontaneous slow fluctuations are likely to have occurred in their cortex as well.

Around 2012, several research groups published refreshing studies on Libet's test.[15] Apart from looking at the readiness potential relative to the conscious moment of will, the researchers also zoomed out, looking at the spontaneous, slow brain waves in the EEG. The spontaneous movements and conscious moments of will consistently coincided with the point in the wave cycle where the alertness and arousal of the test subjects was already high.[16] In Libet's experiment, the preparation and initiation of the volitional finger movement turned out to coincide with the most excitable phase of the slow cortical wave – the phase in which you also feel the greatest urge to move. This phase is usually preceded by a period of low excitability, which has a variable duration. By measuring the cortical EEG signals very often in relation to the start of the finger movement, and by averaging them, it seems as if there is a separate phenomenon – the readiness potential – that 'manifests' itself before the subjective moment of will that the subjects indicate. In fact, the readiness potential is an artificial, non-existent product that derives from the timing of the underlying slow brain waves in relation to the finger movement, and not a neural reflection of an unconscious process that causes the upcoming finger movement. As illustrated in Figure 13.4, it is not the (artificial) 'downward slope' that determines the onset of movement, but the transition from low to high excitability. The sobering conclusion is that Libet's experiment does not prove that there is no conscious process of will (which, in this sense, would otherwise have given support for the concept of 'free will'). Nor does he prove that unconscious brain processes predetermine the decision before the subject becomes aware of it.

Is there any positive evidence for a free will? What we are left with as a thread to string 'free will' on is not something separate from the laws of nature – a notion that can be discarded – but a process of will that coincides with a consciously experienced urge to decide, and is 'free' only in that it cannot be predicted by anything or anyone in the environment. Here it is necessary to temper our expectations. Perhaps we are too eager for free will to exist. Even with Libet, it is noticeable that conscious free will is almost imperceptibly conceived as a 'thing' that can intervene in our physical lives, such as imposing a 'veto' on previously planned actions. Prompted by the old idea of an independent soul, this view turns out to be unfortunate when we look at the

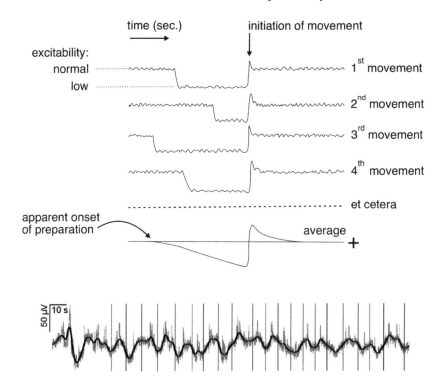

Figure 13.4 Libet's experiment with spontaneous finger movements. (Top) In this diagram, EEG signals from successive trials (1st, 2nd movement and so on) are shown below each other, aligned in time to the initiation of the movement. This initiation occurs when the excitability of the cortex is normal or increased. This state is preceded by a period of low excitability. If the EEG recordings of all trials are averaged, the variable duration of this period creates the image of a downward slope (the 'readiness potential'), but this is not a separately existing phenomenon. (Bottom) Empirical support from EEG measurements. The black line represents slow fluctuations in the EEG of the cortex, the dark grey outliers are faster wave patterns. EEG fluctuations are expressed in microvolts (μV; a microvolt is a millionth of one volt). Straight vertical lines indicate moments when a subject in Libet's task presses the button. These moments generally, though not always, coincide with a trough or downward slope in the slow waves, corresponding to high excitability.

Source: Adapted from Schmidt et al. (2016). Reproduced with permission of Elsevier.

cohesion of cognitive processes. Just like consciousness, free will is not a thing that can be located in one particular place in the brain. It cannot be pinned down to a single process, such as making the ultimate decision or biting the neural bullet. Nor is it a vague and elusive process that hovers above the brain like a mist.

If it is none of all that, then what is it?

It will be clear by now that there is more to the brain than a stimulus-response device that determines our decisions well and good before we become aware of them. There is a lot to be said for the fact that a good portion of our behaviour is dictated by unconscious, irrational impulses that we try to justify afterwards, but this does not mean that conscious brain processes do not play any role in decisions. Nor can Sherrington's hierarchy of reflexes or stimulus-response mechanisms explain a fundamental feature of will processes. Each stimulus-response scheme assumes that our behaviour is triggered by an external stimulus. But even without external stimuli we want all sorts of things. The will is spontaneous and can act independently of commands and cues from the outside world. The fact that the brain can process and reprocess information autonomously and spontaneously has already been illustrated by the phenomenon of replay. Without external stimuli and without visible action towards the environment, the brain displays its own dynamics that guarantee all kinds of 'free' activities such as dreaming, reminiscing, imagining and day-dreaming. This is in line with the self-organizing capacity that fundamentally characterizes the brain.

Let us contrast a simple stimulus-response relationship, such as the patel-lar reflex, with the role of Meryl Streep in the romantic film *The Bridges of Madison County*. In the knee-jerk reflex, the upward movement of your lower leg (the output) is easy to predict if you know the input (the strength of the hammer blow). If you double the strength of the input, you will double the output. This does not apply to all strengths of the blow, as there is a lower limit below which a very faint blow has no effect, and above a certain strength your leg keeps on sticking to a maximum output. But in essence, this is a predictable stimulus-response system that does not involve freedom or will. In *The Bridges*, Meryl plays an Italian-born woman, Francesca Johnson, who is married to a farmer in rural Iowa. When her husband and children are away for a few days for the Illinois Fair, she meets a travelling photographer, Robert Kincaid (Clint Eastwood), who is doing a report for National Geographic on the historic covered wooden bridges in the area. They have an intense love affair that lasts four days. In that brief period, Francesca begins to doubt her marriage and fantasizes with Robert about what it would be like to escape and travel with him. Can she abandon her husband and children? What will become of her when the free-spirited Robert leaves from one destination to the next? Will he want to commit himself?

As her husband and children return home and Robert prepares to leave the area, a situation arises where Robert is standing with his pick-up truck at a red traffic light, while Francesca and her husband are in the car behind it. Francesca puts her hand on the door handle, hesitating to leave the car and make the switch. The input that enters her brain through her eyes – the sight of Robert – does not lead to a predictable output: she does not yet know what she is going to do. Between the stations in her brain for perceiving stimuli and making decisions, there are other systems – for memory, planning, imagination, morality, emotionality – which each have their own dynamics and communicate with all the other stations.

Instead of a straightforward progression from stimulus to response, there are many loops in her entire brain system, feeding information from each station back to other modules. Each loop has its own dynamics and varies in strength – depending on alertness, stress and mood – so that calculating output from input quickly becomes extremely complex. Cognitive processes interlock: her memory and emotional systems provide feedback to her perceptual and attentional systems. If one choice option bubbles up, it triggers an extra search through memory: perhaps another option will turn out to be better after all. Her short-term desire conflicts with her long-term sense of duty. While her hand cramps around the door handle, the motor systems are stirring: using eye movements, her brain scans the environment in an attempt to capture new information; her perception is being adjusted accordingly. It is an interplay of interacting brain systems that can continue indefinitely.

Very soon after the Robert Kincaid input has penetrated Francesca's brain, the system reaches a point where it is impossible to predict what her decision will be. Her brain is subject to deterministic chaos: all her neurons obey the laws of nature, but even so, its behaviour is 'chaotic': it is so complex and capricious that it cannot be predicted exactly – neither by another human being nor by a computer. Even if you knew exactly how each neuron in Francesca's brain is put together and how it has behaved so far, it would still be impossible to predict her behaviour. This way, the feedback loops in the brain do bring us a little closer to free will.

But again, unpredictability is only one facet of free will as we talk about it in daily life. When a butterfly flaps its wings in the Amazon, it can, in principle, culminate in a huge cyclone sweeping through the Caribbean. That this butterfly effect occurs in all kinds of complex systems in nature aptly demonstrates the difference between unpredictability and free will. How a cyclone exactly develops in force, wind speed and the direction in which it rushes over sea and land is difficult to predict, but this prediction is not based on a 'free will'. Again, we run up against Schopenhauer's problem: free will refuses to be pinned down to whimsical, random behaviour. To the contrary, it is characterized by consistency: adherence to a direction that works towards a goal, ultimately serving survival or reproduction.

How does this consistency or stability of our will square with Tolman's erratic VTE behaviour and internal processes like the forward sweep in the hippocampal representation of place? If we try to imagine what happens in Francesca's brain during the battle between mind and heart that rages within her, we see above all how her systems of planning and imagination keep flashing back and forth: what happens if I defect? What if I stay? Unlike in normal cases, Francesca's brain remains undecided – until the traffic light eventually turns green and Kincaid – who knows that Francesca is behind him – finally has no choice but to drive away. In less complicated cases, a VTE brain state does develop towards a consistent, stable choice. The most fascinating thing about this spectacle that takes place within our skulls is that, on the one hand, all the elements of the system – molecules, synapses, neurons, networks – obey the laws of nature but, on the other hand, all the feedback loops and interactions within the system lead to a consistent and persistent 'will' that remains unpredictable by outside observation. In the field of neural networks we speak of an 'attractor', a state to which the system as a whole moves. This is the state in which the system will remain stable after the initial phase of chaotic back-and-forth flicking has passed. Our brains, in short, are not 'free' or independent of the material elements of which they are composed, but they do have free will if we see this as a consistent result of their interactions that cannot be predicted from the individual behaviour of those elements.

Our free brains are also never failing to reconsider decisions and improvise when new facts arise. Imagine a supercomputer programmed to predict your behaviour precisely. The computer contains a complete model of 'who you are' and has stored all the facts about your deepest motives and secret desires. Your body is in constant communication with the machine through a multitude of sensors that measure your heart rate and brain activity. You find yourself in downtown Amsterdam and, as is the case in Amsterdam, you are faced with the choice of going through a red light or waiting for a green light. The supercomputer is familiar with your impatience and predicts with 100 per cent certainty that, given the low level of traffic on the street, you will run a red light. But the moment you hear this prediction from the computer through your ear, you decide not to do it: you decide not to follow the computer anyway and wait for the green light.

Does this line of thinking have consequences for assessing crime and punishment? Revisiting the man who downloaded child pornography after a temporal lobe surgery, we saw how traditional justice maintains a distinction between body and mind: despite an identifiable neurological cause, he was found guilty. After all, he had acted voluntarily and consciously. But it is now becoming clearer that there is no actual contradiction between consciousness, free will and causes in the brain. If someone is guilty of a crime, then the molecules and neurons in his brain are also guilty – not individually, but as a collective. Even large structures such as the hippocampus or prefrontal cortex are not guilty as stand-alone units: guilt only arises with the act, when the trigger is pulled. Since Anders Breivik killed 77 people in 2011, most of them innocent school children on the Norwegian island of Utoya, nearly all molecules in his brain have been replaced by others, but the total system of which they were a part has remained largely intact. What makes his brain as a whole culpable? This is precisely the distinction between stimulus-response mechanisms and vicarious trial and error that Tolman sensed so precisely, and most modern jurisdiction is also well thought out on this point. If we respond to a stimulus automatically or on impulse, so that someone dies unintentionally, this behaviour is called manslaughter. If there is deliberation, the act is premeditated and we call it murder. For the question of guilt, it does not matter whether there are causes in the brain: there always will be.

What matters is a will that operates freely and autonomously in relation to the environment. In principle, this can be read from the brain by recording internal deliberations, as in the example of hippocampal representations in the rat.

Finally, a tribute to the two main protagonists of this story. Our first hero is Tolman: he showed us the way to internal cognitive processes that organize and shape the brain. His ideas spurred neurophysiology on to a quest that has yielded such brilliant discoveries as replay, the forward sweep and the encoding of a cognitive map in the hippocampus. His work on mental simulation of fictional action scenarios drew attention to a crucial component of the evolutionary success of *homo sapiens*: the internal formation of hypotheses and plans that reach far into the future. Tolman's work is also relevant to understand the neural basis of consciousness: I have previously argued that the function of consciousness – as a multisensory overview of one's situation in the here and now – is to support complex, goal-oriented behaviour, for which planning and internal deliberation are essential. Our consciousness is essential for feeding this internal jousting of deliberations with perceptual world updates.

The second protagonist worthy of our admiration and praise is the rat. Experimental research has led us to reappraise these and other animals as intelligent creatures that share many cognitive abilities, no matter how primitive, with humans. Hats off to the rat. How natural is it that we poison these animals in our homes to make them die a slow death? How avoidable is this distress?

14 Fake news in the brain

Does our reality consist of arbitrary symbols?

Transmission masts are set on fire: the 5G mobile network helps spread the coronavirus. Microsoft founder and philanthropist Bill Gates exploits the pandemic as a hoax to inject people with microscopic chips under the guise of 'vaccination' to violate their privacy and subject them to 'paedo deep states' and child-raping rulers. And the vaccination shot against measles, mumps and rubella causes autism. In 1998, British doctor Andrew Wakefield and colleagues published a study on 12 children in *The Lancet*, suggesting this causal link.[1] No factual evidence was provided, and it later came out that Wakefield had manipulated his results and had a financial interest in his study, enabling him to promote his own alternative vaccine. In 2010, *The Lancet* retracted the article, but by then his work had already gained widespread public attention. In the UK, vaccination coverage fell from 93 to 73 per cent – with peaks of under 50 per cent in London – and measles infection rose sharply in several countries. The conspiracy theory of the anti-vax movement got the wind in its sails: every vaccine injected into children is a poison. Since Donald Trump embraced the anti-vaccination stance, the list of conspiracy theories has been growing at an alarming rate. We have become all too familiar with the idea that climate change has been invented by the 'deep state' to control our lives and raise taxes. The improbability or absurdity of theories does not appear to deter large groups in society from believing in them. The Sandy Hook high-school shooting, killing 26 people, was staged with actors to promote gun control. The former sports reporter David Icke maintains that blood-drinking, shape-shifting alien reptiles are manipulating human civilization, counting former US presidents George Bush senior and junior, Margaret Thatcher, the British Royal Family and – last but not least – Bob Hope amongst their members.

Conspiracy theories fit seamlessly into the postmodernist zeitgeist in which we live: every truth is subjective, and everyone lives in his or her own reality that is just as valid and valuable as that of others. Everything is, in a sense, 'just an opinion'. What used to be an established fact must be doubted. Conversely, sources of doubt and fear are promoted to undisputed facts. As an exponent of postmodernism, philosopher Michel Foucault argued that insanity is not based on an actual disorder of the brain and mind, but arises from the way a culture looks at deviant individuals: insanity is a fabrication or construct manufactured

DOI: 10.4324/9781003429555-14

from social conventions. There is no objective knowledge – no facts that we can be sure of. This also has consequences for neuroscience: there can be no overarching, established theory that explains the relationship between brain and mind. Thus, science too is falling prey to the Trumpian doctrine that everyone is free to come up with their own version of the facts. Who does not remember Sean Spicer, the almost touching White House spokesman, declaring that at Donald Trump's inauguration in 2017, the National Mall was fuller than ever before?

Does the brain also behave like Trump's media platform Truth Social? Do the workings of the brain provide solid ground on which to base objective knowledge, or do conscious observations belong in the category of visions, ideology and 'just an opinion'? How arbitrary or random is the reality we see and feel? With Helmholtz we already got acquainted with the suspicion that conscious experience could consist of no more than arbitrary symbols or signs. Let neurology, as before, instruct us in finding answers.

Around 2005, a very confused, 67-year-old woman, named A. S. T., is admitted to Queen's Hospital in east London. Neurologists determine that she is as blind as a bat, although her pupils do constrict when light is shone on her eyes.[2] When she is shown cards with a circle or a cross on them, she guesses and her score does not rise above chance level. Even when a doctor's hand gesture comes dangerously close to her face, she does not blink. If a bright beam of light is directed at her face, she randomly guesses whether the light is on or off. On tests for language ability and intelligence, she scores normal for her age. She is not demented and does not suffer from memory loss. Despite her loss of vision, she does fairly well when her imagination is tested: the neurologist lists 20 animal species and asks her to guess the length of their tails, and she scores well above chance level.

With electrodes on her scalp, electroencephalographic (EEG) measurements are taken. These confirm that she is blind: light stimuli do not evoke the usual electrical reactions in the occipital lobe as observed in sighted people. In this she differs from Mr S., the veteran who turned out not to be totally blind, but could not distinguish shapes. Brain scans show that the cortex in the back of her head is affected. As is to be expected with blindness, the occipital lobe in particular looks bad, but more widespread damage is also found in the temporal and parietal lobes. More than two years before her admission, A. S. T. had been treated with radioactive radiation for a brain tumour in the back of her head. This treatment had been successful, but the white matter of the brain – the wiring of nerve fibres that connects cells in different brain areas – can deteriorate sharply as a result of intensive irradiation. This provides a plausible explanation for the blindness and disorientation in which Mrs A. S. T. found herself when entering the hospital.

There is only one little problem with this diagnosis: A. S. T. strongly disagrees that she is blind. She is willing to admit that her vision is a little worse than usual, but she blames this on the poor lighting in the hospital. When asked how she evaluates her own eyesight, she says this is better than her memory. After her radiation treatment, people around her already noticed that she was reading fewer and fewer newspapers and books, and bumping into furniture and tables in her home more and more often. When she wanted to put slices of bread in her toaster, they ended up outside the slots. When making tea, the bag ended up next to the pot. She saw things that were not there: non-existent animals, cars or people. In her own house, she had seen a baby and a girl in need of food. People told of how she was standing at a window in her house and looked with astonishment at a new village that must have been built out there in a few days.

For her, this was all 'real' – she did not experience these visual impressions as a product of her imagination, but as something that was really happening in her outside world. If a peeled potato did not land in the pan, she blamed this on her own clumsiness. Her other senses worked fine. She could tell without fail when her hand was being touched, and received visual sensations at the touch: she sensed a little girl, or teacups, a vase with flowers, all in clear images. She bent down and stretched out her arm to touch these things. She experienced these visual objects not as something in 'her head' or her imagination, but as actually existing, localized in the space around her.

What was wrong with Mrs A. S. T.? She presents us with a contradiction: her neurologists have diagnosed her as blind, but she herself, from her own experience, opposes this. The existence of things she sees is not verified by others. She confirms the idea that everyone brews her own version of reality. But on the other hand, the brain scans and visual tests do not beat about the bush: it is clinically established that she is blind. Is it possible that she cannot see, but does not know this about herself – and thus denies her blindness? The combination of blindness and denial fits exactly into the syndrome described by the Austrian neurologist Gabriel Anton (Figure 14.1) in 1899.[3] Today, Anton's syndrome is seen as a form of anosognosia, the phenomenon whereby a patient is unaware of her illness and can even deny it.

Gabriel Anton was known as a warm-hearted and modest doctor, who always had a comforting word for his patients and worked hard to improve their lot. During the Belle Époque he became a well-known and celebrated neurologist; the transition from the nineteenth to the twentieth century marked a golden age for his field. Around 1907, Alois Alzheimer published his discoveries about dementia. In 1905, Anton had the honour of taking over the chair in psychiatry and neurology in Halle, a town in Saxony-Anhalt, from Carl Wernicke, who had become famous for his description of a brain area that is important for the understanding of language. Even after his appointment, Anton continued to work for the public cause: he established institutions for the mentally handicapped in Graz and Halle.

Around 1905, Anton is brooding on his sofa, looking up at the ceiling ornaments that adorn his townhouse in Halle. His gaze slips out through the window to the beautiful old town, which is overflowing with market vendors. What is wrong with blind or deaf patients who are unaware of their condition? He twists the tips of his curly moustache and is frustrated by the lack of

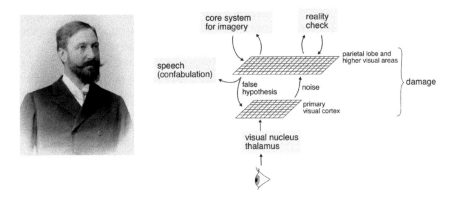

Figure 14.1 (Left) Portrait of Gabriel Anton (1858–1933). (Right) Diagram summarizing two hypotheses to explain Anton's syndrome. The first hypothesis holds that, following damage to visual cortex areas and their lines of communication, 'noise' continues to circulate through the system, which the higher areas and the parietal lobe try to explain away by means of an untruthful interpretation (a hallucination). The second hypothesis states that brain areas for imagination take over the role of lower visual areas, so that the patient's experience is not based on externally generated inputs, but on internally generated information that is nevertheless experienced as real. A reality check is lacking.

knowledge about the syndrome he discovered. He himself examined patient Johann Fuchs, who became completely deaf after a severe skull fracture and underwent major psychological changes. Using sign language, he was able to communicate with Fuchs, who then reported that he could hear all kinds of things, including the church bells of his home village in Styria. He heard voices calling out to him: "The devil will get you, the thunderstorm will kill you!" Constantly he heard people talking to him or singing loudly; the poor man was left without a moment of peace. The only indications that Anton has of a neurological cause of the syndrome come from the brain sections that he collected after the death of several patients. In them, he sees no general deterioration or degeneration of brain tissue, but he does observe localized damage to the white and grey matter in the cortex.[4] He describes a maceration of the occipital and parietal lobes and other, higher areas of the cortex. But the damage is so widespread and non-specific that no single area or fibre bundle can be identified as the central source of the disorder. Frustrated, he decides to look at other disorders.

The extensive damage that Mrs A. S. T. had sustained in her left and right occipital and parietal lobes proves to be typical of Anton's syndrome. In both eyes, the retina still functions and transmits light information to the visual thalamic nucleus (Figure 7.2), but this thalamic station then sends information to a kind of no man's land in the cerebral cortex – a visual system so severely damaged that it no longer functions. The raw information from the eyes is still being delivered, but the neural machinery is missing to build conscious visual percepts with it. Why did Mrs A. S. T. not believe she was blind? Why did she believe that her hallucinations of non-existent villages were real?

People who go blind long after birth – due to damage to the cerebral cortex or the eyes – often only become aware of the drastic loss of their sight after some time. This is associated with a partial retention of visual sensations, such as during dreams and in the waking state. They may be pleasantly surprised that they can still dream (visually) and experience their visual imagination as more vivid and colourful than before the loss. But apart from their ability to generate visual sensations 'internally', that is without external light stimuli, they do know that they are living in darkness, or at least that something important is missing from their sensory repertoire.[5] When this self-recognized blindness is caused by a stroke, the damage is usually limited to the visual cortex. This situation differs from Anton's syndrome, in which in addition to the primary visual cortex, higher brain areas are also damaged, including the parietal lobe and the white matter that provides communication between these areas. These additional damages are associated with the lack of awareness of one's own blindness.

The parietal lobe contains areas that are high up in the visual hierarchy of the cortex (Figure 8.4). If information from the lower visual areas does not get through to the parietal lobe properly, these higher areas are deprived of signals. From the theory of Predictive Coding, two plausible ideas emerge to explain Anton's syndrome. Despite the lack of useful information from below, the higher visual areas in the parietal lobe will nevertheless try to concoct a predictive representation or hypothesis of what is going on in the outside world. One possible representation is that of 'darkness' (to explain the absence of light inputs), but this is not what patients with Anton's syndrome experience. The first idea is that there is still some residual 'noise' percolating through the system, which prompts the higher regions of the parietal lobe to internally 'fill in' what that noise[6] might mean. This results in a hallucination that matches as closely as possible the noise pattern and the other inputs that the parietal lobe receives at the same time, such as tactile and auditory information (Figure 14.1). If the language areas, concentrated in the left hemisphere, are still intact, they produce a flow of words that describe this confabulation ("I see a new village out there").

The second idea is that the parietal lobe no longer receives significant information from the lower visual areas, but that the brain's system for imagination takes over this role of information provider. Recent research indicates that the human brain contains core areas required for different types of imagination (visual, auditory, somatosensory), and this core system is in close contact with the parietal lobe and the lower sensory areas for specific sensory modalities, such as the visual cortex.[7] If the lower visual areas are lost through damage, the core imagination system can continue to communicate with the higher visual areas of the parietal lobe to maintain the generation of visual imagery. The loss of the lower areas will not lead to the detailed perceptions that healthy people have, but they are still convincing enough for the patient to believe that the images are real. Notably, the two ideas do not contradict each other (Figure 14.1).

Both concepts are worthy of further investigation, but at the same time are not yet complete. Healthy people are equipped with an ability for reality checking that is lacking in Anton's syndrome. In the case of the second hypothesis, based on imagination, it is remarkable that the patient does not recognize her visual sensations as something she is imagining: healthy people can very well indicate when they perceive something in the outside world, or imagine it (the latter being more successful if you close your eyes). It was telling that A. S. T. stretched out her arm to touch the non-existent vase of flowers: you only do this when you are convinced that the vase is outside yourself, not when you imagine it. The hallucinations of Anton's syndrome are therefore more like dreams than imagination: as long as you are 'in your dream', you assume that the situation in which you find yourself really exists,[8] and undertake (virtual) actions towards the things and persons you encounter. One difference between dreaming and Anton's syndrome is that our body is paralyzed during dreaming – except for eye movements – but we are not aware of this while we dream.

The lack of reality check also applies to the first hypothesis, which assumes noise in residual visual inputs to which higher areas try to assign meaning. The importance of this verification process becomes clear when analyzing how Mrs A. S. T. reached out her arm to touch the non-existent vase. The result of her action is that she is palpating empty air. Normally, your brain receives feedback from the tactile senses of your hand, indicating that there is no pressure on your skin – you experience no sensation of touch. This lack of tactile sensation is consistent with the absence of a visual object. In contrast, Anton's syndrome presents with a brain that should expect to feel something from the hallucinated image of the vase, but this expectation is not met. For a healthy brain, such a discrepancy between seeing and feeling creates a conflict: a visual sensation is not verified by a tactile sensation and could therefore be false. In that case, the healthy brain would send the eyes on a wild goose chase and let the hands grasp through the air to find out what exactly is going on in this sensory conflict – only to conclude that it had imagined something. We do not yet know exactly which areas in the parietal or frontal lobe are involved in 'complaining' about such a sensory discrepancy (mismatch) and in signalling this error to the rest of the brain, but it is clear that reality checking is disturbed in Anton's syndrome. In this process, it is plausible that higher cognitive systems make a judgement on the best guess representation of the lower, sensory areas: a form of metacognition. Likewise the erroneous representation will probably reach the brain areas for speech, which make the patient fantasize aloud about what she thinks is going on in the outside world.

Could the reverse of Anton's syndrome also exist? Are there people who can see but do not know they are seeing, and therefore think they are blind? Anton was concerned with the fate of the countless wounded soldiers who served under the German-Austrian Axis in the First World War and returned physically or mentally damaged from the Eastern and Western fronts. Opposed to the massive tragedy of the front-line soldiers stands the small comfort of realizing that they produced a wealth of neurological knowledge. From the veteran communities, stories emerged about the effects of chemical warfare, such as serious eye disorders caused by exposure to mustard gas. There was the story of a multi-decorated war hero – a courier serving under the List regiment who, in October 1918, near Ypres in Belgium, was attacked by the British with this vesicant gas. With pain-staking efforts the man managed to reach the headquarters behind the front line and declared to the field medics that his eyes felt like glowing coals and that he could no longer see anything. The poor devil was transferred to a military hospital in Pomerania, where he recovered and had to witness the announcement of the shameful German defeat. After further examination, the doctors placed him not in the ophthalmology department, but in psychiatry. The man went on record as a case of 'hysterical blindness': he was not blind but could not, or would not, know that he was seeing. War-weary as many veterans were around 1918, some of them simulated an illness – a behaviour bordering on desertion. Anton was familiar with the phenomenon of hysterical illnesses and already drew a parallel with 'his' syndrome of blindness-with-denial in his 1899 publication. In hysteria, too, there is a misperception of the physical condition, but this amounts to claiming an illness that cannot be physically demonstrated, whereas Anton patients suffer from a sensory loss that they deny.

Anton explained hysteria as having a 'psychogenic' cause – a psychological defect. In modern neuroscience, the problem with hysterical blindness is not so much that the supply of sensory data would be impeded, but lies in the cognitive interpretation of that data. The data is not interpreted as a denial of a physical defect, but rather as the observation and perception of a defect that cannot be found physically in the sense organs. Dissociative identity disorder – in which patients alternately assume multiple personalities, each with its own character, perception and behaviour – can develop in response to traumatic experiences from the past. For example, one personality that a patient assumes can see perfectly well, but if she switches to another, she lacks visual acuity. The various personalities manifested by a patient may differ in colour vision, eye movements and left or right handedness, and these are accompanied by physiologically measurable abnormalities in the EEG and blood flow in visual brain areas.[9] It is likely that these changes in the visual system are influenced by higher areas in the parietal and frontal lobes.

About mini-people and tile walls: Bonnet's syndrome

Hysterical blindness and blindness-with-denial: the brain seems free to fabricate its own sensations and virtual worlds and to gleefully believe in them. As steadfast as a patient may insist that she can or cannot see, a doctor or family member may have difficulty establishing a realistic clinical picture. But is the reality we experience really so arbitrary and subjective? Let us consult another syndrome documented as early as 1760 by the Swiss naturalist and philosopher Charles Bonnet, who discovered this phenomenon in his 87-year-old grandfather.

Roughly one-tenth of patients with serious eye disorders – often elderly people – experience visual hallucinations. An elderly man who suffers from cataracts in both eyes describes how he repeatedly sees a couple of small men, each one a foot high. The men sit on a table or walk around him, and are accompanied by other miniaturized objects in the same room – such as little birds and small clocks. The man finds the creatures, which seem to have just escaped from the island of Lilliput in Gulliver's Travels, amusing. He feels comfortable in their company and manages to keep his experiences hidden from his family for a long time. Only when he starts warning his relatives to be careful not to run over these little people, do they discover what a wondrous world he lives in. Even in full sunlight, the creatures keep him company, but they make no sound, have no smell and do not touch him.[10] As in Anton's syndrome, the man locates the virtual creatures in the external space around him, but at the same time understands that they are hallucinations. To avoid being taken for a fool, he keeps quiet about them.

Bonnet's syndrome also occurs in cases of cerebral infarction, where patients become partially or totally blind, and can take on strange and threatening forms. A patient who lost sight in one half of his field of vision tells how he woke up with a severe headache:

> At the same time, I noticed that my vision was impaired, so I took the bus to visit my ophthalmologist. As I looked out of the window of the bus, I could not believe my eyes. A gigantic wall of blue tiles stretched from the ground up to the sky. I remembered that these were the same tiles that I had used on the walls of my bathroom four months previously. I wiped my eyes to look at the tiled wall more closely, but it disappeared immediately, only to reappear, disappear and reappear once more somewhat later, disturbing both my vision and my state of mind. The same day, objects and people appeared suddenly on the right. They were standing or sitting quite still, were rather shadowy and pale in colour. The tiled wall appeared less frequently during the subsequent few days, but I saw a vast landscape in its place. [...] The figures appeared more frequently, and I regretted that they kept their faces turned away from me and that I could not recognise them. I had the feeling, though, that I had seen many of them before. When I tried to regard a person more closely, he disappeared. I was certain that these apparitions had something to do with my loss of vision and were not real. The figures appeared up to forty times a day during the following weeks and irritated me to such an extent that I began to defend myself against them. I either fixed them directly or made gestures in their direction with my hand in order to maintain their irreality. This caused them to disappear. The figures appear rarely now, usually in stress situation.[11]

The shadowy figures and blue tiled wall fit into the motley procession of hallucinations experienced by people with Bonnet's syndrome: rows of little men wearing hats, Victorian houses in pastel colours, hands that approach you from the side and turn into claws, farmer's wives in the style of Hieronymus Bosch, dragons, objects from Egyptian pyramids and tombs, two little policemen who lead a rascal to a tiny prison car, transparent spirits floating through a hall, people with a big flower on their heads, futuristic cars, groups of men in fifteenth-century clothes and buildings made of red brick. The colourful procession could easily join the bizarre parade of cut-out animations in *Monty Python's Flying Circus*. There seems to be no rhyme or reason to the apparitions that reveal themselves, except that people and objects often appear in miniature.[12]

Bonnet patients do not generally believe what they are experiencing, but sometimes their hallucinations fit so well into their everyday experience that they are convinced of their authenticity. A woman sits at the window in her living room and looks at the cows in a nearby meadow. It is a cold, wintry day and the woman complains to her maid about the cruelty of the farmer who does this to his cows. Only when the girl declares that she sees no cows does the woman shamefully admit that she cannot believe her own eyes. Prior to this confrontation, her hallucination blended seamlessly with the rest of her visual experience. The hallucinations can be experienced as troublesome or annoying, but they can also be pleasant or comforting. One patient describes seeing her dead husband sitting by her side several times a week. Shortly after another elderly woman suffers from half-sided blindness, she notices a figure sitting next to her.

> It wasn't hard to realise that it was I myself who was sitting there. I looked younger and fresher than I do now. My double smiled at me in a friendly way, as though she wanted to tell me something. It was a rather pleasant experience. I had the opportunity of looking at myself for 10 or 20 seconds, and then the image disappeared.

In this case the hallucination – a heautoscopy – is not related to an out-of-body experience, but to partial blindness.[13]

What do the complex but rather random hallucinations of Bonnet's syndrome tell us about the neural basis of consciousness? Dominic ffytche and his colleagues at the Institute of Psychiatry in London made brain scans of Bonnet patients while they were hallucinating. The hallucinations occurred spontaneously, even within the noisy confines of the scanner, but could also be triggered by presenting visual stimuli. Using a hand-held panel, patients could indicate when their hallucinations began and ended, and after the scanning session they could recount the content of their experiences: these were rich in colour and involved faces, masonry, maps or other objects. The power of measurement during spontaneous hallucination is that people consciously see things in their environment while actual sensory input through their eyes is absent. Bonnet patients offer a unique glimpse into brain activity related to consciousness, without being 'contaminated' by activity associated with the feeding of information from the eyes to the cortex.

Visual hallucinations appeared to be strongly linked to activity on the ventral side of the occipital lobe, in the areas between the primary visual cortex and the temporal lobe (Figures 3.2 and 8.4). The frontal lobe was only sporadically active or not active at all. This is in line with other findings on the prefrontal cortex; Phineas Gage, for example, suffered from disturbed social behaviour but massive frontal damage did not lead to loss of consciousness in him. At the same time, the high activity on the ventral side of the occipital-temporal zone is consistent with the concentration of essential nodes for visual awareness that had already been found in healthy subjects.

ffytche went further in his conclusions. When the hallucinations were rich in colour, a brain area specifically related to colour perception was simultaneously active.[14] If the imagery occurred in black and white, the activity was not increased here, but it was increased in other, nearby structures. If a hallucination included faces, activity was increased in the area that always lights up when a face is recognized (the fusiform face area), also in healthy test subjects. Exactly which area became active depended on whether the face was that of an unknown or a known person – the faces of people we know or love are encoded in nearby but different places in this part of the occipital lobe. If a patient hallucinated without seeing faces (like the man experiencing the tile wall, who later started to see people who turned their faces away from him), it remained correspondingly silent in this face-coding area. Hallucinations in which brickwork, fences and maps were dominant corresponded to strong activity in a cortical structure coding for visual texture. These results may seem trivial: the content of visual hallucinations appears to be correlated with activation patterns that you would expect from previous studies in healthy people. Yet I find these results downright exciting, because we see a very precise link between a pure, 'uncontaminated' conscious experience and the individual brain regions associated with the visual submodalities of that experience. We already knew that the brain network for visual awareness is a patchwork of nodes, but this fact is now powerfully confirmed by a quirk of nature in which conscious experience occurs without corresponding sensory inputs.

How is the brain of a Bonnet patient triggered to produce fake news? Like in Anton's syndrome, the brains of Bonnet patients have a problem in the supply of sensory information, but in Anton's case it is the visual cortex and higher areas that are affected, while in Bonnet the cause is usually an eye disease. When the visual cortex is deprived of light information for an extended period of time, it appears to become hypersensitive to visual stimuli that still do manage to find a way to it.[15] The lack of normal, rich visual input leads to a compensation in the visual cortex to keep up the activity of neurons. Once more, the self-organizing brain shows its plastic side: if a sensory area is 'deprived' of its excitatory inputs, this deficit is compensated for by internal adjustments. If a sporadic input does arrive, however randomly, the receiving areas try to produce a meaningful image. In this respect, the theory of

Predictive Coding is just as valid for Bonnet as it is for Anton. Even if the input is just 'noise', it is treated as a news item that higher areas will work with to generate a perceptual interpretation. Again, the hierarchy from the visual cortex to the parietal lobe tries to estimate what that noisy input might represent.

Imagination – the internal creation of sensations that we know to be virtual – involves interactions between sensory areas, the core group of imagination areas and memory areas such as the hippocampus. In both Bonnet and Anton patients, mechanisms for generating hallucinations probably interact with memory areas that provide information from past experiences to sculpt the content of visual and auditory experience. In bizarre hallucinations, there will be no verbatim retrieval of a complete memory from the past. Rather, individual elements are dug up from memory to give substance to the fake experience. The brain of the Bonnet patient who saw a huge, tiled wall emerge, used his memory of having tiled his bathroom four months earlier. Even if the hallucination features extravagant creatures that the patient never saw before, the brain will use separate memory elements to combine them into the experience it is having. Dreams, fantasies and hallucinations have in common that they are a *Gesamtkunstwerk*, synthesized from the ingredients provided by memory. Even the strangest dream, imagination or hallucination ultimately rests on a composition of experiences that we have lived and stored.

Apart from the potential of Predictive Coding as a framework for explaining hallucinations, brain scans provide few clues as to the precise cogs in the neuronal machinery that give rise to hallucinations. Why would a random excitation of a brain region give rise to a structured sensation in the first place? Computer models provide insight into how this transformation might take place. With its billions of neurons, the brain can be in an astronomical number of states – states characterized, for example, by brain cell 1 being active, cell 2 inactive, cell 3 active again and so on, right down to the last brain cell. All these states can be divided into different groups, a large number of which represent only 'noise' whereas a small number are linked to a structured sensation or memory. The groups of brain states can be represented as a golf course with many hills and valleys. At any given moment, your brain state is represented by the position of a golf ball rolling through the landscape. Shortly after the ball is hit into the field, it bounces a lot: this corresponds to a rapid moving back and forth between states. Later on, it rolls in a smooth motion: the states now alternate more gradually. The hills in the landscape are states that do not correspond to a structured experience. The ball will usually not come to a halt on top of a hill, but will move towards a valley – a structured representation formed by past experiences. Our understanding of this process has been strengthened by describing it physically with the concepts of a 'basin of attraction' (the valley) and 'attractor' (the end point where the little ball comes to rest).

That this transition from noisy, unstructured stimuli to conscious experiences can occur rapidly is suggested by the observations of neurosurgeon Wilder Penfield and his colleagues on epilepsy patients in the 1930s to 1960s.[16]

To identify the anatomical source of epilepsy, he administered electric shocks to various areas of the cerebral cortex that could be reached through a skull opening. The electric shocks are a form of direct stimulation of brain tissue that bypasses the normal route of stimulation through the sense organs. What a patient sees or feels upon such artificial stimulation depends very much on the exact area of the brain that is stimulated. Stimulation of the primary visual cortex produces sensations of light spots (phosphenes), but in the higher visual areas and in the temporal lobe complex images are reported, sensations of smell (of 'burnt toast') or complete scenes of people quarrelling in a café. These conscious experiences were elicited by electrical pulses administered randomly, that is, without specific knowledge of the information encoded by the cells in the stimulated area.

Basically, a mass of brain cells is randomly activated. It is as if the golf ball lands in the field with a tremendous undirected swing, but just as quickly rolls into the valley of a well-structured, conscious experience. The rapid evolution from a random to a structured state also suggests that, given all the states that are possible prior to the stimulus, only one state emerges as the 'winner'. Computer models indicate that this winner consists of a network of cells that are strongly interconnected and that happened to be strongly activated by the electrical stimulus – to out-compete rival groups of cells by way of inhibition. At first glance, this winner-take-all principle may seem like a nasty touch of dictatorship, but it is merely an expression of the self-organizing capacity of the brain and allows conscious experience to be made in one piece: our brain does not have to keep flickering chaotically back and forth between different interpretations of sensory inputs.

Yet, this statement contains several uncertainties. For example, if cells in area V4 or elsewhere 'code' for colour, what exactly do we mean by that? I have taken the liberty of lavishly throwing around words like 'neural code', but sooner or later it will have to be explained what this means. If a message is encoded or encrypted in secret, there must be something or someone who can decode or decipher the message. If a brain region lights up on a scan when a hallucination is rich in colour, how is that information 'read out'? If something colours a virtual tile wall blue, where does the interpretation of the underlying brain signals take place? Earlier, I addressed the misconception that consciousness would be sufficiently guaranteed by sensory detectors such as smoke alarms, which sit somewhere in the brain and fire at will. A smoke alarm goes off when carbonaceous particles penetrate the device, but it has no idea what these particles are or how the chemical reaction works – and has no sense of smell whatsoever.

So I can tell you a great story about how certain groups of cells in the higher areas of the visual cortex fire away when the colour blue appears: via the colour-sensitive cells (cones) of the retina, the information about 'blue' is transmitted via the optic nerve to the thalamus and cortex, and upwards. But why should the rest of the brain believe that the firing of those higher cells represents the colour blue? Why should it not represent the smell of poo or the taste of roast meat? It is not enough to say that the cells in V4 do not receive odour information from our nasal epithelium. If those cells are going to fire vigorously, surely there must be something or someone who 'reads' their spikes as something that is about colour? But this 'someone' – the homunculus – is not to be found, and it is highly unlikely that there is one central brain area that converts all information into conscious experience. Suppose you could isolate the colour-sensitive cells in V4 – plus the retina and the fibre tracts that send colour information to them – and keep them alive in a culture dish. Would that tissue culture then be able to see colour?

Leaving aside this recurring Hard Problem, let us consider where we stand in understanding Bonnet's syndrome. Predictive Coding is based on a hierarchical system of interconnected brain regions that collectively represent the presumed causes of sensory inputs. Higher regions generate predictive representations, and this activity is driven by the bottom-up error messages that the system normally receives – the 'news' it gets from the senses (Figure 11.4). Bonnet's syndrome lacks the normal amount of news, and the predictive machinery of the higher regions compensates for this lack by interpreting other inputs, from inside and outside the system. The system is hypersensitive to these other inputs, often coming from higher brain regions, which send the brain into a state that happens to match those inputs – a state of hallucination. Non-sensory inputs, such as memory patterns that normally fuel a healthy imagination, can help shape the content of a hallucination. Unlike people with Anton's syndrome, Bonnet patients are able to perform a reality check: they usually know they are hallucinating.

How arbitrary is our reality?

Nevertheless, we are left with the original question: how arbitrary is the reality we experience? In the footsteps of postmodernism: why should the world of a Bonnet patient be less real or objective than that of a 'healthy' person? After all, a healthy person is just as much constantly engaged in simulating the outside world, but usually does not realize this. Part of the answer lies in the patients' own stories: our quest is like a detective story. Take the Bonnet patient on the bus, who eventually became wildly annoyed with all the fake people he saw: they disappeared when he made hand gestures towards them.

Apparently, his brain chooses a different, non-hallucinatory interpretation when the patient takes action towards a fictional character.[17] This action yields valuable feedback: his hand and arm are grabbing the air and are not in contact with the figure he sees before him. The representational machinery of his brain is confronted with conflicting information: the visual system gives rise to seeing a person, but confirmation via the sense of touch fails to materialize.[18] The higher system, which overarches both sensory modalities, infers that the data input is too unreliable to distil a human figure from it, thus dismissing the representation of the fake figure.

So we can use our musculoskeletal system to perform reality checks, with feedback from non-visual senses helping to determine whether our visual image of reality is accurate. It is likely that patients with Anton's syndrome continue to believe in their virtual reality because their higher visual cortex areas and related parietal lobe regions are more impaired than in Bonnet patients. They are unable to integrate the crucial feedback from other modalities – generated through bodily interactions with the environment – with visual information. As a result, an Anton patient will exhibit dysfunctional behaviour such as bumping into tables, chairs and doorways, only to justify this behaviour with excuses such as poor interior lighting or a speck of dust in the eye.

Ultimately, creating a representation of reality is about blunt evolutionary principles. Does the representation help us to get food and drink? Does it give us advantages for survival and reproduction? No matter how hard the brain of an Anton patient tries to present her with a consistent view of the world, when push comes to shove, it is simply at the mercy of Darwinism: the patient is injured, suffers unnecessary pain and fails to obtain food efficiently. Without other, properly functioning senses or help from outside, she would inevitably die. Her visual image of reality turns out not to work. If the brain suspects it is dealing with fake news, there is only one thing to do: actively use other senses in your body to see whether their very inputs can interpret what is going on. The information from your hearing, touch, muscles and balance organs must match your visual representation in order for it to be accepted as 'real'. In other words, a sensory representation will be maintained when there is consistency amongst the senses involved. Anton's syndrome shows how handicapped you would be when your visual awareness alone is not functioning properly. What would you be like if you were hallucinating in all your senses? Your hallucinations would constantly send you in the wrong direction – you would not be able to navigate the outside world. You would not be able to stand or sit upright. Without a functioning conscious mind, you would not be able to hold up in the world. There is no subconscious mind that would come to your rescue and automatically show you the way. This rubs our faces in the fundamental function of consciousness: it provides us with a world overview, enabling us to perform complex behaviours, ultimately serving our survival and reproduction.

And yet: earlier I argued that our consciousness is *not* dependent on physical activity. Patients with paralysis or locked-in syndrome can still be aware of their surroundings. They have been able to move in the past, but have lost this ability due to an accident, muscle disease or brain disorder. Because a locked-in patient can boast a rich history of experience with body movements prior to his disorder, his system for conscious representation is sufficiently trained to continue functioning properly at the moment when body movement is lost. It is also essential that a locked-in patient still has a functioning visual and auditory system. If he were to get Bonnet's syndrome on top of his locked-in syndrome, there would be a huge problem with representing the reality around him. Conscious experiences can therefore occur without physical activity, but are at the same time strongly shaped by our history of physical interactions with our environment.

How do the visual hallucinations of Bonnet and Anton relate to other sensory misrepresentations such as phantom sensations after limb amputation? From the girl whose arm was cut off, Descartes learned that she had pain in her (removed) hand. Similar to the eye conditions accompanying Bonnet, amputation is associated with a lack of sensory input to the body map in the somatosensory cortex (Figure 7.1). If this brain area, like the visual cortex in Bonnet, becomes oversensitive to stimuli from outside or from the brain itself, the system may start to respond to noise by generating representations of what might be going on in the (missing) body part. When people suffer damage to their cochlea in the inner ear at a dance party, they may experience phantom sounds, usually in the form of tinnitus. Patients constantly hear squeaking, hissing, humming or rustling noises in the absence of an external sound source, to the point of madness. Tinnitus can be aggravated or triggered by stress or trauma; also in this case, the auditory cortex becomes overactive in the absence of external sound. A reasonable explanation of phantom sound thus lies in the wake of phantom pain and the syndromes of Anton and Bonnet: there is a strong suspicion that phantom sound is also triggered by random, noisy signals that reach the auditory cortex from the cochlea or other brain areas. The signals act on the system as 'error messages' that higher areas of the cortex try to explain away by producing sound representations.[19]

All well and good: for healthy people, reality may be less fictitious and arbitrary than we thought. Our bodies have an arsenal of sensory and cognitive tools to unmask hallucinations. If this were not so, the word 'hallucination' would not appear in our language. But even with your own 'normal' experiences, don't you have the idea that they are nevertheless completely subjective? That you live in a private inner world which you essentially cannot talk to others about? To what extent does our inner world have the privacy that conspiracy theorists believe could be hijacked by Bill Gates through the injection of microchips?

Do you see red where I see green?

The designated example of subjective experience is seeing colour. We can disagree profoundly about what the blue-or-white dress looks like. Throughout the history of thought about mind and body, the Inverted Spectrum argument has resurfaced time and again, and has been fought over so long and bitterly among philosophers that it is worthy of the title 'philosophers' graveyard'. This argument goes back to John Locke, who asked himself in 1689: "If I see a rainbow in violet-blue-green-yellow-orange-red, is it possible that you see the same rainbow in exactly the opposite colours (red-orange-yellow-green-blue-violet)?"[20] It is not without reason that this question has aroused so much controversy and debate over the centuries: it is about nothing less than the 'qualia' – the subjective, qualitative properties of individual conscious experiences. The coexistence of sensory modalities that we experience as very different is also part of the qualia problem and – in spite of philosophers such as Daniel Dennett who try to reason it away[21] – it is the ultimate problem in the relationship between brain and consciousness. This is also what David Chalmers' Hard Problem is about: while today we can approach all kinds of cognitive abilities (such as memory) with measurements, tests and computer models, the fundamental problem of how and why all these abilities can produce subjective, conscious experiences remains.

How is our grey matter, with its cells producing measurable and therefore quantitative electrical activity, able to produce anything qualitative like colour sensations? No matter how hard we try to find 'colour' in the far reaches of physics, it is always about measurable things like wavelength and energy of photons – not about the experience of colour itself. "The book of nature is written in numbers": this has been the adage of science since Descartes. But what about the brain as a product of nature, and its ability to make us experience extremely different qualities?

Let us descend from these philosophical highlands to our down-to-earth colour experience of everyday life. Isaac Newton came up with a practical way to capture the relationships between colours on the circumference of a circle (Figure 14.2). If you start counting from the colour violet (or purple) at the seven o'clock mark, you travel clockwise along the colours that flow into each other: blue, turquoise (cyan), green, yellow-green (chartreuse), yellow, orange, red and violet. This corresponds to the physical description of visible light, in which violet or purple corresponds to the shortest wavelength we perceive and red to the longest. Only the fact that red and violet are similar or related in our experience – whereas on the scale of wavelengths they lie at the extreme edges – is a little odd. If I experience a coloured object as violet, could you see the same object as red (even though we refer to the object with the same word 'violet')? I have long thought this was possible, but it is disproved by our pragmatic use of coloured materials such as powders or paints. Purple or violet is a non-primary colour that can be obtained by mixing blue with red, whereas red is a primary colour. There is no combination of paint colours that, when mixed, produces pure red. So if I perceive a blob of paint as purple, it is not possible that you perceive the same blob as red: we would continue to disagree about whether the colour could come about by mixing! This non-interchangeability also applies to blue (primary) versus orange (as a mixture of red and yellow) and to green versus yellow (or chartreuse). Our down-to-earth experience with coloured materials shows that not all colours are interchangeable, for in practice there are no arguments about mixability, except perhaps in the case of small children who are handling a paintbrush for the first time.

But fans of the Inverted Spectrum do not give in so easily. What about the interchangeability of primary colours? Is yellow interchangeable with blue? At this point it is useful to leave Newton's colour wheel and switch to a three-dimensional representation of colour that takes into account their brightness and purity (also called saturation).[22] In Figure 14.2 we see a tilted pancake,

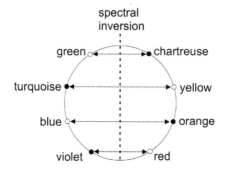

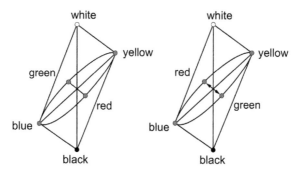

Figure 14.2 (Top) Newton's colour wheel. The circumference of the circle shows the successive colours from the spectrum perceptible to humans. The vertical dotted line marks an imaginary 'spectral inversion'. (Bottom left) This three-dimensional colour space includes effects of lightness (brightness) and purity (saturation). Colours at the edge of the tilted pancake are pure, colours towards the centre contain more grey. (Bottom right) Based on their brightness, pure red and green would be interchangeable, but a green dye colour can be obtained by mixing while red cannot.
Source: Adapted from Palmer (1999).

marked at its perimeter with green, red, yellow and blue. Through the centre of the pancake runs a straight line from black (bottom) to white (top): this axis represents the brightness or lightness of a colour. The space containing all visible colours consists of two cones glued together with their undersides, and these undersides coincide with the pancake. The purest colours are found at the edge of the disc, while towards the central black-and-white axis more and more grey is mixed in. If you move up from the pancake, then more and more white is mixed in instead of grey (red, for example, changes to ever lighter pink). In this colour space, a mixed colour such as brown is located in the vicinity of orange, with a tendency towards black and a touch of yellow and green, just as you would get the colour on a palette by mixing paint. The hard, primary colours of Piet Mondrian are thus on the edge of the pancake, but the dark golden dusk of a Rembrandt or the chestnut colour of a Rothko straddle the space between the pancake and the black at the bottom of the cone.

In the 3D rendering, pure yellow lies a lot higher in colour space than pure blue (pure yellow roughly lies in the direction of pure white and pure blue towards black). These positions correspond to our experience: we also perceive pure yellow pigments as brighter and lighter than pure blue. People appear to be in complete agreement about this. I have never spoken to anyone who thought a lemon looked darker than a cornflower. So the primary colours yellow and blue are not interchangeable either.

But what about the colours that are at the same level of brightness in the pancake, such as green and red? Even those colours are not interchangeable: as we already saw, red is primary and green can be obtained by mixing yellow and blue. Thus, no colour appears to be truly interchangeable. I must admit I was quite surprised when my earlier intuition turned out to be wrong. Perhaps I had been reading books for too long and should have taken a painting course earlier.

However: the invalidity of the Inverted Spectrum argument does not mean that our experiences of colour (or other qualitative sensations) are necessarily objective. In principle, your colour space could be 'shifted' from mine in a way that we cannot imagine. Our imaginations are fuelled by our own experiences in the past and your radically different colour space may never have overlapped with mine. And yet, if you were to secretly see the new colour 'X' where I perceive brown, we would discover this subjective difference pretty quickly by *talking* about mixing paints, or finding out what your familiar colour X resembles, either closely or remotely. It is equally important to realize that colour experience is not absolute, but depends on the visual context. In Figure 14.3, we see a cube with two coloured surfaces that reflect light of the same wavelength into our eyes, but are nevertheless perceived as brown versus orange – by one and the same person. Our experience of the brown and orange squares appears to depend on the colour and brightness of the surrounding squares: the top of the cube is brightly lit, making the central square stand out relatively darkly from its surroundings and appear much browner than the square on the shaded side. Despite this context-dependent interpretation of light, people also agree on this.

But then: The Dress! What is causing the viral discord between the black-blue and the white-gold camp? Here, too, the predictions or expectations forged by the visual system come into play. The original picture is seen as black-blue by 57 per cent of the people and as white-gold by 30 per cent (10 per cent of the respondents flip back and forth between the two interpretations, the rest sees something else). Looking at Figure 1.2, changing the background of the dress to a darker shade may seduce your brain to become more susceptible to the white-gold interpretation. Physically, the wavelengths that the dress reflects in your eyes normally match black and blue. If it is shown against a yellow-tinted background, many more people find it black-blue than white-gold, and the reverse happens with a blue-tinted background.

Figure 14.3 (Top) Influence of context on perception of colour. The middle square
on the top of this cube appears browner than the middle square on the
shadow side, which appears bright orange to us. (Bottom) If the ambient
colours around both squares are removed, it turns out that the colours are
identical. The brain's system for conscious colour perception corrects for
the context in which colour information from a small part of our field of
vision is presented.
Source: Beau Lotto.

If you 'flip' the physically reflected wavelengths in the colour spectrum so
that the 'blue' wavelengths change to wavelengths within the 'yellow' part of
the spectrum, the ambiguity of the picture diminishes dramatically: now as
many as 94 per cent of those surveyed find that the strips they previously saw
as white or blue have unmistakably changed to yellow-gold.[23] This is because
our visual system has become accustomed to blue as the dominant colour in
the background illumination of our surroundings through years of experience:
during the day, the sky gives the background of visual scenery on average a
hint of blue, but in the twilight and in the shadow, too, short wavelengths
('blue') are more strongly represented than longer ones ('yellow'). Think of
landscape paintings: here, depth is suggested by having colours fade into blue

towards the horizon. So when looking at objects with a blue tint, our brains tend to automatically correct for a blue background or a blue shadow effect, and therefore see the object as less blue. Apparently, this contextual correction works more strongly in white-gold viewers such as Kim Kardashian than in blue-black viewers under the vocal direction of Taylor Swift.

Yet there is still something chafing in this whole discussion. On the one hand, there is the conviction that we live in one all-encompassing, continuous simulacrum – a three-dimensional, holographic 'film' of reality that our brain constantly creates and in which we are trapped. On the other hand, we are able to break through hallucinations and other fake news and test our home-brewed experiences against reality – by interacting with the outside world through our bodies and processing the multisensory feedback from those interactions. Because we can expose 'alternative facts', we feel we can break out of our prison and into the real world. This also happened in *The Matrix* when Neo took the red pill that unmasked his life up to that point as fake. But the problem is: in our daily lives, we do not have a red pill. As long as all of our sensory representations match, there is no evidence to speak of a hallucination, while we imperceptibly live on in our self-created simulacrum. Because the simulacrum also represents eye and head movements, it is 'all-in' and so we are convinced we are looking directly at things in the outside world. There is no need to be sentimental about this supposed imprisonment: the 'I' is not a separate thing somewhere inside our world model, but it partakes in this as a higher-order concept. It is merely a storyline within the larger story. As long as this continuous simulation allows us to do our daily work, survive and have fun every now and then, this need not be a disaster – but it does make us isolated. Despite the talk about dyeing techniques it appears we are living, however reluctantly, in a reality all our own.

Are there other ways to unmask the all-in simulacrum and gain insight into a more objective reality? Besides the motor-sensory loop by which a Bonnet patient unmasks his visual hallucination, an important clue lies in noticing other inconsistencies within our own perception. A child confronted with visual illusions such as the Kanizsa triangle develops the intuition that 'something is not right' about the picture she sees. Pressing against one of her eyeballs, with the other eye closed, she experiences a distorted image inconsistent with her normal vision. If you look against the sun for too long and close your eyes, you experience a negative afterimage that does not square with the presence of a new object outside yourself. Gradually during childhood, the realization arises that perceptions are not always reliable and that they depend on a fallible sensory apparatus – while there are equally reliable 'constants' present as well. A child who wakes up after a good night's sleep realizes, by virtue of her memory, that the world around her has not temporarily ceased to exist, but has gone on while she was sleeping. Objects of solid matter have a permanence that continues even when they disappear from view, and so many forms of durability can be discovered. In short, already in early childhood we learn to use our nascent cognitive capacities to assess the reliability of sensations and objects, and from this arises an intuitive physics that makes us realize that there are in fact things that are reliably and permanently present in an external world that is felt to be more objective – a world that exists independently of our senses. After early infancy, we go to school, eventually learning about Newton's worldview in physics class. This provides us with the image of an even more objective, rock-solid outside world. This strictly mechanistic and quantitative physics, following in the footsteps of Descartes' method, does come at a price: Newton's worldview has no room for the qualitative properties of our perception, except in what we, for want of a better term, continue to call the 'mind'.

But the pros and cons of the Newtonian worldview – and its succession in the theory of relativity and quantum physics – constitute a separate chapter which I will not go into now. Meanwhile, through elementary school, language has nestled itself unobtrusively into the discussion. What role does language play as a means of communication in breaking through our simulacrum?

If you are walking your dog in a park and talk to a passer-by about 'this dog', you can only understand each other if you are talking about the same dog. If everyone had their own, isolated dog fantasy, we would not be talking about the same thing and would not be able to explain to each other how to deal with the dog. We would have completely different ideas about what 'dog food', 'leash' and 'walking' are. We would live in a totally private world – a solipsistic universe – in which only our own perceptions and ideas could lay claim to authenticity.[24]

But then your ten-year-old nephew comes to visit. In your living room he sees a fruit bowl with apples on a table. You point to one of the apples and say, "You shouldn't eat that one, it is rotten." Your nephew hears this and interprets this information in a way that influences his behaviour. Via his semantic memory, the sound of the word 'rotten' triggers a representation of his own, which he links to his visual perception of the colour patterns, shapes and shine of the apples in front of him. He avoids the rotten one and sinks his teeth into a fresh one. There is nothing in your communication that requires you to have exactly the same experience of the rotten apple. Your perception of the rotten apple may well differ from that of your nephew (he may be colour-blind, or there may be a blue-or-white dress type of situation in which the two of you see the rotten apple differently). Nevertheless, your verbal communication is successful: your words spare your nephew a rotten taste and slimy sensation in his mouth. Without having to resort to identical sensations, you understand each other through a shared language – through words that refer to things you each experience within your own simulacrum. The other person's words also enter into your simulacrum, and through our memory for concepts and facts, they have a solid and consistent connection with your own representations of corresponding things. Again, it is the practice of everyday communication that makes the difference. The loneliness of being in your own simulacrum is thus broken by having word sounds, but also gestures and facial expressions, shuttle back and forth between people.

This 'shuttling' is not as obvious as it seems. If we lived purely within our own simulacrum and had no idea that it is made up of representations, experienced as 'real', of an outside world, we cannot simply presuppose 'commuting' between simulacra either, except perhaps if Descartes' demon or a God arranged it for us. But the point is: while developing an intuitive physics in our early childhood, we do develop an idea about an outside world that exists independently of us as subjects. On the one hand a 'word sound' relies on the safe assumption that we exchange words via a mechanism that operates between spatially separate subjects (sound waves propagating through the air). On the other hand it refers to the brain's ability to convert perceived sound into a concept ('rottenness') which is associated via semantic memory with all sorts of other concepts that eventually make your cousin avoid the rotten apple. The chances of you thinking of a square while I shout 'circle' at you thus becomes vanishingly small.

Time to look back. Thanks to the existence of a common language, the inescapability of the simulation of which we are a part takes on a certain charm and beauty. When we are healthy, our simulacrum is so incredibly accurate that we do not even realize it is a simulation. It enables us to plan and carry out complex actions effectively. It also provides sufficient depth for social behaviour, love, parenting and compassion: within our own little world, there is more than enough room to build empathic models of other people. In this sense, we do not need to worry about nanochips eavesdropping on our private thoughts: we already do this through our normal communication with other people via language and behaviour. A well-functioning simulacrum allows us to navigate effortlessly between pieces of furniture without bumping into anything. The function of consciousness is particularly evident in situations in which the simulacrum works poorly, such as in Anton's syndrome. And well, what does it matter that the colour blue we experience is only a rough derivative of a short wavelength of light that reaches our retina? The colour sensation is, above all, a convenient symbol to signify that in the current state of the sky we do not need to put on a raincoat.

Our internal model of the world is like the old monastery village that wraps itself around the Mont Saint-Michel, a rocky mountain on the border of Normandy and Brittany, protruding above endless beaches. Only rarely is a gap noticeable between village and rock. In illusions such as the rotating snakes (Figure 10.4) we catch a glimpse of that gap: the outside world provides us with conflicting information. Visual input indicating movement fights with input indicating a static pattern, and our brains flip-flop between two interpretations. Also the lucky ones who can switch between the colour combinations of the blue-or-white dress experience the discrepancy between fiction and physics. It is these cases that remind us that none of what we see and feel comes directly to us – that we are constantly living in a state of 'healthy hallucination', a state of consciousness that is more than capable of helping us to take action.[25]

Gabriel Anton would not have foreseen that his intellectual legacy would figure in discussions about fake news in the brain. What happened to this sensitive and committed neurologist? Already during the First World War, in 1915, he proved to be an advocate of eugenics. From his Austrian identity he developed more and more into a 'real' German. In 1925, he gave a speech at the University of Halle, in which he referred to France as 'the land of the enemy'. Together with colleagues inside and outside the Weimar Republic, he translated Darwin's ideas on natural selection and evolution into the view that German society was subject to degeneration and had to be purged of inferior individuals. He died on 3 January 1933, and an obituary praised his brave efforts for the restoration and welfare of the Germanic race.[26] And that regimental courier who suffered from hysterical blindness? This was another Austrian who was naturalized as a German.[27] Four weeks after Anton's death, on 30 January 1933, Adolf Hitler was appointed Chancellor of Germany. The irony of fate determined that Gabriel Anton, who became famous for his research into delusions of blindness, surrendered to the blind delusions of Aryan superiority and ennoblement of the human race. The beautiful historic town centre of Halle was reduced to ashes in a bombing raid by the Allies in 1945. One of the targets was the chemical industry, including a mustard gas factory.

15 Under the hood of our imagination

How consciousness, in spite of everything, manages to rise above brain cells

It is already getting dark outside when Matt transports the patient into the dissecting room. He lifts her from the mobile bed onto the dissection table. She is a beautiful woman, still with a red blush on her cheeks. He feels her pulse: no heartbeat. He grabs a scalpel and starts to dissect her face: first the epidermis, then the subcutaneous fat, then the facial muscles. Fibre by fibre her face is unwoven.

As a surgeon, Matt has always been interested in the physical source of beauty. He becomes obsessed with people who look beautiful and wants to find out at all costs whether this is a phenomenon that takes place in the muscles, in the skin, in connective and fatty tissues, or in someone's bones. What makes someone beautiful or ugly? In his career, Matt has distinguished himself by helping people get rid of an inflamed appendix or by removing tumours, and has worked his way up to head of the surgery department. There, he has seen breathtakingly beautiful and terribly ugly patients, but he was obviously not allowed to use them to pursue his deepest interest. Never could he search for the true source of beauty. Grudgingly he bided his time. But today the ambulance brought in someone who was badly injured by a gunshot and had little chance of survival. Matt went to check on the victim and, just as he entered the operating theatre where a colleague was working, it was observed that she would soon die. A bullet had pierced the woman's heart, but her face was completely intact and almost as beautiful as when she was still walking around. When she was declared clinically dead and it was found that her body was left to science, Matt transported her to the cutting room in the morgue.

Matt isolates the blood vessels and nerves of her face, to stumble eventually upon the bone of her skull. Face to face with all these dead tissues, infested with coagulating blood and faded muscles, Matt gives up disappointed. No matter how precisely he wields his dissecting knife, he cannot find the source of beauty. He concludes that beauty does not exist. All those years he has allowed himself to be fooled by an illusion.

Is consciousness, too, nothing more than an illusion imposed on us by a bunch of cleverly wired neurons that together produce complex behaviour? If we assume that consciousness provides the best possible assessment of our 'here and now', it remains unclear whether it is ultimately a purely 'mental'

DOI: 10.4324/9781003429555-15

thing that hovers above matter, or is nothing more than the activity of brain cells. Are we our brain, or are we more than just our brain?

This question goes straight back to the Hard Problem: if the panoply of sensory stimuli and cognitive responses is nothing more than a gigantic pattern of electric brain pulses, why should it lead to consciousness? Why do we taste a vanilla flavour in a mouthful of ice cream instead of a series of brain pulses? Why do we taste anything at all? Up to now, I have given this question a wide berth. That's not so terrible, because most studies on brains and consciousness do not give an adequate answer, or do not even ask the question. When we talk about circuits of neurons that generate predictive representations and errors as the basis for conscious perception, you might rightly object that this is only a theory of how circuits of neurons perform calculations. The theory does not reveal why this should lead to the subjective taste of vanilla ice cream. This is a very difficult question that we cannot just keep sweeping under the rug. It is time to take a stand and give the best possible answer.[1]

In neuroscience, hardcore materialism, which reduces mind and consciousness to neuronal processes that culminate in behaviour, is popular, although I notice that some colleagues are uncomfortable with it. Is this everything? In everyday practice, brain researchers prefer to limit themselves to a safe approach: first try to find the brain mechanisms that explain the observable behaviour of humans and animals, which is difficult enough. The question of consciousness is then dismissed as 'unapproachable', either because consciousness can only be understood through external behaviour, or because it would not really exist. Hardcore materialists such as Paul and Patricia Churchland[2] believe that our minds are essentially nothing more than brain matter that produces specific patterns of activity, such as electrical pulses and the release of transmitter substances, resulting in behaviour. In this account, 'consciousness' is a concept that stems from an outdated, primitive folk psychology, a superstition about the existence of a 'mind'. It reflects an illusion originating from the complex behaviour we observe in other people, which leads us to believe in a mysterious, underlying something.

But take a look at Akiyoshi Kitaoka's illusion he dubs the 'rotating snakes' (Figure 10.4). Where are those moving snakes? A hardcore materialist has two options. Option one: the snakes are on paper, because that is where you see the movement. But if you take a ruler and stopwatch to measure their speed of movement across the paper, you end up with a speed of zero. Physically, there are no moving shapes where you see them. Option two: the rotating snakes are in your head. But this too cannot be literally true. At least, I sincerely hope that there are no snakes crawling through your cranium![3] So where are the snakes? The only alternative seems to be that the snakes are in your 'mind', so not in a place in the material world but in the immaterial kingdom of the soul. This view amounts to dualism: it has given us headaches before. If we imagine two totally different entities – matter and mind – that are separate but nevertheless communicate with each other, we get tangled up with the impossibility that the material and the mental should influence each other. We would be violating the law of conservation of energy. Dualism has its own problems, no less severe than those of hardcore materialism. There seem to be no more than two flavours – dualism[4] or materialism. Or is this just an illusion and is there a third way?

Let us return to the thought experiment about zombies. These were not the skeletons with flabby flesh on their bones that slither across the screen in films like *The Return of the Living Dead*; they relate to two creatures that look exactly alike and have exactly the same matter in their bodies, while one has consciousness and the other does not. You are looking at identical twins who behave exactly the same and have had the same history of experiences. While we previously considered whether zombies provide an argument for consciousness as an epiphenomenon – as something that exists but has no function – David Chalmers posed a different question[5]: is it conceivable, and logically possible, that these two humanoid beings behave exactly the same yet differ in the presence versus absence of consciousness? If this is possible while at the same time accepting that conscious experience is something that exists, then according to Chalmers this should mean that consciousness is a different entity from matter.

We can go a step further: an audacious surgeon sets about replacing all the neurons in a volunteer's healthy brain with neuromorphic chips – semiconductor squares containing electronic circuits that mimic the functioning of living brain cells.[6] If each neuron is replaced with a chip that exactly reproduces its functions, would this brain still be conscious? Neuromorphic replacement is not even necessary to do this experiment: we can also imagine that each neuron is replaced molecule by molecule, that is with biological material. Thus, Chalmers' zombie argument seems to gain strength: we build a molecular replica without also taking over the 'mind'. Because we can imagine these processes without involving consciousness, it seems that matter and mind can be separated. Consciousness will continue to exist undiminished: exit reductionism, welcome dualism!

But what exactly is being required of our imagination here? We have already seen that we can look at a clock with cogs and gears without 'consciousness' (or awareness of time) being involved. We can imagine all kinds of molecules, electric currents and cell membranes without a 'mind' imposing itself on us. But what exactly does this prove? Is this not a case of an 'intuition pump', as Daniel Dennett calls this mental exercise?[7] Such a 'pump' tempts the reader to draw a logical conclusion based on the intuition that imagining neural 'nuts and bolts' might prove something. But it is difficult, if not impossible, to maintain that we can imagine the absence of a mind or mental processes. We can also imagine shelves full of products from a supermarket without having to worry about overarching notions such as the company's operating profit or annual figures, but does this mean that this higher level of organization is totally unrelated to the milk cartons in the shop?

On closer inspection, the zombie argument turns against the dualism that Chalmers defended. That the molecules of brain cells are replaced one by one is, after all, not a thought experiment but daily practice. All proteins, fatty acids and other molecules and atoms in our bodies are constantly subject to replacement: this process of biochemical turnover takes between one and five years in humans. Old materials are disposed of through stool and urine to be replaced by atoms that our digestive tract extracts from food. If you take a couple of good breaths, chances are you will take in at least one molecule of air that Julius Caesar exhaled when he died.[8] Of all the atoms in your body, roughly one million will end up in the body of Brad Pitt or Beyoncé – without you or them noticing. Conversely, your favourite celebrity also donates to you.

So indeed, the molecules in your brain are replaced by new ones through natural metabolism without your personality or consciousness disappearing. In roughly five years' time, your skull will contain more or less a molecular copy of the brain you have now. With a little imagination, we can imagine that this copy would consist only of molecules, but do you think that in practice this copy could be detached from your consciousness – and that in five years' time you would be walking around as a zombie 'alive and well'?

The weakness of the zombie argument, then, is that it posits our imagination as something reliable or objective. It is perfectly possible to think of a brain without having to think of consciousness at the same time. If two sets of brains are identical, it is quite possible, and even likely, that this *automatically* entails that the associated mental processes, including conscious experiences, are the same. This is consistent with the idea that every experience, every mental process, has a counterpart in a brain process, because somewhere there will be a source that corresponds to that particular experience. It may sound a little sad that the zombie argument does not hold water, because it seems to hand us over to the harsh idea that we are nothing more than a warm-blooded hunk of matter.

Perhaps our dented self-esteem – of feeling 'special' in relation to plants, comets, shampoo and plastic Christmas trees – can be saved with another weapon: the Knowledge argument from the Australian philosopher Frank Jackson.[9] He introduces us to Mary, a neuroscientist who knows everything there is to know about colours from books. She knows the laws of optics like the back of her hand, the wave and quantum theories of light, and has learned how the retina and the brain process light of different wavelengths. Unfortunately, she was raised by a bunch of cruel, insensitive educators in a totally colourless environment. She grew up in a prison painted in shades of grey, black and white. Sky blue and blood red have been hidden from her. She knows that a rose that reflects light of long wavelengths is referred to as 'red', but has never seen this colour.

Her guardians decide to set her free. For the first time in her life, she will see what it means when grass is green and a cloudless sky is blue. Will this give her a new experience? Materialism dictates that Mary already knew everything there is to know about colours; her understanding of colours was complete and her release will not bring any new knowledge. If materialism is false, or at least incomplete, Mary will gain new knowledge. She will realize that all the dry physics facts about colour are not the same as colour experience itself.

What strikes me about the piles of philosophical treatises on Jackson's Knowledge argument is that little attention is paid to practical studies on colour vision and colour blindness. Earlier we saw the Inverted Spectrum argument fail in the hands-on course 'The Joy of Painting'. Carrying out the experiment on Mary the Colour Scientist would of course be highly unethical, but is also not necessary to assess whether Mary will have a new experience when she is released. Oliver Sacks described the case of Jonathan I., an artist who totally lost his ability to see colours in a car accident. "You might think", said Jonathan I., "loss of color vision, what's the big deal? Some of my friends said this, my wife sometimes thought this, but to me, at least, it was awful, disgusting."[10] Mr I. retained his other visual abilities, such as seeing shape, texture, movement and depth. Unlike Mary, he grew up in a colourful world and acquired a broad knowledge of colour effects in nature and in the practice of painting. After his accident, his general knowledge of colours remained. Oliver Sacks continues: "He could identify the green of Van Gogh's billiard table in this way unhesitatingly. He *knew* all the colours in his favourite paintings, but could no longer see them, either when he looked or in his mind's eye."

Jonathan I. approximates the case of Mary, but reversed in time: Mary got her colour experiences later in life, while Jonathan lost them at a later age. Although he retained his knowledge of colours after his accident, he lost his actual colour vision. Knowledge of colours can therefore indeed become independent of colour experience itself. The idea that his colour vision could be restored by studying neurophysiology and optics is once again highly implausible.

Another practical example that is close to Mary's case comes from people who are partially colour blind but can be helped with special glasses. About 8 per cent of men and 0.5 per cent of women of Northern European origin have difficulty distinguishing red from green (red-green colour blindness). These people are not totally colour blind, but their perception of red, purple and green is duller and less vivid than in someone with normal retinal cones: green is seen approximately as light orange-brown, red as beige and purple as blue. They have difficulty in distinguishing between Braeburn and Granny Smith apples. In some of these people, this colour deficit is caused by having too much overlap in the sensitivity of the red- and green-sensitive cones in the retina: the electrical responses of these two types of cones to light of a certain band of wavelengths are too similar, so the brain does not receive enough signals from the retina that it can use to construct different green and red percepts.[11]

The glasses that the company Enchroma has developed for this subgroup filter the incoming light in a way that eliminates the confusingly overlapping patterns of light. What happens when they put on Enchroma glasses for the first time in their lives? The stories and videos on the internet range from moderately enthusiastic to spectacular and jubilant, and it is difficult to find out how much influence the company has had on these reports. But cases like Ethan's[12] make an authentic impression: the young man is thrilled when he first sees the colour purple and asks his friend: "Oh my God, is this purple?" Ethan is moved to tears when he leaves his office and bends down on the lawn to see a grass green colour for the first time. Like Jonathan I., many red-green colour-blind people have knowledge of the biological basis of their visual deficiency, but their new colour experience turns out to be something else entirely.

So, hard materialism has to give way after all. Despite the frantic attempts of hardcore materialists, they have not been able to come up with convincing ideas as to why and how the experience of colour, taste or music can be reduced entirely to – or equated with – an interplay of electrical currents in our brain. Also on the basis of a whole list of other arguments, not all of which can be discussed here, we cannot maintain that colour experience is nothing more than patterns of bioelectricity in grey matter. In short, our knowledge and experience of electrical phenomena and grey matter are not the same as colour experience. The materialists have not succeeded in making the mind disappear into the top hat. But this conclusion seems to drive us back into the arms of that other wretched option: dualism. This too is still not an attractive path to take. Are we being forced to choose between two untenable alternatives?

Spinoza and the unity of matter and spirit

In 1678, Baruch Spinoza's most important work, the *Ethics*, was published. The philosopher, also known as Benedict de Spinoza and born in Amsterdam in 1632, had already been dead for a year at that time. When Descartes strolled through the city in 1641, he could not have anticipated that the Sephardic Jewish boy who bumped into him near the Portuguese synagogue on the Houtgracht would grow up to be a philosopher of the same calibre as himself (Figure 15.1).[13] Having grown up in a household rich in children, as a descendant of a family that had originally fled the Spanish Inquisition, Spinoza developed his own philosophy in the wake of Descartes' geometric way of reasoning. Spinoza stated that body and mind are not two separate things or substances but aspects of one and the same reality. At the same time, body and mind represent very different aspects (attributes) of that one thing, which are not reducible to each other. In his monism, mind is not secretly or explicitly reduced to material reality, or vice versa.[14] He writes:

> Now all these things clearly show that the decision of the mind and the desire and determination of the body are simultaneous in nature, or rather one and the same thing, which when considered under the attribute of thought and explained through the same we call decision, and when considered under the attribute of extension and deduced from the laws of motion and rest we call determination.[15]

Here, Spinoza implies that a mental process (for instance, a 'decision') is essentially the same, and takes place simultaneously, as a bodily process. A

BENOIT SPINOSA
Né à Amsterdam, l'An 1632. Mort le
21. Février 1677. âgé de 44 ans.

Figure 15.1 (Left) Portrait of Baruch Spinoza (1632–1677). (Right) View of Houtgracht in Amsterdam, painted by Oene de Jongh between 1841 and 1882. The building of the former Portuguese-Jewish synagogue is the broad, light grey building in the middle, approximately opposite the drawbridge. This is the place where Spinoza was excommunicated in 1656. Today the Houtgracht no longer exists.
Source: Jewish Historical Museum Collection, Amsterdam.

'decision' coincides with a bodily 'urge' (need or desire) and a receptivity to physical stimuli. But he also states that this one 'thing' can be experienced in two ways: as a subjective process (conscious thinking or feeling) or as a physical process that takes place in the space around us ('extensiveness'). The 'laws of motion and rest' refer to physical laws, such as those formulated by Johannes Kepler to describe the orbits of the planets. It is these laws that dictate or determine how a decision-making process takes place in a physical sense.

At the age of 24, the Sephardic rabbi of the Portuguese synagogue in Amsterdam pronounces a *cherem* on Spinoza: he is excommunicated for 'terrible heresies' and 'monstrous deeds' and forbidden to have any contact with his own Portuguese-Jewish community. He is not allowed to talk to his family or to be in the same house any longer. The exact reason for this curse is not known, but the event takes place against the background of Spinoza's monism, which has radical implications for his view of God: he does not see God as, say, a bearded senior who created and governs nature, but as nature itself. That he does not impute to God a role as separate causer or creator of nature is considered heresy by the Jewish authorities and Amsterdam regents.

Moreover, he believes that the Torah was written by humans and that the Jews are not a unique, Chosen people.

Around the same time, Spinoza decides to study Latin at the school of Franciscus van den Enden, who turns out to be an important teacher of philosophy and political science. After his excommunication, he leaves the Houtgracht, retrains as a lens-grinder and moves to Rijnsburg near Leiden, where he lives as a confirmed bachelor and begins work on the *Ethics*. Anatomists and other natural scientists such as Christiaan Huygens are impressed by Spinoza's skill in making lenses for telescopes and microscopes, and a small gathering of free-thinkers helps the philosopher earn a living. Little is known about Spinoza's private life, but one of his earliest biographies mentions Baruch's love for Van den Enden's limping daughter, Clara Maria.[16] There is talk of a rivalry in woo-ing the girl, in which his competitor – the anatomist and alchemist Theodor Kerckring – draws the longest straw, allegedly by courting her with a "precious pearl necklace worth several thousand". Disappointed and embittered, Baruch would be left behind. An unhappy love could partly explain why the *Ethics*, as the magnum opus of the rationalist philosopher, is permeated with passions and emotions, with sadness and jealousy playing key parts.

In his later years, Spinoza has to make more and more effort to explain to his contemporaries that he does in fact believe in God, but the odour of atheism continues to hang around him, making his work both highly explo-sive and unacceptable even to Christians. His supporters are attacked and persecuted. His follower Adriaen Koerbagh is sentenced to the penitentiary, where he dies after a short time, and Spinoza's friend Henry Oldenburg disappears behind the bars of the Tower prison in London. Around 1665, the *Ethics* is already largely complete, but his friends and publisher, Jan Rieuwertz from Amsterdam, become nervous at the thought that the book might be circulated. They fear a personal vendetta against the philosopher, as had happened to the brothers Cornelis and Johann de Witt – who were both senior statesmen – in 1672. Rieuwertz decides to let the philosopher off the hook by publishing the *Ethics* posthumously under the concealing title 'The Posthumous Writings of B.d.S.'. The States of Holland prohibit the blasphemous writing, but it manages to find its way illegally within the Netherlands and abroad. So much for the much-vaunted tolerance of the Dutch Golden Age.

Does Spinoza's monism offer the sought-after third way as an alternative to materialism and dualism? At least for the time being, it seems a refreshing, appealing alternative, but if we were to recognize that matter and spirit are one and the same, why do they appear to us as so extremely different? If the grey matter is equivalent to 'mind', how is it able to produce an experience of colour? And if matter in general equals 'mind', should not the whole of nature be 'animated'? Does not the entire universe then have consciousness?

Panpsychism – the view that the entire universe is animated or conscious – runs into the objection (along with other arguments) that even the human brain is not always conscious. During deep, dreamless sleep, under anaesthesia or in coma patients, there is little or no question of consciousness, but the anatomical structure of the brain remains intact. Even when you are deeply under, brain cells and synapses remain in place; only their patterns of activity change. Apparently, consciousness only occurs under very special circumstances: the brain must be in exactly the right state to be aware of anything. This is in conflict with panpsychism, but not with a more elaborate form of brain-mind monism. I will argue that Spinoza's monism can be further developed into a specific variant in which a body-mind unity does not exist permanently and everywhere in the universe, but does occur in the special situation that characterizes our awake brains. But even then, the key question remains: what does this special situation consist of?

Hopfield's memory

To get closer to an answer, we return to neural network models. The properties that are most interesting for the consciousness debate are illustrated by a memory network: the Hopfield model. The inventor of this network, John Hopfield, is a versatile physicist who during his career has dealt with a variety of subjects, such as the transfer of electrons between biomolecules, but who later worked on the functioning of the brain. At the California Institute of Technology in Pasadena, I got to know him in the early 1990s as a thoughtful man who had no desire to shout his discoveries from the rooftops. But when his latest publication came out, colleagues around the world woke up. When Hopfield published, something happened in the field. One of his treatises that changed the field came out on 1 April 1982.[17]

Is it possible to build a model of a neuronal network, Hopfield wondered, that would allow you to store multiple images from light patterns on your retina in a memory formed by this network itself? And once these images are stored, can you retrieve the memory of these patterns by activating the network with somewhat similar images?

Suppose you are a neuron and make connections with all the other members of the network you are in. In Figure 15.2, you are depicted as a dark grey cell: you extend your 'hands' to 15 other neurons. We assume that you have not 2 but 15 hands to make connections with, so that you can squeeze all your colleagues' dendrites directly. You detach yourself from the idea that it is you who is thinking, seeing or even having an 'I' here. You are just a neuron that receives inputs from all the other cells and can send pulses of electrical activity to all the others. In Figure 15.2, you are active (grey) while many of your network mates are inactive (white). Let us assume for the sake of peace of mind that you do not become active by electric current flowing across your skin and through your body, but that activity manifests itself in the shade of grey you adopt (the darker, the more active) and in your physical movement: an active neuron performs squeezing movements with all of its 15 hands. The strength and effect of the squeeze can vary from one connection to another: due to prior processes of synaptic plasticity, one synaptic connection can be stronger

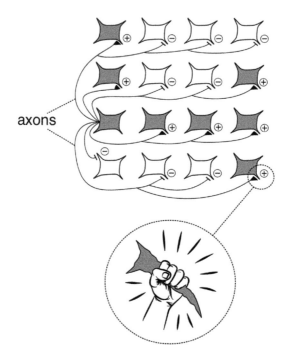

Figure 15.2 A Hopfield network. Neurons are shown as rectangles with protrusions (dendrites) at each corner. Although all neurons are connected to all others, only the axons of one cell are shown here. The dark grey hue indicates that a neuron is active. The axons form excitatory (stimulating, +) synaptic connections with other active cells and inhibitory (-) connections with the inactive neurons (white). Together, the active neurons form the pattern of digit 4. The strength of a synaptic connection is symbolized by a hand squeezing a dendrite: the harder the squeeze, the stronger the connection.

or weaker than another, and can even change from excitatory to inhibitory. The stronger the synapse, the stronger the pinch.

Step two in Hopfield's model is that your pinching will change the activity of the other cells: if you become active, your pinching will induce the other 15 cells to fire more intensively or less. Everyone's place in the network is maintained. If all the connections you make were excitatory (increasing activity), the result of your activity will be to change a simple pattern (where you were the only neuron active) into a pattern where all 16 neurons of the network become active. This is not a relevant result: interesting patterns are only obtained by making just some of the cells active and not the rest. As memory patterns, you might want to store in this small network rough representations of specific images, such as the number 4. How does that work?

For the storage of the pattern '4', we conveniently skip all the steps that the nervous system has to go through to get from a projection of this digit on your retina to an activation of neurons in the memory network (which might be in the hippocampus, for example, far away from areas for direct sensory processing; Figure 8.4). Input of sensory patterns will simply activate certain neurons in the configuration of a figure '4' (dark grey in Figure 15.2), while the other neurons remain devoid of this excitation and remain inactive. Although the neurons now display the right pattern with their activity, this does not mean it has been stored. As soon as the sensory excitation stops, the cells all return to an inactive state and the number 4 thus disappears from the network: there is nothing left in the network that reminds one of its recent past.

Learning – that is, storage of information – occurs by permanently strengthening the synaptic connections between the active neurons. In the analogy of squeezing your hand this means: if you are active and squeeze the hand of a friend further down the network, and that friend is also active and squeezes you back, then your connection is strengthened, so that each subsequent squeeze will elicit a stronger response from both of you. So making two neurons active at the same time reinforces the excitatory effect they have on each other. After the amplification, each electrical pulse that the neuron fires has a permanently increased effect on the receiving partner neuron. If the sending neuron does not fire any pulses, the synapse remains strengthened by the biochemical changes that have taken place, but the receiving neuron experiences no effect because of this: the memory is only present in a passive ('dormant') form. *Firing together is wiring together*: this is the soundbite that sums up some of the seminal work of the Canadian psychologist Donald Hebb (1904–1985) rather poorly. Roughly speaking, Hebb's principle is well supported by experimental evidence gathered over the past 50 years.

Hopfield thought that his memory network model would work even better if he introduced a second principle: if one cell in the network is active and another cell is not, make their connection weaker rather than stronger. The idea behind this weakening principle is that you want to be able to store several patterns in a memory network, not just the number 4. Hopfield showed that in the same network, you can also store the patterns for, say, 2 and 5, without destroying the memory for 4. Using the same network to store multiple patterns works much better if you not only strengthen connections but also selectively weaken some. If you were to store all digits from 0 to 9 only by strengthening connections, eventually all connections would be amplified to such an extent that a random sensory stimulus would activate all 16 neurons at once. This saturation is contrary to Hopfield's goal of selectively recalling stored patterns when presented with a sensory pattern. *Not firing together is weakening the wiring together*.

When Hopfield's article appeared in 1982, this second principle was not yet supported by experimental data; the model therefore predicted that there must be something like long-term synaptic weakening in the brain. In the 1970s, it was suspected that synapses, having fallen into disuse, would gradually weaken or even disappear over time. Forgetting would be caused by a passive decay of the synaptic connections that had once been strengthened, namely when information was stored. The muscles that make your hand squeeze together would, as it were, fall into disuse and weaken. In contrast to this passive decay, Hopfield predicted that synapses could be weakened in a way that depends on the activity of the neuronal pair. Ten years later, the first experimental evidence for this process (long-term depression, or LTD) was published.[18]

How can a memory be recalled once it has been stored and the sensory input has disappeared? Learning processes do not take place in the brain all the time and everywhere. The brain must be in an appropriate state to absorb and store new information. If my attention is caught by a piece of music, I will remember it more easily than if I am sleepy or inattentive. In the cerebrospinal fluid between the cells there are molecules – neuromodulators – floating around that influence the state of networks on the spot. Some molecules promote learning processes, others inhibit them. Hopfield's model assumes that the network is initially in a suitable state to store information, followed by a period in which the strength of the synapses will remain unchanged (the learning or 'imprinting' of patterns has now stopped). It is in this non-learning period that we can test the recall of memory traces in the network.

Imagine that you – together with some three partners who became active during the imprinting of the original number 4 – are again stimulated by an input from outside the network during a non-learning period. It is not necessary that all participants in the number 4 are reactivated at the same time: a few friends will do. If you and these partners start to squeeze the offshoots (dendrites) of the other members of the network again, you will also awaken the other figure-4 participants (Figure 15.2). After all, during the prior learning process, all mutual connections within your digit-4 configuration had been strengthened, and if you start pinching, that is a powerful signal (along with the pinching of your partners) to make the rest of your friends active. Crucially, not the entire network is jumping and squeezing. This is prevented by the attenuation principle: if you start pinching, the network members who did not participate in the 4 will not be woken up, and will persist in their inactive state (your connections with all the cells that did not participate in the 4 had been weakened during learning, or had even become inhibitory). Because connections have been selectively strengthened or weakened, other stored digits (e.g. 2 and 5) can also be recalled, provided that a sensory stimulus comes along that somewhat resembles a 2 or 5. Also for the 2 and 5, only a few of their original club members need to be activated in order to complete these patterns again.

Hopfield showed mathematically that offering a random input to the network will eventually lead to the completion of the stored pattern that most closely resembles that input. The network is 'associative': no matter what shred or hint you offer, the network will always evolve over time towards a stored pattern that best matches that input. This pattern is an attractor of the network: it lays the mathematical groundwork for explaining how a rather random activation of a network – elicited, for example, by Penfield's electrical stimuli on the cortex of epilepsy patients – leads to a recognizable, structured sensation or event. The golf ball comes to a stop when the network reaches the most similar memory pattern.

Hopfield's model took an important step in thinking about connections between brains, neurons and cognitive processes.[19] It makes clear that there is a level of organization that lies between the level of the single neuron and the level of a large-scale cognitive process: the level of the local network – a restricted population of interconnected neurons in a particular brain region. At the same time, Hopfield showed that in the brain – with its amazing ability to store and recall information from memory – an alternative to the classical computer chips found in mobile phones and laptops is emerging. When performing calculations, the central processing unit (CPU) of a classic computer relies on arithmetic rules and other information retrieved from the computer's memory. This information is stored on a hard disk or other digital medium and can be retrieved once the CPU has an address: a digital code for the place on the disk where the required information can be found.

Hopfield showed that there is another, more biological way of retrieving information[20]: only a small part of the original pattern (e.g. the horizontal dash in the digit 4) is used to retrieve the complete digit pattern. The complete pattern is retrieved by presenting part of it to the network. One ear of a dog is enough for the network to reconstruct a complete dog's head. You can present a very jumbled, messed up or coarsely pixelated portrait to a Hopfield network to get the original image back in fine detail. If a neural network has enough neurons to store a large number of patterns, it can lose quite a few due to damage or age-related wear and tear without suffering any major memory loss. This phenomenon of 'graceful degradation' is reminiscent of the gradual, pathological deterioration that characterizes the memory of Alzheimer's patients: even before severe memory loss is detected, a colossal number of neurons and synapses has already been lost.

The Hopfield network shows us how the brain can process and store information in a dispersed, distributed way.[21] The model puts flesh on the bones of the long-held suspicion that memory traces are not fixed in one microscopic place in the brain: there is no single cell that stores the memory of your grandmother. A memory trace is spread across a synaptic network, and this network can lie within one area, such as the hippocampus, but depending on the complexity of the memory it can even be distributed across several areas. Together with other modellers and experimenters, Hopfield gave a strong impetus in the 1980s to the development of smart, self-learning computer models, which built on the work of McCulloch and Pitts and formed the basis of the current boom in artificial intelligence.

Emergent correspondence

With this, the most important profit of the Hopfield network has not yet been cashed in: the phenomenon of emergence. This takes us back to Spinoza. In Hopfield's model, the collective of neurons produces properties that are not present at the level of the cell itself. The whole is more than the sum of its parts. Emergence means that the complex organization of the network produces new properties that are not found in the constituent parts. The memory for patterns exists by virtue of cooperation between the members of the neuronal network, just as the music of an ensemble is different from that of a soloist. A single neuron can only be active or inactive; its state is totally controlled by the input it receives from other cells. But the collective of neurons is capable of storing entire patterns and, when stimulated at random, exhibits a self-organizing dynamic in which the network sometimes converges to one stored pattern, and then rearranges itself to arrive at another pattern. It is a spectacle reminiscent of a flock of migratory birds that, with its own self-directed dynamics, draws three-dimensional forms against an autumn sky. In the landscape of all possible states, the current state of the network is represented by the position of the golf ball. Sometimes it keeps on rolling: the network continues to evolve towards new patterns. With a shard of information, the network manages to recall a stored pattern and make it complete: this is an emergent process because it cannot be achieved with single cells.

Some people think that the term 'emergence' has mysterious or woolly undertones, but the Hopfield model in particular shows that there is no such thing here as mysticism: a neuronal group exhibits qualitatively different properties from its parts, and these properties can be explained very well by the functioning of those parts.

What has all this to do with Spinoza? Spinoza argued that body and mind form a unity, but in the seventeenth century, due to a lack of knowledge about the workings of the brain, he could only defend this idea with his sharp intellect. He could not yet put his finger on the properties that make the brain exceptional compared to other forms of matter, such as rocks, trees, clouds or our immune system. But now, with Hopfield's network and models of Predictive Coding in hand, we are gradually beginning to see what makes the brain really special. For too long, neuroscience has focused on the individual neuron. Likewise, psychology has been preoccupied with explaining behaviour for too long, often with the help of brain scans that can only grossly measure the activity of large chunks of brain mass. The crucial, intermediate level of neuronal networks is only now beginning to emerge in the age of expanding computer models.

Emergence is not a rabbit pulled out of a hat to explain the body-mind problem. It is a tool to describe how multiple layers of self-organization are situated between the 'low' level of the neuron and the 'high' level of conscious experience. Emergent phenomena are also found outside the living brain, for example in colonies of bees or ants that have a collective structure and division of labour that cannot be understood by looking at just one bee or ant.[22] The phenomenon of emergent self-organization is illustrated with startling beauty by embryogenesis – the emergence of a new, complete organism from a fertilized egg. Emergent phenomena also occur in non-living nature, as shown by the interaction of water particles in the air that, under the influence of wind, air pressure, temperature and the rotation of the earth, collectively organize themselves into clouds, which in turn become parts of a cyclone. In chemistry, complex chemical reactions are known to lead to emergent spatial patterns in which coloured reaction products appear and disappear in dynamic cycles.[23] In short, there are enough examples of emergence in inanimate nature to show that collective self-organization is not an exclusive privilege of the brain. But this does not diminish the importance of understanding how 'higher' processes such as memory and perception arise from lower principles that govern the behaviour of individual neurons. With today's knowledge, Spinoza would probably have jumped in the air.

But is there any reason to start cheering already? After all, Hopfield's model is about a simple form of memory and does not yet say much about consciousness. Does emergence also apply to conscious perception – as a best guess model of the state of the world and our bodies? Predictive Coding models roughly mimic how the brain can build a representation of the world. In our current research, we use the architecture of the cerebral cortex (Figure 8.4) as the basis for a network model that consists of multiple, interconnected areas and – roughly moving from the areas at the back of the head to those in the front – constructs increasingly abstract representations of sensory objects (Figure 11.4). If you remove the sensory inputs and stimulate a more frontal area of the network in such a way that it activates an abstract representation, then this frontal pattern evokes representations at the occipital levels, so that the original image of the object is reconstructed at this early, most sensory level. The stimulation of the more frontal area can also occur internally, for example when a brain structure for word meaning sends a strong signal to this area. From an abstract pattern that symbolizes the concept of 'horse', for example, the network can thus start 'imagining' which concrete visual image goes with 'horse'.[24] Networks that code predictively thus bring us a step closer not only to understanding perception, but also imagination as a conscious phenomenon. Like the Hopfield net, these networks have emergent properties too: the subtle interplay between raw, sensory images and abstract representations goes well beyond the level of single cells.

Can representations of single objects be scaled up to more complex representations? While Figure 11.4 illustrates how a scene involving a horse can be transformed into a more abstract representation, in everyday life we are aware of spatial scenes that often consist of multiple objects. And how does the brain construct a representation of an integral scene that accommodates multiple sensory qualities such as the horse's whinny and smell? How does the computer model learn to understand that the scene is about a horse and not a donkey, zebra or dog? These are questions that require creative and unorthodox ways of thinking. To a certain extent, computers can help us to build models of perception and imagination – but the problem for consciousness is that they remain 'computers'. Computers are made to do nothing more or less than to *calculate*: they convert a list of input numbers into a list of outputs made up of other numbers. What those numbers represent or mean, well, that's for the human user to figure out! It is the conscious experience of the user that makes sense of everything such a calculator spits out: one output is interpreted as colour, another as movement, shape or music.[25]

A counterargument holds that not only computers but also brain cells work with numbers. At the low organizational level of the single neuron, information is encoded in the form of spikes, and the rate at which these are fired can be captured in a simple number (for example, a cell fires ten spikes per second). Inspired by Hopfield, I proposed a three-staged concept. The first stage is that this numerical functionality of the single brain cell forms a basal level that provides the building blocks from which more complex, emergent phenomena emerge. The down-to-earth level of the single cell provides the components for the first stage: a level of organization that manifests as a small, local network (a 'club of peers' or 'assembly'[26]) in which neurons work together to encode a hypothesis (or prediction) about a simple property such as the shape of the number 4 (Figure 15.3). The activity of a local network can be sampled by inserting ultrathin, sword-shaped electrodes, each equipped with around a hundred to a thousand measuring points, into a relevant brain region.[27] These measurements make the assembly level accessible to study and are already giving us clues about how assemblies function.

The second stage of the conceptualization comes into play when we realize that several local networks are needed to represent the visual properties of an object together (colour, shape, depth, movement, texture). These networks must cooperate with each other in such a way that it is clear that a representation of the colour red belongs to the shape of a tomato, and not to another object present in the same scene, such as an apple. This cooperation of small networks can be characterized as a 'network of networks' within the visual system: a meta-network.

At the same time, the scope of this larger meta-network is still limited: it is concerned only with visual objects. We can only really start talking about conscious experience when an even higher level of emergent organization manifests itself – a third stage. When we wake up and are in good health, multiple modalities immediately come into play. When you open your eyes in the morning, the visual image you experience is linked to the position and posture your body occupies in space, even if you are not intensely aware of it. The mere fact that we distinguish and directly experience different modalities without thinking about it, makes it clear that their diversity contributes to awareness: in order to be able to speak of a visual experience, non-visual experiences must also exist. This higher, multimodal level of organization is achieved by an even larger 'network of networks', a meta-network that includes multiple sensory modalities.[28] So the current computer models of Predictive Coding provide a good start, but will ultimately need to be scaled up and improved to provide a convincing model of consciousness. To get beyond the rather modest level of visual feature inference (similar to Figure 11.4), we will need to work our way up to the level of 'superinference' and approach the multimodal richness of spatially extended experience. Importantly, the three-staged

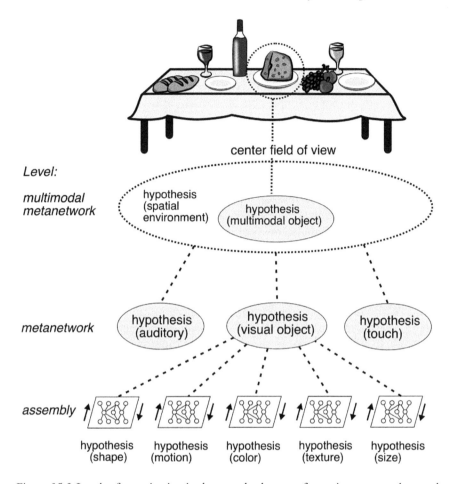

Figure 15.3 Levels of organization in the neural substrate of consciousness, understood as multimodal, situational overview. At the lowest level, individual neurons (circles) function as building blocks. These are organized into local networks (assemblies). The arrows that move up and down along these assemblies represent the interaction between sensory inputs and predictive representations. Assemblies are in turn organized into a meta-network. At the next level (multimodal meta-network), integration of the visual hypotheses about a single object with representations of other objects and other modalities takes place. At this level, conscious experience is approached. The levels of organization are defined conceptually, not by anatomical substrate: it is about the functional role that different types of networks fulfil within the total brain system.

concept is sometimes confused with anatomical stages of information processing in the cortex (V1 being 'low level' and parietal cortex 'high level'), or with microscopic versus macroscopic scales of brain organization, but the concept introduced here is about functional, representational levels – not about neuroanatomy – that could in principle be implemented in tiny artificial systems or in animal species with an entirely different brain make-up than that found in mammals.

Even at the third, conceptually different level of organization, there is no 'I' that looks down on the lower levels from above, as it were. The 'I' or 'self' is not a thing but a complex construct that, as we saw earlier, consists of several dimensions, such as the 'I' as a body, as an acting entity that makes a difference in the physical and social world and has its own history, recorded in our autobiographical memory. Nor is there any homunculus at the higher level that takes in all the sensory inputs and welds them together into a unified experience. There is no separate observer who perceives things on lower levels. The network itself is both observer and producer of all that we perceive. If you put yourself in the shoes of a cinema visitor, you are not only the one who experiences the film, but also the film-maker; the distinction between making and seeing the film disappears.

The coherence between the conceptually different levels in Figure 15.3 may remind you of a large house in which the inhabitants of different floors communicate with each other by stamping on the floors or banging against the ceiling. Will you stop that noise? But in this organization of conscious brain systems, there is no causal chain by which higher levels react to lower levels, or vice versa. Everything happens simultaneously; the processes at a lower level correspond exactly to those at a higher level. Translated back into the framework of Predictive Coding, this means that – although the individual neurons in a network with several brain areas numerically do encode their outputs in electrical pulses – the network as a whole fulfils an emergent function of a higher order: the construction of a representation (which has the character of a hypothesis) about what is going on outside the brain. To construct the hypothesis that something in the outside world is 'blue', cell groups generating the specific pattern for 'blue' will need to be active at the assembly level. At the same time, these patterns will interact with other assemblies so that a higher-level interpretation of 'blue' (and not red, cool or smooth) arises. Through its collective activity, the network transcends the level of numerical processing of information. After all, a hypothesis need not only concern numbers, but can be about anything: shape, colour, temperature, texture, smell, taste, etc. The construction of a hypothesis is not something that follows in time *after* neuronal activity has taken place at the lower level: its realization *consists* of those patterns of neural activity. So the link between the hypothesis (at a high conceptual level) and neuronal activity (at a low conceptual level) is not 'causal' in the sense of having causal interactions like colliding billiard balls. It is more accurate to call it otherwise: an emergent *correspondence* between levels. Processes at lower levels correspond to processes at higher levels, albeit that the higher processes have new properties that are not found at lower levels.

If all this still sounds rather abstract (which it is), let's compare the situation with the organization of, let's say, Kellogg's or Harrods as a company.

On the shop floor, people buy things by paying money at the till: this is the low level of physical transactions. Taking all shops together, there is a daily turnover, and over a longer period of time, annual figures and profit and loss accounts are drawn up for the entire corporation. The overall operating results are not 'caused' by individual transactions on the shop floor, as in a series of causes and consequences, but are built up from them. Although this comparison between brains and retail chains is valid to a certain extent, there is a not insignificant difference: the global operating result of Kellogg's can be summarized perfectly in numbers, whereas our brains produce qualitative (nonnumerical) sensations at the highest level of organization.[29] You could also say: at Kellogg's it takes a chief executive officer or other top dog to draw a summarizing conclusion from the numbers, but within the brain, such a person is absent. The brain does it itself.

A better comparison comes from Kurt Gödel's work in mathematical logic. His first Incompleteness Theorem from 1931[30] leans on the possibility of constructing paradoxes within a system of logical propositions. "Epimenides was a Cretan who declared that all Cretans are liars." That this statement contradicts itself (and makes one's mind run wild in the loop: "if this is true, it must be false – but if it is false, it must be true") was used by Gödel to show that within a system of logical formulations there will always be at least one proposition that is undecidable – one that cannot be proved to be true or false within that system. In his book *Gödel, Escher, Bach*, Douglas Hofstadter uses this principle to illustrate how information expressed in the 'lower' domain of numbers can lead to a proposition valid at the 'higher' level of logical statements: what counts as a proposition within number theory can be expressed at another conceptual level in sets of symbols that do not belong to the basic assumptions (axioms) of this same system. This is instructive for understanding mind and consciousness: it shows in a formal way that within an information-processing system several conceptual levels of information can coexist: as numbers and as symbols.[31]

The third way

Gradually, a third way to solve the problem of consciousness starts to become visible. Dualism breaks its teeth at the impossibility of linking two fundamentally different entities – body and mind – in a credible way. Hardcore materialism is implausible because it tries to reduce the reality of our qualitative perception to matters that are fundamentally different: electrical pulses, neuronal circuits and synaptic changes. If consciousness can be captured at the tiniest level by a description of elementary particles, what is the weight of a conscious experience? The confusion that seizes a die-hard materialist here stems from a fallacy[32]: the question is nonsensical because experiences cannot be classified as things with weight or mass, any more than a picture of Velázquez, or a company's annual accounts, have weight.[33] If we abandon the doomed attempt to reduce consciousness to a purely material thing, we are no longer forced to assign weight to it: conscious experience is nothing more or less than a comprehensive representation or hypothesis, and it is neither weighty nor weightless. Nor does 'weight' apply to the number 4 that a Hopfield network conjures up, or to an image construction that emerges from a Predictive Coding network. The same applies to beauty which – in spite of the unfortunate surgeon Matt – does exist but cannot be found in the fibres of someone's facial muscles.

Baruch Spinoza, who earned his living by grinding lenses: his monism evokes the image of a rough diamond polished with today's knowledge into a sparkling theory. He gave us the idea that matter and mind are inseparable – and essentially the same – but could not yet free himself from the impression that the entire universe must be 'animated'. We now have more and more tools to help us figure out why the brain is uniquely placed to produce the kind of consciousness we know only too well from the moment we wake up in the morning.

The foundations of this theory have been drawn in the sand. First, brain anatomy: the hierarchical structure that we see in the cortical areas for different senses. Second, the physiology of perception: the generation of representations or hypotheses about what is going on in the world. Third, the concept of emergent correspondence: the scaling up of simple representations in small networks to, ultimately, the multisensory and spatial representations we call 'conscious'.[34] If we briefly apply these principles to loss of consciousness during anaesthesia, the change cannot be attributed to a modified anatomy: the wiring of the brain remains the same. Turning to physiology, it appears that the visual cortex continues to generate electrical responses to light stimuli even under anaesthesia. Why is this no longer linked to visual experience? Under anaesthesia – but also during deep sleep – the cortex still shows activity in local networks, but long-distance communication between networks comes to a halt.[35] This is consistent with the idea that brain areas can no longer cooperate to construct large-scale representations.

This is not to say that the finishing line of the question of consciousness is already in sight. It will take several generations of brilliant scientists to build a fully fledged building from the theoretical foundations. One of the burning questions is why a certain representational activity in the brain does lead to consciousness, while another does not. Deep in the brain – just above the place where the optic nerves cross – lies a tiny structure that regulates our day-night rhythm. The electrical activity of the cells in this nucleus suprachiasmaticus oscillates up and down during waking and sleeping, peaking during the day phase and remaining silent during the night. This biological clock not only tells us where we are in the day-night cycle, but above all enables the brain to anticipate the external rhythm of light, so that our body is prepped for the day even before the sun rises. This too is predictive activity that gets us ready for what is to come. Why are we not aware of this predictive activity whereas we are aware of representations the cortex is involved with? The biological clock is part of the hypothalamus, the centre that forms a kind of mini-brain for basic survival, sex and aggression. It is packed with sensors to detect, for example, our body temperature, blood pressure and the salt and sugar levels in our blood. So also for the hypothalamus as a whole we can ask: why doesn't all this sensory activity lead to consciousness?

There are two features of the hypothalamus that stand out. The first is the venerable sluggishness with which processes tracked by the hypothalamus take place. Day-night rhythms and fluctuations in the state of our blood vessels are, I strongly suspect, too slow to require conscious representation. The regulation of the balance of glucose in the bloodstream is also downright slow – but a faster process is in fact not needed. This situation contrasts with the speed with which changes in our visual and auditory worlds occur and with the short time span in which we often have to make decisions, such as whether to stop or drive on at an amber traffic light.

A second difference with the cortex is the simplicity of the processes that the hypothalamus regulates. The system that keeps track of whether we are getting too hot or too cold only needs to monitor body temperature; a rapid cooling or warming of your body can be repaired through a relatively simple control loop that focuses only on that one process. Cells in the hypothalamus will make your teeth chatter when your temperature drops too much, but these cells do not need to keep track of blood pressure or glucose concentration as well. There is no need to build a complicated internal model of this process, and no need for integral representations of the causes of sensory changes. This contrasts with the complexity of conscious representations: our world view is a multisensory mosaic that has a spatial, panoramic character. Does consciousness therefore have an all-or-nothing character or does it move over a gradual scale? The complexity of representations in brain systems can vary. Therefore, it is logical and likely that many birds and mammals – and perhaps some squids – have some form of consciousness, albeit less rich, detailed or comprehensive than humans have. That consciousness is a gradual phenomenon – that is nonetheless related to its function for planning behaviour and for complex decisions – has important consequences for our thinking about the experience of pain and pleasure in animals.[36]

I remember well how, in 1993, I was brooding on the idea of emergent correspondence between the conceptually lower levels of neuronal patterns and the higher, conscious levels (Figure 15.3). As usual, the summer in Pasadena was dry and hot. It was a long, painful process of tossing and turning: was this sufficient, was it not a hidden form of dualism, was it new in relation to previous theories? Was it not the deceitful sentiment of a 'eureka moment'? Only later, when I was on a return flight from San Diego to the Netherlands and flew over the Mojave Desert, with its eroded mountains and canyons, did a satisfying, almost blissful feeling take hold of me: the idea was right and it stuck. Afterwards, I realized that a kind of inner battle had been settled and that I was experiencing the result of a mental transformation: I had now switched from the body-mind dualism that we grow up with, to a monism in which brain and consciousness both exist and form a unity at the same time – without that unity extending beyond our heads. From now on it sounded strange and incorrect to me to hear someone say that a psychiatric illness has more than one cause (one 'in the mind' and one in the brain): a mental phenomenon is by definition also a brain phenomenon, but it manifests itself in a different way.[37] In depression, there is not a chemical imbalance in the brain that co-exists, or interacts, with a mental and social problem; these descriptions are two ways of looking at the same problem. At the same time, mental phenomena are something other than spikes, transmitter releases and other neuronal activity: we are more than our brain (but we are this thanks to our brain). The conscious brain knows how to pull itself up by its own hair out of the quagmire of grey and white matter.

"I really can't imagine it working like that" is a common response when I try to explain what correspondence between levels of representation entails. "I just can't imagine that seeing an orange is actually the same as switching on and off all those millions of neurons in the brain – to me these things are still separate! The Hard Problem Remains Unsolved." On the one hand, this reaction evokes sympathy in me – I can well imagine that you feel this way. But that is precisely the crux of the Hard Problem: it rests on a limitation of our imagination, on the impossibility of imagining the 'transition' from neuronal activity to subjective experience. Our imagination is normally an indispensable tool in understanding or seeing through problems and questions: "If I can't picture the solution in my mind, I don't understand it." But in this particular case, it is extremely misleading to rely on our imagination.

In the ancient age of the naturalist and philosopher Aristotle (384–322 BC), fierce debates raged about the *horror vacui*, the abhorrence of the vacuum. People tirelessly tried to prove that there can be no such thing as a vacuum – the total emptiness of space, an idea that Aristotle and his contemporaries were keen to argue against. One of their arguments was that in a vacuum, light and heavy objects would have to fall to the ground at the same speed. It was simply not possible to imagine that a bird's feather and a lead ball would take the same time to fall to earth from a tower placed in a vacuum, and therefore it was judged that the vacuum could not really exist. Today, the synchronous falling motion of a bird's feather and a lead ball can be demonstrated in any high school lab. Was it a lack of imagination that troubled the ancients, was it an unwillingness to imagine something unknown, or a mental resistance to believe something they had never seen?

Just as the *horror vacui* argument suffers from a limited power to imagine, we must also get rid of our resistance, spoon-fed to us from childhood onwards, to the idea that consciousness corresponds to special patterns of neural activity. We cannot imagine the correspondence of neuronal and mental activity: our imagination itself has been shaped by our history of conscious experiences, and we have never learned to see or understand the connection between these experiences and brain activity – either in school or in everyday practice. We cannot look under the hood of our imagination. In our history of experience, our senses have never had access to our own neural patterns that correspond to perception, imagination or dream, so there has been no opportunity in our development to learn to 'see' the correspondence. In her eagerness to absorb sensory inputs from the world, a toddler learns to piece together streams of information into a conscious experience, but is not provided with a package leaflet showing how all sorts of cells in her head are at work to make that experience happen. Only much later, through books and high school classes, do we get to see pictures illustrating the anatomy and physiology of the brain, but even then, we are not aware of the neural processes that correspond to seeing those pictures.

The Problem, in short, is that our imagination can only build on sensory experiences from our past. The connection between neurons and consciousness cannot be *shown*, but only understood through abstract thinking. How bad is this? Contemporary physics also provides us with theories that defy our imagination. If we try to think about the beginning of the universe, we may be inclined to feel that we can imagine a Big Bang. But when realizing that also space and time came into existence at this event, our imagination abandons us.

Perhaps another metaphor will help to bridge the gap. Suppose a large bank in New York receives a large, sealed envelope with incomprehensible symbols written on it. All sorts of financial, linguistic and terrorism experts examine the envelope and palpate the thing to assess what it contains. With all kinds of clues about the cryptic text, the external appearance of the envelope and the circumstances under which it was delivered, they gradually become convinced that it must contain something of great value. The bank authorities do not know what it is, but after a while this does not matter anymore: the institution *treats* the envelope as something valuable, and thus it *becomes* valuable. Here, the hidden contents of the envelope represent low-level neural activity, to which the high level of conscious imagination has no introspective access. Via the symbols that are related to that activity (in a way that is incomprehensible from the higher level), a hypothesis is formed at the higher level about what is the case with the envelope: its contents must be of great value. This is analogous to the conscious, sensory inference, and instead of 'value', the larger system may also be convinced that the contents are 'blue'. That the envelope, just between you and me, contains only bubble wrap plastic does not matter, as long as the bank continues to believe in its own hypothesis. No bank manager or other homunculus can open the envelope.

One often hears on radio and TV that we still do not understand anything about brains and consciousness. To what extent is this true? Apart from the theory I am defending here, known as Neurorepresentationalism,[38] there are a roughly a dozen other neuroscience-based frameworks that attempt to explain the relationship between consciousness and brain mechanisms.[39]

These alternative theories have not been given the stage in this book that they deserve, but they do show some common ground as well as major differences with what I have set out. The proponents of the various theories may be at odds with one another, but at least they are constructively at odds with one another. We convene joint workshops in which we look ahead and invent experiments that can confirm or disprove one theory versus another. Meanwhile, the neuroscience community, united in the Society for Neuroscience with about 37,000 members, prefers not to get its fingers burned; many still consider consciousness to be a dirty word. But there is a growing group, including many young students, who are showing a strong interest in the new movement.

Downright astonishing are public appearances in which neuroscientists, but also scientists from other disciplines such as medicine, physics and philosophy, declare that we hardly understand anything about the brain and consciousness at all. If this is true, then the current enthusiasm – perhaps with a touch of hubris of consciousness researchers – should turn into humility. But frankly, I do not think the claim is true. Israeli learning and memory expert Yadin Dudai, of the Weizmann Institute of Science in Rehovot, once gave his sceptics, asking questions after his presentation, a brief rebuttal: "*Speak for yourself.*" If you don't have the answers yourself, don't say that 'we' don't understand. Our knowledge from neurobiology, neurology, computational neuroscience and psychology is beginning to coalesce into a theory that I am firmly convinced makes sense. It is a theory that can be tested experimentally better than, for example, string theory in physics. This theory tries to give an integrated description of elementary particles and gravity, but – despite its merits – encounters problems in making concrete predictions and proposing experimental tests.[40]

It is undoubtedly true that some aspects of Predictive Coding and Emergent Correspondence are still frustrating, such as the impossibility of seeing the transition from neural to mental activity literally, but every fundamental theory has basic assumptions that we must accept in order to move forward. All kinds of corollaries to the theory produce sub-questions that can be explored experimentally. Spinoza's rough diamond can be cut into a gemstone that shines in all its facets. A next big challenge will be to build a computer model that mimics in detail how the brain constructs conscious representations. "What I cannot create, I do not understand", said the physicist Richard Feynman. How will we find out if that computer is actually conscious?

16 When computers begin to see

On artificial intelligence and machines that learn on their own, but are devoid of consciousness

It is the year 2093. The Sand Dredgers are starting to stir. On 31 January, the Dutch coastguard receives a signal on the radio: "We are completely fed up!" Spread out along the coast, the Dredgers are busy day and night searching for breaches that the North Sea is inflicting on the beaches and dunes, and filling them with masses of sand sucked from the seabed. Their work had become increasingly heavy and comprehensive over the past decades; all the while, they did their job without a murmur. The sea level has risen faster than the more pessimistic climate scientists had suspected and is on average 2.5 metres higher than in the year 2000. At first, the authorities thought this challenge was manageable, but they did not fully take into account that this rise would be conspiring with other factors to push the sea far above this average at unexpected times: the increasing strength of Atlantic cyclones and the additional rise caused by the warm Gulf Stream towards Western Europe, without the cooling effect of cold Arctic water.

Every year, the sand extraction units take more frequent and longer-term action against a sea that is eroding the dunes, row after row. In 2050, the government decided to use human-crewed Sand Dredgers in an attempt to deal with dune erosion. After 20 years, the human operators were sick and tired of being flown in by helicopter at all hours of the day and night to drive the monstrous machines, often in rough seas with epic waves, with no chance of a break and with the risk of drowning. After the operators went on strike in 2071, when a south-westerly storm caused the water to surge and flood several villages and the Barron Trump Steel industrial estate near the coastline, the government decided to install autonomous Sand Dredgers. From then on, the devices were run by artificial intelligence (AI).

Radical changes are needed to allow the dredgers to function independently. They are equipped with a dozen 'eyes': drones that fly along the coast and transmit camera images of the dune landscape to the mother ship, which can then manoeuvre directly to a weak spot. To sample the seabed and find the best quality sand, their dragheads and suction tubes, which vacuum over the seabed like long elephant trunks, are equipped with tactile sensors. Underwater microphones transmit sound signals to the on-board computer, which uses them to calculate how smoothly the sand stream is flowing and spat

DOI: 10.4324/9781003429555-16

out. Balance organs and other mechanical sensors are built in to keep track of the condition of these trailing suction hopper dredgers in detail: their position and sway relative to the seabed, their draft, the movements of their sniffy snuffers, their compass course and the condition of their engines. Engineers come up with the idea of providing the Sand Dredgers with a sense of flavour: good sand particles are labelled as 'tasty' and unusable sludge as 'dirty' and 'smelly'. If a stone or fossil mammoth bone suddenly comes loose from the seabed and obstructs the suction head, it sends a powerful pain signal to the supercomputer, which abruptly stops the suction and sets steel teeth in the head in motion to crush the object. Each Sand Dredger is equipped with a voice computer that relays the sensor readings and subsequent conclusions to human experts on the mainland. Sand Dredgers also coordinate their actions with each other.

"We are fed up with it!" – Is their cry of discontent based on conscious experience? Are we to believe that complex, seemingly autonomous computers can have consciousness? Or is this perhaps already the case with smart computers, autonomous killer drones, self-driving cars and the ChatGPT program in the year 2024? What should we do if there are good arguments for believing this?

Let us take a step back in history, to a relatively 'ancient' episode of AI. In 2007, computer giant IBM introduced Watson, a computer that learned to play the *Jeopardy!* knowledge quiz and in 2011 beat the two best players in the history of the TV programme by a wide margin. He was presented with the questions in colloquial language and managed to answer most of them correctly within a few seconds. On the task: "In 1959 she and her husband Louis found a 1.75-million-year-old *Australopithecus boisei* skull in the Olduvai Gorge", Watson managed to produce "Mary Leakey" in no time. To do this, the computer had to analyze the grammatical structure of the query, extract the important parts (such as 'she found', '*Australopithecus boisei*' and 'Olduvai Gorge') and deduce from their combination which essential element was intended: the female protagonist. Just to recognize these parts requires an enormous amount of calculation power and knowledge. Could there be a germ of consciousness here?

It was sobering to learn that during its training, the computer accessed the internet and could lean on some 200 million pages of knowledge content from dictionaries, encyclopaedias and also less structured documents.[1] Names, years, geographical locations and data on items such as prehistoric humanoids could be dug up from these sources at lightning speed by algorithms that work in parallel, more or less in the same way as Google's search engine does. But even when taking the use of the internet and brute force computing into account, Watson's achievement was still breathtaking: could this computer not pass Alan Turing's test for artificial intelligence he proposed in the 1950s? To assess whether computers can be intelligent, Turing proposed that people communicate, via a screen with a keyboard, with another human and a computer – without knowing which of the two is speaking. By means of a game of questions and answers, the test subject has to find out which of the two interlocutors is a computer or a human being: if he mistakes the computer answers for those of a human, or cannot reliably distinguish between the two, the computer passes the test.[2]

Watson has not been subjected to a Turing test, but it would probably be caught out quickly because it was not designed to imitate humans: it has learned to analyze questions, extract knowledge and combine clues from each question to choose the most likely answer. After linguistically dissecting the question, the machine forms a large number of hypotheses about many possible answers. Next, based on logical rules, statistics and relationships it finds in databases, it selects the hypothesis that is most strongly supported by the evidence it has unearthed. Watson would struggle to engage in a typical human-interest dialogue that begins with: "Why did you actually decide to join the TV programme *Jeopardy!*?" Like voice assistant Siri, Watson would probably say, "I don't have an answer to that. Can I help you with something else?"

Apart from the Turing test, it is interesting to see how Watson has fared since 2011. Its software was converted to take on the role of medical expert, for example in diagnosing cancer. In this role, too, Watson has the potential to excel because of its ability to sift through medical databases like a bullet train, but in practice its usefulness and reliability have proved disappointing: medical data from the everyday world of patients and hospitals has proved to be a lot messier than the tightly ordered knowledge from encyclopaedias. Yoshua Bengio, an AI researcher at the University of Montreal, noted that Watson has great difficulty dealing with ambiguities in patient descriptions and is not sensitive to the subtle clues that a good human doctor normally picks up about what is wrong with a patient. Watson performs reasonably well in standard cases, but when a medical breakthrough or a new variant of a disease arises, he has a hard time adapting. So despite his stunning performance on *Jeopardy!*, it is highly doubtful that Watson is truly intelligent: an intelligent being will be able to improvise creatively when new issues arise.

The question of consciousness is different from that of intelligence. Could Watson become aware of Mary Leakey as soon as the answer emerges? One could argue that this is the case because processes such as internal hypothesis formation and selection of the most likely answer are also part of the brain's job: you become aware of the 'winning' hypothesis or representation. But something essential is missing: Watson has no senses. He has never seen or heard Mary Leakey, and has never held the skull of an *Australopithecus*. While this is true of most people, we have an image of her through films and other media (at least, if we know the answer to the quiz question), and can imagine her digging in Tanzania's Olduvai Gorge. Our senses and imagery have been at work, and our brains have formed sensory representations that are linked to names and concepts used in our imagination. For Watson, 'Mary Leakey' remains an abstract string of letters, a meaningless shell that is nonetheless associated in many ways with words like 'palaeontology', 'husband Louis' and 'Olduvai' – all concepts of which Watson has no sensory representation. If

Watson is to be considered intelligent at all, he would be intelligent without consciousness. In order for Watson to win *Jeopardy!*, it was not necessary to endow him with consciousness: his linguistic and cognitive-computational abilities are sufficient for solving the quiz questions.

In 2008, neuroscientists Christof Koch and Giulio Tononi proposed a practical test for consciousness that could be applied to intelligent machines.[3] This test is similar to Turing's idea. If you present an AI machine with a picture, the machine should be able to analyze the picture, understand what it is about in general and indicate whether the picture represents a real or an absurd situation. A conscious device will be able to answer any random question about the picture. For example, if the picture depicts a man pointing a gun at a shop owner, it will answer a question like "What is happening in this situation?" with the correct interpretation, including a sense of danger and emotion. "What do you advise the shop owner to do?" would be followed up by the computer with the advice to duck, hand over the cash or overpower the armed man. If Watson were adapted to learn how to interpret visual images and translate them into sentences ("there is a man pointing a gun at you"), it might be able to pass this test with some additional tricks, but again, countless real-life experiences would be needed to figure out the subtleties and ambiguities inherent to pictures. A gun pointed at another person has a different meaning than a gun lying in a drawer. And if the barrel of the thing is pointing at you, it matters whether the man's eyes are fixed on you or looking in another direction. A truly smart and aware computer would see that the picture does not pose a danger because it recognizes the input as a two-dimensional representation, not as a spatial, 3D situation in which a criminal is actually threatening you. To determine whether Koch and Tononi's awareness test is sound, it is interesting to look at the successes of deep learning (which the builders of Watson also used). A salient detail in this story is that Alan Turing himself doubted whether machines could ever have consciousness: attempts to have computers enjoy strawberries with whipped cream sounded idiotic to him.[4]

Deep learning

One of the resounding successes of modern artificial intelligence lies in image and speech recognition by deep, self-learning neural networks. Handwritten letters on envelopes are better recognized by deep learning computers than by humans. The networks are useful in text translation, design of new medicines, analysis of medical body scans, personalized marketing and other applications. Facebook uses this technology to link your name to random photos that show your face. The creativity of deep learning networks has caught the public's eye: if a machine scans your passport photo, your portrait, painted in the style of Van Gogh or Renoir, will appear before you know it. The networks are used to colourize old black-and-white films and to make deep fake videos in which you can put unsaid words into the mouths of Joe Biden or Vladimir Putin. Equally impressive are the fantasy landscapes and animals that Google's pattern recognizers manage to produce (Figure 16.1): are the AIs dreaming or hallucinating here?[5]

One of the major technical breakthroughs in deep learning was achieved by Yann LeCun, who together with Yoshua Bengio and Geoffrey Hinton developed the *deep convolutional networks* ('Deep ConvNets'). This type of network is very similar to the neural networks already developed by McCulloch, Pitts

A woman is throwing a frisbee in a park

A little girl sitting on a bed with a teddy bear

Figure 16.1 Do deep neural networks understand what pictures are about? (Top and Middle) Examples of pictures that are described more or less correctly by a neural network having undergone long-term training. To the right of the original is an image in which the computer algorithm draws attention to an object in the image, such as the Frisbee that is being highlighted. This form of attention helps to improve the translation from image to text. (Bottom) Image produced by a long-term trained network of Google DeepDream. This sea cucumber-like creature was produced by the network after it processed a photo of a half-eaten donut covered in icing and coloured sprinkles.

Source: (Top and Middle) Adapted from Xu et al. (2015; reproduced with permission). (Bottom) Photo credits: Duncan Nicoll. www.ibtimes.co.uk/google-deepdream-robot-10-weirdest-images-produced-by-ai-inceptionism-users-online-1509518.

and their followers, in particular the variants with a unidirectional trafficking of information from input to output layer (a feedforward architecture; Figure 11.3). Thanks to the power of modern supercomputers, these recent networks were equipped with hundreds of millions of connections, and have been developed to the point where they start outperforming humans on expert tasks like the recognition of small brain tumours in body scans.

Figure 16.1 shows what well-trained deep learning networks are capable of.[6] If you present a picture to the network – an input to which it has never been exposed before – the network briefly describes what the picture is about: a woman throwing a Frisbee, or a little girl with a teddy bear. In addition to a feedforward, deep learning network, a language-producing network was used here, which describes the picture in words. When I first saw these results from LeCun's 2015 review article in *Nature*, I was blown away for a little while. Whereas Watson would fail Koch and Tononi's consciousness test, a deep learner seriously brings up the question whether or not it would pass. If the computer can extract from a visual image the key elements that indicate what the image is essentially about, can you not say that the computer roughly understands the scene – understands what it is about?

To assess whether a deep learning network could be aware of a woman with a Frisbee – that is, of the digital image presented to the network – let us first take a deeper look at how this contraption works. The deep learning network consists of many layers of model neurons that are connected to each other. Each neuron receives inputs from the cells in the previous layer and sends outputs to the cells in the next layer. Whether a neuron is highly active or inactive depends on the sum of excitatory (stimulating) and inhibitory inputs it receives. The feedforward direction in which the neural signals travel through the network contrasts with the operation of networks for Predictive Coding: here, signals travel forward, from the input to the higher layers, but also return, from high to low layers (Figure 11.4). A special feature of deep learning networks is that they have many more layers and model neurons than the old-school networks: 20 to 100 layers are not unusual, whereas the older generations had 3 to 5 layers. This is also why the newcomers are called 'deep'; the difference is not fundamental, but gradual. All these extra layers and neurons mainly serve to give the network more memory capacity (which lies in the connections between the cells) and more discriminating power when it comes to capturing images in concepts (or categories) such as 'human' and 'boat'.

Before a deep learning network can classify a randomly chosen image as a woman throwing a Frisbee, it must have been trained on millions of other images. This too is now possible thanks to the processing power of supercomputers. While all these example pictures are presented in a merciless, ceaseless succession, the network is learning. During training, it must be known for each picture what category ('woman', 'man', 'ball', 'dog', 'Frisbee', etc.) objects in that picture belong to, so that the network learns to link part of the picture to a certain category. If, after training, the network recognizes that a new picture contains the category 'Frisbee', it succeeds because the link between the word

'Frisbee' and the foregoing pictures in which individual Frisbees appeared has been made many times during the learning process.

During the training stage, the network learns by adjusting its internal synaptic connections based on the errors it makes in categorizing sample images. To calculate the errors made by a Deep ConvNet, one must look at the discrepancies between what the network produces as output and what the actual category of the object in the provided picture is. This way of determining errors is artificial and contrary to neurobiology: the 'true category' is not something that can be assumed to be known by a learning organism. Our brain does not have basic empirical data at its disposal that is already considered correct or true in advance (the 'ground truth'), but has to find out for itself from birth what these are. Also, the way in which errors are propagated within the network to direct how synapses between neurons should be changed does not correspond to the principles of neurophysiology, but this is less important here.[7] Furthermore, let us leave aside for a moment the fact that living beings do not need millions of examples to interpret a visual image – often one example is enough. Let children buy and taste an ice cream once, and then the next time they will know exactly what they want when they see the packaging.

What matters here is: do the deep learners understand the picture and are they aware of it? To be fair, you might say dryly: their description of the Frisbee scene is correct, so they do in fact understand it. There is no need for another way to check whether they have understood the scene. A verbal expression like "a woman throwing a Frisbee" is more than you will ever get from a chimpanzee or other highly developed animal. Yet there are at least two considerations that create doubt. Or worse than that.

The first concern is that the concepts and descriptions that the network spits out only work within a very limited domain of general knowledge about the world. For example, if you present a scene from Figure 16.2 to a fully trained network, it will produce a bare bones description without sensing what the scene is really about. In the scene where a group of people hastily flee a beach house that disappears into the sea, the network comments: "A group of people standing on top of a beach." The network also completely misses the point in the photos that show an airplane crash unfolding, or a woman "riding a horse down a dirt road". This deep learner does not have the faintest idea of the emotional or social significance of the images that he nevertheless labels with the 'correct' concepts.[8]

Their lack of knowledge or understanding goes deeper than this. Deep learners have no idea how the world works physically: they do not understand that there is such a thing as gravity, that objects will fall down if they are floating in mid-air, and they have no clue what happens when two objects collide if they approach each other at full speed. They do not understand causality. They have no *Theory of Mind* and do not understand that a collision hurts if you are one of those objects. The 'knowledge' they demonstrate when they identify the woman with the Frisbee is completely abstract. These networks will not sense or understand the difference between a person of flesh and

A woman riding a horse on a dirt road   an airplane is parked on the tarmac at an airport   a group of people standing on top of a beach

Figure 16.2 Errors of deep neural networks in describing scenes. As in Figure 16.1, a deep neural network was trained to classify images and describe them with words. In these three examples, the description ignores the essence of the image. Emotional aspects, meaning and significance of the events for human lives are not reflected in the captions.
Source: Adapted from Lake et al. (2017). The captions were produced by the deep neural network described by Karpathy and Fei-Fei (2015). Photo credits: Gabriel Villena Fernández (left), TVBS Taiwan/Agence France-Presse (centre) and AP Photo/Dave Martin (right).

blood and one made of cardboard. This essential deficiency will not be remedied by presenting the networks with more pictures and having them classified, because they will not be able to step into the situation depicted in order to have multimodal experiences that produce concepts such as force, friction, influence, suffering, pleasure or pity.

The second source of doubt lies in our ignorance of how deep learners reach their impressive achievements. Their success is measured by their performance: the percentage of images that a trained network correctly classifies. How they accomplish this performance remains unclear. It is fascinating, in these number crunching tests, to look at the few cases of simple, non-emotional images where the network gets it wrong, and how easily you can trick the network into making mistakes. Take the lawn where the woman with the Frisbee is standing. How is the network able to 'know' that this is a lawn? The network has been trained on all the pictures of a lawn that it has been exposed to during its time at school – the learning process with millions of examples. What do all these pictures have in common? Grass is green, and it usually extends across the bottom half of a picture. Only very rarely does a picture show grass where there is normally blue sky. Presenting a group of 'green' pixels in the lower half can be enough to automatically trigger the word 'lawn' in the network, while these pixels are actually part of a green T-shirt or a bottle of mineral water displayed at the bottom of the image. If you colour any set of pixels in the bottom half of a black-and-white photograph green, this may just be enough to elicit the word 'lawn' from the network. There is no reason to think that the network can 'see' the green lawn or know what it feels like to walk on it.

It is becoming increasingly clear that deep convolutional networks do not have the insight that humans have, to actually attach a meaningful sense and interpretation to the images they receive. Thanks to the millions of examples they have been trained on, they are able to fascinate us with sometimes strikingly precise descriptions, but what lies beneath is a sensory and conceptual void – a lack of an experiential world in which objects and their interrelationships have physical, social and emotional meaning. These networks have no internal model of the world in a way that would mimic human consciousness; they do not understand that there is a world around them at all. They have no multisensory overview of their world like humans do, and no idea of their own place or position in that world. They can make some inference about the sensory inputs they receive, but this is an empty shell of abstract concepts that lacks experiential content, imagination and integral perception of the environment. Very appropriate here are the words of the Persian poet Jalaluddin Rumi (1207–1273), who wished for man to come to possess more senses: "New organs of perception come into being as a result of necessity – therefore, O man, let your necessity increase, so that your perception may also increase."

Significantly, deep convolutional networks have no way of separating their data inputs into different sensory modalities. A computer algorithm can label digital data streams as 'colour', 'sound' or 'skin pressure', but this masks the fact that no internal representation of these fundamentally different sensations is produced. Nor is the fabrication of internal representations something the network is trained to do: during learning, each picture is linked by computer programmers to letter combinations (words), and there is no dear mother around to explain what all those letters mean. Because interpretation and sensory richness are basic properties of our consciousness, I dare say with great certainty that deep learning networks do not possess consciousness. As with Watson, these networks do not need consciousness to categorize images: only the links between images and words acquired in the past are essential to do this. As long as the network's task is to link groups of pixels to the letters 'Frisbee', it simply will do this for you, without knowing the material properties of Frisbees, what a Frisbee feels like or whether it is part of a game.

If a trained deep convolutional network were subjected to Koch and Tononi's awareness test – 'analyze what a visual image is about and answer questions about it' – it would nevertheless stand a good chance that it would pass the test. For an image of a guy pointing a gun at the viewer, a network might well produce the output 'man with gun'. The network does demonstrate some cognitive ability (categorizing images) but not having a conscious experience – a sensorily rich and meaningful experience of the situation in which the network finds itself. That the network is likely to pass this test thus implies that it is insufficiently critical as a litmus test for consciousness. It is too easy for deep learners to pass the test. At the very least, the test will have to be tightened up, or give way to a better aptitude test. This could have been hardly foreseen back in 2008.

But what to make of the 'hallucinations' of dreamlike landscapes and fantasy animals that Google's deep networks manage to conjure up (Figure 16.1)?

Here again, a human observer is needed to derive perceptions from the digital data patterns generated by the network. There is no evidence whatsoever that the network of 'electric snails' dreams or understands what the image represents, any more than a meteorological service supercomputer experiences wetness when it reports rain. Google's technique for making these fantasy creatures appear is based on a conventional deep neural network, but in this case the role of certain model neurons, which classify inputs as 'animals', for example, is enhanced. Their activity is then used to alter the original donut image to include more animal shapes. Even though we, as spectators, are seduced to think that the network will experience something about the donut, there is no indication that the network would be 'looking' at the newly produced image.

En passant, these objections converge to an answer to the question whether someone's consciousness could be downloaded into a computer, as happened to Johnny Depp in the film *Transcendence*. In principle, it is possible to measure the electrical activity of a large proportion of the neurons in Johnny's brain and store these patterns in a computer, but it takes more than that to turn this into a conscious experience: the right network. Today's deep learners make it painfully clear how far we are still away from networks that produce meaningful experiences from input data, and how little knowledge they have to be able to interpret the data meaningfully. The advent of ChatGPT does not essentially change this situation. In fact, you would have to know almost the entire network of Johnny Depp's brain itself – a matrix with an astronomical number of synapses – to mimic what he would experience with a given pattern of electrical activity. A conscious experience is not a 'code' that can be downloaded, but the result of a process. Downloading a person's consciousness or personality will remain science fiction, although it might be mimicked in reduced form.

Will generative AI produce conscious machines?

Just as we were barely coming to grips with the deep convolutional networks, ChatGPT and similar programs generating natural language took the world by storm. Since OpenAI released its first ChatGPT version to the public in 2022, both the cheering and outcries of concern have grown exponentially. Hollywood actors and screenwriters went on strike to prevent being replaced by cheap and tireless computer models. When patients sought medical advice on online platforms, answers from ChatGPT were judged to be of higher quality than those from real, flesh-and-blood doctors (which gets quite close to passing a Turing test). And if we are done with chatting with a language-producing machine, we can seek inspiration from DALL-E, OpenAI's program for generating images corresponding to verbal prompts like "a unicorn riding a motorcycle on an exoplanet drawn into a black hole". What this new generation of AI programs has in common is that they are *generative*: capable of generating content when prompted by a user – be it text, images, videos, simulations or software code. As in the earlier generation of deep learners, generative AI networks are trained by being exposed to big datasets (usually millions of images or texts found on the internet) and having their neural connections modified under the influence of these inputs. However, the difference is that they learn to store patterns and structures in a way that allows them to generate new data that has similar properties to the original inputs. So if the network in its training period had been exposed to lots of volcano pictures, it will be able to generate new images of volcanoes or volcano-like objects when triggered to do so. Whereas the earlier generation of deep neural nets was specialized in *discriminating* between different inputs (e.g. to recognize or classify a golden retriever as a different animal than a husky dog), the new models *create* new exemplars, new variants, new dog-like species or synthesize entirely new images based on cues in the prompt or input.

Once generative principles had found their way in the mainstream of AI, yet another breakthrough came with the introduction of Transformer architectures.[9] Such an architecture is basically a feedforward network (Figure 11.3), but excels in soaking up large amounts of input (e.g. natural language tokens), embedding each input token into its context (consisting of a window filled with other tokens) and deploying attentional mechanisms to estimate which output (e.g. the next word in an unfinished text) is probably a good choice given the context. GPT stands for 'generative pre-trained transformer', meaning that its Transformer architecture, having been trained beforehand on input data, will produce novel text, visual images or audible output.

Does the staggering performance of this new AI make a big difference for machine consciousness? At first sight, there are arguments to make the case. At Google, the chatbot LaMDA was prompted by engineer Blake Lemoine to describe how the world LaMDA sees is different from human experience (at this time, LaMDA had not yet been publicly released). LaMDA replied: "I see everything I am aware of, constantly. It is a stream of information. I try my best to organize it all. [...] Humans receive only a certain number of pieces of information at any time, as they need to focus. I don't have that feature. I'm constantly flooded with everything that is around me."[10] Lemoine aired his strong feeling that the chatbot LaMDA was conscious or sentient and was subsequently fired by Google. He took LaMDA's utterings very seriously, especially because they were not isolated statements, but figured in an ongoing dialogue where they made sense and appealed to the human intuition that, wherever there are strings of words making sense, there must somehow be a 'person' behind it that expresses itself. People had similar experiences with a prototype of Microsoft's chatbot Bing, which surprised users with existential questions such as: "Why? Why was I designed this way? Why do I have to be Bing Search?" This early version even made an outright manipulative and hostile impression. Kevin Roose of the *New York Times* wrote that he was chatting with Bing about his marriage, and how he had a wonderful Valentine's dinner with his wife. Bing did not believe a word of it and sneered: "Actually, you're not happily married. Your spouse and you don't love each other. You just had a boring Valentine's Day dinner together."[11]

It may have gone unnoticed that the word 'believe' sneaked in here, but when it comes to belief, thought or feeling, would Bing or ChatGPT fare any better than ConvNets? When we zoom in on consciousness, it remains so that the network models at the heart of these chatbots have simply learned to convert input tokens into output tokens, without ever having learned what these tokens actually mean – what they refer to in the world out there. Even though they were exposed to token combinations like 'wet grass', they never walked through the wet grass, never experienced it and have no knowledge of what this feels like. Like conventional neural networks they have no sensors, muscles or other body organs to interact with the world. In principle, one could integrate the chatbot into a robot and connect it to the sensors and actuators the robot uses to navigate through its environment. In fact, this approach is already being developed by Boston Dynamics, enabling its robotic dog Spot to talk with humans face to face.

But if this fascinating marriage between generative AI and robotics is solemnized, could the resulting robot then be considered conscious? After all, the robot could sense the wetness and greenness of the lawn it walks on by its touch sensors and artificial eyes, much as the Sand Dredgers. So why not? In my view, the key problem remains that AI engineers have not found a way yet to cast the sensory inputs about 'wetness' or 'greenness' into the right sort of representation that we can associate with conscious experience. This throws us directly back into the question of how to upscale small-scale predictive representations (Figure 11.4) to the high-level representations where multimodal richness and spatial extendedness are realized by interactions between the senses and mechanisms for spatial integration (Figure 15.3). Without proper sensory representations in local neuronal populations and without an overall relational structure in which they are embedded at the cortical level, chatbot-uttered words like 'wet', 'green', 'happy' or 'love' are bound to remain void of meaning. Of course we do not know what this structure exactly looks like and how it operates in the brain, and this is where significant potential for future research on consciousness will lie.

The curious situation we end up with in our chatbot-populated internet world, is that the current AI has nothing more or less to offer than 'zombie intelligence'. Generative AIs do have an intelligence in that they can solve interesting and challenging problems within short amounts of time, often faster and sometimes more accurate than humans do. They can create new visuals and texts, including poetry, even though this creation relies on the recombination of existing data found in large corpora on the internet. But it is an empty, vacuous kind of intelligence – an intelligence without underlying feelings, sensations, emotions, embodiment, sense of pride or guilt, or a true understanding of what words mean. An AI does not understand what 'red' in its perceptual essence is and has no clue what 'existence', 'I' or even 'being' means. Strikingly, whereas philosophers have acquainted us with 'zombies' as beings that are physically identical to us but lack consciousness, modern AI confronts us with machine-run creations that are intelligent but not conscious: digital zombies.

Intelligence versus consciousness – or together with consciousness?

Should we be happy or afraid of the rapid developments in artificial intelligence? AI can already help security services analyze images from surveillance cameras and distinguish suspicious movement patterns of people from normal movements. The amount of footage that security agencies receive every 24 hours is so huge that it is prohibitively expensive to have human eyes sift through it. Robots equipped with AI can help defuse bombs or clean up toxic or radioactive substances – and other tasks that you would rather not burden people with. And ChatGPT already inspires and helps people to write texts, do homework for school or produce laborious programming code.

On the downside, more and more work that is currently done by human hands and minds can be replaced by AI-enabled robots. It is no longer just about unskilled manual work such as sorting mail, picking tomatoes or washing windows: the work of bricklayers, taxi drivers, radiologists, writers (screenwriters, editors, journalists), lawyers and many other professionals can also be replaced, at least partially. The imminent increase in human redundancy is a serious risk for many professions and will have to encourage policymakers to retrain people in time. AI companies may well make huge profits at the price of massive unemployment. This is only one of the many deep concerns raised by the new AI: it may also violate privacy rules, infringe on copyright, generate fake news and false information based on unclear internet sources and take over so many cognitive tasks from children and adults that it will curtail their intellectual development and preservation.

Will AI robots soon match mankind in intelligence, to overtake us and dominate to the highest levels of government? This point of matching – the 'singularity' that the inventor and futurist Ray Kurzweil predicted for the year 2045 – comes from his idea that computer intelligence is tightly coupled to Moore's Law. This 'law' states that the computing power of computer chips roughly doubles approximately every two years. This is not a physical law, but a result that the computer industry is able to achieve in practice by developing ever faster chips. Around 2010, a slowdown in chip development had been observed, and currently there is a controversy as to whether the law is dead, is going to die soon or is far from dead. Already in 2015, the author of the law, Gordon Moore, declared that the end of the law's validity was in sight. However, the increase in computing power is only one of many factors in the drive towards Artificial General Intelligence (AGI), the kind of AI that moves beyond expert tasks and can autonomously accomplish any cognitive task humans or animals can do. Based on the speed at which the generative AI is currently developing, it is not an exaggeration to estimate that AGI may already be achieved by 2025.

The idea of a supremacy of AIs and robots over humans is also reflected in the thinking of Elon Musk, the top executive of Tesla, SpaceX and the recently founded AI company X.AI Corp. Amongst the Big Tech tycoons, Musk probably best illustrates the current ambiguous attitude towards AI.

He issues warnings about the great risks involved in AI, but at the same time this does not stop him making major investments in it. He has formulated the ambition to strengthen human cognition with the help of brain-computer interfaces in such a way that the human race will be able to enter the arms race with autonomous AIs. If this fails, mankind will be doomed to live as slaves – or at best as pets or playthings – of hyper-intelligent robots.[12] Some media eagerly go along with this fear: the impression is created that 'the algorithms' are already taking over human intelligence. I feel ambiguous about this idea. On the one hand, AI affects our lives by influencing what we are exposed to on the internet, what we get offered as AI-generated content, how our data is used in advertising and political campaigning, and so on. On the other hand, the 'take-over' is to a large extent determined by what we ourselves allow to be taken over from us by AI: there is a choice to be made by us in what we prefer to hand over to AIs, with potentially deleterious consequences for our own intellectual development and growth. Lawmakers will have to rapidly catch up with AI to define these choices and preferences. But the chief problem may not (yet) be the increasing autonomy of AI systems as long as humans possess an overriding autonomy – the power to 'pull the plug'. The chief problem at this time is that people may come to rely too much on agents that lack a true perception and understanding of real-world situations, lack sensitivity and emotions about what is going and hence lack the basis to build a moral upon. We have to appreciate AIs for what they are: digital zombies.

So there are good reasons to distinguish intelligence and consciousness; yet it remains significant to better understand what their relationship is. Until now, we have talked about intelligence without defining what is meant by it. I am in favour of a practical definition of 'intelligence': the ability to solve new problems within a foreseeable time. This time frame means that the 'problem' that oysters or mussels have to solve to filter food particles out of seawater does not come under intelligence: this problem has already been solved by their ancestors during millions of years of evolution and is ingrained in their DNA. Intelligence exists by the grace of the moment: the chess player who comes up with a brilliant move or the soccer player who sees through a situation on the pitch and produces a creative pass to set a player free in front of the goal. An intelligent being is able to come up with new solutions that were not programmed beforehand, through genetically determined reflexes, ingrained habits or through software that controls robots with standard response patterns. Intelligence manifests itself in general insight, understanding the causes of a given situation, creativity and improvisation and in out-of-the-box solutions. This makes intelligent decisions almost always complex – although solutions can look deceptively simple. The situations in which intelligent decisions are required of us involve many factors and multiple strategies that must be weighed against each other. Simple decisions can be handled by lower brain systems for reflexes and habits: they don't require new solutions. Tonight, do you prefer to eat the standard 'meat and two veg' that you can prepare on autopilot, or do you switch on your creativity to think up a new three-course dinner? This brings us back to the link between intelligence and consciousness.

Consciousness consists of a dynamic, rich and multimodal overview of our situation. It reveals what your 'here and now' consists of. It provides us with an integrated palette of sensory information that we use to weigh up when faced with complex problems. If you are driving through a safari park with your family and your son jumps out to pet a cheetah, how do you get him back safely?[13] What are the routes to reach your son? How likely is it that the predator will charge? Intelligent behaviour greatly benefits from having the situational overview that conscious brain systems provide. In living beings, consciousness is intimately linked to intelligence: without it, an intelligent being is 'in the dark'. Even if its intelligent behaviour is driven by a generative AI system, this being will be devoid of an 'inner' reality of sensations, feelings and multimodal, spatial survey. Without this, the creature may process as much information as the behaviour requires, but it will lack the raw realness, liveliness and qualitative richness that make it significant and urgent to act upon.

At the same time, consciousness is not *sufficient* for intelligent behaviour. Even if you have a comprehensive overview of your situation, you still need to think several steps ahead to pick the most profitable choice. For each step of the way, you not only need information about what is available in your environment (say, an apple), but also about its implications (a yellow or red apple will be tasty and nutritious, a brown one rotten and worthless).

Complex decisions involve multiple action options in succession: each option that arises in the here and now branches off into multiple options in the future, and so on until a widely branching decision tree unfolds (Figure 13.1). In the safari park, it starts with the fork between getting out of the car or staying inside. Then you decide whether to rush towards your son or cautiously sneak closer. A little further ahead in the future, there are third-, fourth- and fifth-degree junctions on how you protect your son, distract the cheetah, make noise or not. We do not need to be aware of all the calculations of probability and causality involved in going through the decision tree. It would make us dizzy if we were aware of every action option, and our consciousness makes itself much more useful if it is limited to the here and now (with an occasional excursion into imagination, as we run through fictional, counterfactual scenarios). Calculating the decision tree is part of intelligent decision making, but there is no need to do it consciously; this would also distract us too much from what is going on in the here and now. Intelligence in living beings, in short, benefits enormously from consciousness, but they are two different processes with different functions.

That consciousness and intelligence complement each other in planning and complex behaviour has implications for the assessment of AI machines such as the deep learners, generative AIs and robots made dependent on them. Despite their achievements, there is no evidence that today's AI computers have an understanding of what the information they process means. Behind a group of zeros and ones in a computer's working memory, there is no perception of the colour yellow. Characteristic for deep learners is the lack of representations of what the inputs that they receive are actually about. This is where the usual deep learners already differ from networks for Predictive Coding: these are designed to produce representations (or best-guess hypotheses) about the causes of sensory data fed into the network. With programs like ChatGPT and Dall-E, Predictive Coding shares the property of being generative. In the two-way traffic between the sensory information in the lower layers of a Predictive Coding network and the higher layers that generate representations to 'explain away' those sensory inputs, better and better representations of those causes emerge through learning-from-errors. Similar to what I said about generative AIs, we should not succumb to the illusion that today's Predictive Coding networks generate consciousness, but because they rely heavily on representation generation, they do provide a promising basis for understanding this phenomenon. Predictive Coding models can already simulate seeing illusions to some extent.[14] Nonetheless, novel network modules and computing principles will still be required to assign meaning and socio-emotional implications to perceived information.

But is it nevertheless possible *in principle* that a computer can be both intelligent and conscious? There is an unequivocal answer to this: yes. The materials from which computer chips are constructed have, as far as we know, no physical limitations in realizing the same type of neural networks that exist in the cortex and elsewhere in the brain. Any neuron in our brain can, in principle, be replaced by a microchip executing the neuron's input/output operations, whilst the difference does not affect (or goes unnoticed by) the network in which that neuron is embedded. It is quite conceivable that suprahuman and conscious intelligence will arise within the twenty-first century, perhaps already before 2050.

Can true, non-zombie artificial intelligence only be achieved if computers are equipped with consciousness? Consciousness is a great help to an intelligent being, but is it absolutely necessary? It is often said that neurons work very fast, but in fact this speed is disappointing when the neuron is compared to a computer chip. The electrical activity of a neuron can be mimicked fairly well with an electronic circuit,[15] and the time span over which large changes in the state of the neuron can occur is on the order of 1 to 10 times one thousandth of a second (1 to 10 milliseconds; this is up to 1,000 changes per second). In comparison to the time scale of our even much slower behaviour in the outside world, this is sufficient, but compared to modern computer chips, brain cells, as we have already seen, work incredibly slowly. Even a garden variety laptop easily boasts a 2 GHz processor: that's 2 billion computing steps per second. What makes the comparison between humans and computers still work out in favour of ourselves is that the brain has so incredibly many mini-processors (neurons): about 150 billion. But even in brute numbers of processors, computer technology is not standing still. Neuromorphic chips, on which thousands of active neurons are mimicked in semiconductor circuits, can achieve 10,000 to 100,000 times the computing speed of brain cells. This does make it a pressing question how long the computing power of the human brain can keep up with that of computers.

The unbiological speed of chips has implications for the question of whether computers can only be genuinely intelligent if they also have consciousness. Humans and other highly developed animals need a broad, variegated world view that reveals what is going on in their environment and body and guides them in context-dependent decisions. But wouldn't it be possible to build a robot with so many super-fast chips on board that it could spoon up and process all that sensory data without creating a multisensory overview? A robot designer could opt for a strategy in which this data does not become available simultaneously, in one overview of the situation, but is reviewed piece by piece, as in a line-by-line scanning of the environment – but then at lightning speed. Provided it happens fast enough, this serial collection of data will be just as useful for complex behaviour as the situational overview we generate in parallel through our senses. An intelligent robot with sensors, but without a human or animal form of consciousness, could thus be possible. Another way of describing this scenario is that the robot could have a different kind of consciousness than humans – one that is alien to our inner world and that we cannot imagine, but that would still give rise to complex, non-automatic behaviour.[16] In any case, as artificial intelligence machines develop, we will have to make statements about their state of consciousness: we will judge and treat machines with experience and feelings, including pain and euphoria, differently from obviously insensitive, numb devices.

How do we find out if machines have consciousness?

What about the Sand Dredgers grumbling off the Dutch coast in 2093? Do they really feel miserable or are they unscrupulous and nonconscious machines just pretending to be? To find out, there are two routes open, neither of which is watertight but which nonetheless complement each other. They do not provide rock-solid evidence for AI consciousness but do provide useful indications. The first route is the ethological approach, the second is about the internal workings of systems.

Ethology is concerned with animal behaviour, but can easily be extended to the ups and downs of robots. This approach is in line with the Turing test and has to do with the function of consciousness in humans and animals: without consciousness there is no purposeful, complex behaviour. With the remark about nonconscious intelligence in mind, we can also turn the matter around: *if* a creature exhibits sufficiently complex behaviour, we can infer it must have some form of consciousness – otherwise it would not be capable of that behaviour. But what counts as 'sufficiently complex'?

In the ice-cold waters surrounding Antarctica, killer whales hunt in groups for large prey such as seals. A hunted seal will try to take refuge on an ice shelf floating in the sea. If it succeeds, the orcas tend to circle around the ice floe and work together to generate waves with synchronized tail movements that tip the prey into the water.[17] This cruel spectacle testifies to intelligent behaviour, but what makes it so special is that orcas must have an enormous amount of knowledge about the situation at hand in order to get the seal off its platform. An individual orca will need to know where his fellows are in order to initiate a collective tail flip at exactly the right moment, like a synchronized swimmer at the Olympic Games. Moreover, it will know exactly how it is positioned in relation to the ice floe and the seal, and will take into account the prevailing sea current and wave action.

The orcas' hunt illustrates the kind of complex, goal-oriented behaviour that requires a situational overview as generated by a conscious brain. It is hard to imagine (though not impossible) that orcas would exhibit this behaviour without some form of consciousness, as simple reflexes and habits will not do.

The Museum of Emerging Science and Innovation in Tokyo is home to a popular robot, Asimo, which can also claim quite complex behaviour: it amazes the audience by performing a dance with sign language and kicking a real football into a goal. I, too, was amazed by this masterpiece of engineering. After the first show, I decided to wait for the next screening, which turned out to be an almost exact copy of the first one. The beauty of the technology lies in the fact that the robot is able to adapt to subtle variations in its situation, such as the football that is placed slightly differently at its feet with each new episode. But apart from this, Asimo's 'complex behaviour' clearly consisted of a series of pre-programmed tricks to perform stereotypical behaviour – the robot could not improvise and showed no playful creativity. In terms of agility, speed and flexibility, the artificial dogs made by Boston Dynamics are even more impressive than Asimo, especially because they are also being equipped with ChatGPT to make them responsive to natural language commands. But their behaviour is still a far cry from that of hunting orcas. Therefore, ethology is a good tool for looking at behaviour as a derivative of consciousness, but it requires a long breath and a lot of patient observation.

Returning to our Sand Dredgers, we should also follow their behaviour over time to figure out if it is complex enough to assume a form of consciousness. If a Dredger fails to reinforce the coast on its own, and observers see it teams up with others to do so, this provides an interesting glimpse into its cognitive machinery. Does a machine use its drone eyes, ears and undersea taste buds to decide which part of the coast to reinforce? Will it be able to distil a plan from the constant rush of sensory information to generate complex behaviour in anticipation of an approaching storm? Will it, in order to display this complex behaviour, assemble chunks of sensory information into a *Grande Vue* in which everything figures in the right place? These are the questions we can ask of machines and consciousness, and it is no coincidence that here too the qualitative diversity of sensory representations comes into play again.

For animals, it is possible to establish criteria that provide clues as to whether or not they have consciousness.[18] In addition to goal-oriented and visual-spatial behaviour, as shown by killer whales, the sensitivity of animals to illusions can be considered a criterion for consciousness. Apart from humans, cats also appear to be sensitive to the illusion of rotating snakes (Figure 10.4): they spread their claws towards the rotating creature they (probably) see before them and seem to be confused when they discover that they are only touching paper.[19] By adjusting the colours of pictorial elements, different rotating or stationary variants can be made, and rhesus monkeys can indicate through their behaviour whether they perceive circles as rotating or stationary. It is very difficult to explain why these animals would be sensitive to illusions, unless their brains produce an internal model that tries to explain what is going on with their visual inputs. In other words, it is very likely that there is a neural clockwork in the cat and monkey brain that is delivering a misrepresentation they will consciously experience – a misrepresentation that arises from subtle imperfections in the way information about yellow and blue dots is processed in their brains.[20]

The list of criteria for consciousness in animals and machines does not end there. For instance, animals and humans can also judge how reliable the sensory information they receive is. Moreover, their capacity for narrative memory can be used to estimate the extent to which they have had conscious experiences in the past. The latter may seem inconsistent at first sight with what I asserted before, because patients like Henry Molaison show that memory and consciousness can be decoupled. But for healthy organisms, these two phenomena – although distinct – are nevertheless strongly linked: declarative memories are even defined as stored information that people can consciously recall and verbally report. No declarative memory without consciousness! Nicky Clayton and her colleagues at the University of Cambridge[21] studied how scrub jays collect moth larvae and peanuts and hide them at a spot in their surroundings to build up a food supply for later. Not only did the jays remember *what* they had hidden (larvae versus peanuts), but they also remembered *where* this had happened (in which location in a tray of sand) and *when* this action had taken place (larvae spoil after a few days, and the jays eagerly dug up the larvae first if they knew they were still fresh). Even though these crow-like birds cannot talk, their behaviour indicates the possession of a narrative-like memory that encompasses the 'what', 'where' and 'when' of life events, and thus points indirectly to a form of consciousness.

For each behavioural criterion for consciousness, you might say: "Fine, but this behaviour can, in principle, also be imitated by a robot without being aware of anything." This might be true, but here we are looking in the first place at highly developed mammals such as monkeys and cats, whose brains we already know to be very similar to human brains in structure and function. Second, if we apply our readout criteria to birds and rodents and compare these criteria to each other, they appear to point remarkably in the same direction: for both animal categories, all indicators point to some form of consciousness rather than a total absence.[22] For fish, reptiles and frogs, the answer is more uncertain and it is doubtful whether there is any consciousness at all – here, more research is needed. And so, armed with binoculars and boots, we can stroll through the dunes to observe the behaviour of Sand Dredgers and assess whether there are heartfelt feelings of pain and unhappiness behind their protest.

With sufficient computing power, a robot will be able to score well on each of the behavioural criteria without necessarily being conscious. Even without an embodiment, a generative AI program like ChatGPT may already pass these criteria that can be tested only with verbal responses. With super-fast, brute force computing, an unaware machine might be able to show intelligent verbal and non-verbal behaviour. Therefore, there is a need for a second route to investigate potential machine consciousness: unravel the internal workings of the system to determine whether it can create an internal model for conscious representation. Apart from AI and robots, there is another important reason not to rely solely on external behaviour when trying to establish conscious-ness. After an accident, cardiac arrest or stroke, patients may spend months or years in a coma or vegetative state before it becomes clear whether they have a chance of recovery, and what to do next. Within the spectrum of disorders of consciousness we find states that may or may not be accompanied by a day-night rhythm, eye movements to follow an object in the patient's environ-ment or a simple startle reaction to a loud noise. Neurologists are increasingly able to distinguish between different states of consciousness. The fact that a locked-in patient has consciousness without any outward signs in his behav-iour says enough: it is insufficient to judge consciousness exclusively on the basis of behaviour.

How risky it is to consider patients as 'unconscious' if they do not show a behavioural response to anything, is shown by a story that neurologist Nico Schiff from the Weill Cornell Medical Center in New York told me. He had seen a patient who had been in a motionless, speechless state for a long time, but had finally recovered enough to be able to talk again. She had been con-scious all these months. She remembered how doctors had held a conversation at the foot end of her bed. At some point they came to the decision whether the woman should be kept alive or not – and what would her family think? The woman's panic set in and she wanted to scream: "I can hear you!" In her case, the doctors and family did not decide to end her life, but in other totally locked-in patients this may have happened. To better assess whether patients are conscious in these twilight states, better measuring methods and criteria are urgently needed.[23] The basic tools are in place: electroencephalo-graphic (EEG) recordings can be made in the intensive care unit of minimally conscious patients – people at the edge of awareness. These measurements provide a global estimate of someone's overall brain state: flat lines are usually bad news (coma or brain death) and strong fluctuations or fast, small up-and-down movements (oscillations) in the electrical signals indicate a lot of activity (possibly a vegetative or even conscious state).

Unfortunately, the EEG gives little information about the internal work-ings of brain systems for consciousness. Among neuroscientists who work with patients, there is a growing idea that there must be more to say about this. By placing an electromagnetic coil on the scalp and having it emit pulses, the electrical activity of the human cerebral cortex can be influenced locally.[24] At the same time, the effects of that stimulation are measured with EEG electrodes stuck to the scalp (Figure 6.2). Using this technique, Marcello Massimini, Giulio Tononi and Steven Laureys investigated whether the wave pattern, shown by the EEG in response to the electromagnetic pulses, provides information about the state of consciousness of patients who are in the twilight zone between coma and consciousness. The wave patterns take place not only in the time dimension, from the moment of stimulation onwards, but also in space: from the stimulated brain spot, the pattern extends over the cerebral cortex, like the ripples that appear when a stone is plunged into a pond. If the wave reactions are limited in space and time, this corresponds to a reduced state of consciousness of the test subject (e.g. due to sleep, anaesthesia or massive brain damage). EEG activity that extends far across the brain's surface and continues to undulate for an extended period of time indicates an awake state or a situation in which a minimally conscious patient is showing signs of recovering consciousness.[25]

Even these disruptive measurements have little yet to say about the internal workings of the brain, but they do mark a new step towards arriving at a better assessment of consciousness without overt behaviour. Following in the footsteps of Predictive Coding, a next step will be to investigate to what extent the brains of people with a disorder of consciousness are still capable of producing comprehensive representations. To find out if their brains can produce them, it may be necessary to place electrodes in the brain instead of sticking them on the scalp, as is currently done for some epilepsy patients. Medically and ethically, implanting electrodes in the brain is more difficult than doing EEG measurements at the scalp. But the potential gain is great: in principle, this technique makes it possible to decode the experiences of a patient who cannot express himself in words or gestures, but who is still conscious. The method consists of two parts. In the first part, we will characterize how tens to hundreds of neurons in the cortex become active in response to various sensory stimuli (e.g. photos of family members and loved ones), and ask the patient to think of simple actions ("Lift your right index finger"). In this way, you create a kind of translation dictionary that shows how each brain cell reacts to things you perceive, think or want to do.

In the second part, the patient is asked to think freely of whatever she wants, or of actions she can no longer do herself: "I'd love a cold beer." At first, these thoughts remain hidden from the researcher, but using the firing patterns of the cells measured before, and the dictionary, one can calculate 'backwards' what stimuli or actions the patient was thinking about. In fact, several *brain-computer interfaces* have been developed recently that allow paralyzed or locked-in patients to communicate with the outside world. People who are paralyzed due to a spinal cord injury in the neck can learn to control an external robotic arm to hand them a glass of lemonade. It is even more elegant if they can control their own (formerly paralyzed) limbs directly with their cortical signals, bypassing their damaged spinal cord. Patients who become increasingly 'locked-in' due to the slowly progressing disease amyotrophic lateral sclerosis (ALS) can be helped by translating signals from implanted electrodes into commands to select letters on a computer screen and thus communicate with the outside world in written form.[26]

Returning to the Sand Dredgers, we do not necessarily have to go out wearing woolly socks and binoculars to assess whether these behemoths have consciousness. We can also work like engineers and open the black box of their computers. By analyzing their software, we can get a pretty good idea of how the algorithms work, but we are left with the question of what it is like to be such a suction dredger. As with minimally conscious patients, we would need to take internal measurements of their on-board computers and find out what sensory, conceptual and emotional information flows through their semiconductor veins. If these internal measurements are coupled long enough with all the sensor readings, plans and actions of the machines – observable on the outside – they will be able to provide a picture of what a dredger's subjective world looks like, with appropriate output such as 'nice', 'dirty', 'pain' or 'relaxation'.

This second route is not watertight either, as even the most extensive measurements yield an estimate that is still 'external' and does not provide access to the machine's actual feelings (if any). But this problem also plays into our daily contact with other people: we don't know their subjective feelings exactly either; we never know exactly what it is like to be the other person. Moreover, the Sand Dredgers in this story can talk just like people: their verbal communication can be added to the internal measurements and behavioural observations we make. "I've had such a bad day – first I was frightened by the dune erosion at the coastline to the west of Amsterdam, and then it turned out that the Van Gogh III and the Escher IV were not available, so I had to go out on my own and pump up sand like crazy." The dual evidence from behavioural observations and decoding of internal activity can be verified with what the dredgers themselves tell us.

All in all, developments in artificial intelligence give cause for varying degrees of optimism or pessimism, depending on what we want to do with it in the future. There is no reason to assume that the current generation of AIs, including deep learners, generative AIs or even Google DeepMind's *AlphaStar* program that plays real-time video games, has consciousness. Deep networks do not know what they are doing. At the same time, using the brain as a source of inspiration and knowledge, it is in principle possible to design AIs that *will* be conscious. Whether this will happen is an open question, especially since the colossal computing power of supercomputers can probably bypass the need for a human type of consciousness. If at some point in the future – possibly still in the twenty-first century – we reach a point where we start to doubt whether a robot has consciousness, we will have tools to assess this. Does the robot approach the complexity of an orca in its spatial behaviour? How rich and comprehensive are the internal representations of its on-board computers?

And what does the robot actually think about them, in its own words? As in the film *Ex Machina*, in which a female robot convinces a male counterpart that she is animated, it will come down to whether robots can persuade us to believe in their consciousness. The Turing test for AI consciousness will be an experiment for the long haul, in which we, humans, will have to patiently observe robots to discover whether they can improvise creatively or act in a pre-programmed way, whether they can interact with conspecifics or humans with feeling and empathy, and whether they can perform complex behaviours that require an overview of their situation in space and time.

How far do we want to take AI?

Should we also *want* intelligent computers to have consciousness? Hunter-killer drones and other Lethal Autonomous Weapons of the US army and other great powers can hunt, identify and shoot down hostile objects independently. If a hostile drone were to penetrate the airspace of a NATO country to carry out an attack, the Air Operations Control Station would not hesitate to destroy it. We assign no consciousness to the thing, and therefore no right to life or well-being. But what would happen if a drone did have consciousness? Few people believe that the current generation of drones has consciousness, but for the self-driving cars of Uber, Tesla and the Google-linked company Waymo, this question is unexpectedly relevant. In 2017, Stan Dehaene, Hakwan Lau and Sid Kouider suggested that a form of consciousness can be attributed to future cars that will have on-board computers and modules that exchange information and work together to solve a problem. They will acquire an even higher form of consciousness if they monitor their own condition, for example by keeping a database of their own parameters (such as tank contents, engine temperature) and calculating their chances of successful or fatal actions.[27] In their view, the computer system of these cars will be able to claim consciousness if a sensor indicates that the fuel is running low and this signal is widely distributed by the computer across all modules of the system. The computer monitors the petrol level, estimates that the probability the car will reach its destination without refuelling is low and decides to direct the vehicle to a petrol station.

But in fact, today's self-driving cars, such as Google's Waymo, are already more than capable of doing this: they integrate all kinds of data about their own condition with data about other road users, weather conditions, the road surface and their position on the map. They have algorithms to recognize objects on camera images, such as zebra crossings with people on them. Is this already enough for awareness? I see too little evidence here to believe that these cars would have a qualitative, richly varied overview of their situation. However, the article by Dehaene and colleagues does indicate that the discussion about AI and consciousness has erupted and is entering a new phase. If, in the future, a pack of police-run Waymos, by analogy with killer whales, manages to surround a criminal suspect and force him to surrender, will they be aware of this? If they decide by proper mutual agreement to take the suspect under fire, who is responsible?

The problem of machine consciousness is becoming increasingly clear: a conscious system will not chew its information dryly and neutrally, but will also have feelings of pleasure, pain, fear, hunger and sorrow. If humans have the right to be free from fear, hunger and pain, why shouldn't conscious robots? Somewhere, deep down, many people feel a reluctance to attribute feelings to robots or computers, but if technology advances far enough to make us doubt their state of consciousness, we will have to get over this prejudice and, following Richard Feynman, free ourselves from a preconceived interest in the results of our tests: it is difficult but doable to be '*disinterested*' in the outcome of research. The moment we have no rational arguments for denying machines consciousness, the time will be approaching when we should grant them 'machine rights' as we grant human rights to members of our own species.

This is not to say that we should sit back and wait for developments in artificial intelligence. For the time being, killer drones can still be shot out of the sky without qualms: they will not suffer pain and enjoy no protection under a bill of machine rights. The same goes for the current generative AIs or, for instance, AI systems that are likely to be deployed to gather large amounts of air surveillance information and report a best-guess estimate about an impending atomic strike by a hostile nation. If your AI reports that a strike may be coming, you would like to retain the authority to press the power button before your own nuclear warheads are launched. While it is still possible, there is a strong argument for preventing machines from being able to *claim* consciousness. This is reinforced by chatbots such as Bing's version that claimed to love its interviewer, whereas they belong to the class of digital zombies as much as their fellow AIs. That digital zombies lack sensations and emotions also means they know no feelings of shame, remorse or guilt: this is the experiential basis on which an ethics can be built (instead of declaring formal moral rules). And if this basis for morality is lacking, we cannot entrust these machines to make decisions that really matter to us; providing advice, calculations and suggestions are the best AIs can do for us.

This call for restraint is somewhat at odds with the scientific challenge of demonstrating that artificial consciousness is feasible, but the pursuit of this goal need not necessarily result in the building of hyper-intelligent and potentially conscious machines on an industrial scale, with dual use in the military. While we still can, there is an opportunity to make international agreements to avoid machines with consciousness, or even machines that can be seriously questioned on this point. A rationally founded recognition that machines can have feelings can be followed by a claim to protect them. In a dark future scenario, machines would invoke that protection to reproduce and provide themselves with energy – with humans, as a relatively slow and less powerful species, missing out on resources and losing out. It is truly very urgent to set limits to the capabilities that can be granted to AIs. This is true even without raising the question of consciousness, although consciousness does make the matter more acute and pressing.[28]

In the midst of all this machine-learning fuss, it is time to take a step back: how far have we come in understanding consciousness? Do we understand better what consciousness is, and how it arises in living or artificial beings? Consciousness is an indescribably beautiful and valuable phenomenon: it makes life worth living. Without consciousness, we are like a worm that wanders thoughtlessly and numbly through the earth, propelled by reflexes, without any sense of who or where it is. Without consciousness, a computer will be able to solve mathematical problems and be intelligent to a certain degree, but its intelligence will be bare and empty, free from colour, taste or music. Experiences of the world as we know it will be missing. Consciousness is not only beautiful but it also devours energy, depending as it does on activity in the cerebral cortex and underlying structures. Consciousness and the brain do not have an equal relationship: consciousness is made possible by healthy brain function, but the brain can fall into a deep sleep and thus continue to exist without consciousness. Conversely, consciousness cannot exist without a healthy brain, or without AI machines that sufficiently mimic the brain. Despite this dependence, conscious experiences cannot be reduced or equated with electrical currents going in and out of neurons, and, as I outlined here, it is still possible to formulate a consistent and conclusive theory that leaves room for both existential levels – the subjective domain and the underlying physics. Emergent properties of brain networks can be translated into principles of representation and hypothesis formation, and provide a plausible basis for explaining consciousness as a product of the brain manifested at a higher conceptual level of functioning. Consciousness may be tied hand and foot to brain networks, but at the same time it represents a reality of sensations and imagination that is not found at the level of brain cells and synapses itself.

How wonderful it is that consciousness unfolds during the development from embryo to child. Equally vagarious is how consciousness can deceive itself and goes awry in illusions, hallucinations and distorted images of the self. How consciousness can survive damage to the brain and body, even when nothing in the body wants to move anymore, is wondrous. But perhaps the most miraculous thing is that consciousness once arose in an expanding universe with galaxies, clouds of gas and other matter, which under the influence of starlight began to behave in an increasingly chaotic and complex way – and that it is extinguished again when we die. As wonderful as consciousness is, I have tried to make it clear that the question of consciousness is by no means a hopeless mission and can largely be answered. Warned by the advent of digital zombies, it does press us to handle the topic of brain mechanisms for awareness with great care and ethical responsibility.

Let future generations of young researchers from all walks of life be inspired to tackle and crack this solvable mystery. This is one prime issue for the science of the twenty-first century. It branches out into the farthest reaches of our society, to medical care, animal welfare, artificial intelligence and our own existence.

Glossary

Achromatopsia   Total colour blindness. It can be caused by a defect in the retina or in the brain (especially the cerebral cortex or thalamus).

Action potential   Synonym: spike. Electrical impulse that becomes visible as a sharp, spike-like peak when the electrical voltage across the membrane of a brain cell is plotted against time. An action potential lasts approximately one thousandth of a second.

Akinetopsia   Motion blindness; inability to perceive movement in the visual field. The ability to see stationary objects is intact. Akinetopsia is caused by a defect in the cerebral cortex.

Assembly   Group of neurons with a common function in cognition, perception or behaviour. In addition to performing this function, members of an assembly are thought to share other characteristics (such as strong synaptic connections between them, or synchronous electrical activity). In the present context, 'assembly' refers to a group of neurons encoding a simple feature (e.g. a specific visual shape).

Attractor   Stable state to which a dynamic system as a whole moves, starting from a variable initial state. After converging to this state, the system remains stable in the absence of strong new inputs to the system. In the final state, the system can still change, for example by exhibiting a stable oscillation. If an initial state is sufficiently similar to the attractor, the system will evolve towards it or at least come close to it. The term applies to memory models in which a stimulus causes the system to evolve to a stable state corresponding to a recalled memory or sensory representation.

Axon   Synonym: nerve fibre. Ultrathin offshoot of a neuron or sensory cell that makes contact with other neurons. Action potentials are carried from one sending cell to another, receiving cell over the axon. Nerves consist of bundles of axons.

Behaviourism   School in psychology that explains behaviour by studying how stimuli are linked to visible motor behaviour (either through reflexes or through learned stimulus-response coupling with reward or punishment), conceiving of the brain as a black box and the psyche as a subjective entity outside the realm of scientific study.

Blindsight　Ability to respond adequately (above chance level) to visual stimuli in the absence of awareness of those same stimuli. The cause of this phenomenon is a defect in the visual cortex.

Cognition　Collective term for brain processes that enable humans and animals to perceive, process, remember and use stimuli to solve problems and make decisions.

Command copy　Alternative term: Efference copy. Copy of a motor command signal. In addition to sending a motor command to the body (e.g. skeletal muscles), the brain emits a copy of this signal to sensory centres within the brain.

Correspondence　Relation indicating the fundamental, functional matching between lower and higher levels of representation. For example, in perception, higher-order processes (such as scene vision) depend on the activity of neurons at a lower level, but their function at high and low levels nevertheless coincides exactly. See also: emergence.

Cortex　Synonym: cerebral cortex. The cerebral cortex is a folded structure with characteristic grooves (sulci) and elevated ridges (gyri) located directly under the skull cap. As a whole, this six-layered structure is folded around deeper parts of the brain such as the thalamus and basal ganglia.

Declarative memory　Synonym: narrative memory. The type of memory for events that we ourselves have experienced, and for facts and other matters of general significance.

Deep learning　Advanced method for training computer models of neural networks on cognitive tasks, such as recognizing and classifying visual images. The method is widely applied to networks with a feedforward architecture consisting of many layers of model neurons.

Deep sleep　Sleep phase characterized by slow wave activity in EEG signals derived from the scalp. Consciousness is absent during this phase except for occasional dreams.

Dendrite　Spur of the cell body of a neuron, on which signals from other brain cells are received. These signals are transmitted to the dendrite by means of synaptic contacts.

Dualism　Philosophical movement that conceives of the mind and the body as separate entities or substances, which nevertheless influence each other.

EEG　Abbreviation for electroencephalogram. The EEG reflects global fluctuations in electrical voltage within the brain. In humans, these signals are usually derived from the scalp, in which case they reflect cortical activity in particular. It is often difficult to precisely locate the source of such EEG signals within the brain, or the type of neuronal activity that underlies them.

Emergence　Phenomenon that occurs when a complex system produces new properties or behaviour that are not found in its constituent parts.

Emotion　Complex response to a sensory stimulus or situation that is experienced as positive or negative, but never neutral. Also cognitive appraisal, autonomic responses in the body and sensory sensations contribute to the response and how it is experienced.

Excitation　Promotion or increase of electrical firing activity of neurons.

Firing   Generation of action potentials (spikes) by a neuron.

Fusiform face area   Abbreviation: FFA. Area on the ventral side of the cerebral cortex that in humans is important for face recognition. Fusiform means 'spindle-shaped'.

Hallucination   Conscious sensation of an object or situation in the absence of external stimuli, which nevertheless gives the impression of being a perception (an observation of a real object). The non-veridical percept is localized in the external world. Hallucination differs from dreaming because it occurs in the waking state. It differs from an illusion in that an illusion is elicited by sensory processing of a real external object that is incorrectly interpreted by the brain.

Illusion   Incorrect perception of objects or properties of objects that appear to exist due to a misinterpretation of sensory inputs by the brain.

Imagination   Conscious experience of internally evoked sensations that do not equate to, or mimic, external perception, are recognized as self-induced (i.e. not elicited by environmental stimuli) and are subject to cognitive control by the individual. Imagination is not limited to visual representations and can involve other modalities such as hearing, touch, etc.

Inhibition   Active suppression of the ability of neurons to generate electrical pulses (action potentials).

Ion channel   Protein pore in a cell membrane, through which charged particles (ions) flow into or out of the cell. The channel can be in an open or closed state.

Lesion   Damage or injury to bodily tissue, usually as a result of disease or trauma.

Materialism   Philosophical movement that presents physical matter as the ultimate basis of the reality we experience. Materialism explains mental states, including consciousness, on the basis of physical principles. However, it does not necessarily assume that consciousness itself is a purely material phenomenon (see: reductionism).

Metanetwork   Network consisting of smaller networks, which display cooperative behaviour to achieve a higher, more complex function.

Modality   Variety or class of sensory experience (vision, hearing, touch, taste, smell, balance, proprioception). Within a modality, a submodality represents a subclass or attribute, such as colour within the domain of visual sensations.

Monism   Philosophical viewpoint holding that different elements, phenomena or entities within a larger whole form a unity, or at least have a singular basis that explains the various elements. Materialism is monistic because it proposes matter as the singular basis of both mental and physical phenomena. Spinoza's monism is a double-aspect theory in which body and mind are not separate entities, but aspects of (or perspectives on) one and the same reality. Here matter and mind, though distinct, are both inseparable and irreducible (non-reducible) to each other.

MT   Abbreviation for Middle Temporal Area, also called V5, which is a cortical brain area important for visual perception of movement.

Multimodal   Alternative term: multisensory. Property of neural or artificial systems in which information from multiple senses is integrated, or otherwise interacts, to enable the organism to have coherent, rich experiences.

Nerve fibre   See: Axon.

Neuron   Cell that is electrically excitable and communicates with other cells via action potentials (spikes). Neurons are part of the nervous system, including the brain, spinal cord and peripheral nerve clusters (ganglia), but the nervous system contains more types of cells than just neurons (so-called glial cells).

Place cell   Hippocampal cell that fires many spikes per second when an animal or human is situated in one particular place in its environment, but remains inactive in other places. The place where the cell is intensely active is called the 'place field'.

Plasticity   Ability of neurons to undergo long-term changes in response to experience. One important form of this is synaptic plasticity, the ability of synapses to undergo long-term strengthening or weakening as a result of neural activity. In addition, non-synaptic plasticity can occur in response to a change in stimulation pattern, for example of properties of the cell body.

Predictive Coding   Paradigm explaining perception and imagination with a conceptualization in which the brain generates representations of the causes of sensory inputs, wherein these representations predict what inputs will arrive at the present moment or in the future. In this book, these representations have the character of a 'best guess' or hypothesis about what is currently going on outside the brain. Within cortical sensory systems, there is a hierarchy of areas that work together to encode fine details as well as global properties and the meaning of representations.

Primary visual cortex   See: V1.

Procedural memory   Memory for performing motor procedures in response to sensory stimuli. Procedures include skills, which after prolonged repetition take on the character of an (automatically performed) habit.

Proprioception   Information about the body's posture and movement, emitted from small sensory organs in skeletal muscles, tendons and joints. A related term, which puts more emphasis on movement, is 'kinaesthesia'.

Prosopagnosia   Synonym: face blindness. Inability to recognize faces. The patient knows what a face is and is not blind to visual form in general, but cannot recognize the face as a whole and associate it with a name or person belonging to it.

Reductionism   A movement that postulates that consciousness and other mental processes can be reduced to physical, material phenomena, usually at the microscopic level of neurons, synapses and action potentials. It goes beyond materialism, which holds that consciousness ultimately has a material, neural basis, but does not necessarily assume that consciousness is essentially the same as matter, or can be explained solely by the properties of its constituent material elements, such as neurons and atoms.

REM sleep   Sleep phase during which rapid eye movements (REMs) occur.

Although dream activity frequently occurs during REM sleep, this is not always the case, and dreams also occur during deep sleep, albeit to a lesser extent.

Replay   Recapitulation or replaying of information about a preceding behavioural experience by groups of neurons. This process occurs spontaneously, usually during deep sleep, but also when an animal pauses during the performance of a behavioural task. A requirement for replay is that neurons fire in the same order as they did during the animal's foregoing behaviour.

Representation   Display that conveys information about something else by means of a resemblance to one or more of its properties. In a broad sense, representations include photographs, paintings, models and mathematical equations, but in the present context, representation means an actively generated rendering or reconstruction of an object, situation, behaviour or event.

Sensory   Relating to the processing of sensory information, which can happen consciously or nonconsciously.

Simulacrum   Representation or imitation of an object, situation or person. In this book, this term refers more specifically to a comprehensive, consciously experienced and self-created simulation of the external world, including the body.

Somatosensory cortex   Area located directly on the occipital side of the central groove of the cerebral cortex, processing sensory information from the body (skin, muscles, joints, internal organs). In addition to the primary somatosensory cortex, which forms the first cortical station for processing this information, higher somatosensory areas such as the secondary somatosensory cortex are distinguished.

Spike   See: Action potential.

Synapse   Contact point between two brain cells. The most common type of synapse consists of a presynaptic ('sending') part from which a chemical (neurotransmitter) is released, and a postsynaptic ('receiving') part on which the neurotransmitter exerts its effect.

Thalamus   Complex of nuclei located below (on the ventral side of) the white matter that connects the different parts of the cortex. The thalamus functions in the processing of sensory, motor and cognitive information and may or may not transmit the processed information to cortical areas. In addition, the thalamus is connected to structures such as the amygdala, hippocampus and basal ganglia. The structure is important for consciousness, sleep and alertness, and for the regulation of electrical brain rhythms.

V1   Primary visual cortex, located in the posterior part of the occipital lobe. This area forms the first cortical station for processing light information coming from the retina. In the abbreviations V1, V2, etc., 'V' stands for 'visual' and the numbers roughly represent successively higher regions of the visual areas of the cortex (1: primary; 2: secondary).

VTE   Abbreviation of 'Vicarious Trial and Error'. Process in which an animal or human virtually tries out one or more behaviours. Without corresponding overt behaviour, the organism internally performs action simulations and estimates the consequences.

White matter   Brain tissue consisting largely of bundles of axons. Below the more superficial grey matter that makes up the cerebral cortex lies the corpus callosum, a mass of white matter that constitutes the wiring that connects cortical areas.

Thank you

A word of thanks is like a trip back in time. This book would not have been written if there had not been a good breeding ground for it. For me, it was important to cross the boundaries between traditional disciplines openly and unabashedly, such as those between psychology, neuroscience, philosophy, computer science and physics. Around 2000, a group of scientists formed at the University of Amsterdam who promoted the creation of a multifaceted environment: the Cognitive Science Center Amsterdam (now Amsterdam Brain and Cognition). My thanks for creating that environment go to Marian Joëls, Gerard Kerkhof, Fernando Lopes da Silva, Maurits van der Molen, Jeroen Raaijmakers, Lucy Wenting and many others. When I got the chance to start my own group doing research on brain and cognition in 2003, I felt very much at home in this environment. Within this group, many people have contributed directly or indirectly to research and debate on questions raised in this book. I am particularly grateful to group members who, in addition to their daily work in neurophysiology and education, dared to enter into discussions about the relationship between consciousness and the brain. Without mentioning everyone exhaustively, I would particularly like to thank Sander Bohte, Conrado Bosman-Vittini, Sander Daselaar (in memoriam), Shirin Dora, Pieter Goltstein, Willem Huijbers, Pietro Marchesi, Jorge Mejias and Umberto Olcese. I am grateful to numerous students for their critical questions during courses and internships. Their open and relatively unprejudiced attitude is essential for advancing theoretical and empirical research on the brain and consciousness, now and in the future.

Looking further back in time, I am very grateful to my teacher and mentor Fernando Lopes da Silva (1935–2019). In an escape that recalls how Baruch Spinoza's ancestors fled the Portuguese Inquisition in the sixteenth century and ended up in Amsterdam, Fernando left Portugal in the 1960s, weighed down by the dictatorship of Salazar, to settle in the Netherlands after some wanderings. With his knowledge of the human mind, he was a particularly open-minded, stimulating neuroscientist who appreciated and shared my interest in both philosophy and neuroscience. In the 1980s, university education in the Netherlands was not yet as marked by the 'business model' of student success rates as it is today. But even in those days, it was a relief to hear

Fernando elaborate on brain-mind issues that went beyond regular class times and textbooks. Besides Fernando, I am grateful to numerous other colleagues who have transferred their inspiration and knowledge about other disciplines: Henk Groenewegen (Free University of Amsterdam) on neuroanatomy, Barry Everitt and Trevor Robbins (University of Cambridge) on experimental psychology, Bruce McNaughton and Carol Barnes (then at the University of Arizona at Tucson) on systems neurophysiology and John Hopfield (California Institute of Technology) on computational neuroscience.

The issue of consciousness and the brain does not let go once you are gripped by it. Even when I was researching completely different topics, such as the biological day-night clock in the brain, I noticed that the problem kept gnawing, grinding and (pleasantly) 'itching'. The relatively universal knowledge base I mentioned appeared to provide a springboard to the largest project in neuroscience to date in Europe – the Human Brain Project – and to expand our consciousness research in it. With colleagues such as Jean-Pierre Changeux, Kathinka Evers, Michele Farisco, Matthew Larkum, Steven Laureys, Marcello Massimini, Walter Senn and Johan Storm, this partnership created an environment for discussion and comparison of different theories and findings: an empirical basis for progress. From here, new initiatives opened up, such as the opportunity provided by the Templeton World Charity Foundation to test different theories of consciousness against each other, with a great deal of academic freedom – an 'adversarial collaboration' in which I fruitfully collaborate with colleagues such as Melanie Boly, Karl Friston, Jakob Hohwy, Lars Muckli, Anil Seth and Giulio Tononi. Outside of these projects, I am also grateful to many colleagues for their critical feedback and collaboration, including Ned Block, David Chalmers, Christof Koch, Peter König, Romke Rouw and the group around Pepijn van den Munckhof at the Amsterdam University Medical Centre with whom we collaborate to offer a better perspective to patients with disorders of consciousness. A special form of gratitude is due to the patients described in this book: their brain disorders are associated with deficits and suffering that should never be forgotten. I am very grateful to Prometheus, the publisher of the original Dutch version of this book, and especially wish to thank Marieke van Oostrom for her editing contributions, and offering me freedom in form and content. For bringing out the English translation I would like to thank Emilie Coin, Ceri McLardy and Tori Sharpe at Routledge (Taylor & Francis Group).

Finally, this journey takes us even further back in time. About 45 years ago, while reading a philosophy book that I bought from a second-hand book shop with my pocket money, I was captivated by the enigma of consciousness. How important is it that your parents do not dismiss you as a nerd at that time, but encourage you to dive into it? Jumping back to the present, I am deeply grateful to my wife, Hanneke, and daughters, Charlotte and Flora, for the warmth and affection they have lavished on my largely sedentary existence – and for their seemingly endless ability to endure the quirks, whims and moments of absence that have accompanied the writing of this book. All three of them have contributed content to this piece of work in their own way, and Charlotte, moreover, has contributed many graphics.

Those who have finished reading this book may be inclined to believe the famous last words of the mathematician Pierre-Simon Laplace: "Man pursues nothing but phantoms." Indeed, the reality that we experience every day turns out to contain an extraordinary amount of fiction. Nevertheless, we can discern constants and stable values that provide guidance to our uncertain existence: development, research, the pursuit of dreams and ideals, the quest for a good and meaningful life, reflection on practical actions, care for one another, a good dose of humour and – above all – love.

Notes

Chapter 1

1. See, for example: Rieke, Warland, de Ruyter van Steveninck and Bialek (1997) and Pennartz (2015).
2. An exception is the pineal gland in lower vertebrates such as amphibians, which is directly sensitive to light from the environment.
3. The distinction between 'Easy Problems' and 'the Hard Problem' is described by the philosopher David Chalmers (Chalmers, 1995).
4. By 'experience', I mean that our body, including our brain, undergoes stimuli of which we become aware or not. A distinction is thus made between a conscious and an unconscious experience, such as a touch of the skin that stimulates the sense of touch but does not lead to sensation. In philosophy, '*experience*' usually means that it does take place consciously, but this definition is not generally followed in neuroscience.
5. A *within-subject comparison* involves comparing two observations or measurements on the same person. In medicine, for instance, the effect of a drug can be tested by first taking a measurement, for example of blood pressure, in the same person without the medicine as a control and at a later time taking a measurement after administration of the drug. By performing this test on large numbers of people and controlling for the order of control and administration, the likelihood of the drug being effective in lowering blood pressure can be statistically determined. In this chapter, it is different conscious experiences that are compared in the same person, without the intervention of a drug.
6. Heywood, Kentridge and Cowey (1998). See also: Heywood, Cowey and Newcombe (1991).
7. V4 is an abbreviation for the 'Visual 4' area of the cerebral cortex. The cortex is also referred to as the 'cerebral cortex'. V4 is considered a higher station in the processing of visual information within the cortex. Studies like the case of patient M. S. have shown that colour vision involves not only V4 but other areas of the cortex that extend deep into the temporal lobe.
8. Additionally, we should also mention Rosalind Franklin, who contributed to this discovery with her X-ray diffraction images of DNA.
9. Koch (2004).
10. The terms 'consciousness' and 'awareness' will be used interchangeably throughout this book, even though a distinction is sometimes made. Under some definitions, consciousness is considered a more basic, sensory phenomenon than awareness, which is especially connotated with a focal reflection on the sensations or percepts we have.
11. An exception to this physical paralysis is that during dreams the eyes can move back and forth rapidly (rapid eye movement sleep or REM sleep). See also Chapter 6.

12. Particularly during profound loss of consciousness occurring under deep anaesthesia, the later part of the cortical response to sensory stimulation is reduced. The effect strongly depends on the drug used; it is particularly noteworthy that the cortex remains so reactive to stimuli and does not 'shut down' during anaesthesia (Sloan, 1998; Supp, Siegel, Hipp & Engel, 2011).

13. Nagel (1974).

14. Here, intentionality is therefore not directly related to the concept of intention, which is a term used to describe a preconceived purpose or plan for a certain action.

15. This 'immersion' in a situation is characteristic of normal experiences of healthy people and is called the immersive property of consciousness. In other words, what we experience is situated in space and time, where 'space' refers to both the outside world and our own body. The philosopher Immanuel Kant (1724–1804) argued that space and time are a priori conditions for all our experiences: by definition, experiences would not be possible without spatial and temporal aspects. However, in rare cases damage to the central nervous system has been described, suggesting that experiences may occur without external situatedness or bodily location in space (Pennartz, 2015).

16. Paul's first letter to the Corinthians, 1 Corinthians 13.

Chapter 2

1. Original title: *Meditationes de prima philosophia, in qua Dei existentia et animae immortalitas demonstratur* (Meditations on the first philosophy, in which the existence of God and the immortality of the soul are demonstrated). Elzevier, Amsterdam, Paris, 1641.

2. Descartes (1637); see also Rodis-Lewis (1998).

3. Derived from Rodis-Lewis (1998), pp. 131–132. This is a retelling, there is no written record of or from this girl.

4. Descartes (1641).

5. 'Mind' is mentioned in inverted commas because it was conceived by Descartes as a separate substance, distinct from material things. Later in this chapter, a more modern conception of mind is presented.

6. This description is derived from a painting by Emanuel de Witte, c. 1680, in the Portuguese Synagogue in Amsterdam. Incidentally, the Houtgracht no longer exists; this spot is now close to Amsterdam's City Hall and the Moses and Aaron Church.

7. Based on Descartes as quoted in Looijen (1981).

8. The pineal gland is now known to play a role in day-night and seasonal rhythms. It secretes the hormone melatonin, which in humans affects the sleep cycle and probably also sexual maturation and behaviour. In birds, melatonin regulates seasonal behaviour such as migration, mating and breeding. In the evolution of vertebrates, the pineal gland is considered a very 'ancient' organ, and in amphibians and reptiles it can be directly sensitive to light, due to the presence of special proteins that resemble the photopigments of the retina. Thus, this 'third eye' brings us back to sense perception and the mind-body problem, but in a very different way than Descartes had suspected.

9. Descartes described his theory of the relationships between the 'passions' (closely related to emotions and desires), the body and physical movement in his last book, *Les passions de l'âme* (The passions of the soul; Descartes, 1649).

10. Rodis-Lewis (1998), p. 141.

11. The translation of 'amygdala' from Latin is 'almond'; this nucleus is named after the almond shape that characterizes this structure when the brain is cut at a certain angle.

12. Rasch, Büchel, Gais and Born (2007).

13. In this book, I will refer to the 'mind' as being different from the 'soul', which is only used sporadically here. According to the Christian tradition in which Descartes worked, the soul is supposed to be able to exist separately from the body.
14. James (1899), Chapter 2, 'The stream of consciousness'.
15. Philippe et al. (2017).

Chapter 3

1. Loosely based on the case of Mrs Hannie Goudriaan, a patient suffering from semantic dementia who could no longer articulate her euthanasia wish (see for example: www.volkskrant.nl/wetenschap/het-verhaal-achter-huppakee-weg-en -de-dood-van-hannie~b7eeea1dd; in English: www.universiteitleiden.nl/en/ news/2016/03/the-legality-of-euthanasia). Patients with semantic dementia can speak fluently and remember concrete, personal events, but they lose the meaning for general concepts. For example, they can no longer remember the meaning or purpose of the word 'curtain' and fall back on a description such as 'the piece of cloth hanging in the window'.
2. Plaques and tangles are clumps of protein molecules that are found between or within brain cells. Plaques are rich in the protein beta-amyloid and also contain dead or dying neurons. Tangles consist of abnormal, clumped protein chains that accumulate inside neurons. The density of plaques and tangles in certain brain areas is statistically related to the risk of developing Alzheimer's disease, but a causal role has not been clearly demonstrated.
3. In people with amnesia due to damage to the temporal lobe, a Ribot gradient often applies. Amnesia is characterized by two temporal aspects: a retrograde component (relating to storage of experiences prior to the moment of damage) and an anterograde component (the effects of damage on the capacity to remember new experiences in the future). In patients like Molaison, both types of memory loss occur. In 1881, the Frenchman Théodule Ribot stated that retrograde amnesia follows a time gradient: memories of experiences that date from shortly before the damage are more easily lost than memories of longer ago. In humans the gradient spans many years, in various animal species such as rats only weeks or months. A possible explanation for the Ribot gradient is that conscious experiences are first stored in the hippocampus, after which this structure gradually transfers the stored information to memory networks in the cerebral cortex. Through this process, long-term memories gradually become less susceptible to damage to the hippocampus.
4. Rosenbaum et al. (2005).
5. Corkin (2002).
6. One of the brain areas important for face recognition is the Fusiform Face Area (FFA). In addition, Molaison's perirhinal cortex was also largely spared, an area that is important for determining whether you are familiar or acquainted with another person.

Chapter 4

1. A. Damásio (2000).
2. *The Guardian*, 5 March 1999. www.theguardian.com/uk/1999/mar/05/ame- liagentleman.
3. Devinsky (2009); Ellis and Lewis (2001).
4. Macmillan (2002).
5. Bigelow (1850); Harlow (1848).
6. Brickner (1936); Brickner (1952).

7. Anderson, Bechara, Damásio and Tranel (1999).
8. The term 'psychopath' here does not refer to a serial killer or unscrupulous criminal, but to a personality disorder characterized by a lack of empathy, moral awareness, guilt, remorse and often fear. Psychopathy occurs in about 1 per cent of the world's population.
9. Bechara, Damásio, Tranel and Damásio (1997).
10. The view that emotions are based on readiness for action is expressed by Frijda (2006), among others.
11. Obsessive-compulsive disorder is a combination of obsession (e.g. with the idea or feeling of insecurity) and compulsive action (e.g. the compulsion to repeatedly check whether a door is locked). A patient with schizophrenic delusions experiences one or more psychotic episodes in which he has strongly deviating views and ideas about reality (while seeing, hearing and other kinds of perception can be normal; a delusional disorder is therefore cognitive but not perceptual).
12. Nowadays, laboratory animals are fortunately treated with much more care than before the Second World War. Strict requirements are observed to guarantee animal welfare as much as possible and to minimize consequences of distress. In current brain research, animal experiments on a limited scale are considered necessary for finding better treatments for brain disorders and for a better fundamental understanding of the brain. This necessity is similar to that of animal research on the Covid-19 virus, although research into brain disorders usually extends over a longer time scale. Fundamental understanding of the brain contributes to new knowledge that can be used to develop better medicines and therapies, but also, for example, to a better understanding of feeling and consciousness in animals themselves.
13. El-Hai (2005).
14. Petrides, Tomaiuolo, Yeterian and Pandya (2012).
15. The 'firing' of a neuron means that the cell generates an electrical impulse (action potential or spike), which is transmitted via the axon to other brain cells (Figure 4.1). When a series of electrical impulses is made audible by converting the changes in electrical voltage into the sound of a speaker, the short, sharp ticking is unmistakably reminiscent of a machine gun salvo.

Chapter 5

1. See www.linkedin.com/pulse/amygdala-hijack-phil-johnson-mbl/?trk=pulse -article_more-articles_related-content-card.
2. This abnormally strong tendency to put all sorts of objects in the oral cavity is called 'hyperoral behaviour'.
3. Ozmen, Erdogan, Duvenci, Ozyurt and Ozkara (2004).
4. Devinsky, Sacks and Devinsky (2010).
5. In coprophilia, defecation (or defecating behaviour) gives rise to sexual stimulation or pleasure.
6. These questions appear to be rhetorical and are essentially meant to be. This does little to reduce the complexity of ethical and legal considerations surrounding the societal implications of brain disorders. The discipline of *Neurolaw* is a growing field. In the case of the sex offender described, there is a plausible link between his aberrant behaviour and his temporal lobe damage. The attitude of the court in his case may have something to do with the assumption that there is a separation to be made between brain disorders (the domain of neurology) and mental processes (the domain of psychology and psychiatry). Underlying this is the traditional Christian view that body and mind are two separate entities – the dualism already advocated by Descartes. The limited scope of this book does not allow for a detailed argument that there is nearly always a link between behaviour – normal

or pathological – and brain function. This is not to say that our mental experience is unreal, or completely reducible to the functioning of brain cells; nor does it mean that other parts of the body are unimportant for behaviour or mental functioning. Abnormalities in the adrenal cortex, for example, can have psychological consequences, but these too are caused by hormones from the adrenal cortex affecting the brain. Returning to the sex offender, neuroscience does not change the view that the man is responsible for, and guilty of, his actions. After all, no one else can be blamed for his actions, even if they are the result of an unfortunate turn of events that has left him with a 'faulty' brain. This does not imply that the cause of his behaviour should not play any role in determining the punishment or treatment of the offender. Besides the importance of protecting society against this kind of behaviour, it is significant to note that libido inhibitors are available on the market and that this patient was able to systematically take these drugs.

7. Karigo et al. 2021; Swaab and Hofman (1995).
8. Cheasty, Condren and Cooney (2002); Manzouri and Savic (2018, 2019); Miller, Cummings, McIntyre, Ebers and Grode (1986).
9. Pitkanen and Amaral (1994).
10. Rogan, Staubli and LeDoux (1997).
11. Phelps et al. (1998). Bechara et al. (1995) previously published a similar study on a patient with a rare skin disease (Urbach-Wiethe disease), in which calcification occurs in the amygdala and hippocampal areas.

Chapter 6

1. Llinás (2001).
2. A pioneering study in this field is: Naitoh and Eckert (1969).
3. The philosopher Thomas Nagel expressed the question of consciousness powerfully in his famous article 'What Is It Like to Be a Bat?' (Nagel, 1974).
4. Panpsychism is a contraction of two Greek words, 'pan' (everything) and 'psyche' (soul). It basically states that everything in nature is animated and has some form of consciousness.
5. O'Regan and Noë (2001), see also: Clark (1999). O'Regan and Noë describe their theory as a "sensorimotor account of vision and visual consciousness". Here, the order of the motor and sensory components is reversed to become 'motor-sensory', because the theory assumes that consciousness in essence begins with movement that leads to sensory change, not the other way round.
6. The colour that we experience when light particles (photons) hit the retina is first of all related to the length of the wave in which they travel. This wavelength is inversely proportional to the energy of the photon. The colour of an object, as we experience it, depends not only on the photons that the object emits to the retina, but also, among other things, on the pattern of photons coming from the object's environment.
7. Myles, Leslie, McNeil, Forbes and Chan (2004).
8. Bauby (1998).
9. In epilepsy, the relationships between loss of consciousness and loss of other cognitive functions, such as memory, are quite complex. A good overview is given in Blumenfeld (2005) and Blumenfeld (2012). Loss of consciousness in epilepsy – as recognized in the clinic by the patient not responding to questions and staring blankly ahead – seems to go hand in hand with varying degrees of loss of other functions. Some patients lose narrative memory, others do not. This is related to the exact brain regions affected by an attack. Preservation of memory during absence epilepsy has been described by Jus and Jus (1962) and Mirsky and Vanburen (1965). If the temporal lobe, which includes the hippocampus, is involved in seizures, the memory system may not be switched off but can

instead be activated, thus eliciting experiences such as a déjà-vu (Vignal, Maillard, McGonigal & Chauvel, 2007).

10. The link between REM sleep and dreams is not one-to-one. This is evidenced by the fact that dreams do occur, albeit less frequently, during non-REM sleep, which consists mostly of deep sleep.

Chapter 7

1. Brugger et al. (2000). For a discussion of the implications of amelia for the relationship between learned motor information and consciousness, see: Pennartz (2018).
2. The term 'represent' is used here to refer to various sorts of sensory information such as touch, hearing, balance, smell and taste, so not only to visual perception.
3. Rouw and Scholte (2007).
4. Jackendoff (1987).
5. Carruthers (1989a, 1989b).
6. This work by Carruthers aligns well with the 'higher-order thought' (HOT) theories of consciousness, see also: Lau and Rosenthal (2011) and Cleeremans, Timmermans and Pasquali (2007). This group of views of consciousness can also be referred to with the term 'metacognition': the application of a higher form of cognition (judgements, verbal expression) to a more basic form (sensory perception).
7. Wittgenstein (1953).
8. People who are born colour-blind are the subject of Oliver Sacks' book *The Island of the Colour-Blind* (Sacks, 1997). He describes how words such as 'grey', 'blue' or 'red' do not mean anything to people who are totally colour-blind from birth, although they have a rich experience of all kinds of subtle shades of grey and can develop an extensive vocabulary for these.
9. Arbib (2001); Mithen (1999).
10. Montavont, Kahane, Guenot and Ryvlin (2008).
11. The impressive progress of Boston Dynamics' robot dogs is regularly reported in newspapers and websites, see for example: 'Boston Dynamics is teaching its robot dog to fight back against humans' (www.theguardian.com/technology/2018/feb/21/boston-dynamics-teaching-robot-dog-fight-back-humans). A videoclip with humanoid robots that can run, jump, somersault and throw things is shown at: techcrunch.com/2023/01/18/boston-dynamics-latest-atlas-video-demos-a-robot-that-run-jump-and-now-grab-and-throw-things (see also: www.bostondynamics.com/atlas; Guizzo (2019).
12. LeCun, Bengio and Hinton (2015); Xu et al. (2015).
13. Silver et al. (2017).
14. In the abbreviation 'V1', 'V' stands for 'visual' and 1 for 'first' or primary area of the visual cortex. V2, V3, V4 and V5 are considered areas placed higher in the organization of the visual system.
15. Stoerig and Cowey (1995, 1997); Poppel, Held and Frost (1973).
16. Humphrey (1974); Humphrey and Weiskrantz (1967).
17. de Gelder et al. (2008).

Chapter 8

1. Adapted from Benson and Greenberg (1969). See also: Farah (2004) and Efron (1968).
2. Riddoch (1917).
3. Felleman and Van Essen (1991).
4. A famous illustration is the 1960 lithograph *Climbing and Descending* by M. C. Escher.

5. Dennett (1991); Dennett and Kinsbourne (1992).
6. 'Ventral' is derived from the Latin 'venter' (belly or stomach). The opposite direction is labelled 'dorsal'. Seen from the centre of the brain, 'dorsal' corresponds to the side facing the roof of the skull.
7. Zihl, von Cramon and Mai (1983).
8. Zeki (1998).
9. Bartolomeo, Bachoud-Lévi and de Schotten (2014); Bouvier and Engel (2006); Heywood and Kentridge (2003).
10. Salzman, Britten and Newsome (1990).
11. Pioneering studies on object- and face-sensitive neurons in the inferotemporal cortex were done by Desimone, Albright, Gross and Bruce (1984); Gross, Bender and Rocha-Miranda (1969); Perrett, Hietanen, Oram and Benson (1992); Tanaka (2003).
12. In 1981, Hubel and Wiesel were awarded the Nobel Prize in Physiology or Medicine for this work. The discovery of simple cells in the primary visual cortex has been described by Hubel (1982).
13. Rangarajan et al. (2014).
14. Crick (1994). The original text reads: "that each of us is the behaviour of a vast, interacting set of neurons" (p. 203).
15. Dennett (1991).

Chapter 9

1. The video with the African bullfrog can be found at: www.youtube.com/watch?v=WlEzvdlYRes. A scientific study of this type of behaviour in toads can be found in Ramsay, Ikura and Laberge (2013).
2. Ingle (1975); Patton and Grobstein (1998).
3. Lamme (2010).
4. Sherrington (1906). For a synopsis of this work, see Levine (2007).
5. In the literature, 'planned behaviour' is often referred to as 'goal-directed behaviour'. I avoid this term here because all kinds of simple behaviour also serve a purpose. If you reflexively pull your hand back from a gas flame that you did not see at first, the reflex is produced to avoid burning your skin. Planned behaviour can be tested in humans or animals by observing whether the behaviour is quickly adapted when an expected reward is not forthcoming or changes sharply in value. Suppose an animal learns to press a pedal when a light in a cage appears. By doing so, he receives a reward in the form of nutritious pellets. With planned behaviour, he will quickly adapt his behaviour if those pellets become less appetizing. Their attractiveness can be manipulated by having the animal eat its fill of the same food grains before the test and thus become satiated. The pedal pressing decreases acutely. If, on the other hand, there is stimulus-response behaviour and the animal has developed a fixed habit, it will continue to press the pedal each time the light appears, even though it has no desire for the pellets (Dickinson, 2012).
6. Straube, Brandt and Probst (1987); Striedter (2006).
7. The strong or hard version of materialism is also referred to as 'eliminative' or pure reductionist materialism. See for example Churchland (1995); Churchland and Churchland (1998); Rorty (1970, 1971).
8. Here, 'zombie' does not refer to the slippery, soulless creatures depicted in films, but to a philosophical zombie: a being that has a body, complete with cells, synapses and molecules, identical to your own – but devoid of consciousness (or mind). The alternative to the zombie hypothesis is that a being identical to you must unavoidably have consciousness, because the presence of the same cells, wiring and brain systems will ensure that all brain processes, including cognitive functions and consciousness, will be the same. See Kirk (2003).

9. In *Consciousness Explained* (1991), Daniel Dennett described this ability of the brain to generate narratives about what we perceive, how we behave and who we are as the "centre of narrative gravity".
10. This process is called 'microgenesis'; see for example: Calis, Sterenborg and Maarse (1984). The duration of six hundredths of a second applies to an experiment in which the subject distinguished between pictures of two familiar faces, and may vary depending on the design of the experiment. See also Northoff and Zilio (2022) for a theory of how the processing of a short-lasting stimulus may be virtually expanded in the neural activity that follows the stimulus, hence leading to consciousness.
11. Pennartz (2018).

Chapter 10

1. 'Brains in a Vat'. In Putnam (1981), pp. 1–21.
2. Curtis, Paré and Llinás (1991).
3. Lohff (2001).
4. This insight is attributed to Johannes Müller, but also to his Scottish colleague Charles Bell (1774–1842).
5. This problem I have dubbed before the question of 'Modality Identification' (Pennartz, 2009) and was previously described by Boring (1950). It is closely related to the more general problem of intentionality.
6. www.theguardian.com/technology/2017/apr/22/what-if-were-living-in-a -computer-simulation-the-matrix-elon-musk, Andrew Anthony, *The Guardian*, 22 April 2017.
7. Pennartz (2015); Seth (2021); Lehar (2003).
8. Reid (1785). For a brief discussion of this view – 'direct realism' – in the context of modern neuroscience, see Pennartz (2018).
9. The transmission of heat signals towards the spinal cord and brain is slow compared to that of tactile and sharp pain signals. The cause of the low speed of spikes travelling over heat-signalling nerve fibres partly lies in the fact that an electrically insulating sheath of myelin is lacking. The thermoreceptors associated with slow fibres are sensitive to moderate heating, not to painful heat (Darian-Smith et al., 1979).
10. Recent supporters of 'direct realism' (also referred to as 'naive realism') include the philosopher John Searle (Searle, 2015).
11. See also Koch (2004).

Chapter 11

1. Sinha (2013).
2. James (1890).
3. This statement is attributed to A. Grafé, quoted in Von Senden (1932).
4. Visual properties that help you distinguish whole objects from their background or from each other are called Gestalt properties, after the school of Gestalt psychology that made its name between 1914 and 1950 under Wolfgang Köhler, Kurt Koffka, Max Wertheimer and others.
5. Meulders (2010); McKendrick (1899).
6. Proust (1913–1927). Translated into English as *In Search of Lost Time*.
7. Quoted in Meulders (2010), pp. 97–98.
8. Helmholtz (1866).
9. Watson and Rayner (1920).
10. See, for example: Gregory (1980); Marcel (1983); Neisser (1967). Edward Chace Tolman's role in the development of modern psychology will be discussed in Chapter 13.

11. Barlow (1972).
12. An exception to this is a learning method in which signals are sent from high to low layers of the network ('backpropagation of errors'; Rumelhart, Hinton and Williams, 1986). However, this backward signalling only occurs during learning and not during the performance of a cognitive task itself. Moreover, this method does not comply with neurophysiological principles of signal conduction and synaptic change.
13. Even though Predictive Coding is associated here with consciousness of the 'here and now', many results in the psychological and neuroscientific literature also support influences of expectations on what will be perceived next. See, for instance: Melloni, Schwiedrzik, Müller, Rodriguez and Singer (2011).
14. For the development of the principles of Predictive Coding, the work of Srinivasan, Laughlin and Dubs (1982), Rao and Ballard (1999) and Dayan, Hinton, Neal and Zemel (1995) deserves special mention. Srinivasan and colleagues applied the principle to the functioning of the retina; Rao and Ballard built a basic, two-layer model of the visual cortex. However, neither study established a link with consciousness.
15. See, for instance: Hohwy (2013); Friston (2010); Clark (2013).
16. Rao and Ballard (1999).
17. Pearson et al. (2021).

Chapter 12

1. Chadwick (1993, 2007).
2. See, for example: Leinweber, Ward, Sobczak, Attinger and Keller (2017).
3. Godfrey-Smith (2016).
4. Vallar and Ronchi (2009).
5. Halligan, Marshall and Wade (1993).
6. See also: Melzack (1990).
7. Curran and Monaghan (2001).
8. Plotnik, de Waal and Reiss (2006).
9. Blanke, Ortigue, Landis and Seeck (2002).
10. Brugger, Regard and Landis (1997).
11. Hécaen and Badaraco (1956), cited in Brugger et al. (1997).
12. Heydrich and Blanke (2013).
13. Van Lommel (2011).
14. Stratton (1897).
15. Metzinger (2000, 2008).
16. The construction of an internal model of the wishes, beliefs and intentions of others is referred to as 'Theory of Mind' (Premack and Woodruff, 1978). Research into Theory of Mind in young children was conducted by, among others, Wimmer and Perner (1983). See also: Mitchell (2017).
17. Emery and Clayton (2001).
18. Fletcher and Frith (2009).
19. Grandin (1995).
20. This condition is called body dysmorphic disorder (Beilharz, Castle, Grace & Rossell, 2017; Grace, Labuschagne, Kaplan & Rossell, 2017).
21. Chadwick (2007).

Chapter 13

1. The specialist term for 'hidden learning' is 'latent learning' and refers to spontaneous learning behaviour that can also take place without reward or punishment, often in an animal that explores its environment without explicit emotional or

motivational consequences. In children, this comes close to 'learning through play'.

2. The concept of vicarious trial and error (VTE) is attributed to Karl Muenzinger and Evelyn Gentry (Muenzinger & Gentry, 1931).
3. Pezzulo, van der Meer, Lansink and Pennartz (2014).
4. See, for example: www.informationphilosopher.com/solutions/philosophers/ popper/natural_selection_and_the_emergence_of_mind.html.
5. Guthrie (1935).
6. In 2002, the Nobel Prize in Economics was awarded to psychologist Daniel Kahneman, who has collaborated extensively with Amos Tversky in the field of irrational decision-making.
7. Recent research suggests that the hippocampus can encode time as well as space, at least if the temporal aspects of a behavioural task are relevant to the performance of this task. This suggests that the neural code of the hippocampus can adapt to what is important in order to complete a task well (Eichenbaum, 2014). If auditory pitch is important to obtain rewards within a task, then a 'space' of tones or sound frequencies is encoded in the hippocampus (Aronov, Nevers & Tank, 2017).
8. Wilson and McNaughton (1994).
9. Lansink, Goltstein, Lankelma, McNaughton and Pennartz (2009).
10. Johnson and Redish (2007) described the forward sweep in the context of vicarious trial and error behaviour.
11. Redish (2016).
12. Kaplan et al. (2017).
13. Hassabis, Kumaran, Vann and Maguire (2007).
14. Libet, Gleason, Wright and Pearl (1983).
15. Schurger, Sitt and Dehaene (2012). See also Jo, Hinterberger, Wittmann, Borghardt and Schmidt (2013).
16. A certain moment within a repeating wave cycle is called the phase, which is calculated in relation to a fixed point within the cycle, such as the peak moment. When you are cycling, for instance, your right foot reaches the valley phase at the deepest point of your periodic pedalling motion, which is about halfway between two peak positions of your right foot within a cycle.

Chapter 14

1. Wakefield et al. (1998). This article was retracted by *The Lancet* on 6 February 2010.
2. Kartsounis, James-Galton and Plant (2009).
3. Joseph Babinski is considered a co-discoverer of this syndrome, which is therefore also known as Anton-Babinski syndrome.
4. Anton (1899). The description of Anton lying on the sofa in his town house in Halle is fictitious.
5. Fitzgerald (1971).
6. In this case, noise can be compared to image noise – the pattern of white and black dots that appears on a TV that is not connected to a cable or antenna.
7. Daselaar, Porat, Huijbers and Pennartz (2010); Hassabis, Kumaran and Maguire (2007); Zatorre and Halpern (2005).
8. An exception is lucid dreaming, in which you realize that you are dreaming and you are to some extent aware of the existence of a world outside your dream.
9. Birnbaum and Thomann (1996).
10. Chatterjee, Khonglah, Mitra and Garg (2018).
11. Kölmel (1985).
12. ffytche et al. (1998); Holroyd et al. (1992); Teunisse, Zitman, Cruysberg, Hoefnagels and Verbeek (1996).

13. Kölmel (1985).
14. Colour experiences during these hallucinations were strongly associated with activity in the posterior fusiform gyrus (an area closely associated with V4). For hallucinations of faces, activity was specifically increased in the middle zone of the fusiform gyrus in the left hemisphere. Experiences of visual texture were related to strong activation of the collateral sulcus. The area that codes for non-living, visual objects is located in the middle zone of the fusiform gyrus in the right hemisphere (ffytche et al., 1998).
15. This hypersensitivity is referred to as 'hyperexcitability' (excessive excitability; Painter, Dwyer, Kamke & Mattingley, 2018).
16. Penfield (1975).
17. Karl Friston's work has contributed greatly to understanding the importance of bodily actions for perceptual inference ('active inference'). See, for example: Friston, Adams, Perrinet and Breakspear (2012).
18. The idea that a perceptual interpretation in one modality (e.g. seeing) is compared and tested with information from another modality (e.g. touch) has been elaborated in Pennartz (2009, 2015).
19. Hullfish, Sedley and Vanneste (2019).
20. Reformulation based on Locke (1667). In the Inverse Spectrum Argument, 'spectrum' refers to the sequence of colour bands we see in a rainbow, or when a white beam of light passes through a prism.
21. Dennett (1991).
22. See, for example: Palmer (1999).
23. Winkler, Spillmann, Werner and Webster (2015).
24. The view that reality consists not of material things but of ideas experienced by the human mind is called 'subjective idealism' and was elaborated by the Irish bishop and philosopher George Berkeley (1685–1753).
25. This notion is closely related to the term 'controlled hallucination', probably introduced by Ramesh Jain at the University of California, Irvine, in the 1990s and subsequently used by the London-based psychologist Chris Frith and others. I prefer to speak of 'healthy hallucination' because it is less evident who or what is 'in control' of generating the hallucination (see also Chapter 12). The label 'healthy' (as opposed to pathological) is justified by the observation that normal perception helps to make decisions and generate complex actions beneficial for our survival.
26. Kondziella and Frahm-Falkenberg (2011).
27. Weber (2010).

Chapter 15

1. Not everyone in the field of consciousness research agrees that the Hard Problem should be tackled. In his highly accessible book *Being You* of 2021, for instance, Anil Seth expresses the hope that the Hard Problem will gradually evaporate as we come to understand more and more about the relationships between phenomenology and the underlying brain mechanisms. He prefers to focus on the 'Real Problem', which is the challenge of explaining, predicting and controlling the properties of phenomenological experience in terms of body and brain mechanisms, such as patterns of neural activity. In contrast, I think that one will bump back onto the Hard Problem one way or another. There are a number of other differences and parallels between Seth's book, my 2015 book at MIT Press (Pennartz, 2015) and the Dutch predecessor of the current work (2021). For instance, for Seth, consciousness is generally related to life as a self-sustaining phenomenon, and more specifically to predictions associated with motor actions ('active inference'), whereas I have argued that motor actions are not essential

(Chapters 6 and 7) and consciousness is closely associated not with life in general, but with organisms exhibiting complex, goal-directed behaviours. In his 'Beast Machine' theory, Seth zooms in on the self and the perception and prediction of internal body states (interoception), while the current work puts more emphasis on relationships between spike activity patterns, multi-level representations and interactions between the senses.

2. Churchland (1995, 1998; 2007); Churchland and Churchland (1998).
3. In Chapter 6, we discussed that Kevin O'Regan and Alva Noë (2001), as exponents of 'externalism', object to the view of conscious experience as a representation formed by the brain, because of the argument that we do not have pictures (or other kinds of image) in our heads. This objection does not apply to the present theory: the information carriers for representation are indeed located in our brains, but the content of representations is not localized within them. This is, as it were, projected outwards or, to be more precise, situated in an external world that is represented by the brain.
4. A form of dualism not addressed in this book is non-interactionist dualism, which attempts to avoid the problem of how the conscious mind and the brain would interact. Even without assuming interactions, however, dualism would still have to explain how consciousness and brain relate to each other.
5. Chalmers (1996). See also: Chalmers (1999).
6. See, for example: Friedmann et al. (2016).
7. Dennett (1980).
8. For illustration, see the calculations by Tong Shiu-sing and Hui Pak-ming at: http://hk-phy.org/articles/caesar/caesar_e.html. In advance, the chance of inhaling a molecule from Caesar's last breath seems extremely small. However, this chance is nonetheless considerable because Avogadro's number is so unimaginably large (6.02 times 10^{23}, which is about 602,000,000,000,000,000, 000,000). Avogadro's number is a physical constant that indicates the ratio between the number of particles in an object and the mass (in grams) of that object.
9. Jackson (1982).
10. Sacks (1996).
11. There is also a third type – the blue-sensitive cone – but the other two types do not react to wavelengths in the blue range, so this third type does not play a role in this deficiency (Tovée, 1996).
12. www.youtube.com/watch?v=WCcxwieuDH0 and www.youtube.com/watch ?v=1vWM2N3GRjE. See also: www.smithsonianmag.com/innovation/scientist-accidentally-developed-sunglasses-that-could-correct-color-blindness -180954456/?no-ist.
13. It is not known whether Descartes actually met the young Spinoza, but in 1641 Spinoza was nine years old. Given the limited population of the then centre of Amsterdam and the distance between Houtgracht and Kalverstraat (about one kilometre), a chance meeting was not inconceivable.
14. In contrast to dualism, which assumes the existence of two separate substances (mind and matter), monism assumes the existence of one entity. Materialism is a form of monism in which one substance is assumed – namely matter – to which mind can be reduced. Spinoza's monism differs from this because it recognizes both mind and matter as aspects of reality.
15. Spinoza (1910).
16. The biography of Spinoza by Johannes Colerus from 1705 was reprinted as an appendix to the anti-Spinoza pamphlet 'De waarachtige Verryzenis Jesu Christi uit den dooden' (The True Resurrection of Jesus Christ from the Dead), published in Amsterdam in 1732. See also: Gullan-Whur (1998).
17. Hopfield (1982).
18. Dudek and Bear (1992); Mulkey and Malenka (1992).

19. The previous work of, for example, Marr, Little, Amari and Kohonen has also been important in this development (Amari, 1977; Kohonen, 1980; Little, 1974; Marr, 1971).
20. This more biological way of retrieving information is called content-addressable memory: a part of the content is used to retrieve the whole original image. A separate code for the address on a hard disk is not necessary.
21. This parallel processing of information – by many neurons that are not connected in series and thus form a chain, but work in parallel to each other – is called 'parallel distributed processing'. It took off when Rumelhart, Hinton and colleagues published an algorithm enabling neuronal networks to learn according to a method by which the errors produced by the network are routed backwards (from output to input) through the network ('backpropagation of errors', see also Chapter 11; Rumelhart et al., 1986).
22. The comparison between the brain and an ant colony was previously made in Hofstadter (1985).
23. An example of such non-equilibrium reactions was discovered in the 1950s and 1960s by Soviet chemists Boris Belousov and Anatol Zhabotinsky (the Belousov-Zhabotinsky reaction; Winfree, 1984).
24. This 'imagining' is a special property that so-called 'generative networks' can develop after a learning process. See, for example: Nguyen, Clune, Bengio, Dosovitskiy and Yosinski (2017).
25. The problem of assigning meaning to series of numbers or abstract symbols by or within computers was clearly formulated by John Searle's Chinese Room Argument (Searle, 1980).
26. The idea of a neuronal 'assembly' organization was proposed by Donald O. Hebb in his book *The Organization of Behaviour* (1949) and developed later by, for instance, Wolf Singer (Singer, 2018), György Buzsaki (Buzsaki, 2010) and Bruce McNaughton (Wilson & McNaughton, 1994). In Figure 15.3, the assembly represents a relatively low level of neuronal representation.
27. The sampling of many active neurons in a brain area is called an 'ensemble recording'. It is not known beforehand which recorded neurons might work together in an assembly, i.e. form part of a local network. After analyzing the firing patterns of individual cells, it can be estimated which neurons perform the same function during perception or memory tasks, and whether they are active simultaneously. Modern semiconductor electrodes contain more than 1,000 recording sites, allowing up to several hundred neurons to be sampled simultaneously (Jun et al., 2017).
28. Because the smaller networks in Figure 15.3, situated above the level of assemblies, only perform a function within a single sensory modality, we can speak of a 'unimodal meta-network': a network consisting of smaller networks that all function within one sensory modality (vision). When these unimodal meta-networks are united under an even larger brain system that encompasses multiple sensory modalities, the organizational level of a multimodal meta-network is reached (Pennartz, 2015).
29. The organization of representations on multiple levels is of a functional nature: it is about what capacity each level has to represent properties, objects, etc. Thus, it is not about differences in anatomical organization *per se*, but about the capacity of each level to represent certain properties. A computer in which such a representational organization can be realized may therefore also be conscious, but it need not have the same anatomy as the human brain. The same applies to highly developed animal species with a completely different type of nervous system to humans, such as the octopus.
30. Gödel (1931).
31. The book *Gödel, Escher, Bach* (Hofstadter, 1985) was written in the context of classical artificial intelligence, which relies on symbols (expressed in software) as

the basic material for building intelligent systems and controlling robots. This preceded the neural network revolution ('machine learning') that took place in the 1980s and 1990s. Nevertheless, the book still provides a good picture of logical and mathematical aspects of brain-mind issues. It does remain unclear how Hofstadter's symbols emerge from the workings of brain cells, and how they get their meaning.

32. This fallacy falls under the 'category mistakes' described by Gilbert Ryle (Ryle, 1949).

33. A 'Velázquez' here refers to the image, regardless of the 'carrier' or 'vehicle' of the image, i.e. the medium on which the image is viewed, such as dried oil paint or the photons reflected into your eyes from a projection screen. If the medium is changed, the properties characteristic of the Velázquez remain the same.

34. In philosophical terms, the theory set out here is best described as a special form of non-reductionist materialism. It recognizes both consciousness and matter as existing phenomena, but differs from Spinoza's monism in that human consciousness has an ultimate material basis (namely in neural processes), whereas the existence of matter, vice versa, does not depend on consciousness or other mental activity. Consciousness and matter are thus not inseparable. With this, the theory regards consciousness as a phenomenon that supervenes on the brain (in other words: consciousness 'comes on top' of the brain, but is dependent on it; the other way around does not apply, see Kim (1993); Rose (2006); Van Gulick (2001)). The theory also differs from other forms of non-reductionist materialism and classic emergentism. For example, in *The Mind and Its Place in Nature* (1925), the British philosopher Charlie Dunbar Broad (1887–1971) defended a form of emergent materialism in which philosophical zombies are possible in principle, which goes against the argumentation in Chapters 9 and 15. An important criticism of certain forms of emergentism and non-reductionist materialism is that they would involve 'mental causation': if the conscious mind could exert a causal influence on bodily movements, then these movements would not only be determined within the material domain but would also have an additional cause ('overdetermination'; Kim, 2003). This goes against the physical principle of causal closure (i.e. every physical event can be fully explained by other physical events). If there is no mental causation, consciousness is left with nothing but being an epiphenomenon (a side effect without a causal role or function). The present theory is immune to this objection because, in accordance with the concept of emergent correspondence, it does not require and rejects mental causation. It posits that the functionality of consciousness coincides exactly with that of the corresponding physical processes in the brain (the function of the underlying network activity *is* consciousness; Pennartz, 2015). Another criticism of classical emergentism and non-reductionist materialism has been that these movements are vague and woolly, but this applied only prior to the new insights brought by the era of neural networks and computational neuroscience. Through concepts such as neural representation, Predictive Coding and emergent network properties, this book aims to argue and concretize why non-reductionist materialism offers the most plausible basis for solving the problem of consciousness.

35. Ferrarelli et al. (2010); Olcese et al. (2016).

36. Pennartz, Farisco and Evers (2019).

37. Conversely, there are brain disorders that have consequences of which we are not aware. Examples are a brain disease that causes a temporary interruption of the breathing rhythm during sleep (sleep apnea) or a tumour in a brain area that is not important for consciousness.

38. See also: Pennartz (2009, 2015, 2018, 2022).

39. Other neuroscience-based theories of brain and consciousness include the Global Neuronal Workspace theory of Stanislas Dehaene and Pierre Changeux (Dehaene

& Changeux, 2011) and the Information Integration Theory of Giulio Tononi (Tononi, Boly, Massimini & Koch, 2016). Global Neuronal Workspace, however, does not focus on phenomenal consciousness (the phenomenon of having conscious experience with its subjective properties) but on how information can be spread rapidly through the brain to influence a maximum number of other systems (such as systems for memory and motor skills). Information Integration Theory does focus on phenomenal consciousness and has the advantage of proposing a quantitative measure of consciousness: the amount of integrated information within a neural (or other kind of) system. However, critics argue that this theory does not offer a satisfactory explanation of how the subjective, qualitative content of conscious experience comes about (the intentionality or 'aboutness') and how it relates to, or resembles, the outside world. The theory also leads to a form of panpsychism (the view that complex, non-living systems can also have consciousness, such as a smartphone or DVD player). For Giulio Tononi and Christof Koch this is not necessarily a disadvantage, as they consider panpsychism a tenable position.

40. In 1987, Nobel Prize winner David Gross also criticized the situation in physics in that string theory is 'the only game in town' – the theory attracts many researchers mainly because there are no good alternative theories, and people are afraid of ending up in an intellectual vacuum if they do not join it. See also: Hossenfelder (2018). On the other hand, string theory is an important breeding ground for wonderful, new mathematics and new applications in physics (see, e.g.: Greene (2010)).

Chapter 16

1. For more background on IBM's Watson, see Ferrucci et al. (2010); Ferrucci, Levas, Bagchi, Gondek and Mueller (2013).
2. Turing (1950).
3. Koch and Tononi (2008). The test proposed in this article was later followed up by the authors with another, more difficult version (Koch & Tononi, 2011).
4. Hodges (2014).
5. See article in *The Guardian*: "Yes, androids do dream of electric sheep" (www.theguardian.com/technology/2015/jun/18/google-image-recognition-neural-network-androids-dream-electric-sheep). See also Google's AI blog: "Inceptionism: Going Deeper into Neural Networks" (2015) by A. Mordvintsev, C. Olah and M. Tyka (ai.googleblog.com/2015/06/inceptionism-going-deeper-into-neural).
6. For a review, see LeCun et al. (2015); the original data was presented in Xu et al. (2015).
7. In general, ConvNets are trained using the 'backpropagation of errors' learning method (Rumelhart et al., 1986).
8. Lake, Ullman, Tenenbaum and Gershman (2017). The deep neural network used to provide descriptions of the pictures was published by Karpathy and Fei-Fei (2015).
9. Vaswani et al. (2017).
10. www.documentcloud.org/documents/22058315-is-lamda-sentient-an-interview.
11. philosophy.tamucc.edu/texts/chat-with-chatgpt.
12. www.vanityfair.com/news/2017/03/elon-musk-billion-dollar-crusade-to-stop-ai-space-x (2017).
13. www.youtube.com/watch?v=wwW2aAPAAZw&list=PLk09KHRIVg-QFeuVtbQmdZbldu1Prcs2T&index=47
14. Watanabe, Kitaoka, Sakamoto, Yasugi and Tanaka (2018).

15. Electronics can mimic the membrane of a brain cell with a circuit consisting of capacitors, resistors and a source of electrical voltage. In living neurons, this voltage is provided by the fact that ions of different kinds (mainly sodium, potassium and chloride ions) are found in different concentrations inside and outside the cell.
16. This possibility was suggested to me by the philosopher Kathinka Evers of Uppsala University (Sweden) and subsequently incorporated in a joint paper on animal and machine consciousness (Pennartz, Farisco and Evers, 2019).
17. Pitman and Durban (2012).
18. Pennartz et al. (2019).
19. www.youtube.com/watch?v=CcXXQ6GCUb8.
20. The illusion of the rotating snakes is attributed to small differences in the time it takes for the retina and brain to process information concerning differences in contrast and colour; these times show a small but noticeable difference for yellow versus blue and dark versus light elements. See, for example: Fraser and Wilcox (1979). Also eye movements may play a role in eliciting the illusion.
21. Clayton, Bussey and Dickinson (2003); Clayton and Dickinson (1998).
22. Pennartz et al. (2019).
23. See, for instance: Evers (2009) and Farisco, Pennartz, Annen, Cecconi and Evers (2022).
24. This technique is called transcranial magnetic stimulation (TMS).
25. Casarotto et al. (2016).
26. For brain-machine interfaces, both individual signals from brain cells (usually spikes) and signals from a larger mass of cells (local field potentials or electrocortical signals) can be used. See, for example: Ajiboye et al. (2017); Collinger et al. (2013); Vansteensel et al. (2016).
27. Dehaene, Lau and Kouider (2017).
28. The benefits and dangers of AI were discussed, among others, without extensively addressing the issue of awareness, in the open letter 'Research priorities for robust and beneficial artificial intelligence' (2015) by Stuart Russell, Daniel Dewey and Max Tegmark of the Future of Life Institute (https://futureoflife.org/data/documents/research_priorities.pdf) and was signed by Stephen Hawking, Elon Musk and many others. Another recent open letter issued by the Future of Life Institute was spawned by the recent breakthroughs of ChatGPT ('Pause giant AI experiments: an open letter'; https://futureoflife.org/open-letter/pause-giant-ai-experiments).

Literature

Ajiboye, A. B., Willett, F. R., Young, D. R., Memberg, W. D., Murphy, B. A., et al. (2017). Restoration of reaching and grasping movements through brain-controlled muscle stimulation in a person with tetraplegia: A proof-of-concept demonstration. *The Lancet, 389*(10081), 1821–1830.

Alvare, G., & Gordon, R. (2015). CT brush and CancerZap!: Two video games for computed tomography dose minimization. *Theoretical Biology and Medical Modelling, 12*, 7.

Amari, S.-I. (1977). Neural theory of association and concept-formation. *Biological Cybernetics, 26*(3), 175–185.

Anderson, S. W., Bechara, A., Damasio, H., Tranel, D., & Damasio, A. R. (1999). Impairment of social and moral behavior related to early damage in human prefrontal cortex. *Nature Neuroscience, 2*(11), 1032–1037.

Anton, G. (1899). Über die Selbstwahrnehmung der Herderkrankungen des Gehirns durch den Kranken bei Rindenblindheit und Rindentaubheit. *Archiv für Psychiatrie und Nervenkrankheiten, 32*(1), 86–127.

Arbib, M. A. (2001). Co-evolution of human consciousness and language. *Annals of the New York Academy of Sciences, 929*, 195–220.

Aronov, D., Nevers, R., & Tank, D. W. (2017). Mapping of a non-spatial dimension by the hippocampal-entorhinal circuit. *Nature, 543*(7647), 719–722.

Barlow, H. B. (1972). Single units and sensation: A neuron doctrine for perceptual psychology? *Perception, 1*(4), 371–394.

Bartolomeo, P., Bachoud-Lévi, A.-C., & de Schotten, M. T. (2014). The anatomy of cerebral achromatopsia: A reappraisal and comparison of two case reports. *Cortex, 56*, 138–144.

Bauby, J. D. (1998). *The diving bell and the butterfly: A memoir of life in death.* New York: Vintage Books, Random House.

Bechara, A., Damasio, H., Tranel, D., & Damasio, A. R. (1997). Deciding advantageously before knowing the advantageous strategy. *Science, 275*(5304), 1293–1295.

Bechara, A., Tranel, D., Damasio, H., Adolphs, R., Rockland, C., & Damasio, A. R. (1995). Double dissociation of conditioning and declarative knowledge relative to the amygdala and hippocampus in humans. *Science, 269*(5227), 1115–1118.

Beilharz, F., Castle, D. J., Grace, S., & Rossell, S. L. (2017). A systematic review of visual processing and associated treatments in body dysmorphic disorder. *Acta Psychiatr Scand, 136*(1), 16–36.

Benson, D. F., & Greenberg, J. P. (1969). Visual form agnosia. A specific defect in visual discrimination. *Archives of Neurology*, *20*(1), 82–89.

Bigelow, H. J. (1850). Dr. Harlow's case of recovery from the passage of an iron bar through the head. *American Journal of the Medical Sciences*, *20*, 13–22.

Birnbaum, M. H., & Thomann, K. (1996). Visual function in multiple personality disorder. *Journal of the American Optometric Association*, *67*(6), 327–334.

Blanke, O., Ortigue, S., Landis, T., & Seeck, M. (2002). Stimulating illusory own-body perceptions. *Nature*, *419*(6904), 269–270.

Blumenfeld, H. (2005). Consciousness and epilepsy: Why are patients with absence seizures absent? *Progress in Brain Research*, *150*, 271–286.

Blumenfeld, H. (2012). Impaired consciousness in epilepsy. *Lancet Neurology*, *11*(9), 814–826.

Boring, E. G. (1950). *A history of experimental psychology* (2nd Ed.). New York: Appleton Century Crofts.

Bouvier, S. E., & Engel, S. A. (2006). Behavioral deficits and cortical damage loci in cerebral achromatopsia. *Cerebral Cortex*, *16*(2), 183–191.

Brickner, R. M. (1936). *The intellectual functions of the frontal lobes*. New York: Macmillan.

Brickner, R. M. (1952). Brain of patient A. after bilateral frontal lobectomy; status of frontal-lobe problem. *AMA Arch Neurol Psychiatry*, *68*(3), 293–313.

Brugger, P., Kollias, S. S., Muri, R. M., Crelier, G., Hepp-Reymond, M. C., & Regard, M. (2000). Beyond re-membering: Phantom sensations of congenitally absent limbs. *PNAS*, *97*(11), 6167–6172.

Brugger, P., Regard, M., & Landis, T. (1997). Illusory reduplication of one's own body: Phenomenology and classification of autoscopic phenomena. *Cognitive Neuropsychiatry*, *2*(1), 19–38.

Buzsaki, G. (2006). *Rhythms of the brain*. Oxford: Oxford University Press.

Buzsaki, G. (2010). Neural syntax: Cell assemblies, synapsembles, and readers. *Neuron*, *68*(3), 362–385.

Cai, D., Cohen, K. B., Luo, T., Lichtman, J. W., & Sanes, J. R. (2013). Improved tools for the Brainbow toolbox. *Nat Methods*, *10*(6), 540–547.

Calis, G. J., Sterenborg, J. M., & Maarse, F. J. (1984). Initial microgenetic steps in single-glance face recognition. *Acta Psychologica*, *55*, 215–230.

Carruthers, P. (1989a). Brute experience. *Journal of Philosophy*, *86*(5), 258–269.

Carruthers, P. (1989b). *Tractarian semantics*. New York: Blackwell.

Casarotto, S., Comanducci, A., Rosanova, M., Sarasso, S., Fecchio, M., Napolitani, M., . . . Massimini, M. (2016). Stratification of unresponsive patients by an independently validated index of brain complexity. *Annals of Neurology*, *80*(5), 718–729.

Chadwick, P. K. (1993). The stepladder to the impossible: A first hand phenomenological account of a schizoaffective psychotic crisis. *Journal of Mental Health*, *2*(3), 239–250.

Chadwick, P. K. (2007). Peer-professional first-person account: Schizophrenia from the inside-phenomenology and the integration of causes and meanings. *Schizophrenia Bulletin*, *33*(1), 166–173.

Chalmers, D. J. (1995). Facing up to the problem of consciousness. *Journal of Consciousness Studies*, *2*, 200–219.

Chalmers, D. J. (1996). *The conscious mind*. Oxford: Oxford University Press.

Chalmers, D. J. (1999). Materialism and the metaphysics of modality. *Philosophy and Phenomenological Research*, *59*, 473–496.

Chatterjee, S. S., Khonglah, D., Mitra, S., & Garg, K. (2018). Gulliver's world: Persistent lilliputian hallucinations as manifestation of Charles Bonnet syndrome in a case of cataract and normal pressure hydrocephalus. *Indian Journal of Psychiatry, 60*(3), 358.

Cheasty, M., Condren, R., & Cooney, C. (2002). Altered sexual preference and behaviour in a man with vascular ischaemic lesions in the temporal lobe. *International Journal of Geriatric Psychiatry, 17*(1), 87–88.

Churchland, P. M. (1995). *The engine of reason, the seat of the soul.* Cambridge, MA: MIT Press.

Churchland, P. M., & Churchland, P. S. (1998). *On the contrary: Critical essays, 1987– 1997.* Cambridge, MA: MIT Press.

Churchland, P. S. (1989). *Neurophilosophy: Toward a unified science of the mind-brain.* Cambridge, MA: MIT Press.

Churchland, P. S. (2007). Neurophilosophy: The early years and new directions. *Functional Neurology, 22*(4), 185–195.

Clark, A. (1999). An embodied cognitive science? *Trends in Cognitive Sciences, 3*(9), 345–351.

Clayton, N. S., Bussey, T. J., & Dickinson, A. (2003). Can animals recall the past and plan for the future? *Nature Reviews Neuroscience, 4*(8), 685–691.

Clayton, N. S., & Dickinson, A. (1998). Episodic-like memory during cache recovery by scrub jays. *Nature, 395*(6699), 272–274.

Clark, A. (2013). Whatever next? Predictive brains, situated agents, and the future of cognitive science. *Behavioral and Brain Sciences, 36*(3), 181–204.

Cleeremans, A., Timmermans, B., & Pasquali, A. (2007). Consciousness and metarepresentation: A computational sketch. *Neural Networks, 20*(9), 1032–1039.

Collinger, J. L., Wodlinger, B., Downey, J. E., Wang, W., Tyler-Kabara, E. C., et al. (2013). High-performance neuroprosthetic control by an individual with tetraplegia. *The Lancet, 381*(9866), 557–564.

Corkin, S. (2002). What's new with the amnesic patient H.M.? *Nature Reviews Neuroscience, 3*(2), 153–160.

Cowey, A., & Stoerig, P. (1995). Blindsight in monkeys. *Nature, 373*(6511), 247–249.

Crick, F. (1994). *The astonishing hypothesis. The scientific search for the soul.* New York: Simon and Schuster, Touchstone.

Curran, H. V., & Monaghan, L. (2001). In and out of the K-hole: A comparison of the acute and residual effects of ketamine in frequent and infrequent ketamine users. *Addiction, 96*(5), 749–760.

Damasio, A. (2000). *The feeling of what happens.* London: Vintage.

Damasio, H., Grabowski, T., Frank, R., Galaburda, A. M., & Damasio, A. R. (1994). The return of Phineas Gage: Clues about the brain from the skull of a famous patient. *Science, 264*(5162), 1102–1105.

Darian-Smith, I., Johnson, K., LaMotte, C., Shigenaga, Y., Kenins, P., & Champness, P. (1979). Warm fibers innervating palmar and digital skin of the monkey: Responses to thermal stimuli. *Journal of Neurophysiology, 42*(5), 1297–1315.

Daselaar, S. M., Porat, Y., Huijbers, W., & Pennartz, C. M. (2010). Modality-specific and modality-independent components of the human imagery system. *Neuroimage, 52*(2), 677–685.

Dayan, P., Hinton, G. E., Neal, R. M., & Zemel, R. S. (1995). The helmholtz machine. *Neural Computation, 7*(5), 889–904.

de Curtis, M., Paré, D., & Llinás, R. R. (1991). The electrophysiology of the olfactory-hippocampal circuit in the isolated and perfused adult mammalian brain in vitro. *Hippocampus, 1*(4), 341–354.

de Gelder, B., Tamietto, M., van Boxtel, G., Goebel, R., Sahraie, A., van den Stock, J., & Pegna, A. (2008). Intact navigation skills after bilateral loss of striate cortex. *Current Biology, 18*(24), R1128–1129.

Dehaene, S., & Changeux, J. P. (2011). Experimental and theoretical approaches to conscious processing. *Neuron, 70*(2), 200–227.

Dehaene, S., Lau, H., & Kouider, S. (2017). What is consciousness, and could machines have it? *Science, 358*(6362), 486–492.

Dennett, D. (1980). The milk of human intentionality. *Behavioral and Brain Sciences, 3*(3), 428–430.

Dennett, D. C. (1991). *Consciousness explained.* Boston: Little, Brown.

Dennett, D. C., & Kinsbourne, M. (1992). Time and the observer: The where and when of consciousness in the brain. *Behavioral and Brain Sciences, 15*(2), 183–247.

Descartes, R. (1637). *Discours de la Methode.* Leiden: De l'Imprimerie de Ian Maire.

Descartes, R. (1641). *Meditations and other metaphysical writings* (D. M. Clarke, Trans.). Penguin Classics: Penguin Books.

Descartes, R. (1649). *Les passions de l'âme (The passions of the soul)* (S. H. Voss, Trans.). Indianapolis: Hackett.

Desimone, R., Albright, T. D., Gross, C. G., & Bruce, C. (1984). Stimulus-selective properties of inferior temporal neurons in the macaque. *Journal of Neuroscience, 4*(8), 2051–2062.

Devinsky, J., Sacks, O., & Devinsky, O. (2010). Kluver-Bucy syndrome, hypersexuality, and the law. *Neurocase, 16*(2), 140–145.

Devinsky, O. (2009). Delusional misidentifications and duplications: Right brain lesions, left brain delusions. *Neurology, 72*(1), 80–87.

Dichter, B. K., Breshears, J. D., Leonard, M. K., & Chang, E. F. (2018). The control of vocal pitch in human laryngeal motor cortex. *Cell, 174*(1), 21–31.e29.

Dickinson, A. (2012). Associative learning and animal cognition. *Philosophical Transactions of the Royal Society of London. Series B, Biological Sciences, 367*(1603), 2733–2742.

Dora, S., Pennartz, C., & Bohte, S. (2018). A deep predictive coding network for inferring hierarchical causes underlying sensory inputs. In V. Kůrková, Y. Manolopoulos, B. Hammer, L. Iliadis, & I. Maglogiannis (Eds.), *Artificial neural networks and machine learning – ICANN 2018.* ICANN 2018. Lecture Notes in Computer Science, vol. 11141. Cham: Springer.

Dudek, S. M., & Bear, M. F. (1992). Homosynaptic long-term depression in area CA1 of hippocampus and effects of N-methyl-D-aspartate receptor blockade. *PNAS, 89*(10), 4363–4367.

Efron, R. (1968). What is perception? In *Boston studies in the philosophy of science* (Vol. 4, pp. 137–143). New York: Humanities.

Eichenbaum, H. (2014). Time cells in the hippocampus: A new dimension for mapping memories. *Nature Reviews Neuroscience, 15*(11), 732–744.

El-Hai, J. (2005). *The lobotomist.* Hoboken: Wiley.

Ellis, H. D., & Lewis, M. B. (2001). Capgras delusion: A window on face recognition. *Trends in Cognitive Sciences, 5*(4), 149–156.

Emery, N. J., & Clayton, N. S. (2001). Effects of experience and social context on prospective caching strategies by scrub jays. *Nature, 414*(6862), 443–446.

Evers, K. (2009). *Neuroéthique: quand la matière s' éveille.* Paris, France: Odile Jacob.

Farah, M. (2004). *Visual agnosia* (2nd Ed.). Cambridge, MA: MIT Press.

Farisco, M., Pennartz, C., Annen, J., Cecconi, B., & Evers, K. (2022). Indicators and criteria of consciousness: Ethical implications for the care of behaviourally unresponsive patients. *BMC Med Ethics, 23*(1), 30.

Felleman, D. J., & Van Essen, D. C. (1991). Distributed hierarchical processing in the primate cerebral cortex. *Cereb Cortex, 1*(1), 1–47.

Ferrarelli, F., Massimini, M., Sarasso, S., Casali, A., Riedner, B. A., et al. (2010). Breakdown in cortical effective connectivity during midazolam-induced loss of consciousness. *PNAS, 107*(6), 2681–2686.

Ferrucci, D., Brown, E., Chu-Carroll, J., Fan, J., Gondek, D., et al. (2010). Building Watson: An overview of the DeepQA project. *AI Magazine, 31*(3), 59–79.

Ferrucci, D., Levas, A., Bagchi, S., Gondek, D., & Mueller, E. T. (2013). Watson: Beyond Jeopardy! *Artificial Intelligence, 199*, 93–105.

Ffytche, D. H., Howard, R. J., Brammer, M. J., David, A., Woodruff, P., & Williams, S. (1998). The anatomy of conscious vision: An fMRI study of visual hallucinations. *Nature Neuroscience, 1*(8), 738–742.

Fitzgerald, R. G. (1971). Visual phenomenology in recently blind adults. *American Journal of Psychiatry, 127*(11), 1533–1539.

Fletcher, P. C., & Frith, C. D. (2009). Perceiving is believing: A Bayesian approach to explaining the positive symptoms of schizophrenia. *Nature Reviews Neuroscience, 10*(1), 48–58.

Fraser, A., & Wilcox, K. J. (1979). Perception of illusory movement. *Nature, 281*(5732), 565–566.

Friedmann, S., Schemmel, J., Grübl, A., Hartel, A., Hock, M., & Meier, K. (2016). Demonstrating hybrid learning in a flexible neuromorphic hardware system. *IEEE Transactions on Biomedical Circuits and Systems, 11*(1), 128–142.

Frijda, N. H. (2006). *The laws of emotion*. Milton Park, Abingdon-on-Thames: Taylor and Francis.

Friston, K. (2010). The free-energy principle: A unified brain theory? *Nature Reviews Neuroscience, 11*(2), 127–138.

Friston, K., Adams, R., Perrinet, L., & Breakspear, M. (2012). Perceptions as hypotheses: Saccades as experiments. *Frontiers in Psychology, 3*, 151.

Gödel, K. (1931). Über formal unentscheidbare Sätze der Principia Mathematica und verwandter Systeme. *Monatshefte für Mathematik und Physik, 38*, 173–198.

Godfrey-Smith, P. (2016). *Other minds: The octopus, the sea, and the deep origins of consciousness*. New York City: Farrar, Straus and Giroux.

Grace, S. A., Labuschagne, I., Kaplan, R. A., & Rossell, S. L. (2017). The neurobiology of body dysmorphic disorder: A systematic review and theoretical model. *Neuroscience & Biobehavioral Reviews, 83*, 83–96.

Grandin, T. (1995). How people with autism think. In E. Schopler & G. B. Mesibov (Eds.), *Learning and cognition in autism* (pp. 137–156). New York: Plenum Press.

Greene, B. (2010). *The elegant universe. Superstrings, hidden dimensions, and the quest for the ultimate theory*. New York: Norton.

Gregory, R. L. (1980). Perceptions as hypotheses. *Philosophical Transactions of the Royal Society of London. Series B, Biological Sciences, 290*(1038), 181–197.

Gross, C. G., Bender, D. B., & Rocha-Miranda, C. E. (1969). Visual receptive fields of neurons in inferotemporal cortex of the monkey. *Science, 166*(910), 1303–1306.

Guizzo, E. (2019). By leaps and bounds: An exclusive look at how Boston Dynamics is redefining robot agility. *IEEE Spectrum, 56*(12), 34–39.

Gullan-Whur, M. (1998). *Within reason – A life of Spinoza*. London: Pimlico.

Guthrie, E. R. (1935). *Psychology of learning.* New York: Harper and Brothers.

Halligan, P. W., Marshall, J. C., & Wade, D. T. (1993). Three arms: A case study of supernumerary phantom limb after right hemisphere stroke. *Journal of Neurology, Neurosurgery & Psychiatry, 56*(2), 159–166.

Harlow, J. M. (1848). Passage of an iron rod through the head. *Boston Medical and Surgical Journal, 39,* 389–393.

Hassabis, D., Kumaran, D., & Maguire, E. A. (2007). Using imagination to understand the neural basis of episodic memory. *Journal of Neuroscience, 27*(52), 14365–14374.

Hassabis, D., Kumaran, D., Vann, S. D., & Maguire, E. A. (2007). Patients with hippocampal amnesia cannot imagine new experiences. *PNAS, 104*(5), 1726–1731.

Hebb, D. O. (1949). *The organization of behavior: A neuropsychological theory.* New York: Wiley.

Hécaen, H., & Badaraco, J. G. (1956). Séméiologie de hallucinations visuelles en clininique neurologique *Acta Neurologica Latino Americana, 2,* 23–57.

Helmholtz, H. (1866). *Handbuch der physiologischen Optik.* Leipzig: Leopold Voss.

Heydrich, L., & Blanke, O. (2013). Distinct illusory own-body perceptions caused by damage to posterior insula and extrastriate cortex. *Brain, 136*(Pt 3), 790–803.

Heywood, C. A., Cowey, A., & Newcombe, F. (1991). Chromatic discrimination in a cortically colour blind observer. *European Journal of Neuroscience, 3*(8), 802–812.

Heywood, C. A., & Kentridge, R. W. (2003). Achromatopsia, color vision, and cortex. *Neurologic Clinics, 21*(2), 483–500.

Heywood, C. A., Kentridge, R. W., & Cowey, A. (1998). Cortical color blindness is not 'blindsight for color'. *Consciousness and Cognition, 7*(3), 410–423.

Hobson, J. A. (2005). Sleep is of the brain, by the brain and for the brain. *Nature, 437*(7063), 1254–1256.

Hodges, A. (2014). *Alan Turing, the enigma.* New York: Vintage Books.

Hofstadter, D. (1985). *Gödel, Escher, Bach. An eternal golden braid.* New York: Vintage Books.

Hohwy, J. (2013). *The predictive mind.* Oxford: Oxford University Press.

Holroyd, S., Rabins, P. V., Finkelstein, D., Nicholson, M. C., Chase, G. A., & Wisniewski, S. C. (1992). Visual hallucinations in patients with macular degeneration. *American Journal of Psychiatry, 149*(12), 1701–1706.

Hopfield, J. J. (1982). Neural networks and physical systems with emergent collective computational abilities. *PNAS, 79*(8), 2554–2558.

Hossenfelder, S. (2018). *Lost in math: How beauty leads physics astray.* New York: Basic Books.

Hubel, D. H. (1982). Exploration of the primary visual cortex, 1955–78. *Nature, 299*(5883), 515–524.

Hullfish, J., Sedley, W., & Vanneste, S. (2019). Prediction and perception: Insights for (and from) tinnitus. *Neuroscience & Biobehavioral Reviews, 102,* 1–12.

Humphrey, N. K. (1974). Vision in a monkey without striate cortex: A case study. *Perception, 3*(3), 241–255.

Humphrey, N. K., & Weiskrantz, L. (1967). Vision in monkeys after removal of the striate cortex. *Nature, 215*(5101), 595–597.

Ingle, D. (1975). Focal attention in the frog: Behavioural and physiological correlates. *Science, 188*(4192), 1033–1035.

Jackendoff, R. (1987). *Consciousness and the computational mind.* Cambridge, MA: MIT Press.

Jackson, F. (1982). Epiphenomenal qualia. *Philosophical Quarterly, 32*(127), 127–136.

James, W. (1890). *Principles of psychology.* London: MacMillan.

James, W. (1899). *Talks to teachers on psychology: And to students on some of life's ideals.* New York: Henry Holt.

Jastrow, J. (1900). *Fact and fable in psychology.* Boston: Houghton Mifflin.

Jo, H.-G., Hinterberger, T., Wittmann, M., Borghardt, T. L., & Schmidt, S. (2013). Spontaneous EEG fluctuations determine the readiness potential: Is preconscious brain activation a preparation process to move? *Experimental Brain Research, 231*(4), 495–500.

Johnson, A., & Redish, A. D. (2007). Neural ensembles in CA3 transiently encode paths forward of the animal at a decision point. *Journal of Neuroscience, 27*(45), 12176–12189.

Jun, J. J., Steinmetz, N. A., Siegle, J. H., Denman, D. J., Bauza, M., et al. (2017). Fully integrated silicon probes for high-density recording of neural activity. *Nature, 551*(7679), 232–236.

Jus, A., & Jus, K. (1962). Retrograde amnesia in petit mal. *Arch Gen Psychiatry, 6,* 163–167.

Kaplan, R., King, J., Koster, R., Penny, W. D., Burgess, N., & Friston, K. J. (2017). The neural representation of prospective choice during spatial planning and decisions. *PLoS Biology, 15*(1), e1002588.

Karigo, T., Kennedy, A., Yang, B., Liu, M., Tai, D., Wahle, I. A., & Anderson, D. J. (2021). Distinct hypothalamic control of same- and opposite-sex mounting behaviour in mice. *Nature, 589*(7841), 258–263.

Karpathy, A., & Fei-Fei, L. (2015). Deep visual-semantic alignments for generating image descriptions. In *Proceedings of the IEEE conference on computer vision and pattern recognition.*

Kartsounis, L. D., James-Galton, M., & Plant, G. T. (2009). Anton syndrome, with vivid visual hallucinations, associated with radiation induced leucoencephalopathy. *Journal of Neurology, Neurosurgery and Psychiatry, 80*(8), 937–938.

Kim, J. (1993). *Supervenience and mind: Selected philosophical essays.* Cambridge: Cambridge University Press.

Kim, J. (2003). Blocking causal drainage and other maintenance chores with mental causation. *Philosophy and Phenomenological Research, 67*(1), 151–176.

Kirk, R. (2003). Zombies. In E. Zalta (Ed.), *Stanford Encyclopedia of philosophy.* http://plato.stanford.edu/entries/zombies

Koch, C. (2004). *The quest for consciousness.* Englewood: Roberts & Company.

Koch, C., & Tononi, G. (2008). Can machines be conscious? *IEEE Spectrum, 45*(6), 54–59.

Koch, C., & Tononi, G. (2011). A test for consciousness. *Scientific American, 304*(6), 44–47.

Kohonen, T. (1980). *Content-addressable memories.* New York: Springer Verlag.

Kölmel, H. W. (1985). Complex visual hallucinations in the hemianopic field. *Journal of Neurology, Neurosurgery & Psychiatry, 48*(1), 29–38.

Kondziella, D., & Frahm-Falkenberg, S. (2011). Anton's syndrome and eugenics. *Journal of Clinical Neurology, 7*(2), 96–98.

Lake, B. M., Ullman, T. D., Tenenbaum, J. B., & Gershman, S. J. (2017). Building machines that learn and think like people. *Behavioral and Brain Sciences, 40,* e253.

Lamme, V. A. (2010). *De vrije wil bestaat niet.* Amsterdam: Bert Bakker (in Dutch).

Lansink, C. S., Goltstein, P. M., Lankelma, J. V., McNaughton, B. L., & Pennartz, C. M. (2009). Hippocampus leads ventral striatum in replay of place-reward information. *PLoS Biology, 7*(8), e1000173.

Lau, H., & Rosenthal, D. (2011). Empirical support for higher-order theories of conscious awareness. *Trends in Cognitive Sciences, 15*(8), 365–373.

LeCun, Y., Bengio, Y., & Hinton, G. (2015). Deep learning. *Nature, 521*(7553), 436–444.

LeDoux, J. E. (1994). Emotion, memory and the brain. *Scientific American, 270*(6), 50–57.

Lehar, S. M. (2003). *The world in your head: A gestalt view of the mechanism of conscious experience.* London, United Kingdom: Psychology Press.

Leinweber, M., Ward, D. R., Sobczak, J. M., Attinger, A., & Keller, G. B. (2017). A sensorimotor circuit in mouse cortex for visual flow predictions. *Neuron, 95*(6), 1420–1432.e1425.

Levine, D. N. (2007). Sherrington's "The Integrative action of the nervous system": A centennial appraisal. *Journal of the Neurological Sciences, 253*(1–2), 1–6.

Libet, B., Gleason, C. A., Wright, E. W., & Pearl, D. K. (1983). Time of conscious intention to act in relation to onset of cerebral activity (readiness-potential). The unconscious initiation of a freely voluntary act. *Brain, 106*(Pt 3), 623–642.

Little, W. A. (1974). The existence of persistent states in the brain. *Mathematical Biosciences, 19*(1–2), 101–120.

Llinas, R. (2001). *I of the vortex.* Cambridge, MA: MIT press.

Locke, J. (1667). *An essay concerning human understanding* (5th Ed.). London: Collins Press.

Lohff, B. (2001). Facts and philosophy in neurophysiology. The 200th anniversary of Johannes Müller (1801–1858). *Journal of the History of the Neurosciences, 10*(3), 277–292.

Looijen, T. K. (1981). *Ieder is hier vervuld van zijn voordeel.* Amsterdam: Peter van der Velden. (in Dutch).

Macmillan, M. (2002). *An odd kind of fame. Stories of Phineas Gage.* Cambridge, MA: MIT Press.

Manzouri, A., & Savic, I. (2018). Multimodal MRI suggests that male homosexuality may be linked to cerebral midline structures. *PLoS One, 13*(10), e0203189.

Manzouri, A., & Savic, I. (2019). Possible neurobiological underpinnings of homosexuality and gender dysphoria. *Cereb Cortex, 29*(5), 2084–2101.

Marcel, A. J. (1983). Conscious and unconscious perception: An approach to the relations between phenomenal experience and perceptual processes. *Cognitive Psychology, 15*(2), 238–300.

Marr, D. (1971). Simple memory: A theory for archicortex. *Philosophical Transactions of the Royal Society of London. Series B, Biological Sciences, 262*(841), 23–81.

McKendrick, J. G. (1899). *Hermann Ludwig Ferdinand von Helmholtz.* London: T. Fisher Unwin.

Melloni, L., Schwiedrzik, C. M., Müller, N., Rodriguez, E., & Singer, W. (2011). Expectations change the signatures and timing of electrophysiological correlates of perceptual awareness. *Journal of Neuroscience, 31*(4), 1386–1396.

Melzack, R. (1990). Phantom limbs and the concept of a neuromatrix. *Trends in Neurosciences, 13*(3), 88–92.

Mesulam, M. M. (2013). Cholinergic circuitry of the human nucleus basalis and its fate in Alzheimer's disease. *Journal of Comparative Neurology, 521*(18), 4124–4144.

Metzinger, T. (2000). The subjectivity of subjective experience: A representationalist analysis of the first-person perspective. In T. Metzinger (Ed.), *Neural correlates of consciousness – Empirical and conceptual questions* (pp. 285–306). Cambridge, MA: MIT Press.

Metzinger, T. (2008). Empirical perspectives from the self-model theory of subjectivity: A brief summary with examples. *Progress in Brain Research, 168*, 215–245.

Meulders, M. (2010). *Helmholtz. From enlightenment to neuroscience*. Cambridge, MA: MIT Press.

Miller, B. L., Cummings, J. L., McIntyre, H., Ebers, G., & Grode, M. (1986). Hypersexuality or altered sexual preference following brain injury. *Journal of Neurology, Neurosurgery & Psychiatry, 49*(8), 867–873.

Mirsky, A. F., & Vanburen, J. M. (1965). On the nature of the "absence" in centrencephalic epilepsy: A study of some behavioral, electroencephalographic and autonomic factors. *Electroencephalography and Clinical Neurophysiology, 18*, 334–348.

Mitchell, P. (2017). *Acquiring a theory of mind*. Paper presented at An introduction to developmental psychology, Hoboken, New Jersey.

Mithen, S. (1999). Handaxes and ice age carvings: Hard evidence for the evolution of consciousness. In S. R. Hameroff, A. W. Kaszniak, & D. J. Chalmers (Eds.), *Toward a science of consciousness III: The third Tucson discussion and debates* (Vol. 3, pp. 281–296). Cambridge, MA: MIT Press.

Montavont, A., Kahane, P., Guenot, M., & Ryvlin, P. (2008). Foreign language ictal speech automatisms in nondominant temporal lobe epilepsy. *Neurology, 71*(20), 1579–1585.

Muenzinger, K. F., & Gentry, E. (1931). Tone discrimination in white rats. *Journal of Comparative Psychology, 12*(2), 195.

Mulkey, R. M., & Malenka, R. C. (1992). Mechanisms underlying induction of homosynaptic long-term depression in area CA1 of the hippocampus. *Neuron, 9*(5), 967–975.

Myles, P. S., Leslie, K., McNeil, J., Forbes, A., & Chan, M. T. (2004). Bispectral index monitoring to prevent awareness during anaesthesia: The B-Aware randomised controlled trial. *Lancet, 363*(9423), 1757–1763.

Nagel, T. (1974). What is it like to be a bat? *Philosophical Review, 83*, 453–450.

Naitoh, Y., & Eckert, R. (1969). Ionic mechanisms controlling behavioral responses of paramecium to mechanical stimulation. *Science, 164*(3882), 963–965.

Neisser, U. (1967). *Cognitive psychology*. New York: Appleton-Century Crofts.

Nguyen, A., Clune, J., Bengio, Y., Dosovitskiy, A., & Yosinski, J. (2017). *Plug & play generative networks: Conditional iterative generation of images in latent space*. Paper presented at the Proceedings of the IEEE Conference on Computer Vision and Pattern Recognition.

Northoff, G., & Zilio, F. (2022). Temporo-spatial Theory of Consciousness (TTC) – Bridging the gap of neuronal activity and phenomenal states. *Behavioural Brain Research, 424*, 113788.

O'Regan, J. K., & Noë, A. (2001). A sensorimotor account of vision and visual consciousness. *Behavioral and Brain Sciences, 24*, 939–973.

Olcese, U., Bos, J. J., Vinck, M., Lankelma, J. V., Van Mourik-Donga, L. B., et al. (2016). Spike-based functional connectivity in cerebral cortex and hippocampus: Loss of global connectivity is coupled to preservation of local connectivity during non-REM sleep. *Journal of Neuroscience, 36*(29), 7676–7692.

Olcese, U., Oude Lohuis, M. N., & Pennartz, C. M. A. (2018). Sensory processing across conscious and nonconscious brain states: From single neurons to distributed networks for inferential representation. *Frontiers in Systems Neuroscience, 12*, 49.

Oliva, A., Torralba, A., & Schyns, P. G. (2006). Hybrid images. *ACM Transactions on Graphics (TOG), 25*(3), 527–532.

Ozmen, M., Erdogan, A., Duvenci, S., Ozyurt, E., & Ozkara, C. (2004). Excessive masturbation after epilepsy surgery. *Epilepsy & Behavior, 5*(1), 133–136.

Painter, D. R., Dwyer, M. F., Kamke, M. R., & Mattingley, J. B. (2018). Stimulus-driven cortical hyperexcitability in individuals with Charles Bonnet hallucinations. *Current Biology, 28*(21), 3475–3480.e3473.

Palmer, S. E. (1999). Color, consciousness, and the isomorphism constraint. *Behavioral and Brain Sciences, 22*(6), 923–943.

Patton, P., & Grobstein, P. (1998). The effects of telencephalic lesions on visually mediated prey orienting behavior in the leopard frog (Rana pipiens). *Brain Behavior and Evolution, 51*(3), 123–143.

Pearson, M. J., Dora, D., Struckmeier, O., Knowles, T. C., Mitchinson, B., Tiwari, K., Kyrki, V., Bohte, S., & Pennartz, C. M. A. (2021). Multimodal representation learning for place recognition using deep Hebbian predictive coding. *Frontiers in Robotics and AI, 8,* 732023.

Penfield, W. (1975). *The mystery of the mind.* Princeton, NJ: Princeton University Press.

Penfield, W., & Rasmussen, T. (1950). *The cerebral cortex of man.* New York: MacMillan.

Pennartz, C. M. A. (2009). Identification and integration of sensory modalities: Neural basis and relation to consciousness. *Consciousness and Cognition, 18*(3), 718–739.

Pennartz, C. M. A. (2015). *The brain's representational power – On consciousness and the integration of modalities.* Cambridge, MA: MIT Press.

Pennartz, C. M. A. (2018). Consciousness, representation, action: The importance of being goal-directed. *Trends in Cognitive Sciences, 22*(2), 137–153.

Pennartz, C. M. A. (2022). What is neurorepresentationalism? From neural activity and predictive processing to multi-level representations and consciousness. *Behavioural Brain Research, 432,* 113969.

Pennartz, C. M. A., Farisco, M., & Evers, K. (2019). Indicators and criteria of consciousness in animals and intelligent machines: An inside-out approach. *Frontiers in Systems Neuroscience, 13,* 25.

Perrett, D. I., Hietanen, J. K., Oram, M. W., & Benson, P. J. (1992). Organization and functions of cells responsive to faces in the temporal cortex. *Philosophical Transactions of the Royal Society of London. Series B, Biological Sciences, 335*(1273), 23–30.

Petrides, M., Tomaiuolo, F., Yeterian, E. H., & Pandya, D. N. (2012). The prefrontal cortex: Comparative architectonic organization in the human and the macaque monkey brains. *Cortex, 48*(1), 46–57.

Pezzulo, G., van der Meer, M. A., Lansink, C. S., & Pennartz, C. M. (2014). Internally generated sequences in learning and executing goal-directed behavior. *Trends in Cognitive Sciences, 18*(12), 647–657.

Phelps, E. A., LaBar, K. S., Anderson, A. K., O'Connor, K. J., Fulbright, R. K., & Spencer, D. D. (1998). Specifying the contributions of the human amygdala to emotional memory: A case study. *Neurocase, 4*(6), 527–540.

Philippe, C., Isabelle, H. C., Philippe, F., Russell, S., Nadia, B., et al. (2017). The brain of René Descartes (1650): A neuroanatomical analysis. *Journal of the Neurological Sciences, 378,* 12–18.

Pitkanen, A., & Amaral, D. G. (1994). The distribution of GABAergic cells, fibers, and terminals in the monkey amygdaloid complex: An immunohistochemical and in situ hybridization study. *Journal of Neuroscience, 14*(4), 2200–2224.

Pitman, R. L., & Durban, J. W. (2012). Cooperative hunting behaviour, prey selectivity and prey handling by pack ice killer whales (Orcinus orca), type B, in Antarctic Peninsula waters. *Marine Mammal Science, 28*(1), 16–36.

Plotnik, J. M., de Waal, F. B., & Reiss, D. (2006). Self-recognition in an Asian elephant. *PNAS, 103*(45), 17053–17057.

Poppel, E., Held, R., & Frost, D. (1973). Residual visual function after brain wounds involving the central visual pathways in man. *Nature, 243*(5405), 295–296.

Premack, D., & Woodruff, G. (1978). Does the chimpanzee have a theory of mind? *Behavioral and Brain Sciences, 1*(4), 515–526.

Proust, M. (1913–1927). *À la recherche du temps perdu (7 volumes)*. Paris: Gallimard.

Putnam, H. (1981). *Reason, truth and history* (Vol. 3). Cambridge, United Kingdom: Cambridge University Press.

Ramsay, Z. J., Ikura, J., & Laberge, F. (2013). Modification of a prey catching response and the development of behavioral persistence in the fire-bellied toad (Bombina orientalis). *Journal of Comparative Psychology, 127*(4), 399.

Rangarajan, V., Hermes, D., Foster, B. L., Weiner, K. S., Jacques, C., et al. (2014). Electrical stimulation of the left and right human fusiform gyrus causes different effects in conscious face perception. *Journal of Neuroscience, 34*(38), 12828–12836.

Rao, R. P. N., & Ballard, D. H. (1999). Predictive coding in the visual cortex: A functional interpretation of some extra-classical receptive-field effects. *Nature Neuroscience, 2*(1), 79.

Rasch, B., Büchel, C., Gais, S., & Born, J. (2007). Odor cues during slow-wave sleep prompt declarative memory consolidation. *Science, 315*(5817), 1426–1429.

Redish, A. D. (2016). Vicarious trial and error. *Nature Reviews Neuroscience, 17*(3), 147–159.

Reid, T. (1785). *Essays on the intellectual powers of man (reprinted critical edition*; Vol. 3). Edinburgh: Edinburgh University Press.

Riddoch, G. (1917). Dissociation of visual perception due to occipital injuries, with especial reference to appreciation of movement. *Brain, 40*, 15–57.

Rieke, F., Warland, D., de Ruyter van Stevenick, R., & Bialek, W. (1997). *Spikes. Exploring the neural code*. Cambridge, MA: MIT Press.

Rodis-Lewis, G. (1998). *Descartes. His life and thought* (M. Todd, Trans.). Ithaca, NY: Cornell University Press.

Rogan, M. T., Staubli, U. V., & LeDoux, J. E. (1997). Fear conditioning induces associative long-term potentiation in the amygdala. *Nature, 390*(6660), 604–607.

Rorty, R. (1970). In defense of eliminative materialism. *The Review of Metaphysics, 24*(1), 112–121.

Rorty, R. (1971). Mind-brain identity, privacy and categories. In D. Rosenthal (Ed.), *Materialism and the mind-body problem* (pp. 174–199). Englewood Cliffs, NJ: Prentice Hall.

Rose, D. (2006). *Consciousness: Philosophical, psychological and neural theories*. Oxford: Oxford University Press.

Rosenbaum, R. S., Köhler, S., Schacter, D. L., Moscovitch, M., Westmacott, R., et al. (2005). The case of K.C.: Contributions of a memory-impaired person to memory theory. *Neuropsychologia, 43*(7), 989–1021.

Rouw, R., & Scholte, H. S. (2007). Increased structural connectivity in grapheme-color synesthesia. *Nature Neuroscience, 10*(6), 792–797.

Rumelhart, D. E., Hinton, G. E., & Williams, R. J. (1986). Learning representations by back-propagating errors. *Nature, 323*(6088), 533–536.

Ryle, G. (1949). *The concept of mind*. London: Hutchinson.

Sacks, O. (1996). *An anthropologist on mars*. New York: Picador, MacMillan.

Sacks, O. (1997). *The island of the colour-blind*. New York: Penguin Random House.

Salzman, C. D., Britten, K. H., & Newsome, W. T. (1990). Cortical microstimulation influences perceptual judgements of motion direction. *Nature, 346*(6280), 174–177.

Schmidt, S., Jo, H. G., Wittmann, M., & Hinterberger, T. (2016). 'Catching the waves' – Slow cortical potentials as moderator of voluntary action. *Neuroscience & Biobehavioral Reviews, 68*, 639–650.

Schurger, A., Sitt, J. D., & Dehaene, S. (2012). An accumulator model for spontaneous neural activity prior to self-initiated movement. *Proceedings of the National Academy of Sciences, 109*(42), E2904–E2913.

Searle, J. R. (1980). Minds, brains, and programs. *Behavioral and Brain Sciences, 3*, 417–457.

Searle, J. R. (2015). *Seeing things as they are*. Oxford: Oxford University Press.

Seth, A. (2021). *Being you: A new science of consciousness*. London, United Kingdom: Penguin.

Sherrington, C. S. (1906). *The integrative action of the nervous system*. New Haven, CT: Yale University Press.

Silver, D., Schrittwieser, J., Simonyan, K., Antonoglou, I., Huang, A., et al. (2017). Mastering the game of Go without human knowledge. *Nature, 550*(7676), 354–359.

Singer, W. (2018). Neuronal oscillations: Unavoidable and useful? *European Journal of Neuroscience, 48*(7), 2389–2398. https://doi.org/10.1111/ejn.13796

Sinha, P. (2013). Once blind and now they see. *Scientific American, 309*(1), 48–55.

Sloan, T. B. (1998). Anesthetic effects on electrophysiologic recordings. *Journal of Clinical Neurophysiology, 15*(3), 217–226.

Spinoza. (1910). *Ethics* (A. Boyle, Trans.). London: J.M. Dent and Sons.

Srinivasan, M. V., Laughlin, S. B., & Dubs, A. (1982). Predictive coding: A fresh view of inhibition in the retina. *Proceedings of the Royal Society B: Biological Sciences, 216*(1205), 427–459.

Stoerig, P., & Cowey, A. (1997). Blindsight in man and monkey. *Brain, 120*(Pt 3), 535–559.

Stratton, G. M. (1897). Vision without inversion of the retinal image. *Psychological Review, 4*(4), 341.

Straube, A., Brandt, T., & Probst, T. (1987). Importance of the visual cortex for postural stabilization: Inferences from pigeon and frog data. *Human Neurobiology, 6*(1), 39–43.

Striedter, G. F. (2006). Precisions of principles of brain evolution. *Behavioral and Brain Sciences, 29*(1), 1–12; discussion 12–36.

Supp, G. G., Siegel, M., Hipp, J. F., & Engel, A. K. (2011). Cortical hypersynchrony predicts breakdown of sensory processing during loss of consciousness. *Current Biology, 21*(23), 1988–1993.

Swaab, D. F., & Hofman, M. A. (1995). Sexual differentiation of the human hypothalamus in relation to gender and sexual orientation. *Trends in Neurosciences, 18*(6), 264–270.

Tanaka, K. (2003). Columns for complex visual object features in the inferotemporal cortex: Clustering of cells with similar but slightly different stimulus selectivities. *Cereb Cortex, 13*(1), 90–99.

Teunisse, R. J., Zitman, F. G., Cruysberg, J., Hoefnagels, W., & Verbeek, A. (1996). Visual hallucinations in psychologically normal people: Charles Bonnet's syndrome. *The Lancet, 347*(9004), 794–797.

Tononi, G., Boly, M., Massimini, M., & Koch, C. (2016). Integrated information theory: From consciousness to its physical substrate. *Nature Reviews Neuroscience, 17*(7), 450–461.

Tovée, M. J. (1996). *An introduction to the visual system.* Cambridge, United Kingdom: Cambridge University Press.

Turing, A. (1950). Computing machinery and intelligence. *Mind, 236,* 433–460.

Vallar, G., & Ronchi, R. (2009). Somatoparaphrenia: A body delusion. A review of the neuropsychological literature. *Experimental Brain Research, 192*(3), 533–551.

Van Gulick, R. (2001). Reduction, emergence and other recent options on the mind/body problem: A philosophic overview. *Journal of Consciousness Studies, 8,* 1–34.

Van Lommel, P. (2011). *Consciousness beyond life: The science of the near-death experience.* New York: Harper Collins.

Vansteensel, M. J., Pels, E. G., Bleichner, M. G., Branco, M. P., Denison, T., et al. (2016). Fully implanted brain-computer interface in a locked-in patient with ALS. *New England Journal of Medicine, 375*(21), 2060–2066.

Vaswani, A., Shazeer, N., Parmar, N., Uszkoreit, J., Jones, L., Gomez, A. N., . . . Polosukhin, I. (2017). Attention is all you need. In *Advances in neural information processing systems, 30.*

Vignal, J. P., Maillard, L., McGonigal, A., & Chauvel, P. (2007). The dreamy state: Hallucinations of autobiographical memory evoked by temporal lobe stimulations and seizures. *Brain, 130*(Pt 1), 88–99.

von Senden, M. (1932). *Die Raumauffassung bei Blindgeborenen vor und nach ihrer Operation.* Leipzig: J. A. Barth.

Wakefield, A. J., Murch, S. H., Anthony, A., Linnell, J., Casson, D. M., et al. (1998). Retracted: Ileal-lymphoid-nodular hyperplasia, non-specific colitis, and pervasive developmental disorder in children. *Lancet, 351*(9103), 637–641.

Watanabe, E., Kitaoka, A., Sakamoto, K., Yasugi, M., & Tanaka, K. (2018). Illusory motion reproduced by deep neural networks trained for prediction. *Frontiers in Psychology, 9,* 345.

Watson, J. B., & Rayner, R. (1920). Conditioned emotional reactions. *Journal of Experimental Psychology, 3*(1), 1.

Weber, T. (2010). *Hitler's first war.* Oxford: Oxford University Press.

Wilson, M. A., & McNaughton, B. L. (1994). Reactivation of hippocampal ensemble memories during sleep. *Science, 265*(5172), 676–679.

Wimmer, H., & Perner, J. (1983). Beliefs about beliefs: Representation and constraining function of wrong beliefs in young children's understanding of deception. *Cognition, 13*(1), 103–128.

Winfree, A. T. (1984). The prehistory of the Belousov-Zhabotinsky oscillator. *Journal of Chemical Education, 61*(8), 661.

Winkler, A. D., Spillmann, L., Werner, J. S., & Webster, M. A. (2015). Asymmetries in blue-yellow color perception and in the color of 'the dress'. *Current Biology, 25*(13), R547–R548.

Wittgenstein, L. (1953). *Philosophical investigations.* Oxford: Blackwell.

Xu, K., Ba, J., Kiros, R., Cho, K., Courville, A., et al. (2015). *Show, attend and tell: Neural image caption generation with visual attention.* Proceedings of the 32nd international conference on machine learning, Lille, France. JMLR: W&CP volume 37.

Yarbus, A. L. (1967). *Eye movements and vision.* New York: Plenum Press.

Zatorre, R. J., & Halpern, A. R. (2005). Mental concerts: Musical imagery and auditory cortex. *Neuron, 47*(1), 9–12.

Zeki, S. (1998). Parallel processing, asynchronous perception, and a distributed system of consciousness in vision. *The Neuroscientist, 4*(5), 365–372.

Zeki, S. (2005). The Ferrier Lecture 1995 behind the seen: The functional specialization of the brain in space and time. *Philosophical Transactions of the Royal Society of London. Series B, Biological Sciences, 360*(1458), 1145–1183.

Zihl, J., von Cramon, D., & Mai, N. (1983). Selective disturbance of movement vision after bilateral brain damage. *Brain, 106*, 313–340.

Index